The Boundaries of Charity

Cistercian Culture and
Ecclesiastical Reform, 1098–1180

Figurae

READING MEDIEVAL CULTURE

The Boundaries
of Charity

Cistercian Culture

and Ecclesiastical Reform,

1098–1180

Martha G. Newman

Stanford University Press, Stanford, California, 1996

Stanford University Press
Stanford, California
©1996 by the Board of Trustees of
the Leland Stanford Junior University
Printed in the United States of America

CIP data are at the end of the book

Stanford University Press publications are distributed
exclusively by Stanford University Press within the
United States, Canada, Mexico, and Central America;
they are distributed exclusively by Cambridge University Press
throughout the rest of the world

Original printing 1995
Last figure below indicates year of this printing
04   03   02   01   00   99   98   97   96   95

In memory of Daniel U. Newman
1929–1994

Acknowledgments

As this book took shape, over these many years, my friends and colleagues and many institutions have provided invaluable assistance.

I owe my biggest intellectual debt to a man whom I never met and who, unfortunately, is no longer alive to receive my thanks. All scholars of Cistercian history have followed Jean Leclercq's path through the archives, used his edition of Bernard of Clairvaux's *Opera*, and been influenced by his interpretation of Cistercian ideas. More personally, his *Love of Learning and the Desire for God* provided a picture of monastic harmony and order that appealed to a bewildered college freshman and first inspired my interest in monastic history. My understanding of twelfth-century Cistercian *caritas* is no longer so peaceful, but vestiges of this harmony remain.

Many people have read all or part of this book, in one or another of its many forms. Gavin Langmuir and Sabine MacCormack advised my dissertation, shaped my questions, and demonstrated by their own work how discipline, attention to detail, and intellectual excitement combine to produce good scholarship. Giles Constable, Brian Patrick McGuire, Sharon Farmer, Megan McLaughlin, Brigitte Bedos-Rezak, and Barbara H. Rosenwein offered suggestions, comments, and criticisms. My colleagues at the University of Texas—Myron Gutmann, Standish Meacham, Janet Meisel, Howard Miller, Joan Neuberger, and especially the members of the Assistant Professors' Reading Group—provided suggestions and support. I am grateful to Norris Pope of the Stanford University Press for his encouragement, to Lynn Stewart for guiding this book through production, and to Scott Norton for his careful editing. Needless to say, despite all this generous assistance, any mistakes that remain are my own.

I would like to thank the National Endowment for the Humanities, the University Research Institute at the University of Texas, the Charlotte Newcombe Fellowship Fund, the Stanford Humanities Center, and the Fondation Georges Lurcy for their financial support. The librarians at the Perry Casteñeda Library of the University of Texas, the Green Library of Stanford University, and the Widener Library of Harvard University answered my many questions and tracked down my many requests. The librarians, archivists, and scholars at the Bibliothèque Nationale and the Institut de Recherche et d'Histoire des Textes in Paris, and at the departmental archives and municipal libraries in Troyes, Dijon, Auxerre, and Chaumont not only tolerated my French but also offered generous assistance. I would also like to thank the Bibliothèque municipale in Dijon, the Caisse Nationale des Monuments Historiques et des Sites in Paris, and Art Resource and the Artists Rights Society in New York for their photographs and permission to reproduce them. I am grateful to the Western Society for French History for permission to include in Chapter 6 material that previously appeared as "Prayer, Protection, and Politics: The Cistercian Order and Its Bishops," in the *Proceedings of the Annual Meeting of the Western Society for French History* 18 (1991): 70–78. I am also grateful to Brigitte Bedos-Rezak and Constance Berman for sharing what was then unpublished work with me.

Andy Weinberg has lived with this project almost as long as I have. He has done more than I can possibly mention, very little of which had to do with reading, correcting, and commenting on my manuscript.

My father's wide-ranging curiosity; his ability to see connections between visual, intellectual, and political concepts; and his deep concern for social justice have influenced me in ways that I am just beginning to discover. He started to understand my interest in the Cistercians the day we walked from Montbard to Fontenay and stood in the monks' dormitory to discuss the representation of a religious vision in stone. He was almost as eager to see this book between covers as I was, but his sudden death in the spring of 1994 left that wish unfulfilled. To him I dedicate this book.

A Note to the Reader

All translations are mine, except where noted. Where applicable, I have cited both Latin editions and English translations, usually from the Cistercian Fathers Series. Similarly, I have used the traditional numbering for Bernard of Clairvaux's letters but give the number from Bruno Scott James's edition in parentheses. When quoting Latin passages, I have reproduced the orthography used by the editors of the printed editions.

Contents

‿

Map and Figures

for Man is Love,
As God is Love: every kindness to another is a little Death
In the Divine Image, nor can Man exist but by Brotherhood.

William Blake, *Jerusalem*

The Boundaries of Charity

Cistercian Culture and
Ecclesiastical Reform, 1098–1180

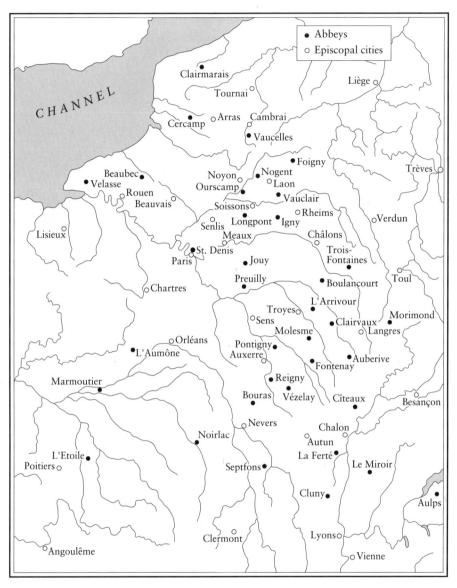

Ecclesiastical institutions in northwestern France, c. 1150. Adapted from Frederik van der Meer, *Atlas de l'ordre cistercien* (Paris: Elsevier, 1965), Table 2.

Introduction

In 1098, Robert, the abbot of Molesme, and a small group of monks left their monastery to found a new community in a forest midway between the Burgundian towns of Dijon and Beaune. Their initial motivations and intentions remain obscure, but when they and their successors defined their regulations and wrote their history over twenty years later, they attributed these actions to a dissatisfaction with prevailing forms of eleventh-century religious life and a desire to return to the purity of the Benedictine Rule. In their new monastery, they curtailed the liturgy to leave time for manual work, wore clothes of undyed wool, and rejected elaborate meals. They refused to accept tithes, to own serfs, to settle near towns, and to associate with women. They celebrated the wilderness and solitude in which they constructed their monastery, and they contrasted their poverty and isolation to the wealth and worldly involvement of the monastery they had abandoned.[1]

This new monastery, later called Cîteaux, remained neither poor nor isolated. By 1115, its monks had spread into four affiliated communities: La Ferté, Pontigny, Clairvaux, and Morimond. By 1119, the monks, now called Cistercians, had composed a document, the *Carta caritatis*, that regulated the relations between these abbeys. The order grew rapidly: by the middle of the twelfth century, there were over 350 Cistercian abbeys spread across Europe; by 1200, despite regulations forbidding further growth, there were more than 500.[2] Many of these houses initially suffered economic difficulties; once they were established, however, most prospered. The monks rejected ornate and expensive decoration in their churches and other buildings, and they reinvested any surplus in their land rather than in the more traditional displays of power and wealth.

Their political activity increased as well. Cistercian monks began to be elected to episcopal positions in 1126; by 1160, there had been more than 50 Cistercian bishops, 10 cardinals, and a pope.[3] Cistercian abbots offered counsel and support to kings, popes, and bishops; they exposed heretics and preached for crusades. Such activities made these monks the most effective servants of the ecclesiastical hierarchy until the Dominicans rose to prominence in the years after 1215.

In this book, I argue that the Cistercians' political activity developed out of their conception of the monastic life. Their "withdrawal" was less an attempt to avoid all social entanglements than an effort to differentiate the social role of monks from that of either the secular clergy or the knightly aristocracy. Unlike many tenth- and eleventh-century monastic communities that responded to a decentralized Church by serving as society's professional penitents, the Cistercians considered the salvation of the laity to be the responsibility of the secular clergy. Yet they also viewed this clergy as lacking the virtues necessary for their positions of authority. The Cistercians envisioned the Church as a moral body, not a legal institution, and they viewed schisms, heresies, and general clerical corruption as rips in the fabric of the Church that endangered the salvation of all Christians. As a result, they worked to create a virtuous and moral clergy that would view its authority as a ministry, encourage the repentance and interior reform of the laity, and repair the social fabric. They believed that if each person fulfilled his or her proper social function, then monks could limit their concern for others to those within their community. However, they also recognized that life on earth was inevitably imperfect and filled with conflicts and tensions, and they thus considered their political behavior inevitable.

The Cistercians have long appeared as important actors in studies of twelfth-century social and cultural developments. Their interest in expressing and analyzing their motivations and feelings, and their empathy for the feelings of others, provide central examples of the period's new affective spirituality.[4] Their biblical hermeneutics illustrate an important aspect of twelfth-century "textuality" in which the written word served as a bridge between divinely created reality and an individual's everyday experiences.[5] Their economic practices and technological innovations put them at the forefront of agricultural developments; their criticisms of the urban schools helped to impel scholars to develop the corporate awareness that eventually led to the medieval university.[6] But despite the extensive literature on the Cistercians and the twelfth century, the question of how a religious group following a tradition of social withdrawal played such a pivotal role in its society remains unanswered. Until now, there has been no study of the social role of the Cistercians comparable to recent works on tenth-century Cluny or the thirteenth-century friars.[7] Those works that attempt to explain the Cistercians' influence usually focus on the activities of one man, Bernard of Clairvaux, and they portray his behavior as unusual, contradictory, or even divinely inspired.[8] But, as Brian Patrick McGuire has recently noted, Bernard exists historiographically as two separate figures, one political and the other theological, and no one has shown how he integrated these two areas of his life.[9]

Most Cistercian historiography considers, either explicitly or implicitly, the characteristics of the Cistercian order that separated it from communities of other monks. This interest in Cistercian distinctiveness received its initial inspiration from the twelfth-century Cistercians who wrote histories and treatises that emphasized their economic and liturgical differences and composed regulations that purported to preserve them. Until recently, scholars have asked whether the actual behavior of the monks followed the ideals expressed in these histories and regulations; they have answered that, by the second half of the twelfth century, the monks had begun to abandon their initial ideals and were corrupted by too much wealth and political power.[10] This interpretation places the story of Cîteaux's foundation and subsequent development within a perpetual cycle of monastic renewal and degeneration that assumes a dichotomy between an unchanging monastic ideal and the corrupting "reality" of social conditions.[11] Within such an interpretative framework, the monks' political activities could only be further evidence of their decline.

In recent years, this paradigm has been criticized and modified in several important ways. Since World War II, historians have raised fundamental questions about the reliability of the documents that present the Cistercians' ideals.[12] It now seems likely that the order's early histories were composed more than twenty years after the events they describe and were modified thereafter; the early regulations, some repetitious and others contradictory, were collected in 1134 but were not edited into a consistent document.[13] One interesting corollary to this argument is that it repositions the central rupture in Cistercian history; rather than emphasize the division between the monks of Cîteaux and the community at Molesme, it posits a split between the legalistic and authoritarian character of Cîteaux's third abbot, Stephen Harding, and the more mystical Bernard of Clairvaux.[14] Questioning the accuracy of Cistercian documents, however, does little to resolve the issue of the monks' political behavior. If the early Cistercian documents were either composed or modified during the 1130's, it is even more important to explain why these monks created histories and regulations that stressed withdrawal while simultaneously increasing their activities outside their monasteries.

A second response to the paradigm of Cistercian ideal and reality has been the careful investigation of the economic activities and patronage patterns of specific Cistercian monasteries. Some of these studies remain influenced by the question of a Cistercian decline and suggest that the variations from the monks' stated economic ideals stemmed from the particular social and geographical environment around each abbey.[15] But many historians now argue that the Cistercians' economic ideals were not uniformly enforced, and they posit other practices, such as an economic organization based on granges and lay brothers and an entrepreneurial attitude toward property, as characteristic of the order.[16] Although these studies are not strictly focused on the monks' political behavior, they nonetheless provide guidance for understanding it, for they remind us that monasteries, no matter how "withdrawn," always need outsiders to provide recruits and economic support. Even more, they suggest that we must be aware of the continuing dialogue between the monks and their patrons. Patrons had their own ideas about the purpose of monastic communities and the types of property they wished to contribute, neither of which necessarily coincided with the monks' stated intentions. Monks were obliged both to educate their patrons and to readjust their own stance to take their patrons' wishes into consideration. Such studies of the Cistercians' economies and patrons demonstrate the importance of examining the monks' behavior as well as their ideals, for they explore the interaction between a supposedly insular monastic community and the larger society around it.

A third approach to Cistercian history, and to the study of monasticism in general, has been to focus on a community's intellectual culture. In his *Love of Learning and the Desire for God,* Jean Leclercq developed the idea of a general monastic culture, based on biblical exegesis and liturgical practice, that contrasted with the new forms of theology developing in twelfth-century urban schools.[17] Over the last decade, historians influenced by cultural anthropology have added analyses of symbol and ritual to Leclercq's initial formulation of "culture" and have found a variety of monastic cultures, but, like Leclercq, they continue to look at monks' ideas and mentalities to understand the nature of their communities.[18] Within Cistercian studies, such an approach has been used to reexamine the idea of a Cistercian "decline" by exploring the way late twelfth-century monks retold their history to present their predecessors as models.[19] It also has been used to analyze elements of the Cistercians' culture, such as the monks' use of maternal imagery or their emphasis on friendship, that were not unique to them, but which they often expressed in an especially clear fashion.[20] Like the historians studying economy and patronage, these scholars have found less of a contrast between twelfth-century Cistercian monks and their monastic contemporaries than had once been posited; the differences have become a matter more of degree than of kind.

The idea of monastic culture is central to my analysis of the Cistercians' political behavior, for I argue that their activities grew out of their interpretation of fundamental monastic symbols and concepts. At the same time, I also borrow the idea of a dialogue between the monastery and the surrounding society from the social historians and explore the process of creating a Cistercian culture and then preserving it within a changing society. Like the scholars of monastic economies and patronage, I recognize that renunciation of the "world" could never entail total social withdrawal, but rather than focus on the process of obtaining more monks and more property, I explore the cultural interactions between the monks and their society. I am interested in how monks who claimed to reject their society's norms still shared with the surrounding society ingrained ideas and customs that they could not conceive of questioning, and I examine the way the very process of forming a new community was both a criticism of certain social values and behaviors and a model for social reform.[21] In comparison with an older historiography that posits an unchanging monastic ideal periodically corrupted by a changing society, I see a continuous tension between the ideal of withdrawal and the monks' social involvement. Thus, instead of asking how the Cistercians' social involvement led to their decline, I explore how they created a monastic culture that allowed them to balance these conflicting impulses. This culture drew on the individual mentalities of the monks, their social environment, and their interpretation of previous models of withdrawal. Examining this monastic culture not only reveals the internal dynamics of the Cistercians' communities but also illuminates their relationship with the society that surrounded them.

To understand a group's religious culture, we must recognize religion as a subject for historical analysis. It is tempting, in studying medieval Christianity, to make assumptions about this religion that we would never make about a religious tradition more alien to European culture. Furthermore, we often take at face value the explanations medieval Christians gave for their actions, and we assume that these are adequate descriptions of their motivations. Whereas historians seldom make such assumptions concerning political, economic, or social behavior, they do explain religious behavior in terms of belief.[22] But the study of religion as a social and historical phenomenon requires studying believers and analyzing their beliefs without either making reference to a supra-empirical truth or accepting their own statements as the limit of our understanding of their motivations.[23]

One of the difficulties in studying religious ideas and behaviors is that they are at the same time sociological and psychological phenomena. In most classic studies of religion, either the social or the psychological aspect predominates at the expense of the other, and their relationship remains unclear.[24] One fruitful response to this problem has been to separate religion, as a social phenomenon, from each individual's religious mentality.[25] In his book *History, Religion and Antisemitism*, Gavin Langmuir connects an individual's religious mentality or "religiosity" to the psychological and social processes that form his or her identity; this "religiosity" is formed from the set of symbols and structures that an individual uses to correlate his or her patterns of thought and emotion with the surrounding social and natural environment in developing and maintaining a coherent identity.[26] Langmuir defines religion, in comparison, as "those elements of religiosity that are explicitly prescribed by people exercising authority over other people."[27] One advantage of this distinction between religion and "religiosity" is that, by considering "religiosity" a psychological condition of all humans, it is possible to explain religious beliefs without either denigrating them as compensatory systems or limiting the explanations of them to descriptions. Using this definition, a person who strives for salvation by becoming "perfect" (Matt. 19.21) seeks to maintain a symbolic unity in all aspects of his or her life and attempts to make all conduct and all experience comprehensible in terms of the symbols through which he or she expresses the most fundamental patterns of thought and emotion.[28] Such certainly was the case with medieval monks; their attempt to organize their life in harmony with divine will was a religious way of expressing their desire to make their world and their conduct in it perfectly coherent. They regulated virtually every aspect of their life and viewed all their behavior as having symbolic value.

Langmuir's distinction between an individual's religious mentality and socially prescribed religion does not, however, explain the relation between the two. Furthermore, his definitions posit a gulf between the individual and society; they place the individual's beliefs at one pole and institutionalized religion at the other but ignore the interesting middle ground where they interact. A person's religious psychology is not particularly accessible historically: if it is difficult to comprehend the symbols that provide coherence for our own identities, it is virtually impossible to analyze the psychological state of people who lived eight hundred years in the past.[29] What is accessible, however, is religious culture: the public expressions of symbolic meaning through speech, action, and ritual that are a dialogue between individuals on the one hand and the traditions of religion on the other. People draw their dominant symbols from a common, and often prescribed, repertoire, but when a person uses a symbol in communication its meaning receives new connotations from the speaker, the audience, and the pragmatic context in which it is used.[30] It no longer is in the realm of individual psychology, but it does not yet have a meaning explicitly prescribed by those holding authority; it exists in a social realm that fits between the spheres of religion and religious mentality delimited by Langmuir's definitions.

An analysis of religious culture provides a partial glimpse into individual minds; even more, it allows us to understand shared meanings—the "webs of significance"—that exist "between the minds" of the members of a group.[31] An individual's actions or expressions might influence the religious mentalities of other people, change the connotations of some of their dominant symbols, and help to bind them into a community. At the same time, as members of a community, people create a shared set of meanings through their communications, their actions, and their collective rituals that are related to, but not identical with, each individual member's religious mentality and articulations of that mentality. This shared religious culture can help to differentiate a community from the rest of its society but need not remain confined to that community. Sometimes the meaning of a symbol is articulated by a person or group with religious authority, or a new meaning becomes so influential that those expressing it are given religious authority; in either case, aspects of a religious culture and, ultimately, aspects of an individual's own religiosity become incorporated into a religion. Such expressions can also be ignored or disputed, or they can be considered authoritative by some, ignored by others, and disputed by still others.

These ideas about religious culture have helped to shape my study of the twelfth-century Cistercians. In exploring how a Cistercian culture was created and transformed, I find an interaction between established religions and the individual monks whose religious mentalities were themselves shaped through the interaction between experience and cultural background. The monks who founded Cîteaux already shared with one another important elements of their religiosity and, over time, began to articulate these shared meanings and to create a new religious culture. This culture developed through the monks' public expression of the symbols and ideas of two overlapping "religions"—Christianity and monasticism. The monks held common understandings of words with important symbolic values—words such as "poverty," the "world," and "monastic peace and quiet"—and this helped them to develop a shared interpretation of canonical religious texts such as the Bible and the Benedictine Rule. The way they expressed their understanding of these symbols and concepts, however, was also influenced by the common elements of their secular culture and experiences, some of which they accepted and others of which they consciously rejected, but all of which made it impossible for them to interpret the monastic religion of withdrawal in a way that would ever truly isolate themselves from their society.

One of the central concepts in the Cistercians' religious culture was their idea of *caritas*. This Christian love was a selfless love that traditionally was associated with both the Christian God's love for humanity and the ideal love felt by a human for both God and other humans. The connotations that the Cistercians associated with this concept illuminate how the interaction between individual mentalities and religious structures creates religious culture. When the Cistercians wrote of caritas, they often used imagery drawn from their knowledge of military and sexual matters, even though these were two aspects of their secular culture that they had outwardly rejected. In fact, their use of such imagery changed the meaning of the word, for while they had abandoned swords and women, they retained the aggressiveness of a knightly elite and understood caritas through this prism. Furthermore, they associated caritas with their efforts to control their own physical nature and their desire to help their fellow monks to do the same. Eventually, the word's meanings came to include the monks' interests in ordering and controlling their material world and their sense of an ideal Christian society. This concept of caritas helped the Cistercians to explain both their material prosperity and their involvement in ecclesiastical and secular politics as consonant with their idea of monastic life.

The Cistercian culture that developed out of the three-way dialogue between the monastic and Christian religions, the mentalities of individual monks, and the cultures and expectations of the surrounding society remained neither static nor uniform nor even limited to the monks in Cistercian communities. Yet, despite the variations in Cistercian practices and the blurred boundaries between the Cistercians and other religious groups, Cistercian monks still identified themselves, and were identified by others, as belonging to a particular order with its own distinguishing characteristics. More than any specific customs, the Cistercians' confidence that their close-knit communities provided them with the best possible environment in which to learn virtue and participate in divine love bound the monks together and provided the people around them with a sense of their identifying characteristics. The monks' efforts to preserve these characteristics as their society changed demonstrate as much about the relationship between the monasteries and the world around them as they do about the variations in the order's culture and practices, for the process of maintaining traditions and culture itself required a dynamic interaction between the values that the monks hoped to retain and the changing context in which they put those values into practice.[32] As will become clear, Cistercians in the 1160's and 1170's preserved essential characteristics of their monastic culture but gradually became less effective political actors as their interpretation of pivotal symbols and concepts no longer had the same importance in the society around them.

Most Cistercian monks have remained historically mute. They left no traces of their voices in historical texts, and others did not record their behavior. As a result, this study focuses on a small group of prominent Cistercians who were known both within and without the order for their spiritual writings and their political activities, and who were responsible for articulating the common elements of their culture, teaching them to other monks, and making them accessible to interested people outside their monastic communities. Yet if the Cistercians were, as Brian Stock has suggested, the outstanding example of a twelfth-century "textual community," then all the monks, however mute, who composed this community were united by a common reading and a shared symbolic understanding of specific texts, especially the Song of Songs.[33] For most twelfth-century Cistercians, Bernard of Clairvaux's commentaries on the Song of Songs provided the model for its interpretation. Yet, although Bernard has dominated the history of the Cistercian order ever since his first biography was composed in the mid–twelfth century, he did not create the Cistercians' culture alone.[34] Instead, he served as the most articulate spokesman for a group of men who shared similar ideas and goals. This group was spread across northwestern, francophone Europe. It included spiritual writers and abbots such as Aelred of Rievaulx, Guerric of Igny, Isaac of Stella, Geoffrey of Auxerre, and Gilbert of Hoyland, and monks who became ecclesiastical officials, such as the bishops Godfrey of Langres and Hugh of Auxerre and the archbishops Henry of Rheims and Guichard of Lyons. Together with Bernard of Clairvaux, these men helped to articulate the central characteristics of the Cistercians' culture and spread it both across the order and into the surrounding society.

The first half of this book explores the creation of the Cistercians' religious culture. It examines the way the monks' communal organization and cultural background influenced their interpretation of Christian theology and monastic traditions, and their understanding of Christian caritas. It shows how the military and scholastic environments that the monks rejected nonetheless provided an imagery that shaped the new individual and introspective character of Cistercian communities. It also demonstrates that the Cistercians' own distinction between an ideal contemplative state and the realities of the human condition led them to insist that the demands of a communal life and a concern for the salvation of others were essential for learning to love the divine. The Cistercians' conception of caritas combined a new emphasis on individual character and conscience with a direct personal concern for the salvation of others. The suggestion that both human nature and Christian society were subjects for reform had implications for the monks' understanding of their order's position in society and made their interest in the society around them inevitable.

The religious culture of these active and articulate Cistercians helps to explain their involvement in the society outside their religious communities but does not by itself explain why others accepted and even encouraged this intervention. The second half of this book examines the Cistercians' religious culture in action: the monks' ideas for an ideal Christian society, their own activities to realize such a vision, and their influence on others. By exploring how the monks gained the authority to transform elements of their religious culture into institutionalized religion, it demonstrates that the monks were not only interested in reforming society but that their close relationship with ecclesiastical officials made their isolation an impossibility.

Like religion itself, religious authority is both a social and a psychological phenomenon: it depends in part on the exercise of power and the control of political institutions, but it also depends on the willingness of other people to accept this authority. In understanding this psychological aspect of religious authority, the definition of "religiosity" is again useful: it helps to explain why individuals are willing to view certain people as especially religious. Most people do not maintain a complete coherence between their dominant sets of symbols and their conduct but instead compartmentalize the various aspects of their lives.[35] Such compartmentalization does not prevent them from admiring and respecting a person who does seek to maintain a completely coherent identity, especially if they share similar understandings of the symbols around which this coherence is constructed. Thus a figure such as Francis of Assisi held authority for many thirteenth-century Christians, not because he rejected all the structures of his society, but because his entire identity was constructed around the imitation of Jesus, and all his actions centered on this symbol.[36] Yet such a Christian saint had little meaning to medieval Jews because the saint's symbols had little congruence with their own. In still other situations, people might actively contest a figure's religious authority, especially if they share symbols but endow them with different connotations.

If religious figures gain authority when other people respect the apparent coherence between their interpretation of important symbols and their conduct and also accept the connotations they give to these symbols, then the Cistercians had authority to the extent that others accepted their interpretation of caritas and believed that the monks had integrated the meaning of this dominant symbol into their lives. Like religious mentality, however, this is a realm that is difficult to examine empirically. We have little, if any, direct information about the religious mentality of the Cistercians' supporters and whether they incorporated elements of the Cistercians' religious culture into their own religious ideas.[37] What we can observe are the interactions between the Cistercians, their supporters, and their detractors: what the monks said and did, and the extent to which others listened to them and encouraged their activity.

The second part of this book explores this sociopolitical aspect of religious authority and the extent to which the Cistercians became allied with popes and bishops who already held religious power and controlled religious institutions. The Cistercians' vision of an ideal Christian society emphasized the need for ecclesiastical reform, and some twelfth-century bishops, who were often benefactors and protectors of the Cistercian communities, accepted and enacted these ideas. This harmonious relationship between bishops and monks was unusual. Throughout most of the early Middle Ages, bishops and monks were, if not actively hostile, at least mutually suspicious, and this hostility certainly reemerged in the thirteenth-century relationship between bishops and friars. The Cistercians, however, established their first monastic community during a period of radical change within the institutions of the Church in which church officials both asserted their monopoly over Christian sacraments and demanded that others recognize the powers associated with this control of salvation. Many of the ecclesiastics who aided the first Cistercians advocated these changes, and they appear to have influenced the monks. Certainly, the Cistercians' regulations prohibiting their control of churches and pastoral care for the laity eliminated many areas of monastic-episcopal conflict, while the monks' unwillingness to act as landlords and possess juridical rights eliminated still other areas of tension. In fact, the Cistercians believed that bishops, not monks, were responsible for the salvation of the laity: a monk's role was to support the reform of the episcopate, not to challenge its authority. This close relationship between the Cistercians and church officials aided the transmission of the monks' ideas and gradually transformed elements of their religious culture into a religion.

Interestingly, it is from the Cistercians' critics that we have the best evidence for how others responded to their articulation of Christian symbols and their vision of Christian society. Initially, the Cistercians' strongest critics were other monks. Many monastic communities were threatened, not only because the Cistercians competed with them for resources and recruits, but also because the Cistercians' own religious culture appeared to challenge the validity of theirs. Much of the famous dispute between the Cistercians and the older Benedictine monks was a fight over how to interpret the dominant symbols in the monastic tradition; the premise underlying Peter the Venerable's criticisms of the Cistercians was that the new monks were mistaken both in their interpretation of caritas and in the rituals that this interpretation inspired.[38] Like these Benedictines, the critics who emerged in the later half of the twelfth century also focused their critique on Cistercian caritas.[39] To both sets of critics, the Cistercians' conduct and symbolic systems appeared inconsistent: both saw contradictions between the Cistercians' aggressive behavior and their stress on Christian love. These criticisms, however, did not indicate that the Cistercians themselves had fallen short of their ideals, but only that they and their critics did not define caritas in the same way.

The boundaries around the Cistercians' monasteries were never impermeable. The monks absorbed without questioning many twelfth-century ideas and assumptions, and a group of active and articulate monks wrote, traveled, and accepted ecclesiastical positions. This permeability explains how a group claiming to withdraw from society could nonetheless be so central to developments within that society. The Cistercians' concept of caritas borrowed from the aristocratic culture in which many of the monks had been raised, and it expressed ideas about the interaction of individual introspection, group cohesion, and a longing for the divine that resonated in the society around them. As such, it provided the underpinning for the Cistercians' vision of a Church bound by the spiritual progress of its members, and it explained the activities of those monks who left their monasteries to enact this vision in the society around them.

Part I

The Creation of Cistercian Culture

Fifty years ago, it was possible for a historian to declare that "few religious orders possess a history of their origins as clear and as simple as the Cistercian order."[1] Today, the early Cistercian documents that had provided this clear and simple history are seen as complex and layered documents whose chronological development is still far from certain.[2] Careful studies of the order's histories and early statutes suggest that the primitive kernels of both the *Exordium parvum* and the *Carta caritatis* were written between 1116 and 1119; the *Exordium cistercii* was composed in 1123 or 1124, probably at Clairvaux; and the statutes contained in the *Summa cartae caritatis* describe decisions of the Chapter General made before 1124. These documents illustrate how the monks defined themselves, and how they wished to be perceived, during the period in which the various abbeys began to consider themselves an order and received papal recognition. Still, they only partially depict the Cistercians' culture: they show the monks' attempts at self-definition but ignore characteristic attitudes and behaviors that were so present to the monks as to be nearly invisible to them. These unconscious but pervasive attitudes influenced much of the Cistercians' behavior and help to explain it in ways that their own regulations and histories do not.

Because much of what we know about the first twenty years of the order is filtered through the lenses of memory and self-justification, there are questions about this period of Cistercian history that remain unanswered and probably unanswerable. For this study, the most important of these is the question of whether the first Cistercians modified their ideas about community organization in response to the influx of novices in the 1110's, or whether these new men converted because they were attracted to the ideas and structures already current in the monasteries. To a large extent, the process by which the earliest Cistercians created their culture remains opaque.[3] What we can see, however, is the monastic culture that began to emerge in the 1120's and the varied expressions of this culture by Cistercian spiritual writers during the next fifty years. The following chapters explore the relationship between the monks' backgrounds, their community organization and economic practices, and the ideas they expressed in their sermons, letters, and treatises. They show that the culture that emerged from these interactions inculcated in the monks an attitude toward the world around their communities that encouraged their interest in societal reform.

A central element of the Cistercians' culture was their interest in the process of conversion. The men who entered Cistercian monasteries were adults; some came from other monasteries, while others had been trained as knights or clerics. In joining a monastery, each had made a personal and often dramatic decision, and Cistercian abbots openly discussed the process of socializing these novices. For them, conversion was not a single act. The creation of a "new man" out of a secular adult became an ongoing process that continued even after a year's probation. To describe this process, abbots and novice masters used imagery derived from life in secular society; they animated their sermons by presenting religious ideas in terms that retained their listeners' interest and portrayed the gradual transformation of knights and clerics into monks.

Not only did men convert to monastic life, but monastic life converted to them. The abbots' recognition and use of secular experiences in their sermons, whether or not they were the actual experiences of their audience, did more than just add vibrant images to the Cistercians' language and aid the reception of their ideas. The language and imagery influenced the culture of the monastery and the meaning of some of the central symbols of their religious life. By presenting religious ideas in images drawn from the backgrounds of their monks, the abbots added new connotations to traditional concepts and rituals and incorporated into the Cistercians' culture a confident, even aggressive, character that further encouraged the monks' interest in reforming the world they saw around them.

This mutual transformation of novices and monastic culture had implications for the Cistercians' understanding of one of the central Christian concepts: the idea of caritas. Best translated as the archaic English

word "charity," caritas is the love enjoined in the two great commandments to love one's God with all one's heart, soul, and mind and to love
one's neighbor as oneself. As such, it refers to both transcendent and
ethical aspects of Christianity. "Caritas" describes the mystery of human contact with the divine, it depicts ideal relations between people on
earth, and it links the two together.

Coined as a Christian term from the Latin word for costliness and es-
teem, "caritas" refers both to the Christian God's love for humanity and
the potential ability of humanity to return that love.[4] Unlike its Greek
counterpart *agape*, however, this Latin word has no accompanying verb:
to express the loving that led to caritas, Latin authors had at their disposal
the two verbs *amare* and *diligere*, both of which had their own associated
nouns. Many medieval authors followed the practice of Augustine of
Hippo, who had used "amare" to express a neutral love and "diligere" to
express a love controlled by the will that could either be good or evil.[5] Bernard of Clairvaux, however, broke this pattern and used the two Latin
verbs interchangeably.[6] He continued Augustine's usage of the noun
dilectio to refer to a love controlled by the will, but he used *amor* to describe both divine and human love, implying an equation between human desire and divine love that Augustine would have found incom-
prehensible.[7] "Caritas," for Bernard, described an abstract virtue. Seldom
did he mention somebody's feelings of caritas; caritas existed indepen-
dently of an actor and did not refer to shared emotions or feelings. Instead, it became an objectified, almost personified concept.

Bernard of Clairvaux's association of amor and amare with both divine
and human love reflected a more widespread twelfth-century shift in
the image of the divine. An older image of a distant, just God the Father
began to fade as people emphasized the loving nature of Christ and
stressed both the sacrifice of the incarnate Jesus and their own feelings
when confronted with this supreme example of caritas.[8] This new image
of God encouraged a variety of religious responses, for embedded in
the concept of caritas was a potential conflict between an individual's desire for a contemplative relation with the divine and a concern for the spiritual well-being of others. Wandering preachers sought to imitate the active ministry of Jesus and his apostles as a means of sharing in his divine
love, while some hermits sought to develop an individual relation with
the divine based on a contemplative understanding of divine love.[9] Others, such as the Cistercians, appear to have been attracted to both re-

sponses; for them, the variety of meanings sheltered within "caritas" provided a means of finding a balance between these potentially conflicting tendencies.

The Cistercians' solutions for reconciling these discordant implications of caritas formed an essential part of their monastic culture. The monks used the word to portray both their striving toward the divine and their insistence on a communal life; it described the bond that linked the monks within their communities but also the bond joining all of Christian society. The Cistercians balanced these conflicting connotations by insisting on the importance of a communal life for an individual relation with the divine, and by differentiating between the ideal toward which they aimed and the realities and compromises of actual life on earth.

Brian Stock has suggested that the Cistercians were the twelfth century's most successful "textual community." By this he means that they were a group organized around a particular interpretation of a text, and that this process of interpretation influenced "their feelings, perceptions and practical ideas."[10] Stock's analysis helps us to understand the relationship between articulate individuals and the historically mute people who shared many of the same ideas but did not leave records expressing them. According to Stock, the Cistercians' central text was the Song of Songs, and its principal interpreter was Bernard of Clairvaux, whose sermons, letters, and treatises resonate with its language even when he did not quote it directly. Bernard articulated the basic themes for the Cistercians' interpretation of this text, and they were repeated, elaborated, and modified by the next generation of Cistercian authors, some of whom had themselves been novices at Clairvaux, and most of whom had been influenced by Bernard's writings and speech.[11] Together, these men expressed ideas that were also reflected in their behaviors and monastic organization, and they helped to create a unified culture that both the monks and those outside the monasteries could identify as characteristic of the Cistercian order.

Stock's conception of the Cistercians as a textual community is further enhanced by the process by which the Cistercians created and preserved their texts. For the most part, their treatises and sermons, as the products of abbots, say little directly about the life and ideas of the majority of men within the monastic communities; they better represent what the monks were taught than how they actually behaved. But even the works of Bernard of Clairvaux do not reflect the ideas of a single man, for they were not solitary compositions. Bernard worked closely with his disciples and secretaries, who at times wrote down what he dictated orally, and at other times wrote down what they remembered him as saying.[12] Furthermore, Bernard, perhaps with the help of these secretaries, edited many of his works, especially his treatises and his sermons on the Song of Songs, so that they were accessible in written form for an audience that could not hear him preach. Although such a cooperative effort may make it more difficult to find the "authentic" Bernard, it aids in the exploration of a monastic culture, for the ideas attributed to Bernard were ideas that had been filtered through the memories of his monks. The multiple versions of the sermons of Aelred of Rievaulx also suggest a complex relationship between oral and written versions.[13] These didactic texts, then, are ideal for illustrating the Cistercians' culture: they not only reflect the ideas and assumptions that an abbot wished to instill in his monks, but also suggest that some monks so internalized these ideas that they then aided in their continued transmission.

Part I starts with a potential monk's entrance into the monastery and ends with the monks' views of the larger society around them. Chapter 1 discusses the conversion of knights and scholars, whether actual or fictitious, and argues that this transformation influenced the culture of the monasteries by adding aggressive and militaristic connotations to the idea of caritas. Chapter 2 explores the double exhortation to love God and neighbor and examines the way the Cistercians conceived of the relationship of the individual to the community. Chapter 3 investigates the continued process of conversion within the monastery as the monks learned that their efforts to transform their wills allowed them to find a potential goodness in both their own bodies and the natural world around them. Chapter 4 discusses the Cistercians' view of their monasteries as diverse communities united by caritas and shows how this monastic organization became a model for the surrounding Christian society. Through the accumulation of ideas and images associated with caritas, we will see how the Cistercians' monastic culture imbued the monks with a concern, not only for their own salvation and that of their monastic brethren, but also for the proper order and well-being of Christian society as a whole.

Chapter I

The Transformation of
the Monastic *Scola*

The prologue of the Benedictine Rule calls the monastery "a school for the Lord's service" (*dominici scola servitii*).[1] For Benedict, the term *scola* implied not only a place of education but also a corps of soldiers; in a "scola" for divine service, a monk both learned and fought.[2] In much of Benedict's Rule, the monastic scola teaches the discipline and obedience necessary to form the monks into a division of a divinely led army: each monk learns to lose his individuality by subsuming his will to that of his abbot, and the community becomes an externalized conscience that gauges his inner spiritual condition by judging his outer actions.[3] Still, Benedict tempered the harshness of this military scola by suggesting that the monastic soldier's heavy burden of endurance, obedience, and patient suffering would become easier through the gradual infusion of divine love.[4] Furthermore, while most of the Rule stresses external behavior, Benedict did imply the possibility of an education that transformed a monk's interior thoughts and intentions; certain chapters of the Rule, especially chapter 7 on humility, describe the process by which a monk could gradually arrive at "that perfect love of God which casts out fear" (1 John 4.18).[5] As the Benedictine Rule became the dominant monastic rule in the Carolingian Empire in the early ninth century, abbots and their monks generally ignored these implications about interior education and instead concentrated on the proper behavior and ritual actions of a military corps. By contrast, when early-twelfth-century Cistercians formulated their understanding of the monastic community, they emphasized this less dominant element within the Benedictine Rule: they stressed interior psychological development and, as a result, reworked the earlier interpretation of both the military and the educative aspects of the monastic scola.

One of the hallmarks of late-eleventh- and twelfth-century religiosity was the new emphasis placed on the interior world of the individual.[6] Many people no longer accepted a simple equation between thought and deed but recognized that outward appearances could be deceptive and that virtuous behavior did not always reflect virtuous thoughts.[7] Men and women were confused by the new and often impersonal relations in an emerging commercial and urban society and felt torn between conflicting ethical dictates; as a result, they read traditional religious texts in new ways, joined already-existing religious communities in the hope of finding certainty, and sometimes established new communities if they found that the older institutions did not resolve their sense of conflict between outward behavior and interior intention.[8] Increased introspection led to new literary forms as people described their emotions, analyzed their intentions, and lambasted the seeming hypocrisy of those whose actions appeared to contradict their ideals.[9] By the mid–twelfth century, these developments had influenced dominant theological ideas about sin. Scholars modified the sacrament of penance by arguing that atonement required not only confession and penitential action but also a mental change. Without inner contrition, penitential actions served for naught.[10]

Because monasteries had been the dominant penitential institutions from the ninth through the eleventh century, they had to adjust to these changes. The corporate liturgical life of the older Benedictine communities helped to expiate the sins of both the monks and the monasteries' benefactors.[11] With this growing emphasis on individual and interior penance, monks reconsidered the extent of their responsibility for their society's spiritual well-being, and they examined the role of their long-established communal life in their individual progress toward salvation. Some twelfth-century abbots from older Benedictine houses defended their communities' intercessory practices but also called for their monks to concentrate on the meaning of their prayers and to develop an inner understanding of divine mysteries through participation in the liturgy. Peter the Venerable of Cluny, for example, justified his monastery's possession of tithes by stressing his community's role in aiding the salvation of lay society, but he also provided a protected space within his monastery for individual contemplation. He revised the Cluniac liturgy, not by reducing the number of commemorative psalms, but rather by eliminating pauses and demanding a correlation between the content of a prayer and its empirical context.[12] Rupert, abbot of Deutz from 1120 to 1129, defended both his monks' pastoral activities and their prayers and masses. He believed that a sincere performance of the chant would open a monk's heart to the divine even more than would biblical reading.[13] At Marmoutier, the monks curtailed the commemoration for their dead, permitted eremitical retreats, and encouraged both personal fervor and interior reform.[14] Some of the new religious communities virtually eliminated intercessory activities; the Carthusians, for example, neither recorded the names of their donors in their martyrology nor performed individual anniversary masses for them, and they met together in chapter only once a week.[15]

The Cistercians charted a middle course between traditional black monks and the new religious groups such as the Carthusians. They curtailed their prayers and masses for the dead and emphasized the importance of the interior development of each individual monk, but they stressed that this development must occur within a community. An early sign of their concern for an individual's interior life was their determination to accept only adults as novices in their communities, and once they began to develop techniques for converting adults, their interest in inner spiritual development became inevitable. Adults who became monks made a conscious choice to change their lives, and they not only renounced their secular activities but also embarked on a long process of mental change and socialization. Yet the acceptance of adults also required the Cistercians to confront and transform attitudes derived from the novices' background. By incorporating these elements into their monastic culture, they reinterpreted the idea of a monastic scola and gradually developed their own conception of the place of the individual in their communities and the role of their monasteries in the wider Christian society.

I

The Cistercians' decision to accept only adults into their communities shaped their understanding of the conversion process. The first rules concerning the age of their novices appear among the statutes collected in 1134. The order's abbots ruled that they would neither teach boys their letters in the monastery nor accept them as monks or novices until they had turned sixteen.[16] No such ruling appears among the earliest statutes, those attached to the *Summa cartae caritatis* in 1123 or 1124, so we can assume that the abbots articulated their decision sometime during the next decade. William of Saint-Thierry, in his *Vita* of Bernard, described Bernard's youngest brother Nivard as too young in 1113 to enter Cîteaux with his brothers, but William wrote in the mid-1140's and may have applied later Cistercian practice retrospectively.[17] It is unlikely, however, that the monks in the new Cistercian abbeys had the time or the resources to provide the special care and teaching that children required, even if they had not yet made a conscious decision to exclude them.[18] This rejection of oblates and monastic schools was not unique to the Cistercians. The Carthusians also refused to accept children, and over the course of the twelfth century, oblation at older Benedictine houses became rarer.[19] For many religious communities, this requirement of adult conversion stemmed from the monks' concern for their own salvation; not only could nurturing and educating children be distracting, but the oblation of children was a family decision, not an individual one, and thus did not involve the personal interior change that adult conversion could foster.

Cistercian sources do not allow a rigorous analysis of the background of the monks. Evidence from charters suggests that the Cistercians' benefactors were predominantly knightly families only recently established in positions of independent power, who had never before donated property to religious institutions.[20] It is likely that many of the monks themselves came from these families; a few charters do specify the donors' relationships with the monks or mention that sons could enter Cistercian communities when they came of age if they wished.[21] The preponderance of evidence about the background of the monks, however, comes from anecdotes drawn from two different types of sources: letters written by monks and abbots encouraging conversions, and bibliographical details contained in saints' lives and in the monks' own accounts of their history. Neither source necessarily represents the actual composition of the communities; both are skewed heavily toward the monastery of Clairvaux and its affiliates, and both were constructed, modified, and edited by monks who had a particular vision of their order's history.[22] Furthermore, as Caroline Walker Bynum reminds us, it is risky to extrapolate from imagery to actual experience.[23] The monks' use of military terms may tell us more about their idea of warfare than their actual experiences at war. It is possible, for instance, that stories about monks as transformed knights appealed even more to men who desired to become knights and dreamed of military exploits than they did to those who had actually lived and abandoned the role. Yet there is no reason to consider the information from these stories entirely fictitious. Such sources suggest that Cistercian monks wished to portray themselves as men who had abandoned knightly or scholarly lives for the true knighthood and scholarship of the cloister: they told tales about groups of knights who discovered that the most challenging fight was the battle against temptation, and they wrote letters teaching clerics that true knowledge could best be found within their monasteries.

Whether knights or clerics, young unmarried men composed the most restless and ambitious element in northern French society. Changes in inheritance patterns that limited a knight's heirs to a single son created a class of youths who sought a livelihood either through clerical appointments or through the profits of military prowess. Youth was defined less by age than by marital status: a knightly youth had neither property nor wife, and even an heir would not be considered an adult until he inherited his father's lands and married. Many knights remained "youths" for their entire lives, existing on tournament winnings and the booty from warfare and hoping that a patron might grant them the marriage of an heiress whose property could support a family.[24] Clerics also had a prolonged period of youth and sought an education that they hoped would lead them to an ecclesiastical prebend or an office with a secular lord.[25] The choice of an ecclesiastical career did not stifle youthful competitiveness: scholars fought as much as their knightly brothers but used their wits as swords to compete in tournaments of intellectual disputation.[26] Intellectual prowess won them jobs but, as the literature of alienated scholars suggests, some students never succeeded in securing a position and, like their brother knights, remained *iuvenes* for life.[27]

The Cistercians' stories about making monks out of knights did not overtly remind young men about the precariousness of their social position. Instead, the stories recognized that the companionship of friends and the love of adventure helped these men survive, but they suggested that such qualities would be even more beneficial if used in a spiritual battle for salvation. The foremost model for transforming knights into Cis-

tercian monks was the famous conversion of nearly thirty men who entered Cîteaux in the spring of 1113.[28] Included in this group were several
of the central figures in twelfth-century Cistercian history, most notably Bernard of Fontaines-les-Dijon, the first abbot of Clairvaux; Hugh
of Mâcon, the first abbot of Pontigny and later bishop of Auxerre; and
Godfrey of La Roche, the first abbot of Fontenay, later prior of Clairvaux,
and eventually bishop of Langres. Although historians once believed
that Bernard and his brothers came from Burgundian nobility, it now
seems clear that they belonged to a less prominent knightly family.[29]
Most were young men. In 1112, when Bernard first considered joining the
monks at Cîteaux, he was 22; his brothers Bartholomew and Andrew were
younger, and his brothers Guy and Gerard and his uncle Gaudry were
older. Bernard's friend Hugh of Mâcon had taken clerical orders and, like
Bernard, had been educated for an ecclesiastical career, but most of the
other men had been trained as knights and had not expected to lead a
monastic life.

When William of Saint-Thierry started his *Vita* of Bernard around 1145,
he detailed Bernard's difficulties in wooing his brothers away from a
military existence and thus made the events into a Cistercian conversion
narrative. In 1112, Guy, Gerard, Andrew, and Gaudry had accompanied
the duke of Burgundy to besiege the lord of Grancey-le-Château. When
Bernard decided to enter Cîteaux, he followed his relatives to the bat-
tlefield to convince them to join him. His uncle quickly agreed, as did
Bernard's young brother Bartholomew, who was not yet a knight. Andrew,
however, had just been knighted and "admitted his brother's words with
difficulty"; only a vision of his mother convinced him to abandon his
hopes for military glory. But Gerard was the most difficult to convince:
"He obstinately rejected the warnings of his brother and the advice
healthy for his soul, considering it to be frivolity, as is the custom for
worldly wisdom." Only after he was wounded in battle and taken prisoner did he promise to become a monk.[30]

Other stories about knightly conversions followed a similar pattern.
Young men gave up opportunities for secular glory with reluctance but,
once monks, retained both the love of companionship and the interest in
adventure that they had possessed as knights. William of Saint-Thierry
related a tale about a band of tournament-seeking knights who arrived at
Clairvaux during Lent and refused to refrain from fighting during the fast.
Bernard gave them beer but told them that they had drunk a potion

for the soul; when they left, he remained confident that they would return. Soon they turned back and entered monastic life, "giving their
right hand to a spiritual army" and abandoning the army of the world.[31]
Whatever the truth of the story, the idea of converting groups of knights
from secular to spiritual warfare constituted an important element in the
Cistercians' own mythology.

Both the anecdotes in William of Saint-Thierry's *Vita* and the sermons and parables analyzed below may have presented Cistercian monks
as transformed knights, but other anecdotal evidence drawn from letters
and biographical vignettes suggests that the preponderance of monks, at
Clairvaux at least, had been trained as clerics. Here the Cistercians ignored
the elements of Benedict's Rule that expressed reservations about accepting priests; in fact, they actively encouraged priests' conversions.[32]
Some of the Cistercians' clerical converts had been monks at other monasteries but many more held prebends in cathedrals or were scholars either at Paris or at other urban schools. The number of Cistercians previously educated in the schools appears to increase starting in the 1140's,
and most of the prominent Cistercian authors of midcentury, including
Guerric of Igny, Isaac of Stella, Geoffrey of Auxerre, and Nicholas of
Clairvaux, had been scholars before they converted to the monastic
life.[33] Many of these men still came from knightly families and had
been raised in a military milieu, but they had been trained in letters
rather than swordplay. This made their transition to monastic life somewhat easier. Still, their conversion required them to quell their ecclesiastical
ambitions, redirect their intellectual interests, and attempt to extinguish
the aggression and competitiveness that their background had encouraged.

All Cistercians were adults, but not all were aristocrats. Within two
decades of Cîteaux's foundation, the monks established a lay brotherhood
that aided the choir monks in their agricultural labors, especially on
lands too distant from the church for the monks to work without shirking their liturgical duties.[34] These men formed a distinct group within the
Cistercian communities: like the monks, they vowed to live in poverty,
stability, and obedience and avoided all contact with women, but they
wore a different habit, retained their beards, followed a different horarium with a shortened liturgy, lived in a different dormitory or in granges,
and were expected to remain illiterate and without clerical orders.

The origins of this lay brotherhood are much debated. Other new
eleventh-century communities had already established lay brotherhoods,

and the Cistercians may have adopted such an institution to help their monasteries to avoid manorial revenues and responsibilities, but this does not resolve the problems of where the men came from and what motivated them to join Cistercian communities.[35] The lay brotherhood has been described variously as a new form of lay piety and as a continuation of the class divisions inherent in a feudal mode of production.[36] Certainly, the Cistercians' lay brothers helped to compensate for the monks' refusal to live off the labor of serfs, and it appears that many lay brothers came from villages near the monastery whose lands were gradually accumulated by the monks.[37] By 1188, the Cistercian Chapter General made the social divisions within the monasteries into a general rule: thereafter, all members of the aristocracy who wished to enter the order had to become monks.[38] Yet in the early years of the order, some lay brothers, such as Bernard of Clairvaux's uncle Milo of Montbard, clearly came from the aristocracy while, even after 1188, the monks told stories about priests who hid their ordination and entered monasteries as lay brothers in order to live a life of greater humility.[39] The Cistercian miracle stories collected in the last decades of the twelfth century portray the lay brothers as especially humble and pious men, suggesting that they were motivated by religious concerns, but these stories were collected during a period of increasing discontent among lay brothers and may have reflected the monks' ideal for the lay brothers rather than the lay brothers' actual behavior.[40]

Whether knights, clerics, or peasants, the adult men who entered Cistercian abbeys could not convert to Cistercian life as a single dramatic act of penance. The creation of a monk entailed more than entering a monastery and being clothed in a new habit. It required a process of fundamental re-education through which the men both learned the prayers and rituals of monastic life and learned to think like monks. More than a matter of changed behavior, it required an interior change by which a man turned his will away from transitory earthly goods and toward the eternal good of the divine. The Cistercians' emphasis on a year-long novitiate illustrates their belief that conversion to monastic life could not be instantaneous, and their sermons and stories suggest that conversion did not end even after this first year but was an ongoing quest for salvation that would occupy a monk for the duration of his life. We know less about the conversion of the lay brothers; most efforts to indoctrinate them into Cistercian life centered around stories proclaiming the honor and spiritual rewards of manual labor and their shared brotherhood with the monks.[41] But the psychological changes implicit in creating a monk out of a knight or cleric form a central element in the Cistercians' culture.

II

Inherent in the idea of monastery as scola was the image of the monk as soldier. The picture of a Christian fighting in a divine army had its source in Paul's epistles and was further enhanced by the warlike language of the psalms that formed the nucleus of the monastic liturgy. Nonetheless, the meanings given to this image reflect specific historical conditions and illustrate changes in monastic life. Barbara Rosenwein has shown that the monks at tenth-century Cluny described their liturgy as a form of warfare in which their corporate prayers assisted God in his cosmic battle with the devil over possession of the human soul; this use of military imagery, she argues, reflected the monks' efforts to transform and control the violence of a warrior class in a society in which centralized authority had broken down.[42] Although twelfth-century Cluniac monks retained this idea of a corps of monks engaged in liturgical warfare for the salvation of humanity, the Cistercians' use of military language reflected their concern with converting adult men and their interest in the interior development of the individual monk. Rather than portray an army of monks fighting for the salvation of their benefactors, Cistercian abbots described each individual monk's battle for his own salvation. Yet this use of military imagery did not only assist the monks' conversion; it also influenced the culture of the monastery and the monks' understanding of their relations with the divine and with one another. Knights abandoned their weapons when they entered the monastery but they did not abandon the aggressiveness with which they had used them. Through their use of military imagery and language, the Cistercians incorporated a knightly aggression into their monastic life and redirected it toward spiritual, rather than material, ends.

In one of his sermons for the Nativity, Aelred of Rievaulx described Cistercian monks as converted knights, and portrayed their conversion as literally fulfilling the prophesy from Isaiah 2.4: "And they shall beat their swords into plowshares and their lances into pruning hooks." He asked his monks, "Do you not see men of worldly nobility coming to conversion, putting aside their lances and swords to work with their hands for their bread as if peasants?"[43] Yet, he continued, this passage referred not only to knights but to all kinds of people, rich and poor, clerical and lay, who beat the sword of iniquity into the plowshare of compunction. Aelred's exegesis suggests that the idea of renouncing one's sword was a potent image even for men who had never fought; even those monks who were not actually transformed knights received an education that considered them as such. At the same time, the passage illustrates the interior aspect of conversion to Cistercian life. Renunciation of the sword was not a simple action but became a symbol for the transformation of secular willfulness into the compunction necessary for spiritual growth.

Military imagery can be found throughout Cistercian writings, but some of the most vivid language is found in Bernard's parables. These stories are primarily concerned with conversion from secular society and are especially good evidence for the way the Cistercians described this process to recently arrived monks. As parables, their imagery is dramatic and elaborate; in other contexts the images did not shape the structure of the text so completely.

Bernard set his parables in a secular milieu. They took place in palaces, besieged forts, and military camps and were peopled with kings, queens, princes, and knights. In one, the son of a king rebelled against his father by eating from the tree of knowledge. As a result, he was captured and bound by the devil in the chains of worldly desire and had to appeal to his father for help. His father's retainers helped him escape from his fetters: first his father sent his servants Fear and Hope, then his prince Prudence, Prudence's friend Temperance, and the distinguished knight Fortitude. With their help, the king's son approached the castle of Wisdom: "A deep moat of humility ringed the castle, above which the strongest and most beautiful wall had been built of obedience and rose to the sky. The wall was marvelously decorated with stories depicting good examples. It was built with ramparts, and a thousand shieldsmen hung from them, all heavily armed. The door of profession was open to all; the porter on the threshold welcomed the worthy and rejected the unworthy."[44] The son entered this castle-monastery, but his trials were not yet over. Pharaoh besieged the walls. The son sent his messenger, Prayer, to his father asking for help, and the father responded by sending his consort to his son's aid. The consort, Charity, vanquished the enemy, and the son and father were reunited. Bernard ended with a moral that described four stages in the process of conversion: first, he told his monks, you are sluggish and stupid, then rash and bold in your prosperity. In adversity, you become timid, and finally, you become "prudent and wise and perfect in the realm of charity."[45]

A second parable, about the continual war between the kings of Jerusalem and Babylon, had a similar theme and was peopled by similar characters. In this story, Charity was not the king's consort but a powerful duke whom the king sent to rescue his besieged son. Charity marched forth accompanied by a noble company of virtues and, passing through the enemy lines, entered the prince's castle. Once there, he grew impatient at the delay: "He organized the army, opened the doors, and while pursuing the enemy, clearly commanded 'Depart to the doors of Hell!' Thus, moving as one, Charity's entire army went forth. The Babylonians could not endure. They fled but could not escape. Temperance felled a thousand on the left, and Prudence felled ten thousand on the right. Fear killed a thousand, and Charity ten thousand."[46]

The military imagery in Bernard's parables served as a pedagogical device. It presented the values of the monastic life in a vibrant language that the converts would understand and remember. As Jean Leclercq has suggested, such language held the monks' attention; in the early thirteenth century, Caesarius of Heisterbach recounted a story of a Cistercian abbot who complained that his monks fell asleep when he talked of God but woke up as soon as he mentioned King Arthur.[47] If an abbot presented a monk's quest for the divine as if it were a story about King Arthur, presumably he would have greater success.

Even if we cannot extrapolate information about monks' backgrounds and experiences from their abbots' use of language, we can nonetheless see how these abbots drew on prevalent characteristics of knightly life and culture. Bernard's portrayal of God as a father who sent his counselor and retainers to aid his rebellious son, for example, both drew on and transformed the common intergenerational conflicts between fathers and their sons. Late-eleventh- and twelfth-century inheritance patterns fostered such tensions: youths tried to wrest control of property and women from their elders, while fathers were torn between their desire for heirs and their fear of their sons' growing strength and possible rebellion.[48] Often fathers and sons did not know each other particularly well; boys were sent from home at eight or nine years of age to receive military training from a relative or lord. Young twelfth-century aristocrats, whether knights or clerics, certainly knew stories of youths such as Robert Curthose or, later, young Henry of England who, like the princes in the parables, rebelled against their royal fathers.[49] God as a father would not have been a particularly comforting idea for men aware of these father-son conflicts. Bernard's parables encouraged the novices' healthy fear of God while also presenting an image of a divine father who appeared to act with more justice and mercy than their biological fathers.

The parables also gave the monks familiar images with which to remember less familiar theological ideas.[50] Wisdom's castle, with its moat of humility, walls of obedience, and pictures of good works, associated familiar objects with religious virtues and taught the monks that a monastery was built out of humility and obedience in which the monks' good works provided examples for others and their prayers elicited divine aid and love in return. In a sermon for the Assumption of Mary, Aelred of Rievaulx used similar images to similar effect. He first described the military interdependence of a castle's moat, walls, and tower and only later explained that this interdependence signified the relationship of humility, chastity, and charity.[51] In another passage, Bernard of Clairvaux taught the monks to remember the virtues necessary for monastic unity by portraying them as armor.

Unity is served by three weapons: patience, humility, and charity. With these the knight of Christ should be armed. He should have patience as a shield, which he bears as a defense against all adversity. Humility should be a corslet with which he protects his heart, and charity should be a lance because, as the Apostle says, everyone who attacks when aroused by charity and does all things in its name fights the war of the Lord. And he should have a helmet of salvation, which is hope, to protect and preserve his head as the place of thought. His sword should be the word of God, and his horse, good desires.[52]

As with the castles, this is no random association of virtues with military hardware. Patience, as a shield, protects against outer adversity while humility guards against inner pride. Hope for salvation protects and directs the knight's thoughts while good deeds actively bear him through life. Charity and God's word serve as offensive weapons; charity pierces like a lance, while the word of God cuts through all resistance. Other Cistercians used similar images in their sermons and letters. Nicholas of Clairvaux, for instance, in a letter to brother Gaucher, described the monks of Clairvaux as knights standing guard day and night over the bed of Solomon, each "wearing a corslet of justice and a helmet of salva-

Figure 1. A knight slaying a dragon. Under the influence of Bernard of Clairvaux, the Cistercians stopped producing such fanciful illuminations. Nonetheless, these early miniatures illustrate the same themes that Bernard drew with words—here, a knight redirects his aggressiveness against evil. Gregory the Great, *Moralia in Iob* (c. 1111). Dijon, Bibliothèque municipale, MS 173, f. 20. Photograph courtesy Bibliothèque municipale, Dijon, France.

tion, having a shield of faith and a sword of spirit which is the word of God."[53] Nicholas ended this passage with one of his favorite conglomerations of biblical quotations, telling Gaucher, "These are the troops of God, and this is none other than the house of God and the door to heaven" (Gen. 32.2, 28.17).

By using military imagery as a pedagogical device to convert adults, the Cistercians modified the idea of monks as transformed knights. They retained the concept that liturgical performance was a form of spiritual warfare, and they, like the monks from Cluny, worked to channel the violence of lay knights into areas sanctioned by the Church.[54] But whereas Cluniac writers had emphasized the battles of a corps of monks who fought for the salvation of their patrons, the Cistercians instead described the monk as an individual knight beset by dangers that threatened his own salvation. The princes in Bernard's parables initially faced danger alone, and when they began to defend themselves, they had to act alone in choosing to use the help sent by their father. Even the descriptions of the knights who came to the young prince's aid emphasized the solitary character of the fight, for these knights were nothing more than the qualities and virtues of the monk himself. Even when Nicholas of Clairvaux presented the monks of his monastery as the troops of God, he still described each monk as fighting on his own behalf with the armor and weapons of his own virtues.[55] The fight was a battle within each individual monk; each struggled against temptations so that he might order his will.

This shift in imagery paralleled a change in the intercessory role of the monastery, in which the Cistercians downplayed their corporate responsibility to pray for the spiritual well-being of others and emphasized instead each individual's responsibility for his or her own salvation. In condensing their liturgy, the Cistercians eliminated many of the rituals by which older communities had associated their patrons with the monks' spiritual benefits. The Cistercians did retain an Office for the Dead, but they removed many of the traditional psalms and collects.[56] They also greatly shortened this office, spreading the nine psalms and lessons over three days, and reducing the collects, which at Cluny could number as many as nine, to four: for those in the cemetery; for monastic brothers, carnal brothers, male relatives, *familiares*, and the recent dead; for mothers, sisters, female relatives, familiares, and the recent dead; and for all the faithful dead.[57] The only time benefactors were specifically commemorated was in chapter, when the monks read a tablet remembering the brethren, familiares, benefactors, and all the faithful dead.[58]

Some benefactors did receive special benefits from the order. In an unusual charter from Pontigny, dated 1118, a Josbert and his sons gave a parcel of land to the abbey "for the soul of my wife Elisabeth, with the agreement that each year on the anniversary of her death—the eve of the mother of St. Gregory—the brothers living there commemorate her memory in their prayers."[59] In letters, the Cistercians mentioned to prominent living benefactors such as Count Theobald of Champagne and King Louis VI that the monks would remember them in their prayers, and in 1152 the Cistercian Chapter General recorded for the first time that the abbeys would offer some benefactors, in this case the king of France and the bishop of Le Mans, the same prayers that they offered a dead monk.[60] Parents, sisters, and brothers of each monk also received commemoration at their death, whether or not they had given property to the monks, but not as full a set of prayers as a monk or a benefactor treated as a monk.[61] Initially, the Cistercians refused to bury outsiders unless a guest or hired worker died within the monastery, although, by the time they issued their collection of statutes in 1134, they had relaxed this prohibition to allow the burial of two friends or *familiares* of each monk.[62] In 1152, the Chapter General decided that no one except kings, queens, archbishops, and bishops should be buried inside their churches, but in 1157 they decided that they would bury no one except their founders.[63] This vacillation concerning the policy of burying nonmonks suggests that the Cistercians' benefactors believed burial in the abbey to be an important privilege and that the monks were unable to convince all of their prominent patrons to forgo such benefits.

Although Cistercian monasteries did not abandon the role of professional penitents completely, their reduction of the rituals and services for their benefactors suggests that they wished to concentrate predominantly on their own spiritual well-being. The stress they placed on fighting for their own salvation further reflects these changes. Not only did Bernard's parables describe an individual monk who accepted and used God's gift of aid, but they also stressed the monk's continuing interior change. A monk began his quest for salvation in the secular world, where he oscillated between fear of divine judgment and hope for divine mercy, but the quest continued in the monastery. There the monk only gradually gained victory as his prayers and divine love vanquished the enemy. This emphasis on the continuing fight and gradual conversion of the individual knight reflected the needs of an order whose novices were adults, but it also illustrated a change toward a more interior conception of conversion and penance.

The Cistercians' use of military language illustrated but also influenced their conception of progress toward the divine. Military images did not merely describe monastic virtues, they shaped the connotations associated with them. The monks had accepted into their communities men whose backgrounds had encouraged violent and aggressive behavior; they succeeded in controlling the violence, but the aggression remained and was even encouraged.[64] No longer knights, the monks renounced the honor, loot, and women that fighting provided, but they redirected their aggression into a battle against temptations and for spiritual rewards and divine love.[65] Virtues themselves took on military and aggressive characteristics. Bernard's description of caritas as an offensive weapon and his picture of it as a king's most powerful duke did not merely satisfy a monk's interest in military affairs, nor did they only create images for remembering the place of that virtue in monastic life. The Cistercians' caritas was no gentle virtue but a monastic weapon with which a monk could slay thousands of his enemies by invoking it in all that he did. By associating charity with military aggressiveness, the image affected the meaning of the word.

Guerric of Igny's sermons contain very little explicit military imagery, but this makes even more striking the penetration of aggressive language into his understanding of a monk's relationship with the divine. In a sermon for the feast day of John the Baptist, Guerric took for his text the passage from Matthew, "Since the days of John the Baptist the kingdom of heaven suffers violence and the violent are even now seizing it" (Matt. 11.12). Rather than lament this behavior, Guerric considered this violent attack on heaven as a model to be imitated. He asked his monks, "For what else ought the repentance of sinners to be called if not violence against the kingdom of heaven? Is it not violence to seize by strength what has not been granted to nature . . . ?" He told his audience that their purpose was to win heaven by force, to wrestle with God, to be armed with the power of love, and thus to conquer the king of heaven himself, "for he seeks to train your soldiers, test your constancy, multiply your victories, and increase your crowns."[66] Guerric repeated this theme in a sermon for Advent, where he told his monks that the "violence of our prayers and the vehemence of our fervor" would draw Jesus into their hearts, and he spoke of the "benevolent violence by which the heavenly kingdom is borne away."[67] Guerric's monks may have given up their swords, but their abbot's sermons encouraged them to retain the attitude with which they had used them.[68]

The conversion of young men to Cistercian life required them to alter their lives in a radical fashion. They not only renounced their former training and received a new education but also reshaped themselves mentally to control their willfulness and their aggression. At the same time, however, the monasteries also adjusted. In developing ways to educate and socialize their new monks, the Cistercians incorporated into their monastic culture elements and assumptions inherent in knightly society. Monks clothed themselves in virtues as if they were wearing weapons and armor; they fought temptations and evils as if they were carry-

ing swords. This association of military aggression with monastic life
had ramifications for the monks' understanding of their role in society,
for they began to work for the salvation of others with an aggressiveness
carried over from the knightly milieu they had abandoned.

III

Just as the Cistercians modified the idea of a monastery as an army of
knights, so they also developed a new conception of the monastic community as a school. Even in their descriptions of monks as knights
searching for salvation, the Cistercians stressed the educative aspects of
their communities.[69] Nonetheless, they did not incorporate aspects of
scholastic culture into their monastic life as easily as they did the culture
of knightly society. Their monastic school did not attempt to transform
the lessons of the urban schools so much as replace them. In creating an
opposition between monastic and urban schools, however, the Cistercians
also began to articulate a new role for monasteries in their society.

The Cistercians' refusal to educate children reflected their acceptance
of eleventh- and early-twelfth-century changes in educational practice.
The establishment of urban schools whose curriculum was unconnected
to the liturgical requirements of monastic life meant that a monastic
education appeared increasingly limited, whereas a scholastic education
in the liberal arts provided the groundwork for more specific studies in
theology, law, or medicine. Even monastic and scholastic theologies
stemmed from different assumptions; monastic theology grew out of
monks' contemplative and liturgical experiences, whereas scholastic theology developed out of intellectual curiosity and a need to define and
teach doctrine.[70] Despite these differences, monasteries and urban schools
attracted men from similar backgrounds. Both offered an education
and the possibility of ecclesiastical positions to younger sons who had little if any inheritance and a pressing need to find a means of support.
These underlying similarities led monks and scholars, like other twelfth-
century groups, to define who they were by emphasizing the differences
between themselves and those groups most like them.

The Cistercians participated actively in this rivalry between school
and monastery and spoke forcefully for the benefits of a monastic rather
than a scholastic education.[71] The monastery was still a school, Bernard of Clairvaux insisted, but unlike the urban schools, which offered

an education with powerful and lucrative positions as its reward, the monastery was a school of piety with Jesus as its master.[72] Bernard's secretary, Nicholas of Clairvaux, repeated Bernard's description of the monastery as a school of piety, and he asked his friend Lecelin to abandon his philosophy of vanities and become a fellow student "under that teacher whose school is on earth and chair is in heaven."[73] Again imitating Bernard, he told Lecelin, "All day, I hear, you read philosophy, rhetoric, and poetry; do you believe that you understand what you read? Believe me, you will find more among us by using hatchets and trowels than you find there in writing and books."[74] Unlike secular education, which wasted a scholar's intellectual talents, pandered to ambition and pleasure, and provoked no fear of God and damnation, a monastic education taught "Jesus crucified."[75] Bernard even offered a competitive goad to a young man who had broken his promise to come to Clairvaux, informing him, "This is not at all easy knowledge to grasp, unless one becomes crucified to the world."[76]

Other Cistercians also emphasized the opposition between monastery and school. Geoffrey of Auxerre, who had been a student in Paris and entered Clairvaux after hearing Bernard preach to Parisian clerics in 1140, described his conversion as moving "from empty studies to the cultivation of true wisdom."[77] His comparison of his two teachers, Abelard and Bernard, exemplifies his understanding of the difference between school and monastery. According to Geoffrey, Abelard saw in the crucifixion both Jesus' virtuous example and the incentive for humans to love him, but he placed no emphasis on its redemptive value. As Geoffrey explained it, Abelard defrauded his students by only showing them Jesus' feet and intestines, whereas Geoffrey's new master, Bernard, entrusted his students with the head as well by teaching that Jesus' willingness to sacrifice himself for human redemption showed his immeasurable love for humanity.[78] This emphasis on the Incarnation and on Jesus' loving sacrifice formed the centerpiece of the Cistercians' theology; as Bernard had told scholars, Cistercian education taught "Jesus crucified."

It is often pointed out that, despite his animosity to the schools, Bernard himself was well educated in the liberal arts and that he and Cistercians such as Geoffrey of Auxerre used scholastic arguments and terminology even when expressing their hostility to scholastic education.[79] A few Cistercians were even open to the mingling of scholastic questions and monastic goals. Isaac of Stella, who probably had studied at Paris and possibly at Chartres in the late 1120's and 1130's before entering a Cistercian monastery sometime before 1147, did not abandon the methods he had learned in the schools but combined speculative theology with a characteristic Cistercian emphasis on God's descent into humanity and the possibility of a human ascent to the divine.[80] Of the twelfth-century Cistercians, Isaac may have gone the farthest in his attempt to balance speculative theology with the monastic life, but he was not the only one to believe that scholastic learning could benefit monastic education. Gilbert of Hoyland, an English contemporary of Isaac's who became abbot of Swineshead just before 1150, wrote a vocation letter to a young scholar named Adam that praised the study of liberal arts as valuable if used properly. He argued that they could be a step toward the "higher and holier and more secret mysteries of wisdom."[81] He criticized Adam's study of philosophy because "this scanty and uncertain acquaintance with natures and principles, which can hardly be reached through long detours and roundabout digressions, has delighted you to excess, snatched your soul, and attracted your love."[82] He did not think Adam should abandon philosophy altogether, but that he should direct it toward its proper end by explaining the nature of the divine and the character of divine blessings. Gilbert suggested that, when Adam had done that, "then I will willingly listen to a fuller explanation and a longer narration of what you think about pardon, grace, and glory, on what the Lord has given, returned, or added for us, and all that he has endured for us and contributed to us."[83] Such a letter suggests that the conversion of a scholar to monastic life required the redirection of his education toward different ends but did not necessarily mean the renunciation of all that he had previously learned. Despite an often-expressed hostility to the schools, the Cistercians accepted scholastic concepts and methods if used within the framework of Cistercian life, and some Cistercians even abandoned this hostility to admit the validity of scholastic questions.

Underlying both the sharp antagonism expressed by Bernard, Nicholas, and Geoffrey and the more temperate comments of Gilbert was a common thread of criticism based less on the Cistercians' suspicion of the scholastic method than on their belief that a scholastic education did not properly train a moral and virtuous clergy. Gilbert, Isaac, and Bernard all believed that the proper end of education was the spiritual growth that led toward salvation, rather than the wealth, honors, and worldly position that could accrue to an ambitious man educated in an urban milieu. Cistercian monks frequently described the immorality of the contemporary clergy, even incorporating such laments into their sermons on the Song of Songs.[84] This also served as a common theme in their letters to clerical friends whose conversions they wished to encourage. Odo of Ourscamp, who himself had been chancellor at Paris before entering Ourscamp in 1165, asked a friend to envision the corrupt behavior of specific clerics whom they had both known: a dissonant cantor, a disobedient scholar, a master who was master only of his errors, all would be scorned by God and cast aside, Odo told his friend, whereas those caught in the net of monastic life would be saved.[85] While ghost-writing a letter for the monk Alquer that encouraged clerics from the church at Périgueux to convert, Nicholas of Clairvaux also warned that those men ruled by comforts, worldly glory, and devilish pride would be damned. He contrasted the religion of the monastery to that of the world: "Worldly people joined to worldly things bring the name of religion into contempt and disgrace, whereas we reject and expel inwardly from our thoughts and deeds the world and things of the world."[86] Urban schools were a path to perdition, but the school of the Cistercian monastery provided a certain road toward salvation.

This opposition between urban schools whose lessons led to damnation, and Cistercian monasteries whose lessons taught virtue and led toward salvation, was not only a rhetorical figure, for it had implications for the monks' understanding of the social function of their religious communities. They had created their monasteries at a time when monks began to lose their traditional role as corporate intercessors for society and secular priests began to assert their role as mediators between the laity and the divine. The stories and sermons told to educate the monks stressed the importance of their inner development and portrayed them as solitary knights concerned for their own salvation rather than a band of knights fighting for the salvation of their society. Unlike many black monks, the Cistercians expressed no regret in abdicating a central intercessory role, and they saw no conflict between monk and clergy.[87] Instead, their opposition to the urban schools was part of a debate over the proper education and behavior of the secular priests who now had responsibility for the salvation of the laity. Although the Cistercians did not suggest that all priests should first be monks, they did present their monasteries as the best schools for an education in virtue, and they offered their monks who became bishops as ideal models for a reformed clergy. The monastery, as a *scola dilectionis*, both taught the monks to love and encouraged them to fight for love. Yet these monks could neither direct this love only at the divine nor confine it to the other men within the boundaries of their communities; this love bound together the entire Church and involved the Cistercians in promoting the reform and well-being of their society.

Chapter 2

"The Consolation
of Holy Companionship"

Individual Progress and Community Support

The Cistercians' image of a monk as a single knight who fought for his own salvation yet relied on the company and aid of a corps of other monks brings into sharp focus questions about the relationship between individual and group. Cistercian authors expressed these questions in religious terms by asking how to reconcile an individual's progress toward the divine with the demands of the other members of their community, or, in other words, how to love both God and neighbor. Ideally, they believed, no conflict could exist between these two objects of caritas: a monk who perfectly loved God loved his neighbors in God. But the Cistercians were at least as concerned with learning to order their lives within the realm of the real as they were with describing their ideals. Their understanding of caritas certainly included the soul's potential for union with the divine, but it focused primarily on the monks' attempts to order their love with the aid of a community and the demands of life on earth. As a result, the Cistercians recognized a possible goodness and order in their earthly existence and suggested that the very process of working to realize these possibilities formed an essential part of each monk's search for his own salvation.

Many studies of the Cistercians' conceptions of love have noted the monks' belief that brotherly love was a necessary component of love for the divine.[1] Caroline Walker Bynum's essays have added greatly to this body of work, for she analyzes the Cistercians' sense of community within the context of the more widespread changes in religious life, especially the emerging twelfth-century concern for serving one's neighbor. By comparing the Cistercians' ideas about service and love to those of other religious groups, she demonstrates that the Cistercians continued to emphasize the Benedictine idea that monks were learners, but that a Cistercian education had an interior component lacking in that of either the regular canons or the black monks. Cistercian monks learned compassion and humility by living in a community and developing an awareness of the example of others.[2] Much of what follows here owes a great debt to Bynum's studies. But, whereas Bynum concludes that the Cistercians responded with ambivalence to the new ideal of service and felt a tension between denying the world and affirming it, I suggest that their community organization made room for a new conception of service in which aiding the spiritual development of others became a necessary component of an individual's own spiritual progress. The Cistercians were not torn between their desire for contemplation and their active concern for others, but they made a distinction between the trials of life on earth and the goal that they sought in heaven. Their goal was union with the divine in caritas, but the process of working toward this goal on earth demanded both individual contemplation and an active concern for the well-being of others. Coping with the sometimes conflicting demands of one's own needs and the needs of others was itself part of learning to grow in caritas. Such a position neither denied nor affirmed the world so much as saw its potential for reform.

I

The Cistercians began to define their communities at a time when many traditional Benedictine monasteries experienced a crisis in their communal organization.[3] The administrative and political duties incumbent on the abbots and officials of large and prominent monasteries distanced these men from the monks and burdened them with secular cares at a time when many also became concerned for their own spiritual development. Monks complained about such duties: Peter Damian, with his satirical tongue, claimed an abbot's real home was no longer his monastery but the back of his horse, and Bernard of Tiron fled his monastery of Saint-Savin for the forests of Maine and Brittany to avoid election as abbot.[4] At the same time, the monastic communities themselves began to fragment. Eleventh-century monasteries had emphasized the performance of corporate rituals, especially the liturgy, as the fundamental means for contact with the divine, but in many monasteries these rituals no longer included the entire community. Peter the Venerable, for example, described Cluny's liturgy as the link between his monks and the army of heavenly saints, but this expression of corporate unity and divine contact was undermined when only one-quarter of his monks attended the daily offices.[5] Some monks who missed offices were monastic officials whose administrative duties took precedence over prayer, but many were priests who performed private masses concurrent with the communal liturgy. Large monastic communities also fragmented physically: monks were sent to distant priories or periodically left their communities for eremitical retreats.[6] The challenge for these monasteries was to find a way of creating cohesion between the brothers as their communities increasingly lost their intimate character.[7]

The early Cistercians responded to these problems only gradually. The erratic behavior of Robert of Molesme suggests that he disliked the duties incumbent on the abbot of a large and prominent Burgundian monastery and enjoyed the character of smaller, less institutionalized communities of hermits but had no idea how to preserve their spirit as his monasteries began to grow. In comparison, Stephen Harding, the third abbot of Cîteaux, and the abbots of the new Cistercian foundations developed regulations for their abbeys that held the potential for new community relations. It has been suggested that the early Cistercians themselves were split in their ideas about the purpose of their new communities: Stephen Harding stressed a legalistic interpretation of the Benedictine Rule, whereas Bernard of Clairvaux desired a mystical and ascetic life in which he could learn to become "perfect."[8] But the differences between Stephen Harding and Bernard of Clairvaux do not show a division in the order as much as two stages in its development: Stephen's legalistic concerns allowed later abbots, such as Bernard of Clairvaux, Aelred of Rievaulx, and Guerric of Igny, to articulate the possibilities for personal growth inherent in the Cistercian community structure.

Although there is much uncertainty about the Cistercians' early documents, it is clear that the monks established the framework for their community organization during the first two decades of the twelfth century. Therefore, it is necessary to work through the hints and suggestions within these sources to understand the monks' actions and motivations. Much historiography has remained so focused on the Cistercians alone and on the way the monks later explained their behavior that these later justifications have been mistaken for initial motivations. The historical argument has centered on whether the monks intended to follow the Benedictine Rule "perfectly," "strictly," or "to the letter" and has ignored the underlying question of what motivated their interpretation of the Rule.[9] An examination of the Cistercians in the context of a more widespread concern about abbatial burdens provides a different view of their behavior.

The three men considered the founders of Cîteaux all held administrative positions at Molesme: Robert served as abbot, Alberic as prior, and Stephen Harding as Robert's secretary. If a thirteenth-century account of Robert's activities is at all trustworthy, the events of his life suggest a man who disliked the administrative duties of his office but was incapable of restructuring his communities to preserve the life he desired.[10] The *Vita* shows a man who seldom remained long in positions of responsibility: he was elected abbot of Saint-Michel of Tonnerre and prior of Saint-Ayoul at Provins but each time left his office after a couple of years.[11] This picture is reinforced by the comments made by the archbishop Hugh of Lyons when he negotiated the settlement between Cîteaux and Molesme in 1099; he accused Robert of "habitual inconstancy."[12] In 1075, after undertaking to direct a community of hermits, Robert reshaped them into a monastery that he would again abandon. He moved the hermits to the forest of Molesme, built a monastic cloister on land donated by the family and neighbors of Hugh of Maligny, and accepted donations from most of the aristocratic families in the region, including the duke of Burgundy and the count of Troyes.[13] Such connections involved Robert in the affairs of the prominent aristocratic families throughout Burgundy.

From its inception, Molesme differed little from other reformed Burgundian monasteries. For the first ten years, donations were sparse and the monastery was poor, but after this difficult first decade, the community became very popular and attracted both donations and recruits.[14] It accepted donations of villages and manors, received tithes, and controlled churches. It admitted child oblates, maintained families who had donated their property to the monastery, and allowed donors to take the monastic habit on their death beds and be buried in the abbey.[15]

It permitted the duke of Burgundy to hold court within its enclosure.[16] And it expanded very rapidly. In the 25 years between its foundation and 1100, it had established 40 dependent priories spread over 12 dioceses.[17] Not even Cîteaux multiplied so quickly. Molesme's growth and popularity shows the strength of Benedictine monasticism in eastern France in the late eleventh century. Molesme, like Cluny, was closely linked to local aristocratic families—it prayed for them, accepted their extra children, supported them in old age, buried them, and received their lands in return.

According to Robert's thirteenth-century *Vita*, by the mid-1090's Robert, Alberic, and Stephen Harding all temporarily left Molesme for eremitical retreats.[18] The *Vita* describes these men as motivated by their despair over reforming the monks remaining at Molesme; although such an interpretation has been followed by some modern historians, it is also possible that these men were discouraged about their administrative responsibilities and relished the opportunity to live as simple monks.[19] In 1098, these same men again left Molesme, this time with more permanent consequences.

The early Cistercian documents do not clearly define what customs these monks instituted in their new monastery in the forest of Cîteaux. Those who did describe the monks' intentions portrayed their proposals in comparative terms: the archbishop of Lyons wrote that the monks wished "to adhere more strictly and more perfectly to the rule of most blessed Benedict, which you previously held tepidly and negligently in that other monastery [Molesme]," and he allowed them to move in order to "serve the Lord more soundly and more quietly."[20] Although this comparative language suggests that the monks thought of their new community in comparison to the one they had left behind, nothing suggests that they had yet developed a clear idea of what their "stricter observance" of the Benedictine Rule might entail. In fact, Robert's behavior suggests that he was again unable to separate his new monastic community from the monastic tradition he knew so well. Not only did he carry his liturgical books and equipment with him when he left Molesme, ensuring that his new monastery would initially continue to follow Molesme's liturgical practices, but he also accepted land on which two serfs lived, suggesting that he initially had no aversion to manorial exploitation.[21] In addition, he allowed the duke of Burgundy to hold court at the monastery on important feast days.[22] Such an arrangement immediately entangled the monks in social relations similar to those at Molesme and suggested that, once again, Robert's desire for regular discipline was not in itself enough to prevent the accumulation of the responsibilities he found so burdensome. But Robert did not remain long at Cîteaux. In 1099, under pressure from the monks remaining at Molesme, the papal legate, and the bishop of Langres, Robert returned to his former monastery with the monks "who did not love the wilderness."[23] In this resettlement, Cîteaux lost its most conservative members: those men most likely to form the new monastery in Molesme's image.

We know little about developments at Cîteaux over the next two decades. By the time the *Carta caritatis* received papal approval in 1119, however, we can see evidence that the Cistercians had begun to resolve some of the problems Robert had sensed but could not define. Most important, they addressed the issue of the abbot's responsibilities by bringing the abbot closer to his monks and limiting some of his authority. They did this by claiming to return to a strict interpretation of the Benedictine Rule, but in so doing they actually modified the position of the abbot in his community.

The Benedictine Rule gave the abbot discretionary authority in his monastery. The abbot represented Christ, and his monks obeyed his commands as if they were wishes from God.[24] He held the responsibility for both the spiritual and the physical well-being of his monks and would answer for their condition on the Day of Judgment.[25] Although he followed the precepts of the Rule as a means of preventing his abuse of power, the Rule allowed him the authority to take into consideration the local conditions, climate, and needs of his monks, especially in regulating prayer, food, drink, and clothing.[26] In general, the abbot was to distribute goods according to the needs of his monks and with consideration for their weaknesses.[27]

The Rule governed relations between the abbot and his monks, but it did not consider the relations between a group of communities founded by a single abbot, even though Benedict himself had established a number of related communities.[28] The prevalent eleventh-century model for the relationship between a monastery and its affiliates was that used by Cluny, Marmoutier, and Molesme, in which one abbot had authority not only over his own community but over all dependent priories as well. Such an organization put immense burdens on a conscientious abbot—he was responsible for the salvation of all his monks, both those in his own community and those living some distance from him—and may have contributed to Peter Damian's complaints that abbots spent most of their time on the back of a horse.[29]

Establishing connections between affiliated houses became an issue for Stephen Harding with the expansion of his new monastery and the establishment of the communities of La Ferté, Pontigny, Clairvaux, and Morimond between 1113 and 1115. Stephen's solution was to rely less on his own discretionary authority as abbot to bind his communities together, and more on the abstract authority of the Benedictine Rule. In the years following the foundation of La Ferté in 1113, Stephen and his fellow monks composed a charter regulating the relations between the monasteries.[30] By the time the pope confirmed this "Charter of Charity" in 1119, Stephen had given up most direct control over the new Cistercian foundations.[31]

The *Carta caritatis* established that each Cistercian abbey should be an independent entity with its own elected abbot who was responsible for the internal affairs of his house, and it insisted that no abbey could demand revenues from any other.[32] At the same time, it drew the abbeys together into an order by determining "by what bond, in what manner, and even by what love the monks, who were divided in body into abbeys in diverse parts of the world, were indissolubly glued together in spirit."[33] This bond was not common obedience to a central abbot but instead stemmed from a uniform observance of the Rule and monastic customs throughout the order. Stephen ordered all the new monasteries to follow the Rule in exactly the same way as it was followed at Cîteaux: "They shall not introduce any other meaning into the reading of the holy Rule, but they should understand it and hold it just as did our predecessors the holy fathers, that is, the monks of the New Monastery, and as we today understand it and hold it."[34] Stephen understood his own authority as ensuring that each monastery preserved this uniform discipline of the Rule. He did retain the ultimate responsibility for the monks' souls, but he placed it within the context of his obedience to the Rule: he retained the care of their souls so that "if they should ever be tempted to stray from their holy resolve and the observance of the holy Rule, even a little bit," he could help them return to "the right path of life."[35]

This insistence on a uniform observance of the Rule curbed a Cistercian abbot's authority and placed him under the Rule as interpreted by the community of abbots meeting in a yearly general chapter. Whereas

Benedict had allowed the abbot discretion in regulating the liturgy and the amounts of food, drink, and clothing, the charter curtailed the abbot's authority in exactly these areas. It removed the abbot's ability to arrange the order of the psalms by ordering that the liturgical books for all Cistercian abbeys "follow the form of the customs and books of the New Monastery, so that nothing be in discord in our actions, but that we live bound by one love and one Rule and the same customs."[36] Two of the Cistercians' early statutes, probably composed before 1123, limited the abbots' discretion in matters of food and clothing as well.[37] In both cases, these statutes first cited the authority of the Rule, but then transformed its guidelines into orders. Clothing was to be "simple and inexpensive, without fur or undergarments, as the Rule prescribes," cowls were not to be flocked on the outside, and day shoes were to be made of cowhide.[38] Bread had to be coarse, that is, sifted through a sieve, and made with either wheat or rye flour.[39] The Rule itself says nothing about the material for shoes, the composition of the cowls, furs, or the type of bread to be served, and never mentions undergarments.[40] The Cistercians specified practices in the very areas that Benedict had left to the abbot's consideration.

Stephen's use of a uniform observance of the Benedictine Rule as the glue that unified his disparate monasteries actually modified the structure of a Benedictine community by lessening the distance between the abbot and his monks. The abbot still had the ultimate human authority in his abbey, he still witnessed his monks' vows of obedience, and he was responsible for their spiritual welfare; however, like his monks, he was subject to the authority of the Rule. The Cistercian customary, assembled by 1134, shows how the monks' rituals reflected these changes.[41] As in older Benedictine communities, the abbot still promoted or degraded whom he wished, received confessions, judged and absolved his monks of faults, and ate with the guests in the hostel. But unlike monasteries such as Cluny, where the abbot had a special chair in the center of the choir with his monks arrayed along the sides, in Cistercian monasteries the abbot joined his monks by sitting in the first stall on the right of the choir, and he took his turn performing the mass with the other priests in the monastery.[42]

The Cistercians modified some of the ritual behavior directed at the abbot as well. Their description of the abbot in their customary has a very different tone than either Ulrich's customary for Cluny or Lanfranc's for Canterbury. All three customaries enumerate the duties of an abbot, but both Ulrich and Lanfranc were especially concerned with the behavior of the monks toward their abbot. Ulrich began by asserting that "special reverence is to be granted to the lord abbot in all places, as is fitting," and he ended his section by reminding his readers that whatever the abbot decided about customs should be accepted as law. The monks were to rise as the abbot went up to read in choir and as he returned to his seat; they were to kiss his hand whenever he gave anything to them and bow whenever they heard his name recited. Bells for services continued until the abbot arrived, so that he was never late.[43] At Canterbury, wherever the abbot went in his monastery, the monks rose until he passed.[44] The Cistercian customary mentions none of this. In chapter, only the monks sitting beside the abbot bowed to him; the others bowed to one another.[45] They bowed not just to the abbot but also to each other if their paths crossed while walking in the cloister.[46] Perhaps most indicative of the Cistercian abbot's changed position is a statute among those collected in 1134 ruling that the abbot, like his monks, was to be punished if he arrived late for prayers.[47]

By the 1120's, the changed position of the Cistercian abbot had become apparent to other monks. Around 1124, William of Malmesbury described the Cistercians' observances and noted that each monk possessed only two tunics and wore no breeches, that their clothes contained no linen, furs, or fine wool, that they made no additions to the offices except the Vigil for the Dead, that they sang Ambrosian hymns, and that they had so arranged their offices that they did not return to bed after matins but proceeded directly to lauds. "They so watch over the Rule," he concluded, "that they think not one dot or point of it should be omitted." The abbot, he said, "allows himself no indulgence beyond the others: he is everywhere present, everywhere attending to his flock, except that he does not eat with the rest because his table is always with the pilgrims and the poor."[48]

By lessening the distance between the abbot and his monks, the Cistercians placed a greater emphasis on the horizontal relations within their community. These relationships were further enhanced by the friendships the men had established before they entered the monastic life. Stories about young knights stressed the bonds of companionship within bands of knights who had often been raised together; they were united by a common search for adventure, pleasure, and booty and by ties of love and loyalty that often lasted for a lifetime.[49] It is unlikely that twelfth-century knights were ever the solitary knights errant of Arthurian legend; that men such as Chrétien de Troyes's *Yvain* lost their names and their identity when isolated may reflect the fear these young men had of being alone. Furthermore, twelfth-century French literature describes the love and companionship that united these bands of knights. Marie de France's *Guigemar* depicts a youth initially more interested in his male friends than in the romantic love of women, whereas Chrétien de Troyes's *Yvain* so enjoys his life with his companions that he ignores his new wife.[50] In both stories, the young knights eventually learn to balance the two types of love. But, in an early-thirteenth-century account of William Marshal, William and his band of youths seldom spoke of loving their wives or mistresses. This was an emotion they reserved for their relations with one another; they were "friends" who "loved each other like brothers."[51]

The Cistercians incorporated this aspect of the culture of aristocratic youth, as they had so much else. Although originating in secular society, these friendships could be maintained once the men entered a Cistercian monastery. Recent work on monastic friendship suggests that, for a few decades in the mid-twelfth century, the acceptance of such bonds of friendship aided developments in both monastic culture and monastic reform, especially, although not solely, among the Cistercians.[52] Putting on the "new man" of the monastic life did not require abandoning one's friends; instead, these new monks encouraged their old friends to convert as well. Friends offered one another advice and emotional support that furthered their spiritual development without necessarily undermining the harmony of the community. In fact, such friendships could aid the well-being of a community as abbots developed webs of friends who also offered political aid and alliances.[53] In Cistercian abbeys, this assimilation of secular friendships added to the new conception of abbatial authority a new understanding of the relations between monks in which the aid and compassion the monks offered to one another also helped their own spiritual progression toward the divine.

The most famous group of friends to enter a Cistercian monastery was the community formed by Bernard of Clairvaux before he entered Cîteaux in the spring of 1113. When Bernard assembled his brothers, uncle, and friends at Châtillon-sur-Seine the winter before entering Cîteaux, he created a version of the bands of military youths but sought adventure in a monastery renowned for its harsh austerities rather than in the tourney and rapine of knightly quest.[54] The fragments written by Geoffrey of Auxerre about Bernard's life contain an especially evocative picture of Bernard's efforts to convert his clerical friend Hugh of Mâcon: the two men spent the night "in so narrow a bed that there was barely room for both," and after the two men outmaneuvered the clergy who wished to prevent Hugh's conversion, the two "returned hand in hand, having re-strengthened their spiritual friendship."[55]

Other men, both knights and scholars, also entered Cistercian monasteries with their friends; Bernard's *Vita* tells of knights converting in groups, and Bernard himself described the conversion of Geoffrey of Peronne, the treasurer of the church of St. Quentin, who entered Clairvaux in 1131 with a group of his companions (*socii*).[56] The many letters of Nicholas of Clairvaux, which he wrote (or ghost-wrote) to invite friends to enter Clairvaux, also point to the bonds of friendship linking clerics and scholars.[57] Even before the foundation of Cîteaux, Stephen Harding had entered Molesme with his friend Peter, with whom he had traveled on pilgrimage from Burgundy to Rome.[58] When the Cistercians accepted groups of men for conversion, they accepted as well the bonds of fraternal companionship these men had already developed.

The Cistercians were not the only religious group to respond to the problems of abbatial authority and community cohesion caused by the fragmentation and social responsibilities of large eleventh-century monastic houses. Some communities, such as the Carthusians, eliminated the position of abbot altogether and stressed solitude and individual prayer.[59] Other monasteries, such as Marmoutier, tried to reintegrate their liturgically based communities by emphasizing the abstract bonds of shared prayers, especially the spiritual assistance offered to the dead and dying.[60] The Cistercians, in comparison, chose a middle ground and emphasized individual spiritual growth within a communal setting.[61] They downplayed the importance of the liturgy by curtailing the length of the daily horarium, and they stressed the interior response of each individual monk to his prayers by insisting that the chant be sung slowly enough to be understood.[62] At the same time, they tried to maintain an intimate and face-to-face character in their communities. Monks who were priests, for instance, could ordinarily perform private masses only during the times for reading and the period after the conventual mass; on fast days they could perform masses between the conventual mass and nones, if there was time. In either case, the customary ruled that they were not to miss the communal mass and that, if they were in doubt as to whether they had enough time, they should ask the sacristan.[63] Furthermore, the Cistercians did not create priories. All monks were to return to their cloister every night, except the monks who were sent to distant markets.[64] As a result, they lived a life in which they remained physically present to one another: they ate together, prayed together, slept in the same dormitory, and all participated in the daily chapter.[65] As Guerric of Igny described it, the Cistercian community stood midway between life alone and life in a crowd: "In our desert we have the tranquillity of solitude but we do not lack the consolation of a welcome and holy companionship. It is possible to sit alone and be silent . . . but it cannot be said of us: 'Woe to him who is alone,' who has no one to cherish him or lift him up if he should fall" (Eccles. 4.10).[66] With the support of their community, monks and abbots could develop an interior silence in which they could hear the voice of God.

In 1119, when the *Carta caritatis* received papal approval, Cistercian monks had not yet articulated the importance of communal life for their individual spiritual growth. Nonetheless, Stephen Harding's legislation, which placed the Cistercian abbot under the Rule and within a community of brothers, not only responded to a widespread unease with the burdensome nature of an abbot's responsibilities and authority but also aided the formation of a new type of monastic community. Although the implications of this new community only become apparent once Bernard of Clairvaux settled into his monastery and began to write, Stephen helped to create an environment that fostered emotional and affectionate bonds between the monks as necessary components of progress toward the divine. In so doing, he provided the foundation for the later Cistercians' language of love.

II

Whereas Stephen Harding initiated a community structure that modified the character of older Benedictine monasteries, it was Bernard of Clairvaux and the men influenced by him, including Aelred of Rievaulx, Guerric of Igny, and William of Saint-Thierry, who articulated the relationship between individual growth and community life that this monastic organization encouraged. The Cistercians' picture of a monk as a lone knight on a quest in search of God suggests that they broke with an older conception of divine contact as liturgically based and instead advocated an individual contemplative experience of the divine. The process of achieving such an experience, however, took place in a community. Not only did the physical presence of other men help a monk strive toward a union with God, but any lasting union required the perfection of the monk's body and the reform of his neighbors as well as the transformation of his own soul. As a result, the Cistercians' conception of community not only combined individual development with community service but also allowed the monks to recognize the potential in both physicality and social relations. This had important implications for their ideas about reform.

The Cistercian authors wrote about their search for divine union in abstract treatises about the soul and sermons that described the process of transformation. These sermons and treatises had both theoretical and practical components: they described how a human soul could come into contact with the divine and how the monastic life provided the best environment for this contact to occur.[67] They portrayed divine contact in various ways, as the harmony of the will and intellect with the divine, as the contemplative delight of feeling filled with divine grace or love, or as the mystical ecstasy of being subsumed into the divine. Essential to each conception of union was the idea of caritas, for it could refer to the perfection of the human will, to divine grace, and to the divine essence itself. Yet, though caritas could describe an ideal union with the divine, much of the Cistercians' writings about it instead concerned the monks' desire for this union and the process of striving toward it. Such depictions of desire and process suggest that the Cistercians saw themselves as living a life of penance on earth rather than as inhabiting an antechamber of heaven that they had entered when they decided to join a monastery.

Central to the Cistercians' anthropology was the Augustinian idea that humans had been created in the likeness of God and possessed an image of the divine in their souls.[68] The divine likeness had been obscured by sin, but the image remained.[69] As a result, those Cistercians who analyzed the nature and powers of the soul also articulated the abstract theological assumptions that underlay their search for the divine and the organization of their monastic life. They were not alone in making these assumptions; what is particularly striking about their theology is less the particulars of their speculative analysis than the sensitivity with which many of the abbots incorporated their own experiences and inner thoughts into their practical and moral lessons.[70]

Cistercian authors did not agree about the exact location of the divine image within the human soul, but all believed it was possible to restore its divine likeness. Bernard of Clairvaux located this image in the free will, whereas most other Cistercian theologians placed it in the rational soul.[71] Despite such differences, all of these authors assumed there was an innate desire in the soul to turn toward the divine. This was a natural weight (*pondus*) or appetite (*affectus*) by which the soul desired what it thought to be good for it. The dilemma for fallen humanity was that this desire was misdirected. Although wishing to be deiform, each soul nonetheless confused its love of immediate but transient material goods with its love for the eternal and spiritual good of the divine. The process of redirecting this desire involved the reform of both the intellect and the will: teaching the intellect to recognize what was truly deserving of love, and controlling the will so that soul would love what it knew to be lovable. As the intellect learned the proper object of its love, a person developed humility; as the will learned how to love, a person became obedient and filled with caritas. This education in humility and obedience was the central purpose of the Benedictine Rule; what the Cistercians emphasized was the idea that fraternal relations could shape interior feeling as well as external behavior and transform obedience into love.[72]

The different locations of the divine image influenced the authors' conclusions about the potential for a soul's union with God. For some Cistercian theologians, contact between the soul and the divine required an interaction between a person's intellect and desires that involved knowing as well as loving the divine. Isaac of Stella, for instance, described contact with God as a state in which knowledge of the divine increased love and love of the divine increased knowledge:

What he sees will light his way to love; what he loves will enkindle his desire to see. So shall seeing and loving stimulate each other that they will form the infinite round of blessedness that only the godly deserve. This seeing and knowing is the result of love; this love and longing the fruit of knowledge. . . . Knowing and loving God is the religious life in a nutshell, the target of our spiritual exercise.[73]

For Isaac, contact with his God was a dynamic condition in which love and knowledge continued to inspire each other. For other Cistercians, such harmony between intellect and will was an important stage in the process of learning caritas, but was not the end in itself. For Bernard, this was the state in which a monk loved God, not yet as God loved him, but no longer only for the goods God provided; it was a state in which a monk loved God because God was good and lovable.[74] William of Saint-Thierry described a progression from "animal man" to "rational man" to "spiritual man": when a monk was "rational," his will and his intellect were in accord.[75] Aelred of Rievaulx described a similar stage in his *De speculo caritatis*, in which he told his monks that the burden of obedience to the Cistercians' observances would lift once they had learned to control their concupiscence and pride.[76] At such a point, monastic regulations were no longer onerous, for the monk now acted according to his understanding rather than out of obedience and fear.

For Bernard and for William of Saint-Thierry, this harmony between intellect and will did not fully unite the soul with God. Both men suggested that there was a point at which a human's continual longing could be quelled momentarily and the soul could rest in the enjoyment of divine love. For Bernard, the ultimate contact between the soul and the divine was a matter of the will alone and occurred at the point when the will became so infused by divine love that it regained its deiform character and could love everything just as God loved it.[77] For William, such a union required a special divine gift. In his commentary on the Song of Songs, he described the embrace of the soul with Christ not as the culmination of a monk's spiritual development but as a special gift of encouragement from which the soul then declined to be cleansed.[78] The goal of a monk's development, the condition of the "spiritual man," was also a state in which enjoyment of the divine was a gift of grace.[79] For both Bernard and William, the soul existed in unity of spirit with the divine when it could will or desire what God willed. But both also doubted that a human could achieve such a state on earth. When Bernard described a progression in love, he questioned whether anyone could achieve this final step while still alive; William wondered whether the full perfection of charity was ever possible in this life.[80]

Whether contact with the divine required the intellect and the will or the will alone, Cistercian spiritual writers described growth in caritas more than caritas itself. Although caritas could refer to the divine essence that was the end of all human desire, most Cistercian authors emphasized the process of ordering human desire more than the state of fulfillment.

Earthly contact with the divine was dynamic: Isaac of Stella described continuing feedback between loving and knowing, whereas Bernard of Clairvaux portrayed an infinite loop of desire itself. Bernard's great paean to the nature of love describes love as an action rather than an essence: it is desire that wants nothing more than itself.

Love is sufficient for itself; it is pleasing for itself and because of itself. It is its own service and its own reward. Love needs no cause beyond itself and no further return; it is its own use and its own enjoyment. I love because I love; I love so I may love. Love is a great reality, and because it returns to its beginning, reverts to its origin, and flows back to its source, it will always draw again from the place out of which it flows freely. Of all the motions of the soul, the senses, and the affections, love is the only one by which the created can respond to the creator, even if not as an equal, and can reciprocate in a similar fashion. . . . When God loves, he desires nothing more than to be loved, because he loves for no other reason than to be loved and knows that those who love him are blessed by their love.[81]

Even though Bernard began this section of his sermon by stating "Deus caritas est," he used "amor" rather than "caritas" throughout this passage. By using "amor" to refer both to human desire and to divine grace, he described the potential for a mutual love between humans and God and the possibility of transforming the human will. This idea that divine contact was a dynamic process rather than a contemplative rest was a fundamental characteristic of Cistercian thought.

The Cistercians' treatises on the nature of the soul described the spiritual progression of an individual, but their monastic writings made clear that this process took place in communities in which the monks were always aware of the physical presence of other men. The Cistercians had assimilated the bonds of friendship common among secular youth, and their regulations sought to preserve the face-to-face character of their communities; the monks then found in the physical proximity of their brothers essential lessons that aided their progression toward the divine. The physical needs of others taught each monk self-control; the desire to be loved and respected by others aided his conscience and shaped his behavior and thoughts; the desire to love others taught him compassion and mercy and ordered his love into caritas. The physical and spiritual needs of both their own bodies and those of their fellow monks might have distracted the monks from a complete and long-lasting state of divine contemplation, but the social and physical aspects of a monastic community played an essential role in aiding their continual progression toward this ideal, heavenly condition.

Spiritual progress toward the divine started with the body. Cistercian authors certainly described an opposition between body and spirit and believed that the body retained habits established by a misguided will, but they made clear that the fundamental battle was internal; the body itself was not the problem. In fact, the soul needed the body for the knowledge necessary to perfect the intellect, for the created world could only be understood by the mind working in the body.[82] The body could also serve as an example for a sinful soul and spur it toward goodness; Bernard of Clairvaux suggested that the body stood upright and looked toward the heavens while the sinful soul remained mired in earthly dung. Bernard even described the body as scolding the soul, saying that because the soul had abused the body's service and used its help to disgrace itself, it was unworthy to dwell in a human body.[83]

Even more, the body, as a physical presence, aided the soul in reordering its love. An education in caritas started with the physical, for the soul naturally loved its body. This self-love was the most basic of all forms of love and was experienced by all humans.[84] As this love was transformed and redirected, a monk began to offer to his body the possibility of eternal life rather than the transient pleasures of life on earth, but he never ceased to love it. According to Bernard, souls could not be in complete rapture until the resurrection of their bodies as they still felt affection toward their bodies after death and did not want to be perfected without the bodies that had served them.[85]

One of the first steps in the movement of the soul away from a purely self-interested love was learning to love someone else. Eventually, this became a love subsumed into the love of the divine, but its reordering started as a person recognized another person's physical presence and developed a concern for his or her needs. Loving another person as oneself required providing him or her with all the things one wanted or needed oneself. However, because a person's unchecked appetites could be infinite, supplying another person with all the things one wanted served to moderate one's own desires. In his treatise *On Loving God*, Bernard described how this process worked: "If a man is overburdened, not by relieving his brother's needs, but by satisfying his desires, he should restrain his own if he does not want to be a transgressor. He can indulge himself as much as he wishes, as long as he remembers to offer

the same to his neighbor."[86] Not only were there insufficient goods to satisfy people's never-ending desires, there were not enough to fulfill even
their true needs, a situation Bernard may well have experienced in the first
years after Clairvaux's foundation.[87] Bernard's invitation to his monks to
indulge themselves as long as their brothers could be equally indulged was
merely a rhetorical offer because he knew that such sharing instead required the monks to control their desires and reduce their needs so that
everyone could have the essential necessities. As a result, the Cistercians
were taught to control their avarice and self-love not only through obedience to a superior but also through their concern for one another.

In addition to providing a check on each monk's unrestrained desires, the Cistercian community also helped the monks to learn to love
one another.[88] Although certainly aware of the dangers that the love of
someone's physical presence could provoke, both Aelred of Rievaulx
and Bernard of Clairvaux believed that such an affection could also be
shaped for the good. Aelred warned against the dangers of loving another's
appearance, but he did not reject this attraction outright as evil. He instead suggested that it could serve as the first step toward loving that person's virtues.[89] Similarly, the abbot Baldwin of Ford asked how a monk
could love God, who was not present, if he did not first love his neighbor who was present to him.[90] Much more important, however, was
the idea, based on Bernard's assumption that bodies existed to help oneself and others, that physical existence allowed monks to offer each
other aid and solace in a way that they could not if separated. As Bernard
wrote: "It is human and necessary that we feel affection for those who are
dear to us; that we feel delight when they are present and grieve when they
are absent. Social interaction, especially between friends, cannot be pur-
poseless; the dread of separation and the sadness of both when separated shows what the mutual love produces when friends are together."[91]
Bernard and other active Cistercians wrote of their longing for their
communities when absent from their brothers on ecclesiastical business.[92] Such laments suggest that the ties binding the monasteries were
not only abstract ideas of a unity of spirit but also a true enjoyment
and comfort that stemmed from the physical presence of their fellow
monks.

The Cistercian community taught each monk to love, but it also reinforced each monk's desire to be loved. By building on this wish, the monastic community became an external conscience for the monks. In

their lessons for their communities, abbots assumed that each monk wished to retain the regard of his brothers.[93] Bernard, for example, described progress in humility as stemming not only from obedience to the abbot but also from living in harmony with brothers and seeking to gain their respect.[94] Seldom did the Cistercians describe this community pressure as coercive; more often they described their communities as providing each monk with examples and support, and they only implicitly suggested that each monk should strive to be worthy of the love and example of his brothers. Thus, Guerric of Igny described living in a Cistercian monastery as feeding among lilies where each lily was the example of a virtuous soul, and Gilbert of Hoyland suggested that the tears and sighs of those monks lamenting their weaknesses might be noticed by others "so that if it happens that some of those who sit nearby are cold themselves, they may catch fire from the sparks of their neighbors."[95] Aelred of Rievaulx linked a monk's attachment to his brothers, and especially to his particular friends, to their virtuous example, for the example of a friend and the desire for his approval served as an impetus for further spiritual development.[96]

Guerric of Igny made explicit the relationship between a monk's own spiritual progress and the effect of the community's regard. In a sermon for the feast of Saint Benedict, he told his monks:

Everyone must take care to do what is good not only before God but also before men. They should neither neglect a good conscience for a good reputation nor neglect a reputation by trusting only in one's conscience. How can you possibly flatter yourself about a clear conscience unless you are without complaint among your brothers? . . . Do you think it is enough not to cause them to stumble? The fact is, you trip them up if you do not instruct them, that is, if you do not glorify God everywhere according to your own position, and have a witness to your goodness both within your conscience and among your brothers.[97]

Thus the community worked in tandem with each monk's own inner conscience. Although some monks found it easier than others to inspire love in their brothers, all monks were obliged to seek the respect of their fellow monks by teaching them through good examples and virtuous behavior. In such a way, the monks' love and their desire to be loved were linked: a monk loved his brothers by edifying them through his own good example, and he became a virtuous example because of his desire to be loved.

The community did correct the monks, but the monks described this discipline as stemming from their compassion and fraternal charity. In the yearly Chapter General, where the abbots assembled at Cîteaux to correct and improve their observances "and restore the good of peace and charity among themselves," any abbot found faulty in his behavior or in the discipline of his monastery was to be "charitably accused" and punished by his fellow abbots.[98] The idea that the correction of faults was an act of fraternal charity appeared within each monastic chapter as well. There a delinquent monk would be accused by his brothers, who could also intercede for him; if he received a beating as punishment, the brother who struck him would help replace his robe.[99] Other monastic customaries also associated compassion with discipline, but whereas in Lanfranc's customary all the monks who witnessed the beating of a monk were to "bow down with a kindly and brotherly compassion for him," in Cistercian monasteries the individual monk who administered the punishment made the ritual display of compassion.[100]

Figure 2. The cloister and chapter house at Fontenay. © 1995 Artists Rights Society (ARS), New York / SPADEM, Paris.

This direct relationship between the culprit and the punisher illuminates another lesson taught by the fraternal relations within a Cistercian community: the development of feelings of compassion and empathy. Such empathy developed out of self knowledge: once a monk had learned true humility, he could recognize in his brothers reflections of his own situation and have compassion for them. Bernard described how such fraternal love grew out of self-awareness:

When a man considers himself and others, he should become gentle with everyone. Following the counsel of Paul, the wisest of men, he should learn to bend down to those who are caught in habits of sin, while always reflecting on himself lest he too be influenced by them. Is it not in this that love of neighbor is rooted . . . ? For indeed, fraternal love derives from intimate human affections, and it grows and strengthens in that good soil which is the natural and innate sweetness by which a person esteems himself.[101]

Feelings of compassion and mercy were essential to the ordering of a monk's love. Bernard told his monks that they should search for the truth first in themselves, then in their brothers and only then in Truth itself. Other Cistercians also described progressions starting in self-love, passing through love of neighbor, and ending in love of God. These steps were not strictly chronological because the perfection of self-love and fraternal love was impossible without love for the divine.[102] Still, as Aelred of Rievaulx explained, this progression described a growth in a person's capacity to love, which expanded and eventually subsumed all other objects of affection into a love of the divine.[103]

By feeling compassion and empathy for his brothers, a monk progressed toward divine love, for such feelings reflected the love Jesus himself had for humanity. The Cistercians considered Jesus' mercy and forgiveness, even toward those who crucified him, as the perfect example of fraternal love.[104] Jesus loved not only his friends but also his enemies, and loved not only those striving to be good but also those still sunk in sin. For Bernard, Jesus' compassion for his enemies and his willingness to suffer as a human made him a model of mercy: "Our Savior has given us the example. He wished to suffer that he might know compassion, he became wretched so that he might learn mercy. . . . I do not mean that he did not know how to be merciful before; his mercy is from eternity to eternity, but what his nature knew in eternity, experience taught him in time."[105] The Incarnation, then, was the ultimate example of empathy because the Christian God experienced the world as a weak mortal rather than as an immortal and all-powerful divinity. A monk who willingly endured the slights and animosities displayed by other monks and developed a sense of compassion toward his brothers began to imitate Jesus. In so doing, he became further infused with the divine love that brought him closer to God.

The Incarnation also provided the best example of the role played by the human body in spurring people toward love. Jesus took on a human body not only as a sign of his complete humility, nor only as an example of perfect love and compassion, but also as a means of encouraging people to love him. Bernard noted that it was easier for people to love the humanity of Jesus than the divinity of God, and that this was why God took on human flesh and interacted with humans as a human.[106] This was true both for people who knew Jesus in the flesh and for later generations of Christians: people continued to be attracted first to the human Jesus and his living example of charity and transformed this physical love to a more rational and more spiritual one afterward. "That physical love," Bernard claimed, "is good because through it a carnal life is excluded and the world is condemned and conquered."[107] Guerric of Igny made a similar point, although he placed less emphasis on love and more on sensory perception; he argued that the Word became flesh because human minds were incapable of comprehending invisible and abstract things and needed to sense an object before they could believe in it.[108]

The fraternal relations in a Cistercian community educated each monk in charity. They helped the monks to control their self-love, expanded their capacity to love, encouraged their virtues, and supported and corrected them when they were weak. The monks' love for their brothers was inspired by, and further enhanced, their love for the divine; ideally, there was no conflict between the two. As a monk's love for his brothers grew, he increasingly responded to their encouragement and acted in ways pleasing to God; as his love for the divine increased, so did his ability to love and provide an edifying example for his brothers. Furthermore, once a monk transformed his self-love into divine love, he loved the world as God loved it and thus loved himself and his neighbors to the extent that they too loved God. Baldwin of Ford explained that when the bride in the Song of Songs proclaimed that her groom ordered her charity, she referred to both love of the divine and love of neighbor, yet "the love of neighbor refers back to the love of God, because you cannot love your neighbor except according to God, in God, and because of God."[109] Ultimately, Cistercian authors suggested, fraternal love included friends and enemies, fellow monks, all other Christians, and even heretics, schismatics, pagans, and Jews.[110] Imbued with caritas, a monk could love his enemies as Jesus had; he could both endure their unwarranted attacks and continue to hope for their reformation. Only if an enemy made clear that he would never change could he be hated, or rather, be regarded as if he were nothing, for only then had he rejected all possibility of divine love.[111]

This ideal state of union with the divine may have been the goal of Cistercian life, but Cistercian authors made clear that it was a goal toward which monks and abbots constantly strove and never fully reached. The contemplative state was at best a fleeting experience; a lasting experience required not only the perfection of the will but the perfection of the body and neighbors as well.[112] Otherwise, Bernard of Clairvaux explained, when a monk became rapt for a moment in contemplation, "immediately the vile world envies him, the evil of the day disturbs him, the mortal body weighs him down, the needs of the flesh bother him, the weakness of corruption offers no support, and sometimes with a greater violence than these, brotherly love calls him back."[113] As he suggested in another sermon, even in a state of contemplation a mind could become so inflamed by the zeal "to bring to God those who will love him equally well" that it willingly abandoned quiet contemplation in order to preach.[114] When a monk tried to put contemplation ahead of the love of humanity, he still could not help but feel compelled to care for his neighbors and his weaker brothers for, as Bernard wrote, "by human law and necessity we aim more toward earthly peace than heavenly glory."[115] Such a compulsion did not signify badly ordered love but instead illustrated a distinction between affective and active charity. Bernard considered affective charity a mental and emotional love best fulfilled by contemplation; its order was rational, for the greater the nature of the object, the more love it inspired. But affective charity could not be fully achieved by anyone while alive. Active charity, on the other hand, was love shown through action; its order seemed topsy-turvy because it put earthly matters over heavenly ones.[116]

The Cistercians' stress on the importance of fraternal relations for a monk's spiritual progress, and their sense that love, even of the divine, was always dynamic, made clear that this seemingly backward active charity was an essential component of their religious life. The idea that a love that traditionally seemed a hindrance to spiritual growth could actually be beneficial appears as well in two famous laments over the death of a monk: Bernard of Clairvaux's grief for his brother Gerard, and Aelred of Rievaulx's sadness for his friend Simon. These laments appear as spontaneous outbursts of grief, but they interrupt highly crafted texts about love, and thus are less spontaneous than they seem.[117] Both men asked whether sorrow at a friend's death was evidence of their lack of faith, and they wondered that they did not rejoice, now that their friends were at peace in a divine embrace. When Augustine of Hippo asked such questions in his *Confessions*, he saw his grief as a sign that he had not yet learned to love God and his friends "in God"; and this refusal to admit the beneficial nature of such feelings of sadness was repeated in the 1140's by the Benedictine monk Lawrence of Durham.[118] But Bernard and Aelred both believed that the affection enhanced by a friend's physical presence could be worthwhile and thus saw the loss of a friend as a cause for mourning. Bernard even introduced a new category, "tears of brotherly compassion," to supplement the "tears of compunction" and "tears of heavenly desire" described by Gregory the Great; this legitimized tears shed at the death of a loved companion.[119] In mourning the death of their friends, the abbots made clear that they mourned for themselves, not the departed, and that they missed their companions because they missed the encouragement and comfort that their friends' physical existence had provided. Their discussions of their emotions and their dependence on the physical presence of their companions further emphasized the importance of active charity in Cistercian life: spiritual growth was impossible without the love and aid that a monk offered and received from his brothers.

The disjunction between the rational order of affective charity and the necessary order of active charity did provoke some Cistercian abbots to express a sense of discordance between their desire to love God and their responsibility for their brothers. Such a conflict grew out of their efforts to balance pastoral responsibilities with a concern for their own salvation and may have become particularly noticeable as Cistercian communities became larger and more socially prominent.[120] Yet these abbots described this tension in more general terms, as applying to all monks. For example, Bernard of Clairvaux and Gilbert of Hoyland warned their monks not to disturb people in contemplation, but at the same time they worried that, after hearing this warning, monks who really needed help would be afraid to ask for it.[121] By communicating to their monks their conflicting impulses toward contemplation and fraternal aid, the abbots again suggested that there was little difference between the experiences and responsibilities of abbots and their monks, but they also helped incorporate this tension between the ideal and the possible into their general monastic culture.

The Cistercians were more interested in the process than in the goal, in a monk's actual experiences than in the ideal progression of a monk who never faltered. Cistercian writing is filled with a sensitivity to the difficulties of the monastic life, and abbots not only encouraged their monks as they ascended but also helped them to avoid despair if they slid backward. Even more, abbots noted the constant tension between their desire for divine love and the realities of their human condition—the needs of their bodies, their neighbors, and the church as a whole. Although they believed that this tension could only relax after the resurrection of the body at the end of time, they did not scorn humanity or reject entirely the material world. Instead, they found potential goodness in human existence. The physical and social demands that might distract a monk once he had attained an ideal state of contemplation nonetheless provided essential assistance as he progressed toward the divine.

For the Cistercians, these conflicts were characteristic of the life on earth that resulted from fallen humanity. Just as union with the divine was at best a fleeting experience while still on earth, so too the harmony between individual contemplation and community life was only fully possible in heaven. Total peace, whether the harmony of body and soul or the unity of individual and community, was the goal of earthly life but was not an earthly condition. Yet, rather than viewing the human condition as a hindrance to the soul's progress, the Cistercians found a goodness both in the physicality of the body and in the emotions of fraternal relations. Although they occasionally expressed an unease with an order that gave human love a priority over divine love, they assumed that the process of growing in love required not only an infusion of divine grace but also the experience of loving other human beings. Whether it was the love for a friend, the sorrow for his death, or the care for a brother that distracted a monk from contemplation, all helped to lead a monk toward his God.

Chapter 3

"A Garden Enclosed"

The Cultivation of the Soul

The Cistercians' belief that they could order their love by caring for others suggests that they recognized the importance of the physical world in aiding their progression toward the divine. As they worked to control their wills, they never stopped loving themselves or their brothers; instead, this love became subsumed into a shared love of God. They demonstrated this sense of the potential goodness of the material and the physical in two seemingly unconnected aspects of their life—their economic behavior and their use of the imagery from the Song of Songs. Their records of land acquisition show that they believed they could reshape the physical world as they transformed their wills; their understanding of the imagery of sexual desire and cultivation from the Song of Songs implies that the transformation of their wills also changed their perception of the world around them, allowing them to see signs of the soul's harmony with the divine in the fertility of a garden and the absence of uncontrollable desire. Taken together, the Cistercians' economic and exegetical practices indicate that the monks found in human desire and the natural world echoes of divine harmonies that spoke of the paradise they wished to create and foreshadowed the heavenly state they hoped was to come.

I

The records describing the property acquired by the first four Cistercian abbeys illustrate the monks' desire to reshape the material world and remove its secular character. The traditional picture of the Cistercians' economy has suggested that they accepted wasteland from the local aristocracy, cleared it for livestock, sold wool, and rapidly became wealthy despite, or even because of, their desire for poverty.[1] Recent scholarship has shown that much of the Cistercians' land was already under cultivation but still supports the picture of Cistercian productivity and ties with a market economy.[2] Although the Cistercians' stories about taming the wilderness may have had little basis in reality, their records of land holdings demonstrate a confidence that they could remove their land from the layers of claims and obligations normally attached to property and distinguish it from the property of others. Such aggressive policies regarding real estate did not break the regulations of the order, although they did bring some monks into regular contact and negotiations with secular society. Instead, these activities suggest parallels between the Cistercians' material and spiritual concerns. Just as the monks explored the process by which a will tainted by secular desire gradually came into harmony with divine love, so they also described the process by which they transformed secular property into a religious domain.

Since the 1970's, studies of the Cistercians' economic practices and social contacts have flourished. Historians have looked past the monks' regulatory documents and polemical attacks to analyze charters and cartularies for evidence of the monks' activities and their relations with their patrons. Although they stress regional variations, these scholars have generally replaced the earlier picture of Cistercian "frontiersmen" with a new picture of efficient estate managers and entrepreneurs who carefully accumulated already-productive lands, organized their holdings into compact units through purchases and trades, and created networks of granges whose lay brothers, assisted by hired laborers, provided a profitable workforce.[3] Some of these studies still fall within the paradigm that contrasts the Cistercians' ideals with their behavior.[4] Other recent work has portrayed the Cistercians as "holy entrepreneurs" but does not so much connect the monks' religiosity to their socioeconomic behavior as suggest that they did not impede each other.[5] This chapter will explore more fully the relation between the monks' economic activities and their religious ideals. The notices, pancartes, and cartularies that the monks created to record their holdings demonstrate an interest in transforming property that paralleled their attitude toward the body and physicality. Just as Cistercian authors described the process of converting human love into divine love, so the Cistercians' cartularies demonstrate the steps by which they untangled the layers of rights and obligations attached to secular property and made their land into a religious domain. Land, like love, maintained a material or physical character, but it could be stripped of its secular distractions and connections; like the human will, it could be shaped to reflect the harmonies of divine creation.

As the Cistercians began to write their history and establish their regulations, they insisted that their founders had established their monasteries in the wilderness. The *Exordium parvum* described the location of Cîteaux as "inhabited only by wild beasts, and unaccustomed to the approach of men because of the tangle of trees and thorns"; the *Exordium cistercii* called it "a place of horror and vast wilderness"; and William of Saint-Thierry used the same phrase in his description of Clairvaux's valley.[6] Such descriptions express a metaphorical condition more than they do the reality of the monasteries' physical locations.[7] The Cistercians built their first five monasteries in Champagne and Burgundy, regions that had been settled since Roman times, and although the abbeys tended to be on the edges of dioceses, they were located near inhabited areas, along major roads and paths, and often not far from towns.[8] This proximity to settled communities and cultivated land meant that, as the monasteries increased their holdings, the monks had to determine how to approach the layers of rights and obligations that inevitably encumbered such property.

The orders' early statutes show the monks' efforts to distinguish their property from the lands around them. Although the dating of many of these statutes is still unclear, those attached as *capitula* to the *Summa cartae caritatis* probably reflect decisions made by the Chapter General before 1123.[9] These abbots decided to distance their monasteries from thickly inhabited areas, decreeing that "no community is to be constructed in towns, castles, or manors."[10] Furthermore, they strictly enforced both the boundaries of their property and the lines that they believed should separate monks from other groups in society. Neither parish priests nor seigneurial landlords, they refused to perform pastoral duties and to exact manorial fees. An early Cistercian statute declares: "Our name and regulations exclude churches, altar revenues, tithes from the labor or husbandry of others, manors, serfs, land rents, oven and mill dues, and other incomes of this kind, as contrary to the monastic purity of our institution."[11] It is possible that the monks had already decided to reject manorial revenues before 1119, for a notice recording one of the first donations to Cîteaux reports that the property did not include manors, peasants, or returns from the various settlements on the territory.[12] By the mid-1130's, the Cistercians had explained their rejection of tithes: although such revenues were due to the clergy who served the altar, "we monks are obliged by our profession and by the example of our fathers to live by our own toil."[13] Unlike many other monks, the Cistercians claimed neither the portion set aside for the priests nor that reserved for the poor.[14] By insisting that their income derive from their own labor on their own estates, they tried to avoid revenues that entailed obligations toward people outside their monasteries.

The organization of the labor that worked the land further enhanced the separation between the Cistercians and the society around them. Whereas many other Burgundian monks saw the performance of the liturgy as a form of work and depended on manorial revenues and peasant labor for their economic well-being, the Cistercians wanted to live off the products of their own labor.[15] However, because they needed to balance their physical work with their hours of prayer, they followed the example of other new monastic houses such as Vallombrosa and the Grand Chartreuse and instituted a lay brotherhood whose members shared the spiritual benefits of the monastery but performed fewer prayers and more labor.[16] Some of these lay brothers lived in the abbey itself, but as the monks began to accumulate property at a distance from their cloister, they settled the lay brothers in granges that became focal points for the accumulation and exploitation of their land.[17] The monks also hired labor, implying that they had a source of revenue with which to pay and that they understood money's potential power.[18] By distinguishing between living off the labor of serfs, which they forbade, and living off the labor of hired men, which they allowed, they made an unspoken assumption about the relation of money and labor: by paying workers, they made this labor their own. Donors, especially ecclesiastical donors, often noted the difference between the Cistercians' property and that surrounding it; they allowed the monks to keep tithes due from monastic land as long as it was cultivated by the monks themselves, their lay brothers, or their hired workers and not by peasant tenants.[19]

The Cistercians' grange-based economy and their use of lay brothers and hired labor made the formation of compact estates especially im-

portant. Land consolidated around the monastery itself could be cultivated by the monks and the lay brothers who resided at the abbey; land
consolidated some distance away could become the location for a grange
where lay brothers could live without returning to the monastery each
evening. Isolated parcels of land, however, were difficult to exploit.

To obtain and consolidate their property, the Cistercians retained
many of the basic economic assumptions and strategies of older Benedictine monasteries. Even though they curtailed some of the spiritual benefits they offered their benefactors, they accepted the fundamental
premise that their economic foundation depended on their possession of
property rights and their ability to pray for others.[20] Unlike Stephen of
Muret's followers at Grandmont, who refused to control land outside their
enclosure, the Cistercians did not limit the amount of the land they
could obtain.[21] Like most other monks, they entered into negotiations
with their neighbors. They received much of their land as gifts for which
the donors might receive intangible spiritual benefits, but they worked
to consolidate their holdings around their granges by requesting specific pieces of land, by exchanging unwanted parcels for those they desired,
by negotiating with the various family members and dependents who held
partial claims to a property, and by offering money or rents in return for
particular property rights.[22] These strategies did not break any of the order's regulations, but they did demonstrate an aggressive attitude toward property that some observers found unsettling.

If the Cistercians' strategies for accumulating property differed little
from those used by other monks, their treatment of this property once it
became theirs differed greatly. Barbara Rosenwein has pointed out that
land is a unique commodity because it can be alienated without being
moved an inch.[23] Around Cluny, she argues, the "ownership" of a piece
of property only gradually moved from the benefactors to Saint Peter and
his monks. Families remembered that the land had once been theirs: it
remained visible to them, and neither its inhabitants nor its form of
exploitation necessarily changed. A donation to tenth- or eleventh-century Cluny was often a fluid process that established an ongoing relationship between two neighbors rather than a concrete transfer of property from one party to another. For the twelfth-century Cistercians,
however, this was not the case.[24] Although some families did establish ongoing relations with Cistercian abbeys and disputed or reconfirmed earlier donations, once they gave property to the monks, they did not get it

back. Property given to the monks was no longer accessible to the laity or subject to manorial exploitation; it was now set apart from the lands around it.

The Cistercians created and organized the records of their property to emphasize the process of obtaining land and distinguishing it from non-Cistercian property. Recently, historians have become interested in examining charters and cartularies not only for information about actual social interactions but also for the vision of social order that the authors wished to reinforce with the authority of a document and seal.[25] Forged foundation charters, for instance, provide information about monks' conception of their history, even if they say little about the actual events of the monastery's creation. Similarly, the structures of cartularies demonstrate the way the monks organized their property and viewed their patrons.[26] Although most of the Cistercian cartularies were compiled in the thirteenth century, there are twelfth-century documents from the first four abbeys that illustrate how these monks presented their property and its transformation. Whether notices, pancartes, or cartularies, these documents demonstrate the monks' interest in recording the accumulation, consolidation, and ultimate transformation of their property from a worldly to a religious domain.[27]

Cîteaux recorded many of its twelfth-century land transactions in notices containing multiple listings, usually of property transactions within a single region. The production of these notices ended in the last third of the twelfth century when the monks at Cîteaux prepared their first cartulary, but the existing notices were eventually copied into a thirteenth-century cartulary.[28] These notices illustrate the monks' detailed interest in detaching land from seigneurial and feudal obligations and making it their own. One such notice tells the story of Cîteaux's accumulation of property for a grange at Moisey.[29] It lists seven separate transactions that probably took place between 1116 and 1119; because the scribe noted the temporal relations of two transactions to ones he had already recorded, the story may be roughly in chronological order. Even more, it illuminates the gradual unraveling of the layers of rights associated with the property. It begins with the largest donation: for the good of their souls, Bernard, lord of Ruellée, and his sons and wife gave the monks of Cîteaux all the property they held in the *fundo* of Moisey, including fields, woods, meadows, and water rights; Guy, lord of the castle of Saint John, from whom Bernard and his family held the lands, approved the gift. The donors of the second act—the canons of the castle of Beaune (who acted with the consent of Bishop Stephen of Autun), the lord Landric and his brother ("before they had brought home wives"), and a knight Raimund—did not have such extensive rights at Moisey, for they gave only arable fields. There is no mention of a pious motive for their gift.[30]

Although even these first, relatively straightforward transactions demonstrate the untangling of property rights, the next transactions show the lengths to which the monks would go to obtain full control of the land. Four brothers, called the Buscerani, promised their fields and meadows at Moisey to the monks if the monks could obtain for them land currently held by the lord Guy of Trouhans and Ogier of Bessey and his brothers "because the brothers Buscerani had rights there that the knights did not wish to render to them." So the monks bought (*ementes*) these fields, meadows, and woods for the Buscerani brothers and received the property at Moisey in return. They did this with the consent of the eldest brother's wife but without the approval of his sons, "who were very young and could not do this." The brothers placed the gift on the altar at Cîteaux and, in the presence of Guy of Trouhans, Ogier of Bessey and his brothers, and "many witnesses," promised that they would not demand anything from the monks if, in the future, a dispute arose over the lands they now freely possessed. The wives of Guy and Ogier and Guy's son also approved this transaction. In a second exchange, the monks bought land from the lord Pons le Bouteiller and his wife and gave it to the monks of Saint-Bénigne of Dijon in return for the fields that Saint-Bénigne's priory at Palleau held at Moisey. This exchange received the approval of the monks and Pons's brother but not his sons, "who did not know how to speak."[31]

An unspecified amount of time passed before the final three transactions. One of these is another complicated exchange in which Rainald, lord of the settlement at Comblanchien, his wife, and her son gave the monks their possessions at Moisey. In return, the monks asked Duke Hugh of Burgundy to compensate Rainald and his heirs by giving them the revenues due from their manor; the duke's officials agreed. The last two acts record property again given for pious motives. One noted the gifts from a knightly family: Renier of Meursault, his wife Guberanda, their son the cleric, and Guberanda's relatives Bernard the knight and Lambert the cleric gave what they had in the *fundo* of Moisey for the redemption of their souls and those of their relatives. The other recorded donations from villagers and craftsmen: the widow Proema from the settlement of Corgengoux, her sons, daughter, son-in-law, sister, nephew, and the blacksmith of Argilly with his wife and sons, all gave "whatever they had" in the great meadow that lay below the settlement at Marigny. At this point, the scribe concluded, "the entire meadow is now the monks'."[32]

The conclusion of this notice confirms that this land was now out of reach of the monks' neighbors. It listed witnesses, some of whom were the donors or their relatives, but others of whom came from the settlement at Marigny. It defined the monks' lands by noting that all the land given by the Buscerani brothers and by Rainald, Renier, and the widow Proema and her family was called the "lands of the Buscerani." And it made clear that both the monks and their neighbors knew the boundaries of their new property:

It is bounded on one side by the stream called the Vieux-Meuzin, as the old men who know the area, that is, Radulf and Geoffrey and Humbert the foundry worker from the village of Meursault, and Arnulf Cenlitta of Villy and many others in the neighborhood of the Cistercian monks testify, and they now settle the boundaries of these lands and the lands of Bernard of Ruellée for the monks in the presence of many men who live in the neighborhood.[33]

Like the notice itself, this action confirmed the monks' possession of the property. It marked out physically what the notice asserted in documentary form: that the lands at Moisey now belonged to the monks. Just as the monks had carefully obtained the consent of the lords, wives, sons, and brothers of the donors and noted when men lacked wives or when children could not understand the proceedings, so they carefully assembled the people who actually lived in the vicinity and demonstrated the boundaries of the monastic domain.

The one final task left to the Cistercians before this property lost all encumbrances was to settle the payment of the tithe. Although this was often the last transaction in a notice, for the lands at Moisey it was recorded in two subsequent notices whose contents overlap.[34] Again the notices were not dated; again they listed several transactions organized according to a process of unraveling rights. The first notice presents the transactions from the top down, starting with Bishop Stephen of Autun, who acted with the consent of both his cathedral chapter and the two priests from Moisey's parish. Following were the lord Theoderic of the castle of Corancy and his wife, who gave the monks the portions of the tithe that they held from Lord Gozeran the Red of Combertault, which Gozeran held from Bernard of Ruellée. The second notice repeated the information but organized it from the bottom up, from the priests to the bishop.[35] At this point, probably about three years after the monks from Cîteaux first began to acquire lands at Moisey, they had removed the layers of rights and obligations from this land and had demonstrated, by the detailed story of its accumulation, its transformation into property for Cistercians alone.

The notice of the accumulation of land and rights at Moisey is unusual in the complexity of its transactions but not in its overall structure. Notices recording the acquisition of property for Cîteaux's grange at Brétigny and its vineyards and cellars at Gilly and Meursault follow a similar pattern.[36] Because the scribes seldom recorded specific dates, the organization of these transactions reflects the monks' idea of the rational order for accumulating property rather than the actual order in which they obtained it. Cîteaux's monks described a process akin to peeling an onion in which they first acquired the general rights to the property, then uncovered and acquired the inner layers of rights, and finally demonstrated to the local villagers that the property now belonged to the monks.

The documents from other Cistercian communities also reflect the process of unpeeling rights and tenures rather than the chronology of land acquisition. The monks from Pontigny produced a late-twelfth-century cartulary that organized their charters according to important granges and recorded the process of removing property from its secular uses.[37] Yet this cartulary also makes clear that the transformation of land from a seigneurial to a grange-based organization could entail not only removal of lands from the use of a local community, as at Moisey, but also removal of the community itself.

The seventh section of the cartulary, which records the monks' acquisition of lands and rights in the territory immediately around their monastery, makes this process especially clear.[38] This inhabited territory, whose settlements included Sainte-Procaire, Venouse, and Ligny, lay within three kilometers of the monastery. Paths crisscrossed the area, connecting these settlements to one another and providing access to the Serein River; Ligny contained not only a village and parish but also a fortification.[39] The first two acts out of the 41 in this section establish most of the monks' rights to the lands around Pontigny. Both were composed about midcentury, after the bulk of the land acquisition had occurred. The first is a notice written after 1147 that describes the initial establishment of the community and the monks' request that Count William II of Nevers augment their property.[40] William not only gave fields, woods, and fishing and forest rights, but he and the monks also persuaded Lady Gilla and John of the Mill to give arable land and forest and water rights in the area. Lady Gilla also permitted any *rusticus* who held land from her to give or sell (*dare aut vendare*) it to the monks.[41] The second act, a charter issued in 1156, marks the end of the Cistercians' major acquisitions in the area.[42] It records a series of complicated exchanges and gifts that demonstrate the extent to which Pontigny modified the settlement patterns in the region.[43] The monks gave their grange at Lorant to Count William III of Nevers, and in return, William gave them all the rights he and his vassals held around the settlement at Sainte-Procaire.[44] One of these vassals, Guiard the Cat, received twelve livres in compensation from William and then gave seven of these to Viscount Bartholomew of Ligny because Guiard had held the land from him. But William's vassals were not the only ones affected by this trade. The charter goes on, in William's voice, to read, "Because the brothers of Pontigny seem very cruel, as it is because of them that the inhabitants of this settlement are excluded from their possessions, I have agreed to make compensation to these people so that they will depart freely and leave the place to the monks in peace."[45] Furthermore, William moved the paths between the remaining settlements and decreed that no person or animal unconnected to the monks could enter a carefully demarcated area around Sainte-Procaire and the granges of Avaranda and Beugnon. He gave the monks still another field for their exclusive cultivation in return for other land from the monks; he conceded to the monks land he had received in trades with the monasteries of Saint-Michel of Tonnerre and Molesme; and he granted the monks the right to acquire what they could from his vassals for their grange at Acrimont.

The compiler of the cartulary appears to have organized the acts by first establishing the monks' general rights to a region and then recording earlier, smaller concessions that the lords and the knights of the region made for either spiritual or material compensation. After the first two records establish Pontigny's general control of the lands around Sainte-

Procaire, the following acts fill in the holes. They show the monks block-
ing paths between settlements, gaining control of lands near Ligny by
trading territory near the castle there for territory closer to their monastery, and making other efforts to, in the words of one charter, "make the
land uncultivated and empty of human habitation."[46] The last group of
acts recorded concessions and settlements of the disputes that occurred
when earlier gifts were challenged by the children, vassals, or lords of the
donors.[47] Like Cîteaux's notices, Pontigny's cartulary shows the gradual transformation of secular property, with its layers of rights and revenues, into monastic property, now virtually unconnected to the neighboring society and exploited by the labor of the monks, their lay brothers, and their hired workers.

Unlike Pontigny and Cîteaux, the twelfth-century monks at La Ferté
and Clairvaux recorded their acquisitions of property in pancartes: lists
of benefactors and their donations, usually organized around granges
and important agglomerations of land, that were issued and sealed by a
bishop. At La Ferté, the pancartes actually appear to be compilations of
notices, and most appear to have been produced at the abbey and then
presented to the bishop for confirmation.[48] Because few of the individual acts or pancartes were dated, their organization, like that of other
records of Cistercian property, reflects the monks' conception of the
process of acquisition rather than its actual chronology. Again, we see the
monks first presenting the gifts from the lords in a region, then describing the concessions from their vassals and knights and the grants of
the tithes, and finally noting the compensation offered to the peasants and
small landholders. Again, in the process of obtaining their property, the
monks made clear that they wished to untangle all the levels of rights to
the land, for the acts note whether a piece of land was held in fief, or
when a lord gave his peasants permission to sell their rights, and they
mention familial claims to the property.[49] One pancarte for the grange at
Chavals, for example, began by recording a village assembly similar to the
one at Moisey: at the request of the monks, the provosts of the duke of
Burgundy and the count of Chalon re-marked the boundaries of the
monks' property in the presence of the villagers of Saint-Ambreuil and
Varennes and renounced all rights in the territory within prescribed
limits.[50] The rest of the pancarte describes La Ferté's acquisition of small
pieces of land around Saint-Ambreuil for which most of the donors re-

ceived small amounts of money, animals, clothes, or, occasionally, other pieces of land. This pancarte also makes apparent La Ferté's entanglement in secular landholding patterns, for one act lists seven annual rents due to the monastery from villagers at Saint-Ambreuil and Varennes.[51] It is possible, in this case, the monks had received the rights to the property but had not yet convinced the men and women who cultivated the land to abandon it.

Clairvaux's pancartes, most of which were issued in 1147 by Godfrey, bishop of Langres and former prior of Clairvaux, demonstrate the same interest in organizing and transforming property as the documents from the other Cistercian abbeys.[52] Like the documents from other houses, these pancartes began with acts from local families holding feudal rights who gave what they had and "whatever [the monks] either have already acquired or will acquire in the future from those lands which are held from them in fief."[53] In a pancarte that lists property around the settlements of Perrecin and Ville, six of the first nine acts show families giving Clairvaux permission to acquire rights in lands held from them in fief, while only one of the next seventeen acts records such permission.[54] Many of these later concessions were clearly from vassals and dependents, as the person from whom the land was held often recorded his approval. The gifts appear to have been small amounts of property, often held jointly with others: parts of a field or "what they had" in the lands around a particular village. It is clear from hints in these pancartes that the monks did not acquire all of these rights at once; the scribe sometimes located a particular gift by specifying its relationship to land the monks already possessed. Thus Wazo of Longchamp and his family gave Clairvaux "whatever they had below the *divisiones* of our land that are across the Aube"; Stephen of Vignory, with the consent of his son Salomon, gave "whatever he held of Salomon's field, wherever situated, which lay above our divisiones that are across the Aube"; Aimo, brother-in-law of Arnulf, and his wife, gave what he held of woods and fields "among our divisiones"; and so on.[55] In another pancarte, the monks were granted only one man's rights to common land, suggesting that for a time the monks shared fields and vineyards with the laity.[56] Although none of Clairvaux's charters records the sort of peasant depopulation that Pontigny's documents reveal, this gradual accumulation of rights to arable and pastoral land did remove the land from peasants who had cultivated it. In 1150, Henry, son of Count Theobald of Blois, examined the claim of some men from Longchamp to the use of lands at Perrecin and determined that they no longer had any rights there.[57] The land had passed into the hands of the monks.

The pancartes from Clairvaux describe the territory after the monks had obtained most of the rights there. They give the illusion that the monks had fully separated their property from secular society and only hint at the messiness of this process. Yet these hints suggest that the monks from Clairvaux did not use the same techniques for accumulating land as the other monasteries we have examined. They seldom exchanged property, seldom offered to pay a *cens* in compensation for lands or tithes, and seldom asked noble patrons to compensate other donors for their concessions, but they did all of these things just often enough to suggest that they did not systematically abridge or distort their records.[58] Surprisingly few of the donations mention spiritual reasons for the act; none of the transactions on the pancartes record pious motives, and only two of the 53 undated charters issued by Bishop Godfrey mention pious motives.[59] Most of the donors who clearly specified that they made gifts for the good of their souls and the souls of their ancestors were prominent nobles: the counts Theobald of Blois, Henry of Troyes, Galeran of Melun, and Gautier of Brienne; Bartholomew, lord of Vignory; and Emperor Frederick Barbarossa.[60] This lack of recorded countergifts suggests that Clairvaux was even more removed than other Cistercian monasteries from the obligations and relationships that gift-giving traditionally entailed; they received land from their neighbors but seldom recorded that they owed anything in return. It also suggests a social landscape around Clairvaux that differed from that around either Cîteaux or Pontigny; unlike those two communities, Clairvaux did not immediately acquire a powerful patron to help the monks manipulate and consolidate their holdings.[61] The documents leave unclear what motivated the people in the vicinity of the monastery to donate property without compensation; perhaps the prestige, or the pressure, of Bernard of Clairvaux encouraged such gifts, or perhaps these families received compensation, either material or spiritual, that remained unrecorded. The monks' frequent quarrels with their neighbors may have been a consequence of their unwillingness to compensate the donors or their families for gifts; they imply that at least some people who held lands near Clairvaux did not find the monastery to be an easy neighbor.[62]

The monks' disputes with their neighbors and their possession of property forbidden by the statutes of the Chapter General show the difficulties of negotiating donations and untangling land tenures and are signs that the monks' transformation of their property was not complete. We have seen that Cistercian charters and notices carefully recorded the *laudatio* of the donors' wives, children, brothers, and lords, and that they noted the reasons why certain persons' approval had not been obtained, as when sons were too young, or the donor did not yet have a wife. Disputes occurred when people who had rights on a piece of land, such as the donor's children or vassals, claimed those rights on the grounds that they had not consented to the donation.[63] These disputes grew more common after midcentury when a second generation contested some of the donations made by their parents.[64]

Third-party exchanges in which a prominent patron compensated another donor for property given to the monks also caused disputes. If one party did not fulfill the obligations of the exchange, the monks could suffer the consequences. Cîteaux quickly learned the dangers of these exchanges when, in 1098, Duke Odo of Burgundy agreed to give Rainard of Beaune an income of twenty sous if Rainard donated the remainder of his lands around Cîteaux to the monastery. Odo did not pay Rainard his money, and Rainard tried to claim compensation from the monks.[65] In 1100, the duke finally agreed to designate two houses from which Rainard would receive the revenue. In return, Rainard promised that if he had any future complaints against the duke he would not also bring them against the monks.[66] Future grants to Cîteaux involving such three-way exchanges, such as the ones at Moisey, contained a clause stating that the monks were not responsible for any quarrel or claims between the other parties to the agreement.[67]

Just as land disputes were the outcome of incomplete negotiations for property rights, so the possession of forbidden lands and revenues was the result of an incomplete transformation of monastic lands. The Cistercians' acceptance of property expressly prohibited by the Chapter General was, in some cases, a sign that they did not convince a potential benefactor to give them the type of property they wanted. Although it is not possible to trace the history of every donation of manors or serfs, the Cistercians often traded manors and land near settled areas for more desirable property, or they removed or bought out the inhabitants. Occasionally, a monastery retained an isolated manor and its inhabitants, especially if it provided a rare resource for the abbey.[68] Even the monks' possession of rents could be evidence that their acquisition of property rights was not yet complete: although La Ferté received rents from lands at Varennes and Saint-Ambreuil, and Pontigny received rents from a meadow and vineyards, it is possible that the monasteries eventually convinced the people cultivating these properties to give them to the monks.[69] For the most part, however, the Cistercians succeeded in removing their land and rights from secular management; they cultivated their fields and raised their livestock themselves, with the aid of the lay brothers and hired labor and, in so doing, changed the traditional tenures on the land.

The monks' possession of forbidden rights and revenues was still unusual by midcentury, but their active participation in the acquisition of lands and their willingness to defend what they thought to be their rights had been present from the first years of the order. It was this behavior, rather than the breaking of any specific regulations, that triggered late-twelfth-century criticisms of Cistercian greed. Gerald of Wales told a tale in which he emphasized the Cistercians' avarice, and the abbot of Sainte-Geneviève questioned whether the Cistercians should be allowed to acquire lands as aggressively as they had seized hold of heaven.[70] Walter Map painted a picture in which the Cistercians transformed inhabited lands into places of solitude; because they could not govern parishes, he argued, they razed villages and threw down altars to bring all the land under their plows.[71]

This behavior broke no regulations and signaled no degeneration of ideals. From the beginning the Cistercians were reformers, confident in their ability to create from their surroundings the kind of communities in which they wished to live. Their economy was constrained by two factors: their desire to live far from other people without the revenues and responsibilities of manorial landlords, and their need to live off the donations of others. They saw nothing amiss in manipulating donations until they achieved their desired isolation, even if such a process required secular negotiations and worldly contacts. Indeed, they documented these negotiations and manipulations so as to demonstrate the steps by which they transformed their property from a secular to a religious domain. This process of land acquisition certainly had economic effects, for it allowed the Cistercians to create compact and productive estates. But it also had a spiritual component, for the monks' confidence that they could manipulate and transform their land paralleled their confidence that they could transform their wills and create from their carnal love a love of the divine.

II

The Cistercians' records of land acquisition demonstrate their confidence in their ability to unite discrete pieces of property into compact parcels of land and to separate them permanently from the land around them. In doing so, they transformed the secular character of the physical world. Their practices of biblical exegesis show a similar attitude toward the physical world and a similar confidence in their ability to transform it. In their explanations of the language of sexual desire and natural cultivation in the Song of Songs, the monks linked the surface, or historical, meanings to their own experiences of love and nature, and then discussed the underlying allegorical content. By doing so, they suggested two things: first, that as they transformed their own wills they also transformed their understanding of human sexuality; and second, that they found in the natural world echoes of the harmony and peace of the divinely created world before the Fall.

Medieval traditions of biblical exegesis, and indeed medieval attitudes toward the perceived world, assumed that surface meanings and observed objects necessarily pointed toward a deeper and truer reality that was hidden beneath them. Augustine's *De doctrina christiana* had established a philosophy of signs that offered principles for reading both the natural world and classical texts in terms of salvation history; he suggested that even the divine words of the Bible should be read as figures of an inner reality. Augustine's treatise, combined with his exegetical practice and those of Origen, Ambrose, and Gregory the Great, provided models for later medieval preachers and theologians.[72] Throughout much of the early Middle Ages, theologians tended to ignore the historical meaning of a text in favor of its figurative meanings and, as a result, created a sharp dichotomy between letter and spirit, the physical and the spiritual, and left a deep suspicion of things "of the world." This dichotomy began to diminish in the twelfth century as theologians like the Victorines insisted that the historical meaning of a text or the nature of a perceived object or act be understood as a valid analogy for the spiritual truth that lay beneath it.[73] But underlying much twelfth-century exegesis was a second assumption, also drawn from Augustine, which added a psychological dimension to the relation between figure and thing. For Augustine, figures, whether natural, historical, or scriptural, did not inherently point toward a more profound reality but instead contained a reality that could only be grasped by a person with a properly ordered internal life, whose reason was illuminated by faith.[74]

Although the Cistercians did not articulate the principles behind their exegetical practice, their use of analogies drawn from the sensed world suggests that they worked with the same basic assumptions as did their more scholastic contemporaries. Like other twelfth-century scholars, they found signs of divine order and harmony in the sensed world, and following Augustine, they stressed that they could perceive these harmonies because their sight was focused by the lens of faith and an ordered will. As in much of Cistercian thought, however, this focusing was an ongoing process rather than an immediate end. Whereas human experiences on earth could reflect divine harmonies when perceived by a person whose mind was illuminated by faith, the perception of these harmonies aided a person's continuing progression toward the divine.

The Cistercians' use of the nuptial and natural imagery in the Song of Songs demonstrates their belief that the ordering of the will could transform people's sensory perceptions and allow them to use such perceptions to further their progress toward the divine. The Song of Songs was not a text for novices to study. In his first sermon on the Canticles, Bernard of Clairvaux told the members of his audience to consider this text only after they had learned to shun the false promises of the world and had prepared for marriage with God.[75] Yet, two sermons later, as Bernard began to explain the meanings of the bride's desire for the bridegroom's kiss, he admitted that his own soul was still "burdened with sins, still subject to the passions of the flesh."[76] Although this comment might be attributed to false modesty on Bernard's part, it also illuminates the consistent tension in Cistercian writings between the world as ideally constituted and the world as actually experienced. Monks sought to teach their intellects the proper object for desire and to direct their wills toward what their intellects knew to be good; to love God not because of the goods he provided but because he was good and lovable; and to so internalize their monastic regulations that their burdens became light. Only at this point were they prepared to experience the delights of divine love that the Song of Songs expressed. Yet, as men still alive in their bodies and living in a community of other men, they never completely controlled the will nor entirely broke the habits of the body. Their commentaries on the Song of Songs described the goal toward which the monks strove, but they also illuminated the monks' ongoing efforts to bring their desires under control.

Sexuality was only one of the human urges that monks tried to control, and the desire for food, sleep, or comfortable clothes and bedding could often be a more immediate temptation in a life of chronic sleep deprivation, meager food, and few comforts. Nonetheless, the control of sexual desire was at the heart of a life of renunciation because the unconscious movement of the human genitals was the central symbol of human willfulness and disobedience.[77] Furthermore, the body seemed to retain willful habits even after the intellect had started to understand the proper object for its desire. For monks who had dedicated their lives to redirecting their wills and breaking the habits of their bodies, control of sexual desire was the most important sign of their obedience, even if a longing for better food or more sleep persisted after their sexual feelings had subsided.

Neither the act of entering a monastery nor a year's novitiate were enough to teach a monk to control his desires. As we have seen, the adults who entered Cistercian communities had to learn to restrain and redirect the aggressiveness and ambition that secular society had encouraged. They also had to learn to control their sexual urges.[78] Although many of the men who entered Cistercian communities were clerics and knightly youths and thus were not married, they had lived in a secular environment through puberty and were familiar with sexual love, even if they had not actually experienced it. Bernard himself was portrayed as taking cold baths to quench his desires and resisting the seduction of both real and demonic women, and Aelred of Rievaulx told his sister that he had "lost his purity" before he became a monk and hinted that he continued to have erotic thoughts about men afterward.[79] Other monks had been married. Bernard's oldest brother Guy had a wife and two small daughters whom he did not wish to leave; his wife actively resisted the dissolution of their marriage until Bernard warned that her opposition would cause her death.[80] The Cistercian customary, in regulating the reception of novices, ruled that, if a community learned that a novice or a monk had once been married, that man should be expelled until he produced evidence that his wife had released him from his marriage vows and promised to live chastely thereafter.[81] This regulation demonstrates that it was often difficult for the monks to know the life histories of the men who entered their communities, and it suggests that some monks may have abandoned their wives.

As Aelred's comments about his fight against sexual temptation suggest, the Cistercians tended to confront their erotic feelings rather than ignore them. Their stories about monastic visions, which they compiled in the second half of the twelfth century, show a greater concern with the fight against sexual temptation than those collections made by other contemporary religious communities.[82] The message of the Cistercian stories was twofold. They suggest that the effort to overcome temptation could be difficult: it was a battle that even the most holy monks had not always won completely. Yet they also suggest that, in the long run and with divine aid, the monks could conquer their temptations and break the habits ingrained in their bodies, although not, of course, eliminate altogether the needs and feelings of their bodies. Such was the message of a story about a monk who fought for a long time against horrible and disgusting demons but retained his faith in the compassion and aid of God. Finally, one night an angel appeared to him in a dream and offered to cut off the organ that disturbed him and thus heal him of his passions. The monk agreed. When he awoke the next morning he found his body was still whole, but that his temptations had entirely disappeared.[83] A story about an older monk who watched a female demon pass through the dormitory and seduce one of the young men had a similar message although a less happy result. When, the following morning, the older monk told the abbot what he had seen, the abbot asked the young man to confess. The young man refused, and within a few days he had left the monastery.[84] As both these stories suggest, the evil was not temptation itself but a despair that divine aid and forgiveness would be forthcoming.

Once a monk had started to redirect his desires, he was able to recognize his longing for the divine in images that on the surface represented sexual love. He could even draw on his own knowledge and memory of human desire. For example, when Gilbert of Hoyland interpreted the passage, "I have sought him but I have not found him" (Song 3.1), he told his monks to remember their own experiences of such longing: "If anyone has ever experienced such a feeling of love or desire, he can appreciate the plaintive heart with which the bride cried out, 'I have not found him,' by inferring from his own example."[85] Gilbert left ambiguous whether the monks were to remember some past desire for another human or their current longing for the divine; other Cistercians made more explicit that they referred to their monastic experiences, not to their former lives.[86] Yet the Cistercians' ability to use such imagery to describe the longing and union implied by caritas nonetheless added new connotations to the word. It demonstrated their confidence in the possibility of transforming their material and carnal desires into a desire for God and implied that they could read in their human emotions signs that pointed toward divine harmonies.

In using a language of desire, the Cistercians contrasted love and longing for God with feelings of sexual desire; at the same time, they used the physical descriptions to express the nuances of their more spiritual love. Thus, in explaining the bride's initial request, "Let him kiss me with the kiss of his mouth," Bernard described a physical kiss as a "pressing of mouth on mouth" to explain why no person would dare ask for a kiss from God's mouth; this "contact of lips," which usually "signifies the embrace of spirits," here signified the single and unique instance in which the mouth of the Word was pressed against the mouth of Jesus and the human and the divine were joined together.[87] Christians instead were to seek the "kiss of his kiss," an unusual request, as Bernard pointed out. "Don't we usually say to each other, 'Kiss me,' or 'Give me a kiss? . . . When we prepare to kiss someone, don't we offer them our mouth without asking for theirs by name?"[88] The form of this request, which differed from the normal language of lovers, pointed toward the special nature of this kiss as "a gift of divine favor and kindness by which a soul can continue in contemplation to the degree possible in a fragile body."[89] Receiving such a kiss was the culmination of the soul's advance toward perfection on earth.

In a sermon structured around the passage, "My dove in the clefts of the rock, in the crannies of the wall, show me your face, let your voice sound in my ears" (Song 2.14), Bernard drew such an evocative picture of two lovers that he felt compelled to remind his audience that "it is not worth hearing the external sound unless the Spirit within aids our weak understanding."[90] He described the bridegroom's courtship of the bride as he shyly asked to see and hear her and "enjoy his pleasures in a protected spot," and he imagined the groom telling his bride that laboring in the vineyard would not hinder their love because the clefts and crannies in the vineyard walls provided them with private shelters. Yet, after creating this scene, Bernard warned that he and his audience should not concentrate on this surface image of a "deformed love" between a man and a woman but should instead consider the lovers to be the Word and the soul or Christ and his Church. Furthermore, Bernard continued, "you must not think of the 'clefts of the rock' and 'crannies of the wall' as hiding places for wicked activities, lest some suspicion should rise up from the works of darkness."[91]

If such images could provoke dangerous emotions, why create such a picture at all? In fact, the remainder of this sermon, and the next, move away from the theme of spiritual union by providing other interpretations for the clefts and crannies and by describing the bride's longing for her groom rather than their mutual desire.[92] Still, the initial depiction of the lovers did serve a purpose: it reminded the monks that it was only because God loved them that they could love him. Humans returned to God a reflection of the divine love that was already his, and he delighted in hearing the voices of "gratitude, wonder, and adoration" that this contemplation produced.[93] By describing the bride and groom's mutual desire for union in the privacy of the vineyard wall, Bernard was able to emphasize the reciprocal nature of the love between humans and the divine that was a hallmark of Cistercian theology. Furthermore, although Bernard's sermon did not linger on the bride and bridegroom as lovers in the vineyard, his discussion nonetheless remained focused on the body. His later association of the clefts of the rock with the wounds of Jesus directed his audience to consider Jesus' human body as the instrument through which divine grace flowed to humanity. "They pierced his hands and his feet," Bernard told his monks, "they gored his side with a lance, and through these fissures I can suck honey from the rock and oil from the hardest stone. . . . The mystery of his heart is accessible through the openings of his body."[94] By meditating on the wounds in Jesus' body, a person ignored the senses of his or her own body; martyrs who gazed on Jesus' wounds, for example, did not feel the otherwise unbearable pain of their own torture. Bernard made clear, however, that such people had transformed not their bodies but their souls. A numb body did not bring about the lack of feeling; love did. "Sensation is not lost, it is quelled," Bernard wrote. "Pain is not absent, it is scorned."[95]

When Gilbert of Hoyland described the union of the bride and bridegroom, he too moved from a discussion with erotic overtones to a consideration of the corporeal nature of the human Jesus. When explaining the passage, "In my little bed by night, I sought him whom my soul loves" (Song 3.1), he gave a multiplicity of interpretations of the little bed, starting with the comment that the narrowness of the bride's bed provided room only for the bride and the bridegroom and pushed all her other, adulterous lovers onto the floor. The bed could be the human mind, which the bride sometimes shared with her bridegroom and sometimes abandoned for the bridegroom's bed where "aroused by the fire of the bridegroom's love, she bubbles, swells, and overflows."[96] The bed also could be the "lures of carnal weakness," which the bride did not share with her groom. But it could also be Jesus himself, who made himself into a little nest of soft pillows in which the bride could curl up. As Bernard described the bride as hiding in the crannies of Jesus' wounds, so Gilbert understood the pillows of this bed. "The softest pillow for me, good Jesus, is that crown of thorns from your head," Gilbert wrote. "A sweet little bed is that wood of your cross."[97] The bride could not share her bed with Jesus while still fighting carnal desires, but when she did share her bed, the contact was not devoid of physicality. Humans knew Christ "according to the flesh," although not "according to the desires of the flesh"; Jesus shared the physical nature of humans but not their physical desires. "He did not refuse the bed of our pain but he did not recline so far as to feel our pleasure."[98]

The Cistercians' delight in sensual imagery from the Song of Songs was not an expression of sublimated sexual desire that bubbled up despite the repression of a monastic life. In recent years, in fact, there have been more works arguing against than for the idea that the erotic language of the Song of Songs commentaries offered an outlet for repressed sexuality.[99] Bernard's explicit warning to his monks not to be caught by the "allurements of lust" when considering the bride and bridegroom in the vineyard, as well as the collections of miracle stories about sexual temptation, show that the monks were conscious of their sexual feelings and that they did not try to disguise them under a spiritualized use of erotic language. Instead, their graphic use of physical images made clear that a monk's desired transformation was entirely internal. The goal of Cistercian life, as expressed through the erotic language of a spiritual marriage, was not to lose the body but to redirect the will within it and thus make it like the body of Jesus: a body that could feel pain and evoke empathy for others, a body that could inspire others to love through its physical presence, but a body not disturbed by carnal desires.[100] Such a body could then experience the supreme pleasure of being subsumed into the body of Christ. The monks recognized that, although they worked toward this goal, it was unattainable in this life. Still, as a monk, however tenuously, brought his will under control, he could consider both the human body and the sexual desires that had previously been invested with such danger as providing lessons that furthered his progression toward the divine.

<h1 style="text-align:center">III</h1>

Although the nuptial imagery and the language of sexual longing are usually the most noted aspects of the Song of Songs, many of the images in the poem could be disassociated from the themes of desire and union and linked instead to ideas of growth and progress. The traditional interpretation of the poem certainly presented it as a marriage song between the soul and the Word, or Christ and the Church; but, apart from the few central passages that speak of contact between the bride and bridegroom or the bride's longing for her groom, much of the poem expresses the lovers' praise for one another through a long series of similes in which the lovers compare each other to fruits, flowers, spices, and animals—that is, to images drawn from the cultivation of nature. With our modern preoccupation with sexuality, we tend to focus on the erotic aspects of the poem; in the Cistercians' exegesis, however, discussions of the beauty and fruitfulness of nature are as least as prevalent as those concerning sexual love.[101] Just as the monks used the images from the Song of Songs to demonstrate that they could find a potential goodness in the human body that aided their contact with the divine, so their understanding of the poem's agricultural images illuminates their attitude toward the natural world. Not only did the production of fruits and flowers became a model for the cultivation of the human soul, but in the process of cultivating the soul, the monks found in their environment evidence of divine harmonies that could aid them in their spiritual progress.

Images of cultivation and fruitfulness were common in twelfth-century writings and reflected a new confidence in the possibility of rebirth and renewal for individuals and for religious institutions alike.[102] Cistercian authors, like many other twelfth-century writers, found analogies to their experiences of monastic life and spiritual growth in images drawn

Figure 3. The Garden of Eden. God creates Adam within a flowering "A." *The Bible of Stephen Harding* (1109–11). Dijon, Bibliothèque municipale, MS 14, f. 76. Photograph courtesy Bibliothèque municipale, Dijon, France.

from the natural world. Their monasteries were "new plantations," and the monks cultivated their souls as if they were gardens and vineyards. Bernard of Clairvaux described the bride as caring for a grapevine of the soul whose roots were fertilized by tears of repentance, but whose fruits of good works were sometimes spoiled by temptations, and whose branches of virtue sometimes withered through neglect.[103] Gilbert of Hoyland compared the bride's soul to an enclosed garden of perfumed flowers that was surrounded by a wall of love, defended by a rampart of discipline, irrigated by virtues, and perfumed by the fruits of spiritual gifts.[104] These horticultural images may have been especially attractive to the Cistercians because they easily lent themselves to descriptions of the process of spiritual development. The bliss of a spiritual union, though the goal of their life, was something they believed they could experience only fleetingly, if at all, but their spiritual progression was an ever-present part of their existence that could easily be seen as a matter of sowing, cultivating, weeding, pruning, encouraging tender sprouts, and fighting off pests and predators so that the seeds in their souls would flower and bear fruit.

Despite the Cistercians' use of images drawn from the natural world, some modern scholars still consider the monks to be uninterested in their environment and in the lessons the created world could provide about its creator. For M.-D. Chenu, the Cistercians best exemplify the "world-renouncing" strain in twelfth-century spirituality.[105] According to Jean Leclercq, the Cistercians did not describe the natural world around them but drew their pictures from classical and biblical sources.[106] Yet even if the Cistercian authors had not necessarily experienced a pomegranate or the more exotic spices in the Song of Songs, they still worked to make such fruits, flowers, and spices seem real before unpacking their allegorical meanings. Bernard of Clairvaux wrote of a lily as if he were passing it around the chapter house. "If you have not already noticed," he told his monks, "observe the golden stamens springing from the center of the flower, surrounded by white petals, beautifully and becomingly arranged into a crown."[107] Only after he finished describing the material object did he explain that it signified Jesus' gold crown of divinity and the white purity of his human nature. Other Cistercians also analyzed symbols derived from the natural world as if they had experienced the object itself. Isaac of Stella, for instance, addressed his monks as if they sat under an oak tree, and then used the idea of a tree contained in its acorn to explain how the material world reflected the divine mind.[108] Gilbert of Hoyland enjoyed the very sounds of the names of the fruits in the bride's garden and imagined the shade of the trees and the taste of their fruit.[109] That Bernard probably did not have a lily on hand, that Isaac most likely did not preach while sitting under a tree, and that Gilbert probably had not seen a pomegranate or smelled nard, is irrelevant; the authors portrayed themselves in a relationship with the natural world that assumed they observed and appreciated it. Just as Bernard's description of a kiss could help his monks to understand the potential goodness in the human condition, even if they had not experienced the sort of kiss Bernard described, so this use of images drawn from the natural world, whether actually experienced or not, encouraged the monks to recognize the divine harmonies present in the world around them.

A

B

Figure 4. Laborers transformed into letters. Some of these men are monks, others are not. Perhaps they are hired laborers. Gregory the Great, *Moralia in Iob* (c. 1111). Dijon, Bibliothèque municipale. A: MS 170, f. 59; B: MS 170, f. 75; C: MS 173, f. 148; D: MS 173, f. 41. Photographs courtesy Bibliothèque municipale, Dijon, France.

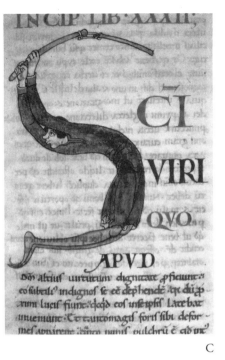

C

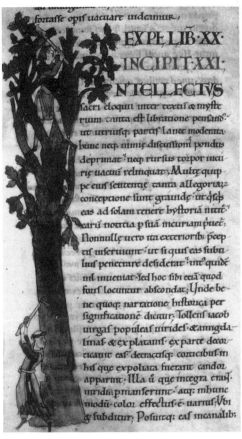

D

Images of gardening provided more than metaphors for the development of the soul. Just as the monks used a language of love and longing to describe a contact between humans and the divine that was devoid of sexual desire but still dependent on the body, so they used the language of natural growth to draw a connection between the cultivation of their soul and the cultivation of the natural world. The idea that the natural world could reflect the condition of the human soul was one with biblical precedents: after the Fall, not only were Adam and Eve cursed with death and the pains of childbirth, but the very ground was cursed, destined to bring forth thorns and thistles that required Adam's labor. In Deuteronomy, the Israelites received divine reward for their faithfulness and were transferred from "a place of horror and vast solitude" to a place where the desert bloomed. Cistercian authors read these passages through the lens of an Augustinian epistemology in which a person's experience was shaped by the condition of his or her soul, and they drew two conclusions. First, they viewed labor as a necessary condition of human existence and the result of human sinfulness; second, they described the beauty and fruitfulness of their estates as divine gifts that mirrored the interior progress of their souls rather than the exterior result of their manual skills and physical efforts.

The Cistercians' sense that humans were always striving for a perfection that they could never fully attain was linked to their view of labor as an inevitable part of earthly existence. "Man is born to labor" was a theme for sermons, and Isaac of Stella introduced and concluded many of his sermons by speaking of the need to go to work.[110] But such labor was a spiritual exercise more than an act of material creation; the monks associated it with the transformation of the soul rather than with the manipulation of the materials around them. Aelred of Rievaulx, for instance, placed labor in a triad with fasting and prayer, and Guerric of Igny wrote of labor as a means of contact with Christ.[111] Sometimes, Guerric suggested, Jesus' presence would come to a monk while he labored rather than during meditation or prayer. Both Bernard and Nicholas of Clairvaux encouraged men to convert by suggesting that they would learn more through their manual labor than they would at their books.[112]

Because labor rather than rest was the lot of humans on earth, Cistercian authors tended to use images of cultivation to describe a dynamic process rather than a static condition. Unlike the monks from Marmoutier who saw their cloister as a restful Eden, Cistercians themselves did not usually describe their monasteries as a place of rest.[113] They either strove to deserve fruitful gardens and lush pastures or, if they had found them, guarded constantly against their loss, for gardens could easily return to desert. By describing Cîteaux's location in the words of Deuteronomy as a place of "horror and vast solitude," the author of the *Exordium cistercii* established it as a place of struggle comparable to the desert that tested the faith of the Israelites, and suggested that the monks, like the Israelites, would eventually be rewarded with a place in which the rocks brought forth oil and honey.[114] Guerric of Igny made the analogy explicit. He told his monks that by following the example of those who dwelt in the wilderness, "the beautiful places of the desert will become fertile,

and the solitude will bloom. . . . Then the desert will be like a paradise
of delights and the solitude like a garden of the Lord."[115] In other sermons, he warned his monks that their sinfulness would transform the
green pastures of their monastery back into a "howling waste of the
wilderness," and told them he did not dwell in a garden on earth but in
a tomb.[116]

The apparent beauty and fruitfulness of the Cistercians' environment,
then, stemmed only indirectly from their labor. God rewarded their efforts to transform their souls by giving them the ability to see the divine
harmonies in the created world around them. Both Guerric of Igny and
Gilbert of Hoyland described how a faithful soul could view the world
as it did the Scriptures, as an entity filled with riches that would further
inspire the soul to love and praise its creator.[117] Gilbert discussed the
necessity of understanding the spiritual meanings hidden under material
objects, but he nonetheless believed that, if the created world were perceived properly by one who was aided by divine reason and love, that person could see the harmonies and order its divine creator established and
thus be further inspired to love God. As he told his fellow abbot, Roger
of Byland, Byland's beauty "so echoes with the sweet songs of birds that
it could revive a dead soul, wipe away the scorn of a delicate soul, and
soften the hardness of a mind lacking in devotion."[118] Walter Daniel, in
his biography of Aelred of Rievaulx, described Rievaulx as a place whose
natural beauty reflected the beauty of its monks' souls. No longer was it
a place of wilderness and thickets:

From the loftiest rocks, the waters wind and tumble down to the valley below,
and as they make their hasty way through the lesser passages and narrower
beds and spread themselves in wider rills, they give out a gentle murmur of soft
sound and join together in the sweet notes of a delicious melody. And when the
branches of lovely trees rustle and sing together and the leaves flutter gently to
the earth, the happy listener is filled increasingly with a glad jubilee of harmonious sounds, as so many various things conspire together in such a sweet consent, in music whose every diverse note is equal to the rest.[119]

Walter could hear in this natural environment the concord of diverse but
equal voices; as we will see in the next chapter, the Cistercians found a
similar harmonious diversity in their monasteries.

The Cistercians' idea that the ordered will could perceive divine harmonies in the natural world helps to explain seemingly unconnected
aspects of Cistercian life: the monks' economic behavior and their tra-

ditions of biblical exegesis. When the Cistercians accepted property, they emphasized the process of stripping from it the customary layers of land tenures and claims so that they could exploit it using their own techniques and labor. Such a process was analogous to their interest in stripping away the layers of misguided love that obscured the image of the divine in their soul. The monks' exegesis made these parallels explicit, for Cistercian authors used sensual and natural imagery to demonstrate that the process of spiritual development also transformed the experience of the environment and the body and allowed the monks to see the divine harmonies contained therein. The goal was to make the monastery a paradise, an Eden where human dominion over a fruitful and peaceful nature reflected control of the will and desire. Although the Cistercians portrayed such perfection as a fleeting experience at best, they emphasized the continued interaction between spiritual transformation and sensed experience: a virtuous soul could find a goodness in both the human body and the natural world that would further aid it in developing a love for the divine. Although the monks themselves never explicitly stated the connection, their actions in the natural world demonstrated the same attitudes that they expressed in their theological texts and would demonstrate in their political activities: that by reshaping their wills and learning the virtues that stemmed from a properly directed love, they could transform the material world to make apparent the divine harmonies that had been hidden beneath its surface.

Chapter 4

Unity and Diversity

The Cistercians incorporated into their conception of caritas two central characteristics of their monastic culture: a recognition that earthly existence was imperfect, and an emphasis on progress toward an ideal, even if that ideal remained unachievable while on earth. The monks used caritas to describe both a union with the divine and their individual desire for such a union, both an ideal fraternal harmony and their actual concern for their brothers, both an ideal transformation of their experiences and the actual process that aided that transformation. Just as the term expressed the relation of the monk to God, his brothers, and his environment, so it also expressed the place and function of the monastic community in its wider society. Caritas united the Cistercian monasteries, ideally because all the monks were bound by their shared participation in divine love, and actually because all were bound in a common quest for the virtues that would lead toward the divine. Yet this unity did not erase all differences within the monastery. The Cistercians' various conceptions of their unified diversity allowed them to present themselves as communities of spiritual elite while at the same time suggesting that their loving unity could serve as a model for the Church as a whole. Similarly, their varying depictions of the diverse groups in their society demonstrated their differentiation between an ideal society and one actually constituted on earth. Such descriptions hinted at the social roles that they believed the needs of fallen humanity required them to play.

By the twelfth century, authors who wished to describe Christian society could draw on a variety of images picturing societal diversity. They could use the Pauline image of a body with many members. They could divide society into two using either the Gelasian distinction between clerical and lay or the still older separation between active and contemplative lives. They could follow Jerome and Augustine in distinguishing groups according to three degrees of sexual purity or, like Gregory the Great, associate these degrees with the three "orders" of bishops, monks, and the married. Finally, they could divide society according to function: those who led and those who followed, those with power and those without, or those who fought, those who prayed, and those who labored. The way authors chose and combined these images reflected their sense of their position in society, their awareness of the political realities around them, and their ideal social order.[1] Yet it is also important to recognize that these social descriptions were not necessarily systems; they could represent unconscious assumptions or form part of a practical response to a current situation rather than depicting a single, consistent social theory.

The Cistercians were not systematic thinkers, and they borrowed whatever images best suited their purposes at a particular time. As a result, it is impossible to pick a single passage from one author's writings and expect it to reflect a Cistercian conception of the social order.[2] Nonetheless, their use of images of unity and diversity, and the particular difficulties they had in classifying the groups that straddled the boundaries between their monasteries and the surrounding society, betrays much about their view of their society and their place in it. When they looked within their monasteries, the monks could not find a consistent place for their lay brothers; when they looked outside, their understanding of the social position of prelates was fraught with contradictions. In both cases, their problems in classification reflect their felt tension between the ideal and the possible: between a contemplative life apart from worldly society and an active interest in reform.

I

A favorite theme of Cistercian authors was the unity of their communities, especially the unity of spirit that derived from their common search for divine love. They described this unity as analogous to the "one heart and one soul" of the early apostles and celebrated it in the words of the psalmist: "Behold how good and how pleasant it is when brothers dwell in unity" (Ps. 132.1).[3] But the unity in these communities did not erase all diversity. In fact, the Cistercians described two types of diversity within their communities: one a diversity of virtue that encompassed the different stages in a progression toward caritas, and the other a diversity of function that separated the duties and customs of the monks from those of their lay brothers. In addition, the Cistercians' proclaimed unity of spirit actually encompassed two different conceptions of unity, one exclusive and the other inclusive. The first derived from the monks' uniform customs and tight-knit communities and allowed the Cistercian monks to present their own search for the divine as the special province of a spiritual elite. The second suggested that all people who progressed toward salvation, whatever their customs, should be bound together in love. Although these two conceptions of unity blended into one another, the Cistercians' difficulties in finding a consistent location for the lay brothers in the rituals and descriptions of their communities illustrate the tension between a caritas that unified the monks alone and a caritas that bound together an entire Christian society.

As we have seen, Cistercian monks relied on the physical presence of their brothers for their individual spiritual development. The order's regulations reinforced each community's cohesion by insisting that monks return to their cloister every night and that private masses not disrupt the communal liturgy.[4] But, although the monks depended on the physical presence of their brothers, they also assumed that a bond of spiritual love would develop out of such contacts and unite them even if they were no longer in close proximity. Geoffrey of Auxerre pictured the monks' virtues as linking them together like jewels in a necklace; their fraternal love "recalled the discordant to unity and contained and preserved the harmonious in the bonds of peace."[5] Bernard of Clairvaux also described the diversity of virtuous behavior in a community in which the brothers lived "as one": "You see one weeping for his sins, another rejoicing in praise of God; this one caring for everyone, that one teaching others; this one praying, that one reading; this one lamenting, that one punishing sin; this one burning with charity, that one powerful with humility; this one humble in prosperity, that one exalted in adversity; this one in active labor, that one in quiet contemplation. . . . You who previously lived in the region of the shadow of death, pass into the region of life and truth!"[6] In a letter to his monks at Clairvaux, Bernard made clear that it was this virtuous behavior that united them, for although he was separated from them in body, he remained united to them in spirit as long as they remained conscientious in their duties and charitable toward one another. But he also reminded them that he was especially present to them during times of prayer for, no matter how distant he was, his voice joined the harmony of Cistercian voices sending their prayers to heaven.[7]

As Bernard's letter suggests, the monks associated the abstract bond of charity with the order's uniform customs. When the *Carta caritatis* determined "by what bond, in what manner, and even by what love the monks, divided in body into abbeys in diverse parts of the world, were indissolubly glued together in spirit," it established identical monastic customs throughout the order.[8] This uniformity provided a tangible sign of the more abstract spiritual bond that tied the communities together; the idea that all Cistercians, no matter how physically separated, prayed in unison and followed the same daily routine served as an important representation of each monastery's spiritual unity.[9] As the charter stated, the monks insisted on this uniformity "so that nothing be discordant in our actions, but that we live according to one charity, one rule, and the same customs."[10]

The bonds that linked the monasteries together into an order were neither fully abstract nor fully dependent on face-to-face contact. The *Carta caritatis* determined that each abbey be independent, each abbot be responsible for the internal affairs of his house, and no abbey owe revenues to another.[11] But it also determined that the abbots meet yearly as a community in Chapter General, and it instituted visitations whereby once a year each abbot received the abbot of his founding monastery and then visited each abbey established by his community. Like each monk, each monastery was to have compassion for the material needs of the others, and each abbot was to consider the welfare of his fellow abbots' souls.[12] According to the *Carta caritatis*, the abbots in Chapter General were to "deal with the well-being of their souls, decide what things should be corrected or improved in the observance of the holy Rule or regulations, and restore the good of peace and charity among themselves."[13] There, if any abbot was found faulty in his behavior or in the discipline of his monastery, he should be "charitably accused" and punished, but only by his fellow abbots.

The order thus reproduced on a larger scale the relations within each Cistercian community. Like each monk, each abbey retained an autonomy within a broader community: each abbot fostered the spiritual growth of his monks just as each monk progressed on his own toward a relationship with the divine. At the same time, each abbot, like each monk, obeyed regulations that he did not have the discretion to modify, received the criticisms of his peers in Chapter General, accepted the watchful eye of another abbot, offered and accepted aid when needed, and sought to maintain peace and harmony among those with whom he lived. The caritas that united the order, then, was a spiritual bond that had its roots in face-to-face contact; the cohesion of these monks and abbeys grew from a common physical environment and from the uniform customs that fostered their progress toward a common goal.

The Cistercians' celebration of their monastic unity, however, existed uneasily with the fundamental organization of their communities. The monks may have claimed to live as one, but each Cistercian abbey was divided in two by an impassable wall. On one side lived the monks, on the other the lay brothers. The lay brothers were not monks, but an early Cistercian statute decreed that, "as our assistants," they were to be accepted "as brothers and partners" and were to share in the spiritual and temporal goods of the monastery.[14] Still, the barrier between monks and lay brothers could not be crossed: the statutes prohibited lay brothers from learning to read and becoming monks, and by 1188, when nobles were formally prohibited from becoming lay brothers, it had become a distinction based on social status.[15]

Initially, the lay brothers' customs seem to have varied with each monastery, belying the uniformity that the Cistercian monks so desired. The prologue to the earliest extant customary for the lay brothers, dated between 1134 and 1150, speaks of the importance of rectifying these variations:[16]

Because it is well known that we have accepted from our bishops the care of the souls of our lay brothers as well as those of the monks, I am amazed that our abbots conscientiously impose the obligation of discipline on the monks, but do not impose it at all on the lay brothers, or at least, very little. . . . Therefore, just as it was necessary for us to write a customary for the monks so that we could everywhere preserve unity in our customs, so one should be provided for the lay brothers for both temporal and spiritual matters."[17]

This customary ensured that the monks and lay brothers had minimal contact with one another. The lay brothers joined the monks for mass on days of two masses and for masses for the dead, and they appeared in the monks' chapter when they made their professions, but they otherwise lived parallel lives, sleeping in their own dormitories or at the granges, eating in their own refectories, dying or convalescing in their own infirmaries, holding separate chapters, and performing their own liturgy.[18] Although such customs were theoretically uniform throughout the order, the very existence of the lay brothers belied the fraternal uniformity the monks celebrated. The diversity of the surrounding society had emerged within the walls of their monasteries, and the Cistercians' attitude toward their lay brothers paralleled their attitude toward Christian society as a whole.

The Cistercians' ecclesiastical rituals displayed some of the ambiguities in the lay brothers' position. In services that demonstrated the fraternal harmony of the community, the lay brothers participated in roles congruent with those of two other major groups in the monastery—the novices and the monks. Thus on Maundy Thursday when the abbot washed the feet of his monks, he did not wash them all but instead washed the feet of four monks, four novices, and four lay brothers.[19] Similarly, on Good Friday, the lay brothers joined the monks and novices in prostrating themselves before the Cross, and in processions for Palm Sunday and for the Purification of the Virgin, the lay brothers followed the novices who followed the monks.[20] Other rituals, however, made clear that the lay brothers remained separate from the monks. When the monks held vigils the night of the Nativity, the cellarer provided two lay brothers to tend the fire to warm the monks; on Palm Sunday, the lay brothers were associated with the guests and *familia* and only received palm fronds if there were enough; on Maundy Thursday, they led the poor into the cloister while the monks were in choir, prepared their feet for washing, and set out the necessary cloths and vessels; and on Good Friday, they cleaned the church after prime while the monks sang the psalter.[21] Such rituals suggest that the lay brothers, the novices, and the monks formed the three major groups within each community, but they also suggested that the monasteries were split between monks and potential monks on the one hand and the lay brothers on the other.

When Cistercian monks described the diversity of their communities, they further reinforced the separation of the lay brothers by ignoring them altogether. Sometimes they divided the monastery into actives and contemplatives; sometimes into actives, contemplatives, and leaders; and sometimes into a greater multiplicity of roles or activities. When they divided the monastery between actives and contemplatives, however, it was the monastic officials or the abbot, not the lay brothers, who held the active role.[22] Similarly, most tripartite divisions also ignored the lay brothers. Bernard of Clairvaux divided the monastery into groups symbolized by Martha, Mary, and Jesus. Again, the officials of the monastery held Martha's active role because, "like the common people, they labor."[23] Aelred of Rievaulx separated the "spiritual militia" of monasteries into cloistered monks, officials, and prelates.[24] Even when monks described a multiplicity of roles in the monastery, the lay brothers were not mentioned. Geoffrey of Auxerre likened the monastery to the body of the bride, assigning monastic counterparts to the body parts mentioned in the Song of Songs, but he moved from the thighs to the hair without finding a place for the lay brothers.[25] Only Nicholas of Clairvaux explicitly linked the lay brothers to an active role in the monastery. In a letter, he described the three same groups demarcated by some Cistercian rituals, telling his friends to "perceive the lay brothers working like Martha, the monks contemplating like Mary, and the novices lamenting like Lazarus, since they were recently revived from the dead."[26]

The Cistercians' tendency to describe their monasteries as divided into novices, monks, officials, and abbot suggests that they saw these groups as reflecting potential stages in the life of a monk rather than more permanent distinctions of social function. Although not all monks became monastic officials or abbots, all had been novices, and all could potentially accept administrative roles. Such diversity was based on variations in virtuous behavior, not on what the monks perceived to be more fundamental differences in function and capability. Within the monks' cloister lived men of similar abilities who progressed in virtuous behavior by pushing themselves to live up to the strict regulations of their monastery, and the uniformity of their customs was one sign of the caritas that united them. The lay brothers, with their separate customary and their different regulations, could not be easily located within these descriptions of the monks' uniform diversity; if they too were to be bound to the monks in caritas, then caritas could not be limited to the bond unifying the spiritual elite. The caritas that united the lay brothers to the monks was the same love that bound people of diverse functions and customs together into a unified Church.

The Cistercians tried to soften their distinctions between monks and lay brothers by suggesting that both possessed the same assurance of salvation. The lay brothers' customary, like the order's early statutes, reiterated that the lay brothers would share with the monks the "same gift of redemption"; this was further reinforced by monastic stories of visions and miracles.[27] Lay brothers were the subjects of many of these stories; they, like the monks, saw visions of saints who assured them they would be saved. In one story, a lay brother demonstrated that "the kingdom of God is not acquired through nobility of blood nor by the possession of earthly wealth, but only by the virtue of obedience."[28] In another, the Cistercians made clear that they did not limit their emphasis on fraternal relations to the choir monks. A dying lay brother, who had lived in peace with his brothers for most of his life, nonetheless thought he had offended a brother who was tending him. He rose from bed and prostrated himself before the man, begged his forgiveness, and asked to die in peace with the love of all his brothers. After the offended brother forgave him, the dying brother saw Jesus and his apostles, the ultimate symbol of fraternal love, around his bed waiting to carry him away.[29]

Other stories proved the holiness of the lay brothers' routine and onerous tasks. In one, a plowman saw Jesus walking next to him, holding the whip and pole used to prod the oxen; in another, a lay brother succeeded in bringing ten large and unusual cattle across the Alps from Italy to Clairvaux because of the efficacy of his prayers to Bernard.[30] Still others hinted that the characteristics separating lay brothers from monks were to disappear in heaven. One dying lay brother suddenly began to speak elegant Latin and gave a lucid sermon on the Bible.[31] Another dreamed that a young girl taught him to celebrate the mass; when he awoke he knew the entire service by heart, even though he had never learned to read.[32] But one story suggests that, even in heaven, monks and lay brothers might not live in perfect equality. A monk and a lay brother died the same day, so they both received the same services and were buried in the same tomb. After this was done

it was shown to a certain holy man in a vision that two most beautiful shrines had been built at Clairvaux, one in the infirmary of the monks, the other in the infirmary of the lay brothers. The first, however, was nobler in length and more graceful. By the construction of these twin shrines . . . the habits of both men are clearly shown to be precious in the sight of God. However, the differences in the shrines indicate differences in merit, because, however holy the one man, we believe the other to exist with more holiness in God.[33]

In this story, the separation of monk from lay brother continued after death. Not only do the two shrines appear in separate places in the monastery, but the story does not clarify whether the difference in holiness was due to an implicit distinction between lay brothers and monks or to the differences in merit between two individuals. Its ambiguity again reflects the anomalous position of the lay brothers. The monks expressed a concern for the well-being of the lay brothers' souls, described them as bound to the rest of the community in caritas, and emphasized that they too would receive a heavenly reward for their difficult life on earth, but they did not necessarily think that their rewards would be the same. Their unwillingness to see the lay brothers when they described the unified diversity of their monasteries, and their identification of their uniform customs with caritas, suggests that the lay brothers did not fully belong to the communities of elite monks who pushed each other to progress in virtue while alive and received the highest reward for their merits in heaven. This perception of the lay brothers foreshadowed the Cistercian monks' attitude toward Christian society in general: they perceived it as united in caritas but divided according to merits. "The just will shine like the sun in their father's kingdom," Bernard explained, "yet because of their differences in merit, some will shine more than others."[34]

The Cistercians' difficulties in placing the lay brothers within their monasteries illustrates the tension between their idea of caritas as a distinctive love that bound together the communities of monks and a more inclusive caritas that united all of Christian society. But the monks' conception of a society unified by caritas did not go unchallenged: by the late twelfth century, some lay brothers did not find the order's promise of salvation sufficient compensation for what seemed an overly difficult life on earth, and they began to protest and revolt.[35] In his *Exordium magnum*, Conrad of Eberbach described one of the earliest lay brother protests, which took place at Schönau in 1168. This account suggests that the lay brothers accepted the monks' offer of shared spiritual benefits; what they objected to were the earthly inequalities.[36] Their protest was triggered by a new abbot who refused to continue his predecessor's practice of giving new shoes each year to the lay brothers as well as the monks. The lay brothers responded that their "arduous and harsh work was intolerable" and plotted to sneak into the monks' dormitory to slash their new shoes.[37] The abbot succeeded in quelling the plot only after his request for divine aid seemingly caused the death of one of the conspiracy's leaders. Conrad's description of the response of the lay brothers' ensuing reaction suggests that they still had great confidence in the efficacy of the community's prayers: the abbot initially refused to provide the dead conspirator with prayers and burial in holy ground and only gave in after the other lay brothers repented of their plot. The final scene of the story took place a year later when a monk had a vision of the dead lay brother. The dead man explained that he was enduring punishment for his rebellion but that he had hope for divine mercy because of his community's prayers. Conrad of Eberbach used this story to portray the dangers of disobedience and to celebrate the power of Cistercian prayer, but the divinely instituted punishment of the lay brother also gave divine sanction to the continued inequities in the Cistercians' customs. The lay brothers' revolt had been turned into a story demonstrating divine approval for the very practices the lay brothers had protested.

Conrad of Eberbach's shaping of the lay brothers' protest at Schönau suggests that the monks and lay brothers had developed different understandings of the language of fraternal harmony. For the lay brothers, sharing in the spiritual benefits of the order implied that they would join their monastic brothers in a heavenly unity that they then wanted to see reproduced in the order's customs on earth. For the monks, however, this offer of spiritual benefits allowed for differences in spiritual ability and heavenly reward, which they then saw replicated in the functional distinctions between monks and lay brothers. Within Cistercian ideology, the lay brothers straddled the line between those within the monastery and those outside. The monks' conception of their lay brothers as a group united to them by love but divided from them by function paralleled their understanding of the order of Christian society, in which they saw many paths toward salvation in a Church whose diverse members were united by caritas but not by equality of merit. But the lay brothers' objections to this social vision reminds us that the Cistercian monks' sense of themselves as a spiritual elite would not go unchallenged by those they ranked below them.

II

The Cistercians used many of the same images to illustrate the unified diversity of Christian society that they used in describing their monasteries. Like their monasteries, Christian society appeared to be divided by a diversity of merit but united into a single Church by caritas. These parallels between monastery and Church suggest that the Cistercians presented their communities as models demonstrating to all Christians that virtue and love could unite diverse individuals and bring them into contact with the divine. Yet hints of the Cistercians' more exclusive sense of caritas are still apparent in their social descriptions, especially in their inability to settle on a consistent ranking of the orders that made up the Church. Such inconsistencies again suggest that they felt a tension between their desire to extend their caritas to all and their desire to reaffirm the distinctiveness of their own contemplative life.

The body of the bride signified the groups within a monastery; it also signified the Church as a whole. According to Geoffrey of Auxerre, the bride's eyes were prelates, her cheeks monastic communities that glowed with virtues. Her hands were almsgivers, her stomach was the common people who lived in conjugal chastity, and her legs were both orders of princes, ecclesiastical and secular, who supported the Church as pillars.[38] Bernard of Clairvaux, Geoffrey of Auxerre, and Hugh of Pontigny all constructed rooms and buildings out of the social orders; for Geoffrey, society could become the bridal chamber in the Song of Songs: "The bed is the quiet of cenobitic churches, the house is the community of the people, the beams are the princes of both orders, who strongly bind them together with just laws, and the paneling is the morals of a well-trained clergy that ornaments the church."[39] Still other images wove the diverse orders of society into the robe that clothed the bride.[40] All emphasized the dependence of these groups on one another, and all stressed that they were unified into a single whole by caritas.

Caritas united the different orders into the Church and linked the Church to the divine, but it also linked each individual soul with the divine. The Cistercians articulated this point by using the same image of the bride for both the Church and the soul. Not only did the Song of Songs celebrate the love between Christ and his Church, but it also expressed "the longing of the soul and its marriage song."[41] This use of the bride to figure both the Church and the individual soul was not new—it had its source in Origen's commentaries on the Canticles—but through much of the early Middle Ages the interpretation of the Song as a marriage between the soul and the divine remained secondary to its interpretation as a marriage between Christ and the Church.[42] The Cistercians were central players in the reemergence of the more personal and interior theme of the soul's search for the divine, and they so merged this theme with the older interpretation of the bride that the image flickered back and forth between soul and Church.[43] Bernard, for instance, often slid between the two or spoke of the bride without noting whether he meant the Church, the soul, or both. This equation between the Church and the individual explained how caritas could unite the Church, for if each Christian sought contact with the divine through caritas, then all Christians would be joined in a shared goal and by the shared virtues that led toward the love of God. Thus, just as the unity of Cistercians' monastic communities derived from each monk's desire for a divine love, the Church's unity stemmed from the harmony of individual Christians, all of whom desired to progress in caritas.

By using the same descriptive language for their own monasteries as for Christian society as a whole, the Cistercians implied that the sense of caritas that they had developed within their communities could be extended to encompass all of Christendom. Bernard of Clairvaux's willingness to distribute his sermons and treatises outside his monastery suggests that he believed that the lessons he developed and learned within his community were applicable to a more general audience. A later abbot of Clairvaux, Henry of Marcy, wrote a treatise on the pilgrimage of the City of God on earth in which he advocated that its citizens renounce worldly values and develop contemplative virtues but never specified that these citizens were monks. Instead, his experience of Cistercian life led him to recommend its fundamental processes to all Christians. Gilbert of Hoyland and Geoffrey of Auxerre made a similar point when they described the bride seeking her beloved in both streets and squares; they took this to signify that both wide and narrow paths could lead to heaven.[44] In fact, Geoffrey strained to reconcile his interpretation with the traditional idea that only the narrow path led to eternal life; his solution divided the narrow path into wider and narrower ways, because "the city of Jerusalem does not have so many streets of those living strictly, but also has more of those living in humbler and flatter squares."[45] Both men insisted that the bride could find traces of her groom in all the orders in the Church, as long as all did good works and were inspired by love. Most Cistercian authors still made clear that they believed the best progress in caritas occurred on the narrow path provided by a Cistercian monastery, but this path was not the only one.[46] Within the monasteries, both the monks' and the lay brothers' customs could lead to salvation; in the larger Christian society, all Christians, whatever their order, could strive toward this same goal.

When Cistercian authors described the diversity of Christian society, their imagery reinforced this point. They often portrayed society as divided into contemplatives and actives, which they associated with Mary and Martha or Rachel and Leah. At times, they used these pairs to distinguish the monastic world from all other social groups: this formed one of the basic assumptions of the Cistercians' commentaries on the Song of Songs because monks, as contemplatives, could lie in the nuptial bed and experience most fully the love of the bridegroom. Other ways in which they used these figures were either more restricted or more inclusive. Gilbert of Hoyland condensed their referent from society to the individual by suggesting that each monk had to attain both Martha's active charity and Mary's contemplative love.[47] Other Cistercians expanded the referent to compare life on earth to heaven. Hugh of Pontigny and Henry of Marcy, for example, implied that all Christians on earth had Martha's active part and would only find contemplation in heaven.[48] Gilbert of Hoyland, in yet another sermon, made all Christians contemplatives, although in his description a tripartite division into contemplation of the divine essence, contemplation of divine signs, and contemplation of divine handiwork began to emerge. "This last manner of contemplation belongs to ordinary people, the second to the learned, the first to the most purified."[49] Used in these ways, the distinction between action and contemplation was inclusive rather than exclusive; it made Cistercian life part of a Christian life on earth rather than separating the monks from the activities of the world.

The inconsistencies in the Cistercians' use of tripartite social images also illuminate the monks' conception of Christian society and their place in it. They used triads—either Jesus, Mary, and Martha or Noah, Daniel, and Job—that pointed toward three distinct social roles, but they used them in ways that were fundamentally binary. They either divided society between actives and contemplatives or between the married and the continent, and then they added to this division a third group, the prelates, that was not fully congruent with the other two. As we will see, their inability to locate prelates within these binary divisions, and their inconsistencies in ranking prelates in relation to the other social orders, again points to the monks' desire for an ideal contemplative life and their concurrent recognition of the need for a virtuous and active life on earth.

Geoffrey of Auxerre's use of triads to describe social divisions illustrates the way he, like other Cistercian authors, viewed society as fundamentally divided into two. In trying to use the queens, concubines, and maidens of the Song of Songs to figure a tripartite society, he began with a distinction between queens and concubines to signify a division between leaders and subjects. He then added a third group, the maidens, whom he associated with contemplatives, and ended up with the triad of Noah, Job, and Daniel.[50] But this triad ultimately contained a binary distinction, as Geoffrey described both queens and concubines, or Noah and Job, as actives who went to the mill and worked in the field; only the maidens, whom he associated with Daniel, were left in bed as contemplatives who had renounced the world.

More often, when Cistercian authors used the triad of Noah, Daniel, and Job, they connected it with the traditional degrees of sexual purity. Origen and Jerome had both associated Daniel with virgins, Noah with the continent, and Job with the married, a pattern that became common again when tenth- and eleventh-century monastic authors associated monks with both Daniel and virgins.[51] The Cistercians, however, seldom used this triad to refer to three degrees of sexual purity, but instead started with a binary distinction between the married and the continent. In so doing, they returned to the classification of Gregory the Great, who had associated Noah with preachers or prelates, Daniel with the continent monks, and Job with the good married people.[52] Perhaps the Cistercians dropped the category of virgins because they, monks recruited as adults, were not necessarily virgins themselves. Bernard, for example, first distinguished between the continent monks and the married people, and made no mention of the sexual status of prelates.[53] Henry of Marcy also associated Noah, Daniel, and Job with the leaders, the continent, and the married, using the same basic configuration as Bernard and, like Bernard, viewing the basic distinctions of sexual purity as binary, not tripartite.[54]

Whether they described their society as divided between actives and contemplatives or the married and the continent, the Cistercians could not find a consistent place for prelates. Leaders fit only uneasily into these binary divisions; like monks, they were continent, while like married people, they were active. Additionally, Cistercian authors could not

decide how to rank prelates in relation to monks. Sometimes the ranking varied even within a single passage. Thus, when Bernard described the
three orders of Noah, Daniel, and Job, their relative position remained
ambiguous.

Just as the prophet Ezechiel foresaw that Noah, Daniel, and Job alone would be
saved, so we should understand in these names the three kinds of people to
whom alone God spoke of peace. They represent these orders: the continent, the
prelates, and the married. But they do so only if the continent turn from carnal attractions to those of the heart, that is, to spiritual desires—as Daniel was
named a man of desire by the Angel; if the prelates strive more to serve [*prodesse*]
than to rule [*praeesse*], because sanctity is especially fitting for them—as in the
psalm they were spiritually called saints; and if the married people do not
transgress the commandments so that they can be named the people of God and
the sheep of the field because of their merits.[55]

Bernard placed Noah before Daniel and the continent before the prelates,
but when he discussed the prelates he suggested that sanctity was especially fitting for them because the psalmist called them saints. He showed
the same ambiguity in a second sermon, in which he described the three
groups of Christians crossing a sea of worldly fluctuations. The leaders, like Noah, crossed by guiding an ark; the penitent and continent, like
Daniel, crossed over a bridge; and the "faithful people administering
the goods of this world" waded across a ford and wet their feet in the sea.
Although prelates led and directed the ark of the Church, the bridge
of continence and penance provided the securest form of crossing.[56]

Other Cistercians were equally inconsistent with their rankings. Sometimes Geoffrey of Auxerre elevated the monks, as contemplatives, to
the highest rung, whereas at other times he elevated the prelates.[57] Hugh
of Pontigny tried to divide the Church into three orders—the leaders, the
contemplatives, and the actives—which he associated with Jesus, Mary,
and Martha, but he varied the number of the orders and their relative positions. The word of God, he suggested,

sprouts in prelates, flowers in contemplatives, and fruits in those who are active. . . . Good listeners are likened to flowers, true teachers to sprouts, and
devotion to pious acts to the fruits. Jesus speaks, Mary sits, and only Martha pre-
pares the meal, because prelates teach, contemplatives are empty for God, and
only the active life administers whatever is necessary in the present. And because
spirituals are indebted to carnal ones for carnal things, Martha rightly asks
that Mary recommend her. Certainly, those who are active depend on the securer

merits and prayers of the contemplatives; they are harmoniously yoked together, because Mary chose the highest part. There are three parts: one good, one better, and the third is the best.[58]

Here, Hugh first created an order based on authority—Jesus first, then Mary, then Martha—that was reinforced by the temporal progression of sprouts, flowers, and fruits. But then the distinction between the active and the contemplative life began to reappear: first Hugh put listeners before teachers and those who performed pious acts, and then teachers dropped out altogether, leaving actives dependent on contemplatives, since Mary chose the highest part. When a triad reappears in the last line, the referents are ambiguous, but the previous statement implies that the three figures were now ranked with actives first, teachers second, and contemplatives as the best.

The Cistercians' unease with using tripartite imagery to describe the organization of their society, and their seeming uncertainty about the relative positions of the three groupings, suggests that their view of their society, like their construction of their monasteries, was essentially binary. As their monasteries were divided between monks and lay brothers, so Christian society split into contemplatives and actives, those who abstained from sexual relations and those who did not, those in the monastery and those in the world. As a category, prelates or leaders fluctuated between these two poles: they were actives who abstained from sex; they ranked above monks in terms of authority but below them in terms of virtue and merit.

This inability to place prelates firmly within one of two categories actually betrays much about the Cistercians' view of their society and their own place in it. Their understanding of caritas distinguished between the yearning of life on earth and the consummation of love in heaven while still providing a link between the two; their variation in ranking the orders in society depended on a similar distinction. A hierarchy based on authority, with prelates at the apex, was an earthly hierarchy, required because fallen humanity could neither live in peace nor develop the virtues necessary for salvation unless it was subject to the authority and guidance of leaders. On earth, then, the Cistercians ranked prelates above contemplatives, for leaders cared for their subjects, who could not learn unaided the humility and charity essential for salvation. In contrast, the Cistercians believed that such positions of leadership were fraught with danger; abbots warned their monks not to seek to become prelates and described the perils of the "world."[59] If the orders were ranked, not according to human needs but according to their potential for heavenly reward, then the monastic life preceded the others, for a life of contemplation provided the best means for growing in virtue and learning charity. In his *Apologia*, Bernard made clear that the bases for these gradations were different in heaven than on earth; on earth rankings were based on authority and function, whereas in heaven they were based on merit.[60] In earthly society, where human sinfulness subjected people to a life of labor and placed them under the authority of others, monks were not preeminent. In heaven, however, where rankings instead depended on virtue and merit, those who had led a contemplative life would be supreme.

Still, these Cistercian authors did not completely separate the orders based on earthly authority from those based on spiritual merit. Their return to Gregory the Great's interpretation of the three figures of Noah, Daniel, and Job also signaled their interest in Gregory's ideas about the relation of the monastery to its society. Writing at a time in which classical distinctions between Church and society had become blurred, Gregory had used the monastery to serve as a model for the Christian community and adapted its ascetic ideal as a model for the behavior of bishops and clergy.[61] He suggested that the position of prelates as Christian administrators was connected to their abilities and merits; his *Regulae pastoralis* described a balance between contemplation and activity in which a good rector learned virtue through study and contemplation, put such virtues into action by preaching and service, and renewed and refreshed himself in contemplative retreats.[62] Gregory's ideal bishops thus had the virtues and merits of monks, only with an added authority. As a result, in Gregory's ranking of social orders, prelates belonged at the top, monks came second, and the faithful married people were third.

As we shall see, the Cistercians, like Gregory, believed that the leaders of the Church were to balance the spiritual benefits of contemplation against the demands of their active life. For the earthly Church to reflect its heavenly form and become the bride united with Christ in caritas, churchmen could not hold authority over others before they had developed the virtues necessary for their own salvation, virtues the Cistercians believed were best learned within their monasteries. Thus, despite their warning to their monks about striving for positions of authority, the Cistercians presented their communities as schools that taught the virtues so essential to men in these positions. Their monasteries demonstrated to the rest of Christian society how best to progress in virtue, but they also helped to train and advise men who accepted positions of leadership so that these prelates would properly use their authority to guide the diverse orders of Christian society and to draw them into a Church unified by the bonds of caritas.

In using Gregory the Great's social classifications, the Cistercians abandoned other monastic expressions of the social order. Tenth- and eleventh-century monks from Cluny and Fleury, and the twelfth-century Rupert of Deutz all associated Noah, Daniel, and Job with three degrees of sexual purity, and consistently placed Daniel, who symbolized the virginal monks, above the orders figured by Noah and Job.[63] For these authors, there was no question that the monastic life was superior to that of clerics, and their social rankings reflect their often strained relations with bishops and their sense of themselves as the source of protection and salvation for their society.[64] But, for Cistercian monks writing in the decades after the Investiture Controversy, at a time when the ecclesiastical hierarchy increasingly defined its powers and roles, the monastery could no longer easily claim such superiority. That they occasionally placed prelates before monks reflects their improved relations with their bishops and their rejection of the pastoral and sacramental responsibilities incumbent on such prelates. Yet, their unwillingness to adopt Gregory's rankings with consistency, and their occasional ranking of contemplatives before prelates, betrays the attractiveness of the older conception of monasteries as worlds apart. Just as the Cistercians' inability to find a consistent place for the lay brothers demonstrated a tension between their sense of the exclusiveness of their communities and their interest in the spiritual well-being of others, so their inconsistencies in ranking the society around them illustrates the tension between their contemplative ideal and their recognition that they were necessarily a part of the Church on pilgrimage on earth.

When the Cistercians used images that abandoned social rankings, they placed themselves at the center of the Church rather than at its head. They lay in a bed of contemplation while the other orders built the rest of the Church around them. But the inconsistencies in the monks' schemes of social classification suggest that they recognized that they could not remain in contemplation but had to take on active roles as monastic officials, abbots, and even bishops. The variation in their rankings of Christian society, sometimes according to degrees of authority and other times according to degrees of merit, makes clear that they did not wish to be leaders of the earthly Church but instead expected to receive the highest reward in heaven. Their communities served as models for the Church both by demonstrating how the quest for caritas could unite a diverse community into a single whole, and by suggesting that the virtues taught by a contemplative life were also necessary for those who were to become society's leaders. Yet their recognition that life on earth always offered a struggle toward the ideal rather than its fulfillment, and often required compromises that reversed the ideal order of caritas, led them to become actively involved in attempts to create a virtuous and united Christian society.

Part II

Charity in Action

The Cistercians' careful definition of the boundaries of their monasteries did not prevent their contact with and concern for the society around them. Twelfth-century social and economic changes, the attitudes of a knightly class, and even the demands of their benefactors all permeated the monasteries and helped shape their monastic culture. But the monks themselves also breached the monastery walls as they willingly intervened in political and ecclesiastical affairs both locally and throughout Europe. They mediated disputes between monasteries, lords, bishops, and kings; they worked to end papal schisms and disputed episcopal elections; they reformed monasteries and condemned theological errors; they preached against heretics and for crusades. Although their literature occasionally celebrated withdrawal and isolation and criticized the worldliness of other monks, their political activities did not contradict their idea of monastic life. Rather, their ideas about ecclesiastical reform and the patterns of their activity were rooted in their monastic culture and their conception of caritas.

Defining the characteristics and boundaries of groups, especially those linked by abstract rather than personal ties, was a concern shared by many in the twelfth century.[1] Churchmen and scholars explored the bonds of both the Church and Christian society; monastic orders sought to understand the unity of people no longer necessarily in face-to-face contact; townspeople and scholars found common interests and strove to be recognized by others; and even kings began, haltingly, to rule kingdoms rather than peoples. Issues of law and jurisdiction played an increasingly important role in establishing the characteristics of such groups. The canonists associated with the Gregorian reform, for example, began to determine the extent of papal jurisdiction and to define a Christendom bound by obedience to the pope and subjection to Church canons.[2] Urban communes and universities defined themselves in terms of their freedom from the jurisdiction of others, whereas kings began to understand their power in terms of law and, eventually, legislation.[3] By establishing the boundaries of their jurisdiction, these groups created bonds that linked their members together and determined who remained outside.

The Cistercians too were interested in defining their place in their monastic order, in the Church, and in Christian society, but they understood the bonds of these societies to be formed by love, not jurisdiction. This vision of a society linked by caritas had a long lineage. Its roots lay in the Pauline figure of Christians as individual members but one body in Christ, and it flourished with both Carolingian clerics and eleventh-century imperial apologists as a description of a Christian society united in peace and harmony under an emperor.[4] It emerged in a different form in the peace assemblies and *concordia* of the late tenth and eleventh centuries, for there it helped to blur the lines between royal authority and the power of banal lordship rather than supporting the divine authority of the ruler.[5] The Cistercians applied this language of unity to their vision of the Church as the body of all Christians, but they added to their predecessors' assumptions their own characteristic interest in an individual and interior spiritual growth. As a result, they articulated an image of a Christian society united by the moral character of its members. This conception of the Church intersected with, but ultimately remained distinct from, the developing ideas of papal monarchy.[6]

The Cistercians' central image for the Church was that of the bride united to Christ her bridegroom by caritas. The meanings they gave to this image were shaped in part by their monastic experiences, for they believed that the source of their monastic unity was the effort made by each monk to participate in divine love. However, by associating the image of the bride with both the Church and the individual soul, the monks implied that their order had no monopoly on caritas. Instead, the goals of the Church and of each Christian were interrelated. Caritas unified the Church because each Christian sought to experience that divine love that joined him or her with God and neighbor; yet, at the same time, Christians were able to experience this love only because the Church already existed as an entity united with the divine. The intertwined nature of individual and ecclesiastical reform influenced the Cistercians' ideas about the Church and the actions by which they effected them. On the one hand, they emphasized and worked for the unity of the Church, because without a unified Church no one could be saved; on the other hand, they encouraged individuals to develop in virtue, because without such individual reform the Church could not be united.

The Cistercians' vision of Christian society and their willingness to accept obligations for people outside their communities do not fully explain their activities. However much the monks' ideas may have predisposed them toward social reform, ideas alone did not motivate them to leave their communities. The impetus instead came from gradually developed networks of friends who channeled information about crises and problems into the monasteries and then provided fellowship and assistance to the monks as they worked to resolve them. These networks of associates furthered the monks' confidence that an ecclesiastical unity of spirit could actually be realized, for they fostered the monks' impression that all people of virtuous character would seek to support the same vision of the Church and the same political aims. For a few decades on either side of 1150, such connections with powerful ecclesiastics gave the Cistercians' ideas authority and influence. Yet these networks also illustrate the limits of the Cistercians' vision, for the political unity of their friends became increasingly illusory and the caritas that the Cistercians believed united them became a contested concept.

The networks demonstrate the limits of the Cistercians' activities in another way as well. Most of their friends and associates were either ecclesiastical officials or powerful secular lords. Although all Christians theoretically were unified by caritas, the Cistercians paid little attention to the spiritual development of the laity. Instead, they worked to ensure that those with authority, especially church officials, had the virtues necessary to administer their offices properly. If monks were ever to rest at the center of the Church, undisturbed by secular responsibilities or the demands of caritas, then others had to take responsibility for the unity of Christian society. Only with a proper exercise of authority by the leaders of society could the Christians on earth be linked to the heavenly Church and bound into a single whole.

The Cistercians' image of a Church united by charity intersected and even occasionally supported the aims of their more legal-minded contemporaries, but it was based on very different assumptions. Whereas the eleventh-century papal reformers tried to establish papal lordship over the Church, and many twelfth-century thinkers sought to define the relationship of secular and ecclesiastical jurisdiction, the Cistercians called for a program of moral regeneration and based their conception of both ecclesiastical and secular authority on Gregory the Great's ideas about ministry.[7] Gregory the Great had borrowed ideas about virtuous authority from Augustine of Hippo but modified Augustine's analysis of power to suggest that inequality and subjection had their roots in individual sin and merit rather than in the fundamental taint of Adam and Eve's fall. As a result, Gregory posited less of a gulf between earthly political society and the eschatological Church than did Augustine, and he believed it was possible for society to be led by holy men, both religious and lay, who had the virtues necessary to make their authority into a ministry.[8]

The Cistercians shared Gregory's association between authority and merit, arguing that the virtuous exercise of authority would unite the earthly social divisions based on power to the heavenly divisions founded on merit and maintain a single Church concurrently on pilgrimage on earth and at rest in heaven. They were, perhaps, less optimistic than Gregory that the Church could locate leaders with the qualities of the holy men of Gregory's *Dialogues*, as well as less confident that they could find an earthly equilibrium between activity and contemplation, between love of the divine and love of one's neighbor.[9] But even if the mixed nature of earthly society continually required compromises, and the ultimate realization of a unified Church was only possible in heaven at the end of time, they nonetheless agreed that this was a goal toward which to strive. If they could convince those with authority to develop the necessary virtues, they believed each order would fulfill its own distinct social function without usurping the functions of others. In such an ideal society, caritas would no longer compel monks into reforming activities, and they could remain within their communities in a life of contemplation and prayer. Around them, prelates would care for the salvation of their flocks, secular princes would keep the peace and protect the poor and weak with a merciful justice, and the Church would unite the diverse orders in harmony with divine love. Until the advent of this ideal, however, the Cistercians' caritas inspired them to advise others on how they ought to behave.

The five chapters of Part II explore the nature of this advice and the actions by which the monks worked to implement it. Chapters 5, 6, and 7 examine their efforts to encourage a unified Church by counseling monks, prelates, and lay authorities on their need for spiritual reform; Chapters 8 and 9 investigate their attempts to preserve ecclesiastical unity from the threats of schism and heresy. Thus, the first three chapters focus on the Cistercians' conception of an ideal earthly society, whereas the last two focus on their behavior in a society in which the human condition demanded that they make constant compromises between the ideal and the necessary, between the desires of affective caritas and the demands of a caritas active on earth.

Chapter 5

"Some Will Shine More Than Others"
The Unity of the Monastic World

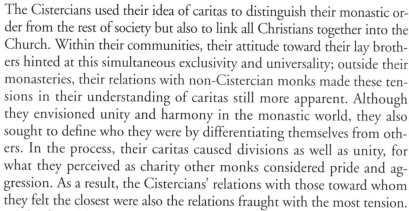

The Cistercians used their idea of caritas to distinguish their monastic order from the rest of society but also to link all Christians together into the
Church. Within their communities, their attitude toward their lay brothers hinted at this simultaneous exclusivity and universality; outside their
monasteries, their relations with non-Cistercian monks made these tensions in their understanding of caritas still more apparent. Although
they envisioned unity and harmony in the monastic world, they also
sought to define who they were by differentiating themselves from others. In the process, their caritas caused divisions as well as unity, for
what they perceived as charity other monks considered pride and aggression. As a result, the Cistercians' relations with those toward whom
they felt the closest were also the relations fraught with the most tension.

The friendships the Cistercians developed with monks from other
communities, and the support they offered one another, enhanced a
sense that the common life and interests of all monks could unite their
communities in peace and brotherhood. In fact, Cistercian abbeys received much early support from other religious communities. Pontigny
and Morimond were established at the request of hermits, while Cluny,
Saint-Germain-des-Pres, Saint-Bénigne of Dijon, and Molesme helped
the monks from Cîteaux and Clairvaux to consolidate their early property holdings.[1] As the Cistercians became more politically prominent, they
began to help other religious communities. Bernard of Clairvaux's exhortation to other monks that they should "preserve in unity the bonds
of peace" was no mere rhetorical formula.[2] Bernard wrote at least 35
letters to bishops, lords, and popes furthering the interests of non-Cis-

tercian monks and canons, and other Cistercian abbots, often working together or with one or two Cistercian bishops, helped to mediate disputes so that these monasteries could live in peace with both their benefactors and one another.[3]

Even more than economic aid, the friendships that Cistercian monks developed with non-Cistercians created an impression of monastic brotherhood. Recent work has pointed to the late eleventh and twelfth centuries as an important period for monastic friendships in which monks explored their emotional feelings for one another as part of both their own self-understanding and their spiritual quest for the divine.[4] For the Cistercians, these friendships often took place within their communities; Aelred of Rievaulx especially celebrated the importance of a friend's physical proximity for his own spiritual development, and many of the letters of friendship written by Nicholas of Clairvaux encouraged their recipients to enter Clairvaux.[5] Still, Cistercians did develop friendships with, and reveal their feelings to, non-Cistercian monks. Stephen Harding, for instance, wrote to his former brothers from the English monastery of Sherborne to express his gratitude that they had raised him and trained him well.[6] Bernard of Clairvaux and William of Saint-Thierry became friends soon after Bernard became abbot in 1115, and William described his delight in Bernard's company when he visited the hut in which Bernard was staying.[7] Letters sustained the connection when the men were physically distant, and their relationship eventually combined personal feelings and political activities. Bernard's secretary, Nicholas, wrote letters of friendship both on his own behalf and for other monks at Clairvaux, and his letters are particularly good examples of the way this genre investigated the feelings of love, longing, loss, and even betrayal. Throughout these letters, he emphasized that the shared love between friends overcame all variations in monastic custom and created unity and harmony. Writing for his fellow monk Gerard of Perona, Nicholas told the Benedictine Peter of Celles, "Although our different order divides us, charity binds us because love of the heart, not color of the clothes, produces unity and even unanimity, most beloved father."[8]

Prayer associations also demonstrated the seeming unity of the monastic world. Just as the uniformity of the Cistercians' prayers created a tangible symbol of the order's harmony, so the exchange of prayers with other religious communities expressed a vision of monastic brotherhood. Formal prayer associations had long existed between monasteries and often

had provided temporal benefits to the communities as well as commemorations for their dead.[9] Although the Cistercians did not record the
individual anniversaries of either their own monks or monks from other
communities, they were willing to commemorate the dead from other
communities collectively on November 20.[10] Often, these agreements
grew out of personal contacts between abbots, such as the "association of
mutual brotherhood" established by Stephen Harding and the abbot
of Saint Waast in Arras during Stephen Harding's travels in Flanders in
1124.[11] Other times, they marked the end of a dispute and the restoration
of monastic harmony. This was the case in 1142, when the Cistercians and
Premonstratensian canons formed an agreement "for the preservation of
peace and charity" and determined to make a yearly commemoration for
each other and hold full offices for the other's dead.[12] Sometimes these exchanges of prayers were less formally established, as in 1150 when Bernard
of Clairvaux told Peter the Venerable of Cluny that "at the chapter at
Cîteaux a commemoration was made of you as our special lord, father,
and dearest friend, and of all of yours, both living and dead."[13] Requests
for prayers could also link individual monks: Nicholas of Clairvaux, for
instance, ended many of his letters of friendship by asking his corre-
spondents to pray for him.[14] With such associations and requests, the Cistercians implied a fellowship with other monks. They recognized features
common to all religious communities—their members sought the same
virtues and spent much of their lives in formal prayer—and, by admit-
ting the effectiveness of the prayers of others, they acknowledged the holiness of other forms of religious life.

At the same time, however, the Cistercians asserted their differences by
distinguishing their customs from those of other communities. Their emphasis on the Benedictine Rule was one such means of differentiation, for
although they may never have intended to follow the Rule exactly, their
emphasis on its authority quickly became a trait that other monks noticed. Around 1124, William of Malmesbury remarked that the Cistercians
intended to follow the Benedictine Rule so that "not one dot or point of
it be omitted"; a year later, the Benedictine abbot Rupert of Deutz
called the Cistercians "zealous investigators of the Benedictine Rule."[15]
Their insistence that they live off their own labor and their refusal to receive either tithes or manorial revenues also differentiated them from other
monks, whose economies relied on the labor of serfs and on manorial and
parish revenues.[16] Their undyed habits further set them apart, as did

Figure 5. Stephen Harding (left) and the abbot of Saint Waast of Arras. In this miniature, the abbots offer their monasteries to the Virgin Mary while the scribe Osbert offers her his book. Osbert copied Jerome's *Super Jeremiam prophetam* and gave it to Stephen Harding after the prayer association between the two abbeys. *Hieronymous super Jeremiam* (1124). Dijon, Bibliothèque municipale, MS 130, f. 104. Photograph courtesy Foto Marburg / Art Resource, New York.

their distinctive liturgy, both of which appeared to be evidence of their presumptuous desire to be different.[17] So did their refusal to allow non-Cistercian monks into their cloister. This regulation dramatically illustrates the monks' sense of their monasteries' exclusiveness and the importance of uniform customs as a symbol of their distinctive caritas. Not even those Cistercians who became bishops could enter the cloister "because of their differences."[18]

The Cistercians' attitude toward Molesme illustrates the implications of a caritas that both united and separated, for they used Molesme as a foil at the same time that they offered it aid and assistance. From its beginning, the foundation of Cîteaux implicitly reproached Molesme, especially because the prelates who described the monks' proposal to form a new monastery compared it to the monastery they had left behind.[19] The *Exordium cistercii*, which was probably written at Clairvaux around 1123, made the Cistercians' criticisms more explicit.[20] Although it began by praising Molesme for its greatness in both virtues and possessions, it then continued: "Because possessions and virtues are not accustomed to be long-term companions, certain men from this holy congregation who were exceedingly wise and understanding of higher things decided to occupy themselves with heavenly studies rather than to be entangled in earthly affairs."[21] Despite the compliments, the passage presents the monks who left for Cîteaux as a spiritual elite, and it hints that Molesme's wealth would, in the long run, hinder its virtues.[22] But soon after the composition of the *Exordium cistercii*, Bernard began to solicit help for Molesme: he wrote the count of Nevers, perhaps during the famine of 1124–26, to ask for food for the monks; he requested donations from his relatives, the lords of Montbard; and he intervened on Molesme's behalf with the archbishop of Sens and the bishop of Langres.[23] Sometimes, Bernard provided Molesme with kinds of property prohibited to the Cistercians: he asked that they be given tithes and be allowed to retain control of some churches.[24] Such actions further reinforced the *Exordium cistercii*'s implication that Molesme, although holy, was not as holy as the Cistercian foundations; Bernard thought that Molesme could accept tithes and administer churches but insisted that the Cistercians avoid such entanglements and remain focused on their progression toward the divine.

The Cistercians' attitude toward monasteries that accepted tithes had similar implications of the Cistercians' superior holiness. Disputes over tithes formed part of a more widespread discussion about the pastoral activities of monks; many eleventh- and twelfth-century religious groups, both monks and regular canons, suggested that monks abandon pastoral responsibilities and the revenues associated with them, whereas many older Benedictine monasteries objected to both the loss of revenues and the curtailing of their social role.[25] The Cistercians joined this debate, arguing that the monastic acceptance of tithes not only confused the role of monks with that of the secular clergy but also adversely influenced the health of the Church by withdrawing revenue from those who truly needed it. Hugh of Pontigny and Bernard of Clairvaux made clear their distinction between monks and the secular clergy in a letter they wrote to Odo, the abbot of Marmoutier.[26] Odo had become embroiled in a dispute over the rights to tithes that he claimed his bishop had granted him, but Hugh and Bernard advised Odo to drop his suit. Clerics served the altar and thus lived off revenues from the altar, they argued, but monks should avoid such responsibilities. Yet they also made an argument that equated responsibilities and revenues: if the monks of Marmoutier actually cared for the laity in the parish, then they could receive the tithes.

O you presumptuous monks, how can you take wine from vines you did not plant or milk from the flock you did not pasture? By what agreement do you take from places where you offered nothing? Certainly, if you wish to do this—to baptize the newborn, to bury the dead, to visit the sick, to marry the marriageable, to teach the ignorant, to correct the delinquent, to excommunicate the stubborn, to absolve the fallen, to reconcile the repentant—then you will open your mouth in the middle of the church, when a monk's role is to sit and be silent. Perhaps such a hired servant will prove himself worthy of his wages. Otherwise it is completely hateful and injurious to harvest where you have not sown or to gather what another has planted.[27]

Marmoutier's fight for the tithe upset two Cistercian assumptions about the right order of the Church: that monks should not usurp the responsibilities of the clergy, and that they should not appropriate the revenues due for another's work. The clergy received tithes because they performed pastoral duties in return, but monks were to live off their own labor.

For the most part, the Cistercians themselves continued to refuse revenues from tithes, although they did receive numerous grants that exempted them from paying tithes due from their lands. However, they

quickly became more tolerant of other monasteries that received such revenues. As early as 1126, Cistercian abbots witnessed a charter confirming
a tithe received by Molesme, and subsequently both Cistercian abbots and
bishops granted or witnessed the grants of tithes and churches to monasteries.[28] Although the Cistercians did not say so explicitly, their position on the monastic reception of tithes appears to have moved away from
a complete separation of monastic and clerical roles to an emphasis on the
relation between revenues and responsibilities. Those monks who abandoned monastic contemplation by accepting pastoral duties could receive
the associated tithes as well.[29]

Over time, papal policy changed as well. By midcentury, the papal exemption from paying tithes that once seemed a reward for Cistercian austerity now appeared as a privilege for a powerful order and a sign of
greed. In 1155, Pope Hadrian IV noted the hardships this exemption
caused for older monasteries and changed the policy of his predecessors by exempting the Cistercians from paying tithes only on *noval*
lands.[30] His successor, Alexander III, reversed this policy and restored the
full exemption to the Cistercians.[31] However, the damage had been
done and the Cistercians' freedom from tithes seemed no longer a privilege due to their poverty and unworldliness, but only evidence of their
wealth and political power. The Cistercians themselves realized this,
and in 1180, "because of the serious scandal which increases daily in all
places because of our keeping of tithes," they ruled that they should
now pay tithes on any lands from which a tithe had previously been
due.[32] In 1215, at the Fourth Lateran Council, this became Church policy as well.

Even in the early years of the order, the Cistercians' insistence on living off their own labor and their criticism of other monks for appro-
priating priestly functions provoked criticism in return. The earliest attack was that of the Benedictine Rupert of Deutz, who pinpointed the
Cistercian practices that would later upset other monks as well.[33] Rupert
accused the Cistercians of bringing scandal by recruiting monks from
other abbeys, and he thought their white, undyed habits were merely an
attempt to set themselves apart from other religious groups—if monks
and nuns had traditionally worn white, he suggested, these new monks
would wear black.[34] He was especially appalled, however, that the new
monks curtailed what he considered the central function of monastic
life—the intercession of the chant and the mass—in order to spend

time at manual labor. For Rupert, a monk approached the divine through the commemoration of the mass, and he could not understand why the Cistercians would neglect this office in order to harvest grain and cut down trees.[35] In his critique, Rupert, like later critics, made clear that his conception of caritas differed from that of the Cistercians: for him, the mass and not private mediation or fraternal compassion provided a monk with the avenue toward divine love.[36]

Rupert also described the Cistercians as false prophets who lured monks to damnation by recruiting men unable to withstand the austerities of their life. In so doing, he touched on one of the most contentious aspects of the Cistercians' behavior: their willingness to convert monks from other religious communities. The Benedictine Rule had addressed this issue, stating that pilgrim monks from a distant monastery could be received as guests and could be accepted as novices if they seemed worthy, but that an abbot should not receive a monk from a "known" monastery without the consent of the monk's abbot or a letter of recommendation.[37] In the tenth century, however, both Cluny and Fleury were granted the privilege of accepting anyone who asked to be admitted, even if they did not have their abbot's approval, and eleventh-century canons permitted the movement of monks to stricter houses, especially if the laxity of the customs of their former communities seemed to endanger their souls.[38] By the twelfth century, however, such movement had become a matter of contention, for the transfer to a "stricter" house did not necessarily mean abandoning a degenerate one, and abbots who lost monks to the Cistercians resented the implications of laxity.

When Bernard of Clairvaux wrote letters to his monks' former abbots, he offered little comfort, for his letters express the confident sense of superiority that non-Cistercians so resented. Despite Rupert's worry that these "false prophets" would attract unsuitable men to their communities, Bernard occasionally refused to admit men to Clairvaux if he thought the life there would be too difficult for them.[39] He even suggested that it would be safer for some monks to remain in their current communities rather than to switch to a Cistercian house and only then discover that they lacked the strength to persevere.[40] But these warnings only enhanced the implication inherent in any transfer, that Cistercian houses were stricter and holier than others. Furthermore, when Bernard did accept a monk, he denied he had actually recruited the man and instead suggested that the monk had finally found the monastic order best suited to his spiritual abilities. He warned the abbot of Saint Nicasius not to resist divine will, and explained to the bishop of Arras after he had accepted a monk from Saint Bertin, "I am not unaware that the brothers at Saint Bertin work toward their salvation, but only those whom God has called there."[41] After telling the abbot and monks of Saint Bertin that "I shall always love you, dearest brothers, in the Lord, and will serve you with all my love in him whose servants you are, and will always honor you in Christ, whose members you are," Bernard then stated explicitly that such love did not create an equality among monasteries. He warned the abbot, "Do not call back one whom the Lord has called, do not try to change one whom God has aroused, nor place stumbling-blocks before one to whom God has offered a hand on his ascent."[42] Such statements did little to soothe abbots who had to endure not only the loss of a monk but also the suggestion of their lesser holiness.

As Bernard's letter to the abbot of Saint Bertin suggests, the Cistercians' phrases of love and unity did not necessarily accompany letters exploring the harmonious nature of friendship. They also initiated letters of criticism and rebuke, for abbots invoked caritas to explain their interest in the conditions and customs of other monasteries. When Hugh of Pontigny and Bernard criticized Odo of Marmoutier for claiming tithes, for instance, they proclaimed, "Charity reminds us to write to you for your good, for although we are very far from you, we are separated by distance, not by spirit," and when Bernard attempted to correct a problem at the Benedictine abbey of Pouthières, he told the abbot, "You should know that I have no quarrel with you but only act out of charity for the peace of your monastery."[43] The caritas they invoked was the same caritas that they associated with the discipline that their daily chapter and the yearly Chapter General offered to Cistercians: a concern for the spiritual well-being of fellow monks included chastising them when they went astray. Within their order, they may have been able to reconcile their conception of caritas with such correction, but monks from other monasteries found this conjunction less comprehensible.

Not only did Bernard explain his criticisms in terms of his love, but he also could turn conflicts with friends into battles over caritas. Such, for instance, was the case when the close relations between the Cistercians and the Premonstratensian canons became strained. The two orders had long been allies; Bernard had helped in the foundation of Premonstratensian houses, and he and Norbert of Xanten had worked together on behalf of Innocent II during the papal schism.[44] By the 1140's, relations between the two orders appear to have soured. When Hugh, the new abbot of Premontré, accused the Cistercians of accepting two canons at Clairvaux, destroying a house belonging to the canons at Basse-Font, burning down a hut used by the canons at Braine, building on Premonstratensian property, and bringing down an interdict on the community at Saint Follian, Bernard replied that, far from trying to injure the canons, he had done his best to help them. He asked Hugh, "What have I done wrong? I have always loved you personally and have always fostered and promoted your order; what, then, have I done?"[45] He suggested that he, not Hugh, had been injured because Hugh's complaints disrupted the peace between the two orders. He told Hugh:

It only remains for you to love those who love you and to take great care to preserve unity in the bonds of peace, those bonds that have been forged between us in the cause of peace and charity, and are perhaps not less useful to you than to us. . . . Once I linked myself to you with a strong bond, with that charity that does not lie, that charity which never fails. When you are angry, I will be peaceful, and I will give the place of anger to those who are quarrelsome lest I should give it to the devil.[46]

The dispute ended with an agreement about property and the prayer association mentioned above, but in the process Bernard had used his claim of charity to turn Hugh's criticisms on their head: the Premonstratensians' complaints, not the Cisterians' actions, had disrupted the peace and broken the bonds of charity.

Even Bernard's friendship with William of Saint-Thierry could become a contest over *caritas*. When William complained that Bernard did not show the same affection for him that he did for Bernard, Bernard's response transposed this accusation into presumption. How could William claim to see into another's heart, Bernard wondered, and he then implied that it was William rather than Bernard who lacked *caritas*. Because William had the greater capacity to love, Bernard argued, then he had the charitable responsibility to help Bernard to learn to love more.[47] Such linguistic "trifling," as Bernard called it, was common in letters of friendship that explored the nuances of the writers' emotions, often with a measure of verbal one-upmanship.[48] Nonetheless, it was characteristic of Bernard's use of *caritas* that he employed it to deflect a criticism back on the critic.

The stormy relationship between Bernard and Peter the Venerable, and between the Cistercians and Cluniacs more generally, illustrates the intermingling of friendship and conflict and the way monastic disputes had both political and conceptual components. The two abbots' expressions of friendship became intertwined with disputes over property, revenues, and political influence and with contests over the meaning of *caritas*. In recent years, many scholars have argued for good relations between the two abbots—the men both supported Innocent II during the papal schism, met at the council of Pisa in 1135, wrote friendly and even loving letters to one another, and shared a strong affection for the secretary Nicholas.[49] But even the affection the two men expressed for one another did not obscure their deep differences, and each used the language of friendship to define his own positions and undermine the positions of the other.

The institutional battles between the two monastic orders concerned customs, recruitment, revenue, and political influence—the standard material of monastic disputes. Bernard, for instance, used the transfer of his younger relative Robert from Clairvaux to Cluny as an occasion to attack Cluniac customs and, thereby, to define those of the Cistercians. His letter to Robert again illustrates the Cistercians' desire to differentiate their behavior as monks from that of other social groups, for Bernard criticized Cluny for confusing monks with laymen. He described the comfortable furs, soft shifts, and ample sleeves and hoods that he supposed the monks of Cluny to be wearing, and he attacked their warm bedding and elaborate foods. "These things are consolations for the weak, not weapons for fighting men," he told Robert. "They who wear soft raiment are in kings' houses."[50] Bernard's *Apologia*, which appears to have been directed more generally against black monks, makes similar points: Bernard satirized the elaborate foods he supposed that the monks in such communities consumed, and he criticized a hypothetical abbot for traveling in lordly state, with 60 horses and more, as if "he were the lord of a castle instead of the father of a monastery, the ruler of a province rather than a guardian of souls."[51]

If Bernard's satires attacked the customs of a monastery that had served previous generations as a model of sanctity, the Cistercians' position on tithes challenged its financial well-being. In 1132, Pope Innocent II exempted the entire Cistercian order from paying tithes on all lands that the monks worked themselves.[52] Before this time, individual monasteries and bishops, including the abbey of Cluny, had often exempted specific Cistercian houses from paying the tithe on a particular parcel of land or on land within a diocese, and had sometimes received a rent in compensation from the Cistercians.[53] The papal exemption, however, removed revenues from both parishes and non-Cistercian monasteries without their consent. In his bulls for individual houses, Innocent II implied that he offered this privilege in part because of the Cistercians' austerity, and the Cistercians themselves tried to reinforce this picture.[54] However, the policy caused financial damage to monasteries such as Cluny, which had long relied on revenue from tithes. Peter the Venerable estimated that the policy deprived Cluny of nearly 10 percent of its income—no small amount for a house already in financial difficulties.[55] Some communities, such as the Cluniac priory of Gigny, still tried to obtain the tithes traditionally owed to them; in 1152, after twenty years of fruitless negotiations, they attacked the Cistercian monastery of Le Miroir, ransacked its supplies, destroyed its buildings, and caused an estimated 30,000 shillings' worth of damage.[56] In 1151, a similar dispute between the Cluniac house of Seltz and the Cistercian abbey of Neuberg was settled in court without violence, but in the late 1170's monks from the abbey of Bourg-Dieu attacked the Cistercians at Noirlac, again in the hope of recovering their tithes.[57]

Yet another area of conflict concerned political influence. In 1138, a dispute between two factions of the cathedral chapter at Langres over the election of a new bishop became a contest between the Cistercians and Cluny over the control of the episcopal seat.[58] The chapter had ignored papal instructions to consult Bernard and had elected a Cluniac monk. Bernard appealed to Rome using all the weapons in his rhetorical arsenal, while Peter entreated Bernard to ignore the hostile rumors about the bishop-elect.[59] Innocent II eventually ordered a new election and the cathedral chapter, after offering the position to Bernard himself, elected Clairvaux's prior, Godfrey, as their new bishop. Peter also entered into and eventually lost a long dispute with two successive Cistercian bishops of Auxerre over the right to invest the abbot of Saint-Germain of Auxerre.[60] In both of these cases, Peter the Venerable watched the political influence in the dioceses pass from Cluny to the Cistercians. He responded by striking at the charity of his rivals.[61]

Peter attacked Cistercian *caritas* to defend Cluny's customs and his own sense of monastic unity. In the process, he presented an alternative conception of *caritas* that opposed both the *caritas* binding Cistercian communities together and the caritas the Cistercians invoked when they spoke of the peace and harmony of the monastic world. In the late 1120's, Peter wrote to Bernard to answer twenty specific criticisms of Cluniac customs and traditions supposedly made by an anonymous Cistercian.[62] It is unclear whether Peter responded to an actual Cistercian attack on Cluny or reconstructed these criticisms from Bernard's writings and the implications about older monastic customs in the Cistercians' foundation stories and early statutes. In any event, Peter justified Cluny's traditions by emphasizing that the legislated, ordered life at Cluny did not depend on the Benedictine Rule alone but rather relied on the divine law of charity, as interpreted to the monks by their abbot.[63] In constrast to the Cistercian Chapter General, whose regulations gave each Cistercian abbot little discretionary authority, Peter argued that an abbot could modify the precepts of the Rule as long as he preserved charity. In contrast to the Cistercian idea that monastic regulations and community life should push a monk to progress further than he could go alone, Peter argued that the Cistercians neglected the salvation of their brothers by creating unnecessary hardships and provoking their monks to grumble and run away. At Cluny, Peter argued, the abbot loved his monks as he loved himself, provided them with the necessities of life, and did not compel them toward "unsuitable and noxious labor."[64] Bernard, in comparison, had argued in his *Apologia* that such modifications of the Rule destroyed charity: "Such love destroys true love; such discretion violates true discretion. Such tenderheartedness is full of cruelty, for it so ministers to the body that it strangles the soul."[65] What the Cistercians perceived as laxity, Peter called charity; what the Cistercians called charity, Peter considered excessive severity.

Peter's argument about an abbot's discretion and charity stemmed from his experiences at Cluny and his view of this monastic community. Cluniac monks had portrayed themselves as "immaculate lambs" who lived on the threshold of heaven and provided for the salvation of their society by joining the heavenly choirs in song and aiding God in his never-ending battle against evil.[66] For Peter, the network of Cluniac monasteries had become virtually coterminous with Christian society: as places "where people of all professions, ranks, and orders exchange worldly arrogance and excess for the humility and poverty of a monastic life," these communities had spread with Christianity to every corner of the earth.[67] In a monastery that viewed itself as the primary avenue of

salvation for the world, whose very size required its abbot to emphasize the importance of preserving the peace and preventing factions, an
emphasis on the uniform observance of unchangeable regulations seemed
coercive.[68] Instead, Peter portrayed Cluniac traditions as creating harmony
out of a diversity of monks by modifying the regulations to a level at
which all could obey.

Cistercian monasteries did not try to encompass the diversity of earthly
society but presented themselves as communities of the spiritual elite. The
Cistercians did not wish to incorporate the whole world into their monasteries but only those capable of enduring the hardships of their life.
Their monastic life was one of penance on earth, not a prefiguration
of heavenly glory. But their sense that they were a spiritual elite who
submitted themselves to a severe penitential life so as to receive special
merits in heaven further provoked Peter the Venerable's wrath. For Peter,
the Cistercians' criticisms of other monks and their claims to a superior
holiness were further evidence of their false charity. He lamented that the
Cistercians were Pharisees who thought themselves purer than all others,
and he singled out their white habits as a symbol of their pride: "But you,
you alone in all the world are truly holy monks; all others are false and
ruined. You alone are established following the interpretation of the
Rule, yet you wear a habit of insolent color, and by displaying a splendor
among the black, you distinguish yourself from all other monks."[69] This
picture of Cistercian hypocrisy, in which the supposed Cistercian claim
to be the only true monks destroyed the humility that was the essential
characteristic of monks, became a popular image among later Cistercian critics.

For Peter, it was not just that the Cistercians were hypocrites, but
that their hypocrisy caused scandal and thus destroyed charity. The Cistercians' exemption from paying tithes seemed to be evidence of their
claims to superiority, as did their willingness to accept monks who had
professed at other monasteries. Peter used the occasion of the dispute between Gigny and Le Miroir to lament the divisions in the Church that
the Cistercians had caused. In the mid-1130's, he complained to the cardinal Haimeric that the Cistercians' exemption from tithes was a scandal
that subverted obedience and destroyed charity, and he continued in
the same vein to the Cistercian Chapter General. "He [the Enemy]
throws the fruit of discord among us," he told the Cistercian abbots, "so
that by the withdrawal of charity alone all kinds of virtues are easily

able to escape, and as the head of all good is broken off, all the limbs will also die."[70]

Peter's position was similar in 1138, when Bernard of Clairvaux opposed Peter's candidate for the see of Langres. Although Bernard was infuriated by this election, he addressed nothing to Peter directly; Peter, in comparison, scolded Bernard for relying on rumors spread by the cathedral canons rather than on information offered by monks. Monks, he argued, were all members of a single family and ought to love and support one another. He called on Bernard not to forget the love "which makes us in accord in the house of God," and reminded him that, in this monastic family, "if one member suffers, all suffer together."[71] He continued to make this argument as late as 1149, when he wrote Bernard to scold the Cistercians for their unwillingness to let black monks into Cistercian cloisters. Again, he could not understand why all members of the same monastic family did not receive the same hospitality, and he suggested that if the Cistercians would only let other monks into their cloister, then "diverse customs would not separate these and those monks whom the same faith and charity ought truly to make brothers."[72]

Over time, Peter began to combine his anger with expressions of affection. He had met Bernard at the council of Pisa in 1135, and the two men exchanged friendly letters in 1137 and early 1138, before the election at Langres. But these expressions of friendship still conceal fundamental differences; in fact, Peter used his appeals for friendship to continue his argument for a monastic world without divisions or rankings. In his letter of 1137, he claimed to be so united to Bernard in caritas that neither could have anything that was not also the other's; Bernard responded in a more restrained fashion, noting that they were joined in their shared labors for the Church but saying nothing about caritas.[73] Later that year, when Peter criticized Bernard for putting rumors above monastic fellowship, he also accused Bernard of ignoring their friendship, and a still later letter that called for Cistercian and Cluniac monks to recognize their similarities began with a long discussion of his epistolary friendship with Bernard and the "honeyed sweetness of charity" that existed between them.[74]

Bernard responded to Peter's requests for friendship, but his personal respect and love for Peter did not translate into acceptance of Peter's claims for institutional equality. In Bernard's treatise *De praecepto et dispensatione*, which he wrote around 1140, he agreed with Peter that the

Benedictine Rule could be altered to preserve charity and accepted that monks who lived "according to the Rule" could modify its precepts as long as they continued to obey the customs of their house. But then he again separated the Cistercians, because they had not vowed to live according to the Rule but had promised "to hold to the Rule in its unadorned entirety, according to the letter, because they truly consider that to be their profession."[75] Bernard disclaimed any intent to encourage monks to leave Cluny for a Cistercian house, but he made clear that he considered the Cistercians to be living "a higher and stricter life" that followed "the pure customs of the Rule."[76]

On the surface, Peter's pleas for peace, unity, and the preservation of charity appear little different from the language used by Bernard. But the assumptions beneath their appeals differed, allowing the two monks to use the same vocabulary and phrases to talk past one another. Peter's unity assumed an essential equality of all monks—no one form of monastic life could be holier than another. When he described the monastic world as united by charity, he saw no distinctions between types of monks: "Charity, derived from the highest unity, repairs corruption, reintegrates schisms, unifies divisions, unifies all. So it is clearly proper that for those for whom there is one lord, one faith, one baptism, whom one church contains and one eternal and blessed life awaits, there should be for them, as according to Scripture, one heart and one soul."[77] For Bernard and the other Cistercians, unity was not the same as the uniform equality within their own cloister. Equality was only possible between people of similar spiritual abilities who had chosen the order best suited for those abilities; unity still allowed for differences in holiness. The Cistercians' image of a peaceful and unified Christian society was a hierarchic one in which each individual belonged to an order, and each order followed the practices that best encouraged the salvation of its members. This ranking applied to monastic society as well as earthly society as a whole. Not all monasteries were equally holy; they varied in the strictness of their regulations and in their heavenly reward. Bernard wrote: "Here on earth, we have a diversity of orders and various forms of labor; in heaven, there are obvious and well-ordered differences in merit. . . . The just will shine like the sun in their father's kingdom, yet because of their differences in merit, some will shine more than others."[78] Even in heaven, where Peter insisted that "one eternal and blessed life awaits," Bernard found differences.

Peter the Venerable's letters demonstrate that the Cistercians' conception of caritas did not remain unchallenged. The Cistercians advocated a united monastic world and, by offering economic assistance and constructive criticism, tried to treat other religious communities as they treated communities in their own order. At the same time, however, they asserted their differences and suggested that their exclusivity and austerity implied a spiritual superiority. It was not precisely the implied ranking of monastic orders that upset their critics, for others had perceived such a hierarchy as well. The author of the *Libellus de diuersis ordinibus*, for instance, not only differentiated between monks who lived close to people and those who lived at a distance but also suggested that the monks who lived far from others were stronger and nearer Christ.[79] Even Peter the Venerable praised and admired what he perceived to be the Carthusians' austere holiness.[80] But after the author of the *Libellus* established a ranking, he also warned the stronger monks "not to look down on other orders of people in the church, even though they are less strong, nor to think themselves higher, but to feel united with the humble."[81] The Cistercians did not follow this advice. What irked other monks was the Cistercians' confidence in their own holiness and their sense that monastic unity did not preclude exclusivity. Peter the Venerable and others attacked this combination of unity and exclusiveness and, in so doing, challenged the Cistercians' ideas about caritas.

The response of other religious figures to the double nature of Cistercian caritas helps to demonstrate both the strength of the Cistercians' ideas and the limits of their influence. Abbots from non-Cistercian communities heard expressions of unity and fraternity in the Cistercians' language, but they could not reconcile them with the Cistercians' aggressive confidence. What the Cistercians called love, these other monks considered pride and hypocrisy. Peter the Venerable's complaint that the Cistercians' habits symbolized their pride was echoed by other complaints that the Cistercians covered their pride in a cloak of monastic humility.[82] Even Orderic Vitalis, who in general praised the Cistercians, commented: "Among the good men are some hypocrites who, clothed in white or other distinctive habits, have deceived men and made a great show to the masses. Many seek to be numbered with the true servants of God by their outward observance, not their virtue; their numbers disgust those who see them and make true monks seem less worthy in the faulty judgment of men."[83] Such criticisms do not stem from a change in Cistercian behavior and are not a sign of an early Cistercian decline. The Cistercians came into conflict with other monastic groups, not because they had abandoned their ideals, but because they envisioned a social order that threatened the long-held ideas and social visions of other monks. But the men most threatened by the Cistercians' claims of superiority were also able to challenge them the most effectively. These created an image of proud and hypocritical Cistercians that far outlasted the specific disputes over tithes and recruitment that had engendered it.

Chapter 6

"A Well-trained Clergy"

When the Cistercians imagined a unified Christian society, they sometimes placed themselves at the center of the Church rather than at its
head. For the monks to rest in this bed of contemplation and remain
undisturbed by secular cares or the demands of caritas, the secular clergy
had to accept responsibility for the spiritual well-being of the social orders that the monks had imagined building the room around their bed.
Furthermore, the Cistercians' ambiguous ranking of ecclesiastical prelates
suggested that such men would ideally combine monastic virtues with
earthly authority so as to create an analogue of the heavenly kingdom on
earth. But the Cistercians also recognized that the prelates around them
did not necessarily have such virtues. Therefore, they wrote treatises
and accounts of saints' lives that offered models of virtuous prelates,
and they worked actively to encourage the spiritual reform of the episcopate as a step toward that day when monks would be able to remain
undisturbed in a contemplative state.

The Cistercians' interest in the reform of prelates stemmed from their
vision of Christian society, but their ability to spread their ideas came from
the close relations they developed with neighboring bishops. These relations expanded into a network of clergy whose sympathy for the Cistercians' ideas encouraged their further dissemination and helped to
draw some of the monks into activities promoting ecclesiastical reform.
Some of the most active of Cistercians were monks who became bishops
themselves. As former contemplatives, these men provided real examples
of the Cistercians' virtuous prelate, and by remaining members of the order, they extended the Cistercians' network of connections across Europe
and furthered the spread of their ideas.

I

The Cistercians' most important allies in the early years of their order were bishops. Unlike many of the important tenth- and eleventh-century monasteries such as Cluny, Fleury, and Marmoutier, Cistercian abbeys maintained close relations with their diocesan bishops. They neither challenged episcopal authority nor invoked papal authority to free them from episcopal control. Many of the Cistercians' first communities were founded with the aid, and even at the request of, local bishops, and the monks often relied on these bishops to record and confirm their property rights.[1] More personal relations and friendships between the monks and bishops developed out of these connections: the Cistercians offered prayers and advice, while the bishops drew the monks into local ecclesiastical affairs. The friendships the monks developed while involved in such matters endured long after the immediate problems were resolved. Although the papal schism of 1130 greatly expanded the range of the Cistercians' activity, the friends and connections that the monks had developed in the preceding fifteen years formed the core of the network within which they worked.

The Cistercians often criticized monastic exemptions, and they supported the authority of the bishop in his diocese, but they gradually became independent of episcopal control. They accepted the bishop's right to consecrate abbots and invest them with the pastoral staff, but the *Carta caritatis* curtailed episcopal interference in the internal affairs of the community by providing the monks with an internal mechanism for enforcing discipline.[2] Cistercian abbots professed obedience to their bishops, but they hinged this profession on the condition that the bishops ask them to do nothing contrary to the rules of the order.[3] Initially they expected their bishops to help them to remove a disobedient abbot, but they also considered the possibility that a bishop might ignore the abbot's transgressions, in which case the monks could settle the matter themselves.[4] They continued to ask their diocesan bishops to perform tasks that could, in theory, be performed by any bishop—to consecrate the monastery's church and altars, to bless its sacred vessels and holy oil, and to ordain the monks who were priests—and they only began to seek the services of other bishops after 1185, and even then only if their local bishop was absent or impeached.[5] By 1132, Innocent II had exempted them from attending diocesan synods except those concerning matters of faith, but a statute collected and reissued in 1134 stated that the monks should nonetheless obey the call of bishops and archbishops unless it conflicted with the scheduled meeting of the order's Chapter General. "We do not deny the obedience due to our prelates," the abbots ruled, "but we ought to observe the rules we have decided to hold in our order."[6]

Rather than bring the Cistercians into conflict with their bishops, this gradual independence from diocesan institutions often came with episcopal approval. Bishops gave many of the first grants exempting the monks from paying tithes. The bishop of Autun conceded to Cîteaux the tithes for the monks' lands at Moisey and Gergueil, the bishop of Langres granted Clairvaux an exemption from paying tithes on all its lands in his diocese and Pontigny an exemption on all its vineyards, and the archbishop of Sens remitted to Pontigny all tithes in his diocese.[7] By 1132, when Innocent II granted the Cistercian order an exemption from tithes, he acted more to approve, codify, and spread an already existing practice than to initiate a new immunity. As we have seen, this exemption created a greater conflict with other monasteries than it did with the secular priests to whom tithes were canonically due.

The geographical positions of the first five Cistercian monasteries exemplify their close yet independent relationship with the ecclesiastical hierarchy. Each house was positioned on the periphery of a diocese: Cîteaux on the northern edge of the diocese of Chalon-sur-Saône, near the dioceses of Langres and Autun; La Ferté on Chalon's southern edge, near Mâcon; Pontigny on the northeastern corner of Auxerre, near Sens and Langres; Clairvaux on the western edge of Langres, near Troyes and Châlons-sur-Marne; and Morimond on the eastern edge of Langres, near Besançon and Toul. The location of these monasteries on the borders between dioceses distanced the monks from the centers of episcopal power and the pull of episcopal politics. Because the monasteries tended to hold lands in two or even three dioceses, no single bishop had complete jurisdiction over all of their property. At the same time, this peripheral position increased the monks' contact with bishops, doubling the number who had some jurisdiction over monastic lands. Thus, rather than avoiding relations with the episcopacy, the first five Cistercian monasteries developed ties with ten bishops.[8]

In fact, the rapid expansion of Cistercian monasteries between 1113 and 1115 depended greatly on the support of these bishops. Walter, the bishop of Chalon-sur-Saône, participated in the negotiations about Cîteaux's foundation and Robert's return to Molesme, received the profession of Cîteaux's abbots, and dedicated Cîteaux's church; he also supported the foundation of Cîteaux's first affiliated community, La Ferté, in his diocese.[9] Hermits initiated the foundations of Pontigny and Morimond, but these foundations too depended on the support of bishops. A hermit-priest named Ansius asked that Stephen Harding send monks to Pontigny to instruct him in regular discipline; Stephen agreed to do so "if the bishop, in whose diocese this place was situated, embraced this idea."[10] At Morimond, Bishop Joceran of Langres and Lord Ulrich of Aigremont advised a lay hermit named John to donate his land to monks from Cîteaux in order to improve his way of life.[11] Subsequent expansion continued to draw on these episcopal connections, for the monks founded many of their early abbeys either in the same dioceses as their first houses or in neighboring dioceses whose bishops they already knew. Only Clairvaux followed a slightly different pattern. Although founded in the diocese of Langres, that bishop played no immediate role in its establishment. William of Champeaux, the bishop of Châlons-sur-Marne, invested Bernard as Clairvaux's new abbot, and the monastery's first affiliates were in Châlons and Autun, not Langres.[12] For all these communities, however, it was through their connections with bishops, especially with the archbishop of Sens and the bishop of Châlons, that their monks began to participate in the ecclesiastical affairs around them.

The Cistercians' relations with Henry Sanglier, the archbishop of Sens, demonstrates the way that interaction with bishops drew them into ecclesiastical politics. Cîteaux, Clairvaux, and Pontigny all lay within this archdiocese, and four of the early Cistercian affiliates were directly subject to the archbishop.[13] By the late 1120's, the archbishop's support of the Cistercians began to bear fruit. In 1127 or 1128, Bernard of Clairvaux wrote Henry a long letter detailing his ideas about the ideal behavior of a bishop and praising Henry for developing an interest in church reform.[14] By the end of the decade, when Henry came under attack from the French king, Stephen Harding, Hugh of Pontigny, and Bernard all came to his defense, asking Pope Honorius to judge Henry's case rather than leaving it to be settled in France, where Henry's enemies dominated the court.[15] The abbots praised Henry for reforming his behavior and warned the pope about the intentions of a king who seemed to reward Henry for worldly actions and accused him of simony now that he had assumed a pious life and a zeal for justice.[16] Bernard wrote a second letter to the pope on his own and sent another to Cardinal Haimeric, from whom the Cistercians had recently received a gift of gold.[17] The ties initiated by the Cistercians' presence in Henry's archdiocese had developed into a closer bond with the archbishop. The monks' support of the embattled Henry turned him into an important ally who worked closely with active Cistercians as they later attempted to resolve ecclesiastical problems and crises.

Clairvaux's relations with William of Champeaux, the bishop of Châlons-sur-Marne, also drew the monks into diocesan affairs. William not only had ordained and invested Bernard and encouraged the foundation of Clairvaux's first affiliate, Trois-Fontaines, in his diocese but also had often visited Clairvaux and convinced Bernard to moderate his asceticism and care for his health.[18] This friendship drew Bernard into the concerns of William's diocese. According to the *Vita prima*, Bernard and William were "of one spirit in the Lord and often took turns having each other as guests. Clairvaux was like the bishop's own house, and not only the bishop's house but, through him, the entire city of Châlons became home to the monks from Clairvaux."[19] Bernard retained his interest in the diocese after William's death. In 1126, he wrote to Pope Honorius, offering his opinion about the new bishop-elect.[20] Later that year, he wrote to the new bishop, mentioned William as a model of virtuous episcopal behavior, and advised him to move quickly in installing an abbot for the canons of All Saints.[21] In 1129, Bernard attended a council at Châlons where he recommended that the bishop of Verdun, who was accused of simony, resign.[22]

William of Champeaux may also have been the source of the Cistercians' connections with Bishop Geoffrey of Chartres. Geoffrey may have studied with William, and he had asked William's aid in resolving diocesan affairs.[23] Geoffrey approved the series of land transactions that resulted in the foundation of Cîteaux's affiliate of L'Aumône in 1121; in 1126 he appeared with Hugh of Pontigny and Bernard of Clairvaux as witnesses to a donation to Molesme; and by 1128 Bernard was writing to Geoffrey to ask for favors and to request his intercession with Count Theobald of Champagne on various matters.[24] Bernard and Geoffrey later worked together during the papal schism, traveled together to combat heresy in southern France, and fought together against the ideas of Abelard.[25]

According to William of Saint-Thierry, William of Champeaux was instrumental in spreading Bernard's reputation not only in Châlons but throughout the archdiocese of Rheims, and it is possible that William of Saint-Thierry's own connections with Bernard came through William of Champeaux.[26] In any case, Clairvaux's influence did spread quickly through the archdiocese. In 1121, with the support of Bartholomew of Vir, bishop of Laon, Clairvaux founded Foigny, its first affiliated house in the archdiocese of Rheims.[27] In 1127, Bernard mediated a quarrel between Archbishop Rainald of Rheims and the people of the diocese, and Rainald, in gratitude, donated to Bernard the land for the monastery of Igny.[28] William of Saint-Thierry and Suger of Saint-Denis witnessed the foundation charter.[29] In 1128, the archbishop of Rheims called a council at Arras to reform the royal convent of nuns of Saint John at Laon; attending were Bernard of Clairvaux, King Louis VI, and the bishops and abbots of the archdiocese.[30] Around the same time, Bernard also advised Fulbert, the abbot of Saint Sepulchre in Cambrai, to resign.[31] The contacts Bernard formed while in Flanders may have influenced the further expansion of Clairvaux's affiliates into northeast France: in 1129 Clairvaux founded the house of Ourscamp in the diocese of Noyon, and in 1132 it founded the houses of Longpont and Vaucelles in Soissons and Cambrai.[32] Thus, from an initial connection with the bishop of Châlons, the monks of Clairvaux developed a series of connections throughout the archdiocese of Rheims and into Flanders that not only aided the further expansion of the order but also drew Bernard into problems of ecclesiastical, and especially monastic, reform.

The Cistercians' support of the Victorines of Paris may also have stemmed from their connections with William of Champeaux. In 1125, Hugh of Saint Victor asked Bernard for his opinion about four questions concerning baptism; by the end of the decade, Cistercian abbots had become involved in the Victorines' disputes.[33] In 1127, Bishop Stephen of Paris had tried to introduce Victorine canons into the chapter of Notre Dame and initiated a long conflict between the cathedral canons, supported by the king, and the Victorines, supported by the bishop. By 1129, the diocese lay under an interdict, the bishop had fled, the king had confiscated his goods, and the Cistercian abbots had intervened. Stephen Harding, writing for the entire order, sent a letter to Louis VI protesting his behavior and warning him that the Cistercians' sense of justice and their fraternity with the bishop compelled them to write to the pope on the bishop's behalf.[34] Louis met with Hugh of Pontigny, Bernard of

Clairvaux, and Archbishop Henry of Sens, but this did little to resolve the dispute. Both sides appealed to Rome, where the king prevailed, and Pope Honorius lifted the interdict. At this point, Hugh and Bernard intervened yet again, scolding Honorius for removing the interdict just when it had begun to have some effect and for doing so after hearing only one side of the case. They advised Honorius to consult his own heart as to whether he thought justice had been done.[35]

Louis VI and Bishop Stephen of Paris eventually came to an agreement, for Suger of Saint-Denis relates that Stephen and the abbot of Saint Victor heard Louis's deathbed confession and performed the last rites.[36] The Cistercians' contact with Bishop Stephen continued; in 1132 Bernard mediated a dispute between Stephen and his archdeacon.[37] Furthermore, although the king may have been reconciled with the bishop and the Victorines, the animosity between the cathedral chapter of Notre Dame and the canons of Saint Victor still ran deep, for in 1133 the prior of Saint Victor, who had continued to try to establish Victorine canons in the cathedral chapter, was murdered by the archdeacon's men. Bishop Stephen took refuge at Clairvaux, and Bernard joined him in writing to the pope to ask for his intervention.[38]

The Cistercians' presence at the ecclesiastical council at Troyes in January 1129 reinforced the connections the monks had already formed and illustrates how quickly they had become important figures in their region. The council approved the formation of the knights of the Order of the Temple, whose rule, according to the author of its introduction, had been composed with Bernard of Clairvaux's advice.[39] There the abbots of Cîteaux, Clairvaux, Pontigny, and Trois-Fontaines joined many ecclesiastics with whom they had already developed close relations, including the archbishops Rainald of Rheims and Henry of Sens, the bishops of Chartres, Auxerre, Châlons, Laon, and Paris, and the abbots of Molesme, Saint Stephen at Dijon, and Saint-Denis at Rheims. Also present were the counts of Champagne and Nevers, important lay benefactors for the order. The Cistercian abbots met other bishops at Troyes, most notably Jocelin of Soissons, with whom Bernard of Clairvaux would later work closely.[40]

The contacts that the Cistercians developed between 1120 and 1130, which were reflected and strengthened by their participation in the council of Troyes, became fundamental to their emerging network of friends and connections. In the 1130's and 1140's, they retained close relations with men such as the archbishops Henry of Sens and Rainald of Rheims, and the bishops Geoffrey of Chartres and Jocelin of Soissons. These were men who had supported the expansion of the order and gained the Cistercians' friendship and trust. They channeled information to the monks about the needs and problems of the people in their territories, and they worked with the Cistercians to resolve these issues. Most of the major events that involved Cistercians during these decades also involved at least one, and usually a number, of these men. Thus, the first decade of Cistercian activity established the pattern for their subsequent behavior. The monks intervened in the affairs and problems of the people around them because they had developed a network of episcopal friends who shared many of their concerns, who brought specific problems to their attention, and who offered assistance and companionship as they worked together to resolve such crises.

II

The Cistercians' episcopal friends and connections expanded as Cistercian monks became bishops. Once bishops, these men left their monasteries and the daily patterns of monastic life, but they maintained close connections with their former communities and retained certain monastic customs. They and the Cistercian abbots brought to each other's attention the problems that concerned them. These bishops not only formed an integral part of the Cistercians' network of information and support but also became instrumental in promoting the Cistercians' ideas about episcopal reform through their example.

Abbot Peter of La Ferté became the first Cistercian bishop when, in 1126, he was elected archbishop of Tarentaise.[41] The first Cistercian cardinal, Martin Cibo, a monk from Clairvaux, may have been appointed cardinal-priest of Saint Stephen in Monte Celio as early as 1130; according to Mabillon, Innocent II also appointed the monk Baldwin as cardinal in 1130. Bernard mentioned Baldwin in his letter of 1137, the same year a Baldwin begins to appear on papal bulls.[42] Hugh of Mâcon, the abbot of Pontigny, became bishop of Auxerre in 1136; Godfrey, the prior of Clairvaux, became bishop of Langres in 1139. Between 1126 and 1180, there were over 60 Cistercian bishops and cardinals, and a monk from Clairvaux was elected pope.[43] The bulk of bishops and cardinals elected before 1160 came from Clairvaux and started their administration between

1139 and 1153—the period of Bernard of Clairvaux's greatest political influence. Some, such as Godfrey of Langres, Henry Murdac of York, and Alan of Auxerre, were Bernard's chosen candidates in contested elections.[44] These and other Cistercian bishops worked closely with Bernard and, with him, made up the group of Cistercians who had the greatest opportunities and abilities to resolve the problems that they perceived in the society around them.

Before their election as bishops, many of these Cistercians had been instrumental in their order's expansion. This is especially true of the prelates who had professed at Clairvaux and then become an abbot of an affiliated house before their episcopal election. For example, before becoming Pope Eugenius III in 1145, Peter Bernard Paganelli had been a monk at Clairvaux and the first abbot of Clairvaux's affiliate Trefontane, founded near Rome. Amadeus of Clermont, who entered Clairvaux in 1125 and became abbot of Hautecombe ten years later, was elected bishop of Lausanne in 1145, and Alan of Flanders left Clairvaux in 1140 to become abbot of L'Arrivour, where he remained until elected bishop of Auxerre in 1152. Hugh of Châlons left Clairvaux around 1147 to become abbot of Trois-Fontaines, and in 1150 Eugenius III appointed him cardinal-bishop of Ostia. In all, nine of the thirteen bishops who had been monks at Clairvaux followed this pattern.[45] One monk from Cîteaux did as well: John, who had professed at Cîteaux and become abbot of Cîteaux's affiliate, Bonnevaux, was elected bishop of Valence in 1141.[46] By contrast, the bishops who professed at Pontigny had not moved to affiliated monasteries but had been abbots of Pontigny itself. Nearly all of Pontigny's twelfth-century abbots eventually left the monastery for episcopal positions.[47] By contrast, no abbot of Clairvaux was elected bishop until 1170, and no abbot of Cîteaux was elected until 1184.[48] As former abbots, these Cistercian bishops had clear administrative skills and a strong interest in the organization and reform of their society. Even had they not been elected to positions outside their monasteries, they, like Bernard, would probably have been active in the society around them.

The monks who became bishops remained members of the Cistercian order. Two statutes issued by the Chapter General formally established connections between these bishops and their monasteries, implying that the abbots believed that these men still fell under their jurisdiction.[49] The first statute determined that no monk could consent to his election as bishop without the approval of his abbot and the Cistercian Chapter General unless strongly compelled by the pope.[50] The second statute ruled on the bishops' dress, food, and behavior.

Bishops who have risen from our order shall hold to our customs in the quality of their food, in the form of their garments, in the observance of fasts, and in the office of regular hours, except that they can have a cloak of common cloth and sheepskin and a hat of similar materials or simply of wool, if they wish. With such things, however, they can only seldom enter our cloister and cannot take part in our chapters, because of their differences. For solace, they can be given someone from our houses, up to two monks and three lay brothers, if so many are necessary, as long as no secular business or cares are imposed on them.[51]

In short, the abbots required that the Cistercian bishops maintain, as much as possible, their monastic customs. By allowing them monk-companions, the abbots hoped the bishops could continue to develop the charity that they believed such fraternal relations encouraged.

Evidence as to whether the Cistercian bishops adhered to these rules comes primarily from saints' lives and miracle stories. Unfortunately, this literature portrays ideal Cistercian figures, not necessarily actual Cistercian behavior. In his *Vita* of Archbishop Peter II of Tarentaise, the former abbot of the monastery of Tamié, Geoffrey of Auxerre describes the monastic customs that Peter retained while serving as archbishop: he continued to eat coarse bread with vegetables, to wear humble clothes, and to hold the vigils he had practiced as a monk. His one major change was to substitute the concerns of pastoral care for other forms of manual labor.[52] Similarly, in the *Exordium magnum*, Conrad of Eberbach described the monks who became bishops as continuing to live in monastic humility and retaining a "monastic lamentation" within.[53]

Cistercian bishops did ask monks and lay brothers to live in their episcopal residences as companions. According to a twelfth-century biography, Bishop Hugh of Auxerre asked a lay brother from Pontigny to administer the episcopal guest house and receive guests when the bishop could not.[54] Witness lists from the bishops' charters also provide evidence for these monk-companions. Four appear on Hugh of Auxerre's charters for Pontigny.[55] Amadeus, bishop of Lausanne and former monk of Clairvaux, issued a charter for Cîteaux in 1145, noting the transfer of rights of lordship and usage in the village, woods, fields, and waters of Latrecy; it was witnessed by Stephen and Willard, "the monks of the bishop of Lausanne."[56] At least two monks lived with Godfrey, bishop of Langres.[57] One of them, Gilbert, served for a time as Godfrey's chaplain.[58] Finally, John de Poré and Isaard, two monks in the company of Guichard, archbishop of Lyons and former abbot of Pontigny, witnessed Guichard's settlement of a dispute between Cîteaux and the canons of Autun.[59] This list is not exhaustive. Other Cistercian bishops may have had monk-companions who either remained more isolated from episcopal business or appeared on charters now lost.

The presence of monk-companions in their bishops' charters suggests that they and their bishops ignored, to some extent, the Cistercian order's prohibition against involving the companions in worldly affairs. In many cases, though, these monks witnessed charters for the Cistercian order, although not always for their own monasteries. Many of the other charters concerned monastic affairs. But even if these monk-companions lived in relative seclusion in the episcopal palace, they must have been influenced by the business negotiations around them. It is possible that such experience trained monks who later assumed administrative positions themselves. Two of Hugh of Auxerre's companions, Garin and Mainard, may have been the same monks who later became abbots of Pontigny and, afterward, bishops; a Garin left the abbacy of Pontigny to become archbishop of Bourges in 1174, and a Mainard, also abbot at Pontigny, was appointed cardinal-bishop of Palestrina in 1188 but died before he was consecrated.[60]

Some Cistercian bishops retired from their episcopal positions and returned to their cloisters before they died. Godfrey of Langres, Alan of Auxerre, and Archbishop Henry of Rheims retired to Clairvaux for the last years of their lives. These retired prelates often were powerful figures within their monasteries; Robert Fossier attributes many of Geoffrey of Auxerre's problems as abbot of Clairvaux to the influence of Godfrey of Langres.[61] Many more Cistercian prelates were buried at their former monasteries or in Cistercian houses they had founded. Bishop Hugh of Auxerre and Archbishops Garin of Bourges and Guichard of Lyons were buried at Pontigny; Bishops Godfrey of Langres, Alan of Auxerre, and Godfrey of Sorra were buried at Clairvaux; and Henry of Troyes was buried at Boulancourt, a house he had affiliated with the Cistercian order.[62]

The bishops' retention of Cistercian customs reminded them of their fraternal bonds with the monks who remained in the cloisters. For their part, the cloistered monks continued to consider these bishops as brothers and assumed that the bishops continued to feel a bond with their former communities. Thus, when Eugenius III returned to the Cistercian Chapter General in 1151, Geoffrey of Auxerre wrote that "the venerable pope was present, not presiding with his apostolic authority, but seating himself among us with fraternal charity, as if one of us."[63] When Eugenius died in 1153, Hugh, cardinal-bishop of Ostia and himself a Cistercian, described the event to the Cistercian Chapter General and asked for prayers. His account vividly portrays the position of these monk-bishops in the Cistercian order and illustrates the responsibility the monks felt toward them:

You, however, from whose fraternity he was elected to sit above the princes of the earth and hold the throne of glory, pray for him and establish a perpetual benefice so that the Lord will show favor to him and increase his crown of glory. Likewise, pray for our guide (*magister*), and for our brother. We ask no less that you pray for us who must remain in this valley of misery, this region of unlikeness, and in the midst of evil peoples, and that you pray for the Roman Church, which, in such a short time, has fallen from the heights into a deep abyss, lest it be submerged in the depths of this great sea in which there are reptiles without number.[64]

Hugh thus separated his request for prayers for Eugenius as the pope from his request for prayers for Eugenius as a brother. Eugenius had moved from his monastic order into an office whose authority placed him well above his former companions, yet he remained a part of their community. At the same time, Hugh reminded the order of the importance of its prayers in supporting brothers who continued to work within worldly society by invoking its concern for the condition of the institutional Church.

Two letters written in the later part of the twelfth century also display the strong emotional ties between Cistercian monks and Cistercian bishops. The letters appear in a collection assembled by Master Transmundus, a papal notary who became a monk at Clairvaux around 1186 and lived until at least 1216.[65] Two letters addressed to monks who had left the monastery to become bishops have neither date nor salutation, but they were clearly written at Clairvaux by someone, probably the abbot, who spoke for the monastery. One letter praised a bishop for his good works, the other scolded a bishop for ignoring his responsibilities to his order, but both used strong maternal and affective imagery to express the links between the monastery and its bishops. The letter to the bishop who retained his connections with Clairvaux begins:

It is an argument from nature that says that she who is a mother loves. If it pleases your most reverend father to reflect on this, we are confident it will be clear to you how sweet and how kind the affection of each and every one of us is for you. We recognize that this affection becomes more greatly inflamed because, by loving you, the desire for your appearance continues to grow. Still, it withstands the grief caused by the mutual difficulty of our great distance.[66]

The maternal imagery in the letter to the bishop who ignored his former monastery is even more elaborate:

If you have not yet rejected from your loving breast all memory of that place from whence God cloaked you in the priesthood with glory and honor, it seems in all ways cruel to your Clairvaux that much time and many years have passed, and you still have not applied yourself to visiting your most sweet mother. You should recall that you suckled her sweet breasts whose infusion of certain sweetness you once considered right for you. Now you offer that fruit of honor and honesty to the people of God, both by word and by example. You know that the prospect of your visit would be desirable for us, so that your Clairvaux, viewing in you the fruit of her womb with maternal exaltation, can revive her spirit with joyful virtue at the sight and kiss of her Joseph and be strengthened by the blessing of her son, rather than lamenting him as if already dead or ruined.[67]

This letter also stressed that, even if affection for his mother did not move him, the bishop was still bound to return to Clairvaux, "out of reverence for your order, from which you ought in no way to consider yourself exempt."[68]

Both letters emphasized that the monks at Clairvaux continued to pray and care for their brothers who had become bishops. They told the favored bishop, "we are greatly watchful of and devoted to you in all our prayers to God, by which the glory of his name is honored," and they threatened the other with the loss of his participation in the order's "universal grace and unity."[69] The monks within the monastery clearly believed that the actions of their monk-bishops grew out of, and reflected back on, life within the monastery. For the neglectful bishop, his pastoral activity "by word and by example" was the fruit of the nourishment he received at Clairvaux; for the other, the monks' prayers aided his ability to administer his office and spread the word of God in foreign places.

Cistercian bishops, in turn, used their positions to protect and further the interests of their former monasteries. The Cistercians' effectiveness in controlling the episcopal seats in both their own and nearby dioceses strengthened these links between monastery and bishop even more. Between 1136 and 1167, two Cistercians administered Pontigny's diocese of Auxerre; between 1139 and 1161, Clairvaux's former prior, Godfrey, administered Clairvaux's diocese of Langres; and between 1145 and 1169, Henry, a monk from Morimond, was bishop of the nearby diocese of Troyes. These bishops maintained close relations with one another and with their monasteries, occasionally working together or with abbots to settle internal Cistercian affairs. Hugh of Auxerre and Henry of Troyes worked with Abbot Rainald of Cîteaux to settle a dispute between the Cistercian houses of Pontigny and Reigny over pasture rights; Godfrey of Langres and Alan of Auxerre negotiated an agreement between Reigny and one of its donors that was witnessed by Abbot Lambert of Cîteaux; and Alan, with the count of Nevers, settled a dispute between Reigny and Crisennone that was witnessed by Abbot Geoffrey of Clairvaux.[70] The bishops issued and witnessed charters describing donations of lands to the monasteries and occasionally solicited donations themselves. In 1139 Hugh of Auxerre, with Bernard of Clairvaux and Abbot Guichard of Pontigny, asked the bishop of Sens to give Pontigny use of the forest of Othe, and in 1157 Alan of Auxerre made peace between Pontigny and Montier-la-Celle by buying the rights to a rent from Montier and giving it to Pontigny so that Pontigny no longer owed money to Montier.[71] They also settled disputes between the Cistercians and other landholders and tended to ensure that the Cistercians emerged victorious.[72]

Although Cistercian bishops no longer lived within the cloister, they and their order still considered them Cistercians, as did canon law. The Cistercian Chapter General still had jurisdiction over their behavior, and the bishops were expected to follow Cistercian regulations. They not only retained many of their monastic observances but also succeeded in preserving the fraternal ties and friendships characteristic of their monastic life. They remained connected to their former communities, in part through shared customs, but, more important, through feelings of affection and a knowledge that they participated in their monasteries' spiritual benefits. Furthermore, many tried to recreate aspects of their former community life by accepting monk-companions into their residences. Finally, some also maintained a communal life while active in the world by assisting and supporting the activities of other Cistercian bishops and Cistercian abbots. By participating in these networks of information and support, these bishops preserved many of the distinctive characteristics of their religious life even when they were no longer in contemplation within the cloister.

III

The Cistercians' networks of friends and former monks provided a way for the monks to spread their ideas, but the ideas themselves stemmed from the context of their monastic life. The Cistercians did not suggest that all prelates be monks first, but they especially celebrated their monks who became bishops, for these men seemed to make real the process that the Cistercians advocated for all ecclesiastical leaders: that bishops should learn to rule themselves before they began to rule others. The Cistercians believed this process was best started in one of their monasteries, for there a monk learned humility and obedience. But even if a prelate was not a Cistercian, he could follow the model offered by such a life and learn to balance his desire for salvation with his responsibility for others. Unless ecclesiastical leaders could combine their authority with virtue, monks could not remain in their monasteries in a life of quiet prayer and contemplation. In order to work toward that eventuality, the Cistercians not only encouraged the moral reform of prelates but also portrayed their monasteries as schools for virtue that offered the training necessary for a reformed clergy.

As communities of people who strove to create perfect societies on earth, monasteries had been a source of ideas for Church reform long before the Cistercians. In sixth-century Gaul, bishops had come from a monastic background, and in Rome, Gregory the Great described an alternation between monastery and world designed to restore the spiritual life of prelates.[73] Tenth- and eleventh-century monasteries were centers of angelic purity, homes of the "immaculate lambs" whose prayers provided for the salvation of their society; as they spread their ideas of purity into the larger Church, these monks worked to separate the clergy from the imperfections of the secular world so that priests would become worthy of their sacramental functions.[74] Many eleventh-century monks associated with the ecclesiastical reform movement were concerned with such ritual purity; men such as Peter Damian, Humbert of Moyenmoutier, and John Gualbert wanted to free the clergy from the contamination of money, sexuality, and secular interference.[75]

The Cistercians, who viewed their own life as a series of compromises through which they balanced their search for personal perfection with the cares of a social existence, did not try to create a pure clergy so much as one capable of attaining this same balance. In fact, they believed that prelates experienced the tension between an active and a contemplative charity even more than monks, for prelates administered an office with both secular and spiritual responsibilities. In a sermon preached at the council at Tours in 1163, Geoffrey of Auxerre clearly expressed this need for a balancing act by comparing prelates to the four-faced beasts in the vision of the prophet Ezechiel. Part lion, part man, part bull, part eagle, prelates needed to temper lionlike zeal with human compassion, a bovine concern for the earth with the soaring contemplation of eagles. Most prelates, Geoffrey suggested, had too much lion and not enough man, too much bull and not enough eagle. They showed too much zeal, especially in administering their secular positions, and could neither care for both earthly and celestial matters nor balance their concern for their own spiritual condition with that of their parishioners.[76]

The Cistercians drew their ideas about the virtues and authority of prelates from Gregory the Great's *Regulae pastoralis*. Like Gregory, they believed that men who developed spiritual abilities through contemplation should then aid the spiritual welfare of others. They also agreed that an active pastor was to develop contemplative virtues so that he could practice what he taught and withstand the temptations and cares of secular administration. Without such virtues, a leader cared too much for his own preeminence and for things of the world and, still ravaged by his own sins, was unable to care for other sinners.[77] In looking back to Gregory the Great, the Cistercians anticipated the positions of the late twelfth-century moral theologians and played a larger role in the twelfth-century attempts to spread Gregory's ideas among the clergy than has often been realized. Along with the Victorines, the Cistercians became the dominant voices for clerical reform in the second and third quarters of the twelfth century.[78]

Cistercian monks presented their ideas about an ideal prelate in a number of different genres. Bernard of Clairvaux addressed two treatises to ecclesiastics with whom he had developed close relations: in 1129 or 1130, he sent a long letter on the customs and responsibilities of bishops to his friend Archbishop Henry of Sens, and at the end of his life, he sent *De consideratione* to his former monk, now pope, Eugenius III. As we have already seen, Bernard and other Cistercian abbots wrote letters to their ecclesiastical connections, some supporting bishops, others complaining about a disruption of what they considered the proper order of the Church. Both Bernard and Geoffrey of Auxerre wrote hagiographical accounts of saintly bishops, and Conrad of Eberbach included short vignettes about Cistercian prelates in his *Exordium magnum*. Finally, both Geoffrey of Auxerre and Aelred of Rievaulx took a more active role as well and appeared at clerical synods and councils to preach sermons advocating ecclesiastical reform. The message of these letters, treatises, saints' lives, and sermons remained remarkably consistent: prelates needed to develop the virtues necessary for their own salvation before they took on the responsibility for the salvation of others.

Repeatedly, these Cistercians insisted that ecclesiastical officials be shepherds or servants who ministered to their people, not lords who dominated them.[79] Prelates who were lords concentrated too much on things of the world and lost track of their spiritual ministry; rather than shepherds, they were hired workers who fled from the wolves and left their sheep in danger, or thieves who stole from and killed those they were to protect.[80] Such churchmen desired to increase their wealth and power at the expense of those whom they were to serve. Cistercian monks frequently criticized the ambition, greed, vanity, and pride of twelfth-century clerics. Aelred of Rievaulx made desires of the flesh, desires of the eyes, and secular ambition into the ropes by which the Philistines tried to bind Samson; Bernard warned archbishop Henry of Sens to avoid the traps of avarice, vanity, and pride; and Geoffrey of Auxerre portrayed clerical wealth, love of pleasure, and ambition as ingrained diseases killing the body of the Church.[81] These snares and diseases tempted prelates to accumulate more power and higher offices, to live in opulence, and to ignore the people they had been chosen to serve. Such men confused the role of a prelate with that of a secular lord and disordered the divinely instituted Church hierarchy. According to Geoffrey, they spoke often, but without effect, thundered but did not fight, possessed the trappings of their position but were hollow underneath.[82]

At the root of this clerical corruption lay a misguided love that desired power and position rather than things of God. An ambitious prelate was forever dissatisfied with his current office and always seeking one higher, often one for which he was unsuited. Geoffrey of Auxerre likened the scramble for such offices to the hump that impeded the camel's entry into heaven, and Bernard of Clairvaux described Parisian scholars as grabbing Peter's keys and, as a result, hindering their subjects' salvation.[83] These scholars wanted positions from which they could rule others, but they had not yet learned to rule themselves. In a letter to clerics at Périgueux, Nicholas of Clairvaux argued that such men should not administer what they themselves had not gained; he warned the clerics, "It is not safe for you to have the care of souls and not care for the soul, to live by the patrimony of Christ and not serve Christ."[84]

Such ambition did not stop with ecclesiastical offices. Ambitious church officials tried to extend their jurisdiction over secular matters, provoking conflicts with kings and princes. Bishops were not satisfied with control of a town, Bernard complained, so they dredged up old privileges to demonstrate their jurisdiction over the countryside as well.[85] This ambition caused prelates to confuse their spiritual ministry with the authority of secular leaders. Bernard asked Archbishop Henry of Sens, "What is this hateful presumption, this great eagerness to hold domination over the earth, this unrestrained desire for preeminence?"[86] He made a similar point in his treatise *De consideratione*, in which he reminded Eugenius III that his power was over sin, not property. "These worthless and worldly matters have their own judges, the kings and princes of the earth. Why do you invade another's territory?"[87] Only ecclesiastical officials who remained content with their position and considered it a burden rather than a glory would use their authority properly and minister to the souls of others rather than further their dominion.[88]

Ambitious prelates loved not only power but also worldly wealth. Aelred of Rievaulx associated ambition with venality, because "when prebend, archdeaconate, episcopacy are empty, the Philistine comes with the rope of ambition, suggesting that the position be sought, suggesting that it be extorted, ultimately suggesting that it be bought."[89] Bernard spoke scathingly about such greed, for he thought prelates who desired worldly pleasures and pomp were like women in their love of extravagant clothing.[90] He protested that their gold bridles and saddles, gleaming spurs, glittering plates and goblets, drunken feasts, and musical entertainment mimicked the trappings of the secular aristocracy: "Their spurs shine more than their altars."[91] Such wallowing in earthly pleasure not only confused social roles and hindered the prelate's own spiritual condition but also harmed his subjects. Aelred lamented that many clerics placed a concern for money before their concern for their flock, and in a sermon on the Song of Songs, Bernard thundered that ministers who thought their stipends insufficient and kept income designated for the needy were "not ashamed to consume the food of the poor to profit their own pride and luxury."[92] This behavior made ambitious prelates doubly guilty: not only did they feed their own desires and vanities, but they stole the goods of the Church to do so.

Ambition disrupted the divinely modeled hierarchical organization of the Church. Bernard described to Eugenius III a vision of the Church in which the ranks of ecclesiastical officials on earth mirrored the ranks of angels in heaven, and Eugenius remembered this lesson, for he used similar language in a letter to the Cistercian archbishop of York, Henry Murdac:

For indeed the catholic Church is established on earth in the image of the heavenly order. For just as some of the heavenly spirits are superior without being proud and probing into divine secrets, and others are inferior without being envious and, at the commands of their superiors, rejoice and humbly submit, so in the catholic Church, some are established as patriarchs or primates, others as archbishops or metropolitans, and others as bishops. Therefore, so that true peace and concord may be preserved undiminished, each one should be content with his rights and not exceed the measure established by the holy fathers.[93]

Any prelate, whether a pope, bishop, or abbot, who attempted to increase his own authority at the expense of another subverted this divinely instituted order.

When Bernard of Clairvaux criticized this disruption of the ecclesiastical hierarchy, he had two specific practices in mind, both of which were linked to the increasing centralization of the papal government. One was the papal practice of exempting monasteries from episcopal control. The pope had the power to do this, but that did not mean that he should. Bernard asked Eugenius, "Do you judge it to be lawful for you to cut off churches from their members, and to confuse the order and disturb the boundaries that your predecessors established?"[94] This dislike of monastic exemptions was not just theoretical. Around 1140, Abbot Rainald of Cîteaux and the entire Cistercian Chapter General wrote to Pope Innocent II to support the efforts of the bishop of Autun to maintain jurisdiction over the monastery of Vézelay.[95] Vézelay, they argued, was provoking a great scandal and injuring the Church in its attempt to deprive the bishop of Autun of his ancient rights. In their insistence on a hierarchy of authority in the Church, however, the Cistercians were swimming against the tide. Their plea on behalf of the bishop was unsuccessful and Vézelay became subject directly to the papacy.

The second practice, the abuse of judicial appeals, provoked similar criticism. The right to hear appeals, like the right to grant exemptions, derived from the special authority of the papacy. Yet it was also the pope's responsibility to ensure that appeals produced justice instead of undermining it. Thus, Bernard criticized people who appealed to Rome to injure others or who appealed before judgment had been passed in an episcopal court.[96] Many of the Cistercians' letters to the papacy concerned what they considered a misuse of the papacy's judicial authority, especially when the pope overrode a seemingly just decision by a bishop or archbishop. Hugh of Pontigny and Bernard of Clairvaux both objected when Pope Honorius overturned the interdict Bishop Stephen of Paris had placed on his diocese.[97] Similarly, Bernard later complained that, when Innocent II reversed the decisions made by the archbishop of Trèves, "justice in the Church is lost, the keys of the Church are abolished, and episcopal authority is reviled by all, because no one among the bishops is ready to avenge the injuries given to God, and no one can punish illegal actions even in his own diocese."[98] It would have been better, Bernard thought, for the pope to support decisions made at the local level.

With these criticisms of an expanding papal jurisdiction and of monastic exemptions, Bernard and his companions fought a losing battle. Papal government became increasingly centralized over the course of the twelfth century, and the papal legal system became ever more important.[99] Bernard accepted the premise behind this centralization, for he agreed that the pope had the ultimate authority to hear appeals and intervene in diocesan matters and accepted the pope's authority to change clerical behavior through church councils and legatine activity.[100] He even admitted that a mechanism for appealing to Rome was both necessary and a sign of papal primacy.[101] In fact, he and other Cistercians acted as papal delegates in disputes that had been appealed to Rome.[102] The disjunction between Bernard's critique of papal jurisdiction and his support for papal authority, as well as his metaphorical descriptions of papal *plenitudo potestatis* and the two swords, have led generations of historians to argue over whether he accepted Gregory VII's jurisdictional claims over the episcopate and Gregory's hierocratic view of Christian society.[103] But recently they have concluded that this is the wrong question.[104] Bernard's use of figurative language, and the Cistercians' tendency to lump all church officials, whether popes, cardinals, bishops, or priests, into the general category of prelates at a time when other people were trying to distinguish the powers of one office from another, suggests that these Cistercians were more interested in determining how ecclesiastical authority was to be exercised than they were in defining the variations and limits of its jurisdiction. Ultimately, these Cistercians did not criticize the extent of papal power but its use; their central concern was not defining jurisdiction but reforming moral character.

The remedy that Bernard of Clairvaux and his companions offered for the ambition and corruption of the clergy derived from their conception of the monastic life: prelates must first attend to their own spiritual condition. Bernard told Henry, bishop of Sens, that "reason demands this order, that he who is ordered to love his neighbor according to his capacity first should love himself."[105] Similarly, he advised Pope Eugenius, "Let your waters be diverted into the streets; let men and oxen and cattle drink from them. . . . But you should drink with the others from the waters of your well."[106] When Aelred warned his clerical audience to guard against the temptations of the Philistines, he preached that they were to beware first for themselves, and only second for those for whom they were responsible. "If a person is not good to himself, to whom will he be good?" he asked.[107]

The process of learning care for one's own salvation by ordering desire and growing in caritas was no different for prelates than for anyone else. Bernard gave bishops the same advice about filling their reservoirs with caritas before dispersing it to others that he had given to his monks, and he organized his letter to Henry of Sens around the contemplative virtues of chastity, humility, and charity.[108] Aelred's sermons to clerics stressed the process of repentance required of all Christians. In one sermon, he called on priests to progress through seven stages in the sacrament of penance; in another, he described how acts of penance helped clerics to break the chains of temptation. "The chains of the Philistine, as long as they are not hardened by sinful habit, are lightened through compunction, freed by confession, and dissolved by fasting and vigils and works of mercy," he preached.[109] Bernard gave similar advice in his parables for a monastic audience, and as we shall see, these ideas appeared in a Cistercian sermon to the laity as well. The virtues that led to salvation were the same for prelates, monks, and lay people.

Although prelates needed to learn the same virtues as other Christians through the same process of humility and penance, they were to use these virtues to ward off temptations characteristic of their own order. Thus, when Bernard advised Henry of Sens about chastity, he said little about the virtue itself, but he made a common association between lack of chastity and love of ornamentation and warned Henry against enjoying the large buildings, the flashy horses, and especially the elaborate clothes that often accompanied episcopal positions.[110] Similarly, whereas prelates certainly had no monopoly on charity, the exercise of a bishop's charity was specific to his office, for he was directly responsible for other people's salvation as well as his own. As Bernard told Henry of Sens, the office of a bishop particularly combined the obligation to love both one's God and one's neighbor: "In all his deeds and words, the bishop should seek nothing of his own but much either for the honor of God or the salvation of his neighbor, or both. In doing this, he not only discharges the office of pontiff but also fulfills the etymology of his name by making himself a bridge (*pons*) between God and his neighbors."[111] A bishop was to offer people's prayers and promises to God and, in return, channel God's benediction and grace to his people. The special danger for a prelate was to help others at the expense of his own soul. As a result, he had to be particularly careful to replenish the reservoirs of caritas that he expended on the care of others.

The other essential virtue for a prelate was humility, for its antithesis, pride, destroyed all virtue. Bishops easily succumbed to pride. Bernard warned Henry of Sens, "Birth, age, wisdom, office, and what is still greater, episcopal prerogative; for whom are not these excessive forms the occasion for pride?"[112] The best remedy against pride was self-knowledge; if pride was the desire for one's own excellence, then humility stemmed from a recognition of one's insignificance in comparison to the greatness of one's God.[113] A prelate ought not confuse the glory pertaining to his office with the frailties of his human nature. As Bernard told Eugenius, "It is a wholesome connection that when you think of yourself as Supreme Pontiff you pay equal attention to the most vile dust that you not only were, but are."[114] To avoid pride, a prelate had to develop a good conscience by finding time for leisure amid all the affairs pressing on him and using the time for contemplation. Only by considering his own spiritual state, God, and the condition of his church would he learn enough about himself and his relation to the divine to develop the necessary humility.[115] This consideration was especially important for the pope, for it was the only check on his use of his power. Bernard reminded Eugenius III that only his conscience could determine when direct papal intervention was necessary and when judgment should be left to those who had a more immediate authority over the matter, and Hugh of Pontigny and Bernard together made the same point in their letter to Pope Honorius: they claimed not to censure him for lifting the bishop of Paris's interdict but suggested that he consult the dictates of his heart.[116]

The Cistercians' remedies for the moral failings of prelates drew on their monastic experience, especially the importance they placed on a communal life. Bernard suggested that prelates live with a group of companions who could offer advice and solace and help to preserve the virtues necessary for ecclesiastical office. Thus, he told the bishop-elect of Geneva, whose character he thought questionable for his new position, "Have good men in council, good men in your service, and good men dwelling with you; they will be the guardians and the witnesses of your life and your integrity."[117] Even the papal curia could serve such a function. Bernard advised Eugenius to fill curial positions with men without ambition who, like the pope himself, would put the interests of God before all things. His description of these advisers must have reminded Eugenius of his life at Clairvaux. With such companions, Bernard thought the pope could exclaim:

What would be more blessed and more reassuring to me than to see such men around me as custodians and witnesses to my life? I could safely entrust all my secrets and communicate my plans to them and pour out myself to them as if to myself. They would not allow me to stray if I should ever wish to, they would restrain me from headlong acts, and they would revive me if I grew lazy. Their reverence and frankness would restrain my haughtiness and correct my excesses; their constancy and strength would support me when I wavered and encourage me when I despaired; their faith and holiness would challenge me to do whatever is holy, honest, modest, lovable, and of good repute.[118]

Just as the Cistercians believed that a communal life taught a monk charity and helped his progress toward his salvation, so they advocated a communal life for popes and bishops in which the restraints, encouragement, and advice provided by such companionship helped a prelate to live a holy life and to fulfill the responsibilities of his office.

Because a prelate had to learn both to order his love and to use it properly, he had to develop active as well as contemplative virtues. Whereas Bernard's letter to Bishop Henry of Sens stressed charity, chastity, and humility, his treatise *De consideratione*, addressed to Pope Eugenius, was structured around justice, prudence, temperance, and fortitude. Presumably, Eugenius, as a former Cistercian, had already internalized lessons about ordered and disordered love.[119] Aelred of Rievaulx also stressed the four active virtues, telling clerics that they were essential for all, but especially pertinent to priests. He drew a picture of a priest getting dressed after bathing in the four waters of humility, knowledge, mercy, and grace: he was to put on the pants of temperance to restrain desire, the tunic of justice to give each person what he deserved, the belt of fortitude to sustain adversity, and the crown of prudence to ward off error.[120] In another sermon, Aelred spoke of prudence, fortitude, and mercy as virtues that influenced a prelate's own resistance to temptation as well as his ability to aid others. Prudence protected a priest from falling and helped him to call back his wandering sheep, sweetness and mercy kept him from irritation and made him a doctor who could heal the sick, and fortitude prevented him from grumbling and gave him the patience to sustain the perverse and willful.[121] Implicit in these texts was still the idea that the contemplative virtues came first; without charity and humility, a prelate could not temper his justice with mercy or restrain his fortitude with prudence.

The Cistercians used stories about former monks who had become bishops to reinforce their message about moral reform. In his *Exordium magnum*, composed between 1190 and 1210, Conrad of Eberbach described a number of Cistercian bishops who balanced their monastic virtues, especially their humility, with a careful and zealous administration of their offices. For example, when Pons, the abbot of Grandselve, was elected bishop of Clermont,

he most commendably restored to the rank of the higher priesthood the purity of monastic humility. In return, the vigor of his religion contributed to his authority as pontiff. Thus, feeding and teaching the people to whom he had been given as bishop by word and example, he appeared remarkable among the priests of his time, and when he had completed the span of his life in praise-worthy labor, he received his reward from God and rested in peace.[122]

Similarly, Godfrey, bishop of the church of Sorra in Sardinia, "actively ruled for seven years and kept his life in all purity, magnificently honored his office, and left to posterity a worthy example of sanctity."[123] Henry, cardinal-bishop of Albano, and Cardinal Baldwin also combined their monastic humility with their obligations as cardinals and became columns of support for the papacy and the Church.[124]

Bernard's *Vita sancti Malachiae*, Geoffrey of Auxerre's *Vita sancti Petri archiepiscopi Tarentasiensi*, and the sermons both men preached about Malachy fleshed out these brief sketches of ideal bishops and demonstrated the relation between good character and good administration. Both hagiographical accounts suggest that virtues were best learned in monastic life. Malachy never became a Cistercian; he had desired to leave his episcopal position for Clairvaux but was prohibited from doing so. Bernard approved of Malachy's obedience to a higher authority, and the Cistercians buried him at the altar of Clairvaux's church. Malachy demonstrated a propensity for monastic life as a child by outdoing his teachers in discipline and virtue; he displayed his humility and discipline as a young man by apprenticing himself to a holy man and sitting in absolute silence; and he undertook the classic action of the humble prelate by refusing to accept all positions of authority. He had to be coerced, first to become a deacon, and later to become bishop and then archbishop.[125] He only accepted the archbishopric of Armagh on the condition that, once he restored peace to the province, he could return to his former position in a community of regular canons.[126] He was physically chaste, and so spurned material ornamentation and glory that, after being elected archbishop of Armagh, he left the episcopal palace to his rival and, for two years, administered his diocese without a permanent residence.[127] Finally, he balanced a concern for his own spiritual condition with a concern for the salvation of others. He combined contemplation and prayer with his pastoral activities and, according to Bernard, oscillated between the cloister and his episcopal responsibilities.[128]

Geoffrey of Auxerre's *Vita* of Archbishop Peter of Tarentaise portrays an even closer relationship between the monastic life and the ideal behavior of a bishop. Unlike Malachy, who had been attracted to Cistercian life but prohibited from resigning his office, Peter had been both a Cistercian monk and an abbot before his election as archbishop in 1141. Like Malachy, Peter demonstrated a great reluctance to assume his new position; he only accepted it under pressure from the abbots of the order.[129] Geoffrey's account of Peter's life insists that Peter "moved little from the form of life to which he had converted."[130] Peter continued to wear his monastic habit, and he gave away any luxurious clothes. He ate the same beans and bread that he gave in alms to the poor, and he kept vigils even longer than those he had kept as a monk. He continued to work with his hands and to maintain discipline over his tongue, but in these cases, Geoffrey made clear that episcopal life demanded behavior different from that of a monk. Once a bishop, Peter's manual labor consisted of traveling and administering the sacrament of confirmation (which he performed "sometimes from morning to nightfall and beyond"), and for the discipline of silence he substituted preaching.[131] These episcopal activities thus developed out of the virtues and behaviors Peter had learned as a Cistercian monk.

Geoffrey transformed even Peter's questionable actions into subjects for praise. At one point in his episcopacy, Peter secretly fled to a Cistercian monastery in order to avoid his responsibilities. But rather than portraying Peter as shirking his duties, Geoffrey considered Peter's escape to be evidence of his humility, his hatred for praise and attention, and his desire to live without the trappings of episcopal privilege. Geoffrey emphasized Peter's melancholy state before his departure and described his laments that the profits of the world were meaningless if one lost one's soul. According to Geoffrey, this retreat was for Peter what the oscillations between episcopacy and monastery were for Malachy: a chance to refill his reservoirs with charity after emptying them in the care of others.

Both Bernard and Geoffrey described the virtues of their ideal prelates but also showed these virtues in action. Bernard suggested that Malachy's Irish subjects were barely Christian: the clergy did not perform the sacraments and the laity was ignorant of Christian doctrine. Malachy restored discipline to the clergy and wiped out pagan practices among the laity. He did this, as Bernard put it, with "the hoe of his tongue," preaching to his subjects both in groups and individually, "sometimes roughly, sometimes gently, whichever way he saw would be best for each one."[132] Closely following the model set by Gregory the Great in his *Regulae pastoralis*, Bernard described Malachy as teaching as much by his virtuous behavior as by his words; his success was due to his example as a humble and apostolic figure.[133]

Geoffrey of Auxerre portrayed Peter of Tarentaise as an ideal bishop who could combine the four aspects of Ezechiel's beast: he balanced the spiritual and temporal demands of his office and combined zeal with mercy. He reformed his diocese after the depredations that occurred under the previous archbishop, asserted his right to the tithes and parochial revenues usurped by secular lords, rebuilt his cathedral in stone, supplied his priests with necessary books and vestments, constructed hospices for the sick and needy, and gave alms. Yet Geoffrey stressed that he did these things without making undue financial demands on the poor of his diocese.[134] Nor did he only care for the material condition of his diocese. He reformed the life of his clergy by introducing regular canons into his cathedral and instructing them in discipline and the celebration of the divine office; he preached to the diocesan priests, insisting that they become examples of virtue for the laity.[135] He ministered to the laity through the sacrament of confirmation and by vernacular preaching. Geoffrey suggested that he presented his sermons with a style appropriate to the fluency of his listeners, and that he was famous throughout the countryside and honored in the vulgar language as a man powerful in deeds and in speech.[136] Furthermore, according to Geoffrey, Peter acted as a virtuous judge and peacemaker, successfully combining justice and mercy as he settled disputes between the counts of Savoy and Toulouse and between the kings of England and France.[137]

The Cistercians' concern for clerical morality and their stress on the clergy's pastoral functions made them intellectual precursors to schoolmen in the second half of the twelfth century who also advocated clerical reform. The circle of masters and preachers associated with Peter the Chanter stressed the clergy's pastoral role as confessors, issued *summae* and handbooks detailing specific sinful behaviors associated with specific occupations, and encouraged preaching as a means of spreading this information to the laity.[138] These men were especially interested in reforming the behavior of students in the schools, with the assumption that they were training potential leaders of the Church who would then spread this program of reform once they obtained ecclesiastical office.[139] The reforms these moralists advocated had important parallels with Cistercian ideas about the training of virtuous prelates and suggests that, despite the legendary animosity between monastery and school, there was a cross-fertilization of ideas between the two environments.

In his introduction to his life of Peter of Tarentaise, Geoffrey of Auxerre compared a bishop to an almond tree. Its roots were words of doctrine, he said, its leaves were an exemplary life, and its fruits were effective preaching.[140] Geoffrey's account of Peter's life echoed both Gregory the Great and Bernard of Clairvaux in that he found the source of this virtuous behavior in a contemplative life; the Parisian moralists' picture of an ideal cleric followed a similar pattern. They too insisted that clerics not only be educated but also live a holy life, and that they teach not just with words but also by their example. Maurice of Sully, bishop of Paris from 1160 to 1196, began his manual on preaching with a sermon that outlined the same three requirements for the priesthood that Geoffrey attributed to bishops: a priest had to be educated in doctrine, live a holy life, and preach frequently. Other Parisian theologians also emphasized that a cleric's knowledge could not be separated from his life, and that he was to use both his knowledge and his good example to instruct others.[141] Whereas monasteries and schools offered very different types of education, the Cistercians and the moral theologians presented similar critiques of scholastic education and drew similar pictures of an ideal priesthood. Both groups placed preaching and instruction at the pinnacle of their educational process; for Alan of Lille and Peter the Chanter, instruction crowned a scholastic education of reading and disputation, whereas for Bernard of Clairvaux, William of Saint-Thierry, and Geoffrey of Auxerre, it grew out of the virtues inculcated in a monastic life. Peter the Chanter denounced the "most dreadful silence" of the non-preaching clergy who, like muted dogs, would not bark; Bernard, although a monk, had barked aplenty.[142]

Cistercian authors celebrated bishops who had once been monks, but they nonetheless insisted on keeping the clerical and monastic orders separate. The communal life of a bishop or pope was not that of a monk; good companions, like monastic brethren, might help teach humility and charity, but unlike monks, bishops then had to use these virtues to perform their episcopal obligations in secular society.[143] In order to keep these orders distinct, Bernard slightly distorted the events of Malachy's life to separate his tenure as abbot from that as bishop, and he ended his letter to Henry of Sens by protesting against monks who sought exceptions from episcopal jurisdiction and thus usurped episcopal privileges.[144] Nor did Bernard advise Pope Eugenius to live as a monk in prayer and contemplation. He only suggested that Eugenius find leisure time for consideration, which was directed more toward activity than was the contemplation of a monk.[145] Even a prelate's contemplation of God and heaven was, in part, directed toward action, for a strong sense of the nature of the divine and the eternal order of things was necessary if the earthly church was to maintain its heavenly image. Thus, monks could become bishops, but bishops were not monks. The Cistercian monks who became bishops retained ties to their communities and continued to follow many of its observances. They even continued to live in fraternal communities within their episcopal residences. Still, the obligations of their office differentiated them from their former brethren. The virtues of humility, charity, and chastity could lead everyone to salvation, but the different obligations of the social orders meant that the members of each order displayed these virtues in different ways.

By celebrating the character and performance of their monks who became bishops, the Cistercians implied that their monasteries provided a training ground for a reformed clergy. Of course, they never stated explicitly that monastic life provided an education for prelates, and they roundly criticized monks who seemed ambitious for either monastic or ecclesiastical office. Bernard of Clairvaux and Gilbert of Hoyland both told their monks that they did not yet have the strength to shoulder the "male burdens" of episcopal positions.[146] Nonetheless, many Cistercian monks did leave their communities to serve in the ecclesiastical hierarchy, some within only a few years of their conversion, and they often used monastic offices as stepping-stones. Few Cistercian bishops had not previously been abbots. But rather than viewing these prelates as ambitious, the Cistercians were proud of these men and offered them as examples of ideal churchmen.

Furthermore, the Cistercian texts criticizing clerical behavior did not always have a clerical audience. Cistercian abbots warned about the dangers of ambition, lambasted episcopal wealth and pride, and praised Cistercian prelates in sermons and stories designed for their own monks. Bernard's comments about corrupt clerics in his sermons on the Song of Songs, the sermons he and Geoffrey of Auxerre preached on Malachy's anniversary, the vignettes in Conrad of Eberbach's *Exordium magnum*, all taught monks about the need for clerical reform and the characteristics of ideal prelates. Even if they were not explicitly designed to prepare

Cistercian monks for those roles, they certainly reminded the monks not to remain isolated in the cloister but instead to be aware of the condition of the Church and have a part in its reformation. They reinforced what Bernard's treatises to prelates and Aelred's and Geoffrey's sermons to clerical synods also established: that the Cistercians believed one of their social functions was to aid in restoring the unity and celestial order of the Church by encouraging the moral and behavioral reform of the clergy.

Chapter 7

"With the Power of Your Right Hand"

Princes and Knights

When Cistercian monks used tripartite images to describe the divisions in Christian society, they lumped all lay people together into a single group identified by its worldly activity, its ability to marry, and its submission to the direction of prelates. Their other images of society, however, differentiated among the lay groups and often linked together secular and ecclesiastical authorities. If the Church was the body of the bride, Geoffrey of Auxerre considered her legs to be the leaders of both orders because they served as columns of support for the Church; if Christian society was the bridal chamber in the Song of Songs, then its beams were secular and ecclesiastical princes who bound the room together with their just laws. The differences between these two visions of society encapsulate the tensions in the Cistercians' view of the laity. On the one hand, they wished to encourage all Christians to progress in virtue so as to bind the Church together in a common striving toward the divine. On the other hand, these active Cistercians were really only interested in those lay people with power—especially those with juridical authority and military might—for they assumed that if such people learned to use their power in harmony with divine will, then they, along with the ecclesiastical prelates, would support and bind together Christian society like good columns and beams, and leave monks at peace in the bridal bed at the center of the Church. Most of the Cistercians' close contacts with secular figures were with kings and princes, but their advice for such men had implications not just for the behavior of rulers but for the development of a knightly ideology and a lay spirituality as well.

I

Although the early Cistercian abbeys received much of their property from the lesser aristocracy and petty knights, the benefactors with whom they established close reciprocal relationships were great magnates and important lords. These relationships had important implications for the Cistercians' political activities, for they augmented the monks' networks of Cistercian bishops and allied prelates, and they provided recipients for the letters and treatises that portrayed the monks' conception of an ideal prince. The great majority of the texts that the Cistercians addressed to secular figures were directed toward kings and queens, counts, and other banal lords. Three-quarters of Bernard of Clairvaux's letters to the laity were sent to people with titles, and other Cistercian abbots were also more likely to write kings, queens, and counts than knights.[1] Unfortunately, Aelred of Rievaulx's letters are no longer extant, but he did send a work on the *Genealogia regum Anglorum* to Henry of Anjou; and even Hugh of Payens, the recipient of Bernard's *De laude novae militiae* was called *dominus* in charters and may well have been an official associated with the count of Champagne.[2] However, by becoming involved in the political affairs of these great men, the Cistercians also risked becoming involved in their conflicts. For a time, the monks sustained relations that cut across traditional political rivalries and maintained the illusion of a unified Christian society, but such contacts eventually led to divisions within the order.

As we have seen, the monks at Cîteaux, Clairvaux, Pontigny, and La Ferté organized their cartularies and pancartes so as to emphasize their relations with counts, dukes, and bishops, and these same men received special liturgical commemoration from the monks and could be buried in the monastic cemetery.[3] Whereas the bulk of the lands given to Cîteaux and Pontigny came from families other than those of the duke of Burgundy and the count of Nevers, these two magnates nonetheless were a presence behind many of the transactions, compensating smaller donors for their gifts. In fact, the monks of Pontigny not only received donations from counts William II and III of Nevers but also relied on William II and his vassals to aid subsequent foundations.[4] The land for Pontigny's first affiliate, Bouras, came from William's seneschal, Hugh of Tilio, lord of Chalmley, and another member of William's entourage, Milo of Courtenay, donated the land for Pontigny's third foundation,

Fontaine-Jean, in 1124.[5] According to the *Exordium parvum*, Cîteaux received much early financial support from Duke Odo of Burgundy, and in a letter written around 1125, Bernard of Clairvaux complimented Count Hugh of Champagne for his "long-standing love and generosity," suggesting that he too may have provided the monks with money.[6] Hugh joined the Knights Templar in 1125, leaving his county to his nephew, Theobald, count of Blois.

In 1121, Theobald of Blois had aided with the foundation of Cîteaux's affiliate, L'Aumône, and he continued thereafter to be a generous donor to Cistercian houses, financing both the rebuilding of Clairvaux in 1135 and the additions to Pontigny's church.[7] Sometime after 1125, the monks of Clairvaux associated the count with their prayers, and these reciprocal bonds of patronage and prayer created a close relationship that worked to both the monks' and the count's advantage.[8] Bernard of Clairvaux asked the count to protect religious men and worked with him on promoting monastic reform; he sent letters to the count, advising him about the administration of justice in his territory; and he later intervened on the count's behalf when Louis VII invaded the county in 1144.[9] Cistercian texts presented Count Theobald as a model prince, and it was this image of Theobald that took hold in later writings, despite Suger of Saint-Denis's attempts to portray him as a coward.[10] The monks maintained good relations with Theobald's son, Henry the Liberal, who continued his father's generosity to the order and received the same sort of lavish praise from a later abbot of Clairvaux that Theobald had received from Bernard.[11]

Unlike most of the first Cistercian abbeys, whose early abbots tended to be unrelated to neighboring families, Clairvaux and some of its affiliates maintained strong connections to the families of their monks.[12] Initially, many of the monks at Clairvaux were related to one another, and the most prominent of the initial donors was Bernard's relative, Josbert of La Ferté, viscount of Dijon and seneschal of the count of Champagne.[13] The foundation of Clairvaux's second affiliate, Fontenay, also depended on the monks' familial connections; its initial donor was Rainard of Montbard, Bernard's maternal uncle, whose brother, Gaudry of Touillon, had entered Cîteaux with Bernard; its first abbot was Bernard's paternal relative, Godfrey of La Roche, who had ties with the family at Montbard.[14] The family's connections with Clairvaux continued; Rayner of La Roche was one of the initial donors for Clairvaux's affiliate Auberive, and Bernard and his brothers appeared on charters when the family donated land to non-Cistercian monasteries as well.[15] This reliance on family ties may have contributed to Clairvaux's economic differences: its initial lack of a ducal or comital patron to help negotiate donations, and its later reliance on pancartes issued by Godfrey, once he became bishop of Langres, to record their property. According to both Geoffrey of Auxerre and William of Saint-Thierry, Bernard worked his first miracle for his relative Josbert and demonstrated that knightly predation against churches and monasteries hindered salvation, but otherwise these families appear only on Cistercian charters and do not seem to have helped to shape the monks' political behavior.[16]

Though the first Cistercian houses lay in regions in which a royal presence was lacking, the order nonetheless quickly established relations with the king of France. It is unclear when they first made contact, but when the order intervened with Louis VI on behalf of Bishop Henry of Sens in 1129, they reminded him that he had already requested to be remembered in their prayers, and made clear what they expected of him in return.

The king of heaven and earth has given to you the kingdom of the earth, and will give you that in heaven, if you try to rule justly and wisely what you have received. This is what we hope and pray for you, so that you rule this one faithfully, and that one happily. Yet, how can you already so bitterly oppose the intention of our prayers for you (which, you recall, you formerly humbly requested)? How can we confidently raise our hand to the Spouse of the Church for you when you have thus, and without reason (so we conclude), saddened us, having dared to disregard us? . . . Thus we boldly, but lovingly, care to make this known to you through that mutual friendship and fraternity of ours, to which you worthily enough associated yourself but are now seriously wounding, that we advise and beseech you to desist quickly from such evil.[17]

The Cistercians' relations with Louis VI remained uneven; Bernard appeared at the council at Etampes in 1130 to help enlist Louis's support for Innocent II, and in 1131 Louis exempted the monks of Pontigny from paying dues on the transport of goods through his territory, a privilege he repeated for the entire order in 1135. But Bernard again wrote a critical letter to Louis in 1134, scolding him for refusing to let his bishops attend the council at Pisa.[18] Louis VII reiterated the exemption from transport dues for both Pontigny and Clairvaux, but he too provoked angry letters from Bernard, first when he hesitated to invest Bernard's candidate for the bishopric of Langres with the temporal regalia, and again when he invaded the county of Champagne.[19] Bernard's relations with the king improved after Louis repented the burning of a church at Vitry and joined the expedition to Jerusalem, but the monks' relations with the French king were never as close as those with their local princes or even with Henry II of England.

The Cistercians' contacts in England started with Stephen Harding, who had remained in contact with his former community at Sherborne.[20] Clairvaux quickly attracted a number of men from northern England, many of whom later helped to found Clairvaux's affiliates in Yorkshire.[21] The first Cistercian foundations in England, however, were made by monks sent from Cîteaux's affiliate L'Aumône: Waverly was established in 1129, Tintern in 1131. In 1131, when in Rouen, King Henry I met with Bernard of Clairvaux and Bishop Geoffrey of Chartres and proclaimed his support for Innocent II; at the same time, he granted the monks from Pontigny freedom from customs on the goods they transported through his territory.[22] Politically, one would expect Bernard and the Cistercians in Champagne and Burgundy to look at Henry of Anjou with some suspicion—their patron Theobald was the brother of King Stephen—but the actions of Stephen and his brother, Bishop Henry of Winchester, during a disputed episcopal election in York did not endear them to either Bernard or the English Cistercians.[23] By 1148 the Cistercian pope Eugenius III had turned against Stephen as well.[24] For northern English Cistercians such as Aelred of Rievaulx, Henry of Anjou's connections to the Scottish king were a further bonus—Henry was knighted at Carlisle in 1149 by his great-uncle, King David of Scotland, in whose court Aelred had served.[25] Between 1152 and 1154, Aelred wrote the *Genealogia regum Anglorum* for Henry, and with the important exception of the Becket conflict, many Cistercians, both in England and on the Continent, maintained good relations with the Angevin king. In the 1170's, King Henry promised Clairvaux a shipment of lead with which to cover the roof of their new oratory, and soon after Bernard's canonization, Clairvaux's abbot, Henry of Marcy, sent Henry II a bone from Bernard's finger.[26]

The first Cistercian houses were founded in a region with scant royal presence, where princely power depended on personal ties with vassals, bishops, and monasteries. The political networks of the Cistercian order also relied on such personal ties, even as many of their princely contacts began to systematize their feudal obligations and to depend on ideas derived from Roman law.[27] For a time, the Cistercians used their friendships and effective moral suasion to resolve disputes between rivals such as Louis VII and Count Theobald. But, as the conflicts between Louis VII and Henry II heated up in the 1170's, the Cistercians' position became more difficult and they were caught between two increasingly powerful and self-conscious kings.

II

Monastic visions of the social order were not always mere images, for they often provided a means of understanding the bonds holding society together and the sources of power and authority that the monks actually saw, or wished to see, around them. In recent years, historians have studied in some detail the importance of such social images in tenth- and eleventh-century French society, and they have examined their relation to the decline in royal power and the emergence of banal lords and a predatory knightly class. The tenth-century monks from Cluny, aware of the increased power of strong men who usurped royal powers and brought the peasantry under their control, created a picture of a restrained lord, but one willing to use his violence for purposes sanctioned by religious men, and thus they contributed to a blurred line between royal and seigneurial power.[28] In comparison, eleventh- and twelfth-century monks from communities such as Fleury and Saint-Denis, which were closely associated with the Capetian royal house, presented pictures of kings that set royal authority apart from the secular powers surrounding it.[29] Still other communities, such as the monastery of Marmoutier, provided genealogies and family histories for their princely patrons that enhanced the princes' emerging positions as the sources of justice and peace within their territories.[30]

In comparison to the monks from Cluny, Fleury, and Saint-Denis, the Cistercians who wrote about secular lords were not particularly innovative in their message. They borrowed the language of Carolingian churchmen who had emphasized the divine source of secular power and who had used images of corporate unity to portray the harmonious cooperation of secular and ecclesiastical authorities, but they used this older language in a new social and political context. Writing at a time in which the great territorial princes began to consolidate their lands and powers, the monks witnessed the princes' efforts to enforce the peace and extend their jurisdiction, and they understood the relationship of secular and ecclesiastical authority through the lenses of the late eleventh-century disputes over church reform and investiture. As a result, they used language that had once described the concord of the emperor and his clergy to portray a prince willing to serve the aims of the Church and to maintain peace in his territory. Following Gregory the Great's portrayal of an ideal rector in his *Regulae pastoralis*, the Cistercians suggested that secular lords, like bishops, could reform their behavior, learn to temper their justice with mercy, and govern, in Augustine's phrase, not out of a lust for domination but out of a loving concern for the well-being of others. The image of a good lord that they presented served to blur what for others were important distinctions between royal and banal power. In fact, when the Cistercians described the way in which these lords could obtain the inner repentance and moral reform necessary for their good rule, they advocated a process open to all men with military power, not just those with judicial authority. In so doing, they contributed to the emergence of an ideology that expressed a new cohesiveness among knights in twelfth-century society.[31]

Ninth-century Carolingian clerics portrayed their emperor as the representative of Christ on earth, but they also stressed the Augustinian idea that his authority was a ministry bestowed by the divine rather than a dominion stemming from his birth. The emperor, with the aid of his bishops, protected and taught the people he ruled; ideally, he united his subjects into a peaceful community symbolized by the body of Christ and led them toward salvation.[32] When the Cistercians repeated this political language of concord, they did so in a twelfth-century context in which rulers such as the duke of Normandy, the counts of Flanders, Anjou, and Champagne, and the king of France attempted to define and expand the limits of their jurisdiction in order to maintain peace in their territories. The Cistercians were not particularly interested in this process of definition and expansion, but they were deeply concerned with the proper exercise of, and potential abuses of, judicial power and argued that a ruler who understood his rule to be a ministry kept the peace by balancing justice with mercy. They thus modified the Carolingian political language in two important ways: they applied it to all territorial rulers, not just the king or emperor, and they found evidence of the rulers' *ministerium* in their behavior and inner conscience, not their anointing. Rather than return to Augustine's idea of the eschatological neutrality of secular institutions, or maintain the Carolingians' sense of a hierarchy of delegated authority, the Cistercians believed that all lords who learned to rule justly became analogues of divine power on earth.

The repetitious nature of Aelred's descriptions of English kings in his *Genealogia* hammers home his message about good lordship. These kings ruled with divine approval and had a loving concern for their subjects, not a desire to dominate. King Aethelwulf "always conducted himself in his earthly realm as if it were heaven, for it was clearly understood that he was not captured by desire but called by charity, and he cared for others by the requirements of ruling, not to satisfy a wish for domination."[33] Alfred was a "knight of Christ" to whom a vision of Saint Cuthbert appeared to tell him that Christ was working to subdue his enemies; Edward the Elder was so friendly and affable to all that even his enemies "elected him with all devotion not so much their lord and king as their father."[34] Aethelstan was devoted to Saint John of Beverly, who helped him quell a Scottish invasion; Edmund was "more of a father than a king"; and after King Edred died, Dunstan heard a voice saying that Edred now slept with God.[35] Edwin broke this pattern of virtuous kings, but his brother Edgar continued his predecessors' behavior and taught his people "not only by word but by example."[36] With Edgar, this lineage reached its apex. Aethelred ruled "most laboriously and strenuously"; Edmund Ironsides, with miraculous fortitude, showed great ferocity toward his enemies and great gentleness to his friends; and Edward the Confessor was "a gentle and pious man who protected his kingdom more by peace than by arms."[37] King David of Scotland, Henry of Anjou's great-uncle and the man who knighted him, returned to the model of Aethelwulf and Edgar; like his forefathers, "he did not desire to be king, but dreaded it, and accepted it on account of the needs of others rather than avidly usurping it like a man conquered by a lust for domination."[38]

The kings in Aelred's *Genealogia* maintained the peace by administering their just laws with mercy and by controlling their officials "so the poor not be oppressed by the powerful."[39] Similarly, Bernard advised both the king and queen of France to administer justice with prudence and mercy.[40] But, whereas Stephen Harding told King Louis VI that "the king of heaven and earth has given to you the kingdom of the earth," Bernard of Clairvaux blurred the distinction between king and count by using almost identical language to tell Count Henry of Champagne, "the ruler of earthly kings has established you as a ruler upon earth."[41] In fact, it was neither the king of England nor the king of France but Count Henry's nephew Theobald who received the most advice about the exercise of justice. In one letter, Bernard of Clairvaux asked Theobald to show mercy to a castellan whose castle he had just gained though Bernard's advice; in two other letters, Bernard asked that Theobald pardon a man he had disinherited and restore his heritage to his family.[42] In still another letter, Bernard wrote on behalf of a woman whose husband had been punished, and for the family of a man who had lost a duel, had his eyes put out, and his goods confiscated; in both cases, he pleaded that the families not be punished for the offenders' behavior.[43] In a later story told about Bernard and Theobald, Bernard prevented Theobald from hanging a convicted thief and took the man back to Clairvaux as a monk, claiming that this too would make him dead to the world. The thief's conversion again illustrated the importance of tempering justice with mercy, and it demonstrated that the discretion of a virtuous man could provide justice more effective than a strict adherence to absolute notions of law and punishment.[44]

These letters and stories made clear the connection between divine and earthly power. The Christian God was both just and merciful, and for a secular lord, the ability to pardon was at least as dramatic a sign of his divinely instituted authority as was his power to judge.[45] As Bernard reminded Theobald, God could disinherit him just as easily as he disinherited his subjects, and the more merciful his judgments, the more merciful God would be in judging him.[46] He advised Theobald to use his judgments not as instruments of vengeance but as opportunities to administer his office with compassion:

Even in such cases in which the fault seems so clear and inexcusable that justice is endangered if the occasion for mercy is not abandoned, you still should offer punishment with fear and sorrow, compelled more by the duty of your office than by the desire for vengeance. But when the criminal charges are either recognized to be less certain or are accepted as excusable, you ought not to avoid this joyful opportunity, but willingly accept that here you can show your loving kindness without sacrificing justice.[47]

Later, in an attempt to hold Theobald to a decision of which he approved, Bernard praised the judgment as "most benevolently just, most justly benevolent," again stressing the balance between mercy and justice.[48]

The Cistercians used the idea that secular power had a divine source not only to advocate a merciful exercise of justice but also to stress that rulers should use their powers to serve the needs of the Church. In so doing, they again repeated Carolingian commonplaces that emphasized the partnership between kings and their churchmen but gave them new meanings. They used ideas that had distinctly dualist implications but used them to describe a cooperation between rulers and churchmen whose purpose was to support the aims of the Church.[49] When Bernard told Eugenius that the apostle Peter had possessed two swords, one to be drawn by his hand, but the other to be drawn by the hand of a soldier, "at the bidding of the priest and the order of the emperor," he made clear that both swords belonged to the Church, "the one exercised on behalf of the church, the other by the church."[50] Yet both times that Bernard repeated this figure, he insisted that Eugenius was not to wield the secular sword, and in still another passage he reminded the pope that his was a ministry over spiritual, not secular, things.[51] Bernard's letters to emperors, in comparison, urged them to act on behalf of the Church. At the same time that he told Emperor Lothar that he had been raised to his position by divine power, he also reminded him that he should both restore the empire and support the Church and thus "work even now for our well-being upon the earth."[52] Specifically, Bernard wanted Lothar to help Innocent II to return to Rome. In a letter to Conrad of Germany, Bernard again described the cooperation of secular and ecclesiastical authorities as if they were partners in a marriage. Bernard told Conrad, "What God has joined together let no man put asunder. Instead, let the human will try to fulfill what divine authority has established so that those who are joined by design are also joined in spirit."[53]

Aelred's *Genealogia* also described a partnership between kings and churchmen in which kings acted on the advice of their ecclesiastical advisors and used their authority to support and serve the Church. Aelred's kings built and repaired churches, founded monasteries, gave alms, went on pilgrimages to Rome with gifts for the pope, reformed clerical behavior, and took advice from churchmen whom they held in greatest reverence but did not try to control. As Aelred said about King Alfred, "he believed that the greatest rank of king had no power in the Church of Christ."[54]

Bernard and Aelred could envision such cooperation between the two powers because they assumed both swords would be used for the same ends if secular and ecclesiastical offices were both filled with people of goodwill who had learned to desire what was best for Christian society. They were less concerned with defining what to do if a secular ruler refused to act at the bidding of a priest than they were with ensuring that he would want to act in harmony with the Church. They put their own mark on the more traditional picture of good lordship by insisting that such virtuous behavior could only stem from a good inner conscience and an ordered will. Secular leaders, no less than ecclesiastical authorities and monks, needed to care for their own salvation first; their actions would then reflect their interior state. Aelred said of King Edgar, "He revealed signs of his interior sweetness in his words, face, and customs," and he described Edward the Confessor in nearly identical terms: "The spirit of interior sanctity shone even in his body, for a certain special sweetness appeared in his face, a seriousness in his step, and a simplicity in his desires."[55] Similarly, Henry of Marcy, while abbot of Clairvaux, described Henry of Champagne's decision to go on crusade as "rich sprouts springing from the garden of his heart."[56] Only when lords' actions were motivated by their concern for the well-being of others rather than their love of power and domination were they virtuous leaders whose acts supported the Church. To become so, they first had to learn to order their own love.

The Cistercians' letters to secular lords and their descriptions of good rulers stressed the importance of reforming the inner self and the human will. Aelred's *Genealogia* started with a discussion of virtue, reason, and the human soul that echoed the ideas in his more theological treatises. Virtue, Aelred argued, harmonized with the divine image in the human soul whereas vice contradicted it, for even a sinful person capable of rational thought could not excuse sinful behavior. The fundamental challenge for Henry of Anjou, as for each Cistercian monk and indeed every Christian, was to mold his will so that he desired what he rationally knew to be good: "Because the love of virtue and a hate of vice is naturally contained in the rational soul, whoever should desire good customs and virtues easily draws them all toward himself and yields his will to them."[57] The purpose of Aelred's *Genealogia* was to demonstrate the good customs and virtues toward which Henry's rational soul naturally inclined, and to show how other kings had learned to control their errant wills.[58] Aelred described the English kings as possessing the same virtues that Cistercian monks tried to inculcate and that Aelred advocated for prelates as well. His kings were merciful, just, chaste, and humble; they spent time in vigils and prayers, gave alms, and took advice from holy men. Bernard offered similar guidance to Melisande, queen of Jerusalem, who was ruling as regent for her son Baldwin, for he told her that her virtues as a widow were inseparable from her virtues as a ruler; he also reminded Henry I of England that he was to serve the king of heaven in ruling his earthly kingdom.[59]

Perhaps in an attempt to show that the many letters Bernard sent to Theobald had an effect, the *Vita prima* portrays Theobald as a model lord. Like Aelred's English kings, Theobald appears as "a servant among the servants of God, and in no way a lord."[60] He endeared himself to the Cistercians by his generosity to their foundations and his willingness to accept Bernard as his spiritual adviser.[61] He built churches, founded monasteries, cared for the poor, defended widows and orphans, settled disputes with justice, and sought to keep the peace. He lived simply and parted with luxuries, breaking up two golden goblets to donate the proceeds to the poor. He gave alms, fed the needy, the sick, and the leprous, and controlled his servants, who "feared God and desired to please him as much as their count."[62] This picture of Theobald embodied all of the virtues that the Cistercians encouraged temporal lords to learn. He was just yet merciful, generous yet personally abstemious, peaceful but willing to defend the weak and oppressed. And, most important, he used his temporal power not to harass the Church but to support it, thus demonstrating that the spiritual and temporal powers be allied because both, ultimately, derived from God.

When the Cistercians addressed princes and kings about the administration of justice and support for the Church, they emphasized the importance of inner repentance and moral reform but did not describe in any detail how such a reform might be effected. When they wrote about warfare, however, they did describe a process of interior reform, for they portrayed warfare as a form of penance through which warriors learned to control their wills and progress toward their salvation. But warfare was an activity for all knights, not just princes, and the Cistercians presented a conception of warfare that applied not only to those in positions of authority but to all who carried arms. Their ideas further blurred distinctions between royal, princely, and knightly power and, as a result, aided the development of an ideology that unified all knights into a single nobility. The Cistercians themselves, however, were more interested in showing how such activities could bind Christian society in caritas than they were in providing a unique identity for knights, and they hinted that the inner transformation that warfare offered to knights could be extended to the rest of the laity as well.

Violence had long been one of the most serious threats to the unity of Christian society, and monks had long tried to control the warfare and plunder of men whose physical power had made them virtually independent of a weakened government. Some monks had used the power of their patron saints to defend their own communities, and the laity dependent on them, from the depredations of violent warriors; monks at tenth-century Cluny had developed a model of an ideal knight who fought only to protect the poor and powerless and for causes sanctioned by churchmen.[63] The Peace of God assemblies offered one way of spreading this monastic ideal among the warrior elites; the papal sanctions for wars against the Muslims in Spain and the Middle East offered another.[64]

The Cistercian order began the year the crusaders captured Jerusalem, and its monks lived in a society that had already started to incorporate this monastic model for an ideal knight into its culture. Cistercian authors both enhanced the model and shifted its focus. Unlike earlier monks, they were less concerned with preventing the oppression of the poor and powerless than they were in encouraging men to fight for causes sanctioned by churchmen, especially in crusades against non-Christians and heretics. But they further modified the older message by adding to it a new interest in inner motivation. As they presented it, Church-sanctioned warfare had more of an inner goal than an outward one; it was part of a personal process of penitence that focused an individual's attention on the humanity and sacrifice of Christ, and thus encouraged warriors to undergo the same interior changes that they could achieve in a still better form if they entered a monastery. Such warfare no longer necessarily divided and fractured the peace of a unified Christian society. Instead, it could be a means of moral reform and yet another way of uniting the Church in charity.

Warfare against other Christians, of course, still divided Christian society. Both Bernard of Clairvaux, in calling for the second crusade, and Henry of Marcy, in calling for the third, scolded warriors who ruptured Christian unity by fighting one another. "They are not knights but evil men [*malitia fuit, non militia*]," Henry exhorted, "who deserve the inextinguishable fire and undying torture of worms."[65] Fighting against the enemies of Christ and the Church, in comparison, contributed to a person's salvation. When Bernard encouraged people to take up their swords in the service of God and join the second crusade, he told them that "now, O strong knights and warlike men, you have a place where you can fight without danger, where it is glorious to conquer and profitable to die."[66] As Bernard saw it, this military expedition to Jerusalem was part of the divine plan for human salvation; it was yet another divine gift to help sinners reform. The primary purpose of such an armed pilgrimage was not to conquer territory from the Muslims or even to protect the holy places of Jesus' life, but to give Christians yet another opportunity to abandon worldly things and turn their will to God by offering themselves for possible martyrdom.[67] God could have protected the holy places against its enemies had he wished, but instead he put himself in debt to humans "in order to give as payment to his knights forgiveness of their weaknesses and everlasting glory."[68] As a form of penance and possible martyrdom, Bernard recommended crusading not only for knights but for all social orders except monks.[69]

Henry of Marcy even more explicitly associated the inner change effected by warfare for a just cause with the performance of the sacrament of penance: "Behold, by your works, the health in the midst of the earth, where already we see the most evil men purified, running to confession, doing penance, making satisfaction for their earlier sins, looking to the future, and promising reform. Not content with the mediocre penance to which they were accustomed, they assemble for complete perfection, freeing their hand for bravery, bearing their cross, and leaving all to follow Christ."[70] Henry's words could as easily have described men entering a monastery as those going on crusade. Both offered to the laity a similar opportunity for personal reform.

Bernard's *De laude novae militiae*, in which he describes the behavior of the Knights Templar, demonstrates most clearly this association of warfare with inner repentance and personal transformation. Bernard's treatise not only honored the Knights Templar but also served as a goad for less virtuous warriors. Bernard contrasted worldly knights, whose silks, gems, and elegant display confused the insignia of warriors with the ornaments of women and inspired only greed in their enemies, to the Knights Templar, who wore their hair short, seldom washed, shunned excess food, clothing, and flashy horses, avoided games, hunting, laughter, and jests, and armed themselves "with faith within and steel without . . . so as to strike fear in the enemies."[71] The greatest difference between worldly knights and the Templars, however, was the condition of their conscience. Worldly knights rode into battle in a terrible state of insecurity, knowing that their wars were unjust. As a result, they could not act boldly, because they feared both to kill and to be killed. In comparison, a Templar as a knight of Christ "may kill fearlessly and be killed even more fearlessly, for he serves Christ when he kills and serves himself when he dies."[72]

Bernard so praised the Knights Templar that he seemingly blurred the line between monastic and secular life that he usually tried so hard to keep distinct. Indeed, he claimed to be unsure how to characterize these men, writing, "I hesitate as to whether it would be better to call them monks or soldiers, unless perhaps I should consider them as equal to both."[73] But Bernard still did not erase the line between monastic and secular. For all their austerities, the Templars did not live a monastic life but rather, like the Cistercians' ideal monk-bishops and virtuous lords, they had organized their lives so as to best aid their salvation while fulfilling their allotted social role. They demonstrated that knights in the world could develop the same virtues as their monastic brethren. Nicholas of Clairvaux, whose letters often reflected Bernard's ideas, made this same point when he ghostwrote a letter for the monks Gaucher and Gerard to a knight named Henry. In Henry, the monks wrote, "we find a man according to our heart, who seeks God in the world, and who professes daily to be a monk under the soldier." Henry was a man "in the world, but not embracing the world"; his inner goodness allowed the monks to see him not with their corporeal eyes but with the "eyes of their hearts in the breast of Jesus Christ."[74]

What made the Templars the most like monks was that they, too, lived in communities in which the concern and example of their brothers taught them to discipline their wills. Bernard described these communities using the same biblical language that William of Saint-Thierry used to describe Bernard and his knightly friends and relatives living together at Châtillon:

So that nothing is missing from their evangelical perfection, they all live in one house according to a single rule without anything of their own, carefully preserving a unity of spirit in the bond of peace. You could say that the entire multitude has one heart and one soul, for no one follows his own will but rather obediently responds to commands. . . . They pay little attention to a person's standing, but defer to goodness rather than to nobility. They surpass one another in mutual respect; and they bear each other's burdens, thus fulfilling the law of Christ.[75]

Yet, just as William had used these images to describe Bernard and his companions at Châtillon *before* they entered Cîteaux, so the Templars' communal life taught the men the virtues necessary to live in concord but did not make them monks. Instead, Bernard's praise for the Templars illustrates the importance the Cistercians placed on a communal life as the best way for a person of any order to progress toward salvation. Like the Cistercians' model bishops, who lived with companions in order to develop further the virtues they needed to administer their office, so the Templars lived communally to maintain the virtues necessary for knights whose primary role was to defend the Holy Land and the pilgrims there. A person could not live concurrently as a monk and a bishop or a monk and a knight: the duties and obligations of these orders conflicted. But whether monk, bishop, or knight, a person could live in a community with others and, through such a life, learn the virtues of humility and charity that were essential for the salvation of every Christian.

Much of Bernard's *De laude novae militiae* provides a spiritual geography of the Holy Land. Bernard moved his reader through the places of Jesus' life and death, giving brief meditations on the feelings and lessons he imagined such places evoking. This itinerary paralleled the process of spiritual development and redemption that formed part of the crusading ideology, but it also further demonstrated the Cistercians' separation of monastic and lay sanctity, for its emphasis differed from that in works composed primarily for a Cistercian audience.[76] When Bernard and other Cistercians preached to their monks, they made the Incarnation and the Crucifixion the central events of their monastic theology—the one symbolized the humanity of Christ, the other Christ's great love for mankind. Bernard's imagined trip though the Holy Land, however, did not elicit the meditations on Jesus' humanity and loving sacrifice that can be found in myriad Cistercian sermons and treatises. Rather than emphasize Bethlehem and Calvary, Bernard concentrated on the Holy Sepulchre and discussed divine judgment and mercy, death and resurrection. He explained that people seemed more drawn to the place where Jesus' body lay than the places where he had lived and were more moved by remembrance of his death than his life. "I think that his life seems harsher whereas his death seems sweeter," he wrote, "and that the quiet of his rest soothes human weakness more than the effort of actions, the security of his death more than the rectitude of his life."[77] Cistercian monks, who did not need to go on crusade because they bore an inner cross on their hearts, had the strength to model their life on the life of Jesus and follow the difficult path it demanded, but crusaders, pilgrims, and even the Knights Templar followed the easier path marked by the hope offered by Jesus' death rather than the demands of his life. As Geoffrey of Auxerre and Gilbert of Hoyland both insisted in their description of the streets and squares that made up the Church, both paths led to salvation, but one was narrow and strict and the other broad and level. Secular life might offer opportunities for spiritual progress and salvation, but the path of greatest merit still lay in the monastery.

The Cistercians seldom addressed the laity in general but focused what interest they had in lay people on knights and lords. In an ideal world, they expected the secular clergy to care for the laity's salvation and the secular lords to provide for the laity's protection; as monks, they offered to these prelates and princes models of ideal behavior so that these men would properly exercise their authority, care for the spiritual and temporal well-being of their subjects, and unite all Christians into a unified Church.[78] The threat to the unity of the Church posed by the Cathar heresy in southern France, however, appears to have inspired some Cistercians to provide religious instruction to lay men and women, for there is extant a sermon delivered in Provençal by an abbot of Cîteaux to a congregation in the church of Saint Firmin in Montpellier.[79] The audience of the sermon was composed not of Cathars but of people whom the abbot hoped to keep from heresy; although he warned about heretical ideas, the bulk of the sermon consisted of the abbot's views about lay behavior. It repeated the same theme the Cistercians presented to bishops, princes, and knights: that the reformation of the soul would restore the unity of the Church.

The abbot called on his audience to arise from sleep, from death, and from sin, especially from pride, ignorance, and love of the flesh. "We rise in the morning," he said, "to care for the things of our household. For humans, such household things are our thoughts and our wills. We ought to rise to set this household and our actions in order, to order our thoughts so as to think good things, to order our wills to desire good things, and to order our actions to do good things."⁸⁰ He stressed inner reformation again later in the sermon when he called on his audience to censor the thoughts that drew their souls toward evil, the desires that drew their souls to sin, and the actions that drew their souls toward earthly delights. In a passage echoing the Benedictine Rule's description of the conversion of monks, he told his audience to leave off the old man and put on the new, although here the process of renewal occurred not through conversion to monastic life but through the sacrament of penance. Through penance, the abbot explained, people scrutinized the corners of their conscience for sins, cleansed the mind of all ugliness, and decorated it with virtues.⁸¹ In general, he told his audience, they should approach the divine through prayers, fasting, vigils, and almsgiving, through good works and the sacraments.⁸²

Just as Bernard's treatise on the Templars suggested that the laity found Jesus' death more comforting than the model of his life, so this later abbot stressed the hope of redemption offered by Jesus' sacrifice more than he emphasized the example offered by Jesus' life. In fact, some Cistercians looked with suspicion on lay people who tried to follow the difficult path that the example of Jesus' life had established for monks, and they considered the preachers and their followers who sought an apostolic life to be hypocrites and heretics.⁸³ Such a distinction between a monastic emphasis on Jesus' life and a lay concentration on his passion and redemptive sacrifice was especially important in the context of combating Cathar ideas, for had the abbot recommended that the laity model their life on the life of Jesus or the apostles, he would have advocated a life similar to that of the Cathar *perfecti*. By stressing the Passion, the abbot instead emphasized a central element of orthodox Christianity that the Cathars had rejected. He thus told his audience to use its God-given reason to judge between what was good and evil, light and dark, and true and false, and called on it to abandon foreign gods, by which he meant heretics, who showed their enmity to the cross by contradicting Christ's incarnation, denying his passion, and holding his cross in contempt. The audience ought to rise to Christ by considering Christ's passion— the sag of his head, the extension of his arms, the nails in his hands and feet, the wound in his side—all of which made it possible for humans to enter the kingdom of heaven.⁸⁴ The abbot ended his sermon by warning about damnation and again advocating penance, obedience, and humility, which, he reiterated, provided a secure path to "the kingdom where Christ is king and his mother queen, where the angels are knights and the saints citizens."[85]

The Cistercians' teachings for the laity thus incorporated many of the same themes as were found in their advice to the social groups whose welfare generally interested them more. They believed that the Church, as the bride of Christ, could be unified only if individual Christians sought to unite themselves with God through a process of inner reformation that turned their desires away from things of the world and toward the divine. For the laity, such a process led to the sacrament of penance, the performance of good works, and a concentration on the salvific force of Jesus' death and passion. For warriors, such a process required fighting for a cause sanctioned by the Church. For people with authority, whether religious or secular, such a process entailed learning to balance one's own needs with the needs of others. Although the Cistercians focused most of their attention on ecclesiastical leaders who were responsible for the spiritual well-being of their flock, they also advised secular leaders so they would provide the peace and security that allowed people to concentrate on their spiritual condition. In each case, the monks followed the picture of an ideal *rector* presented by Gregory the Great: they insisted that proper rule required the proper motivation to rule, and that leaders could not properly administer their offices and aid the reformation of others unless they first reformed themselves. This involvement in encouraging the reform of both ecclesiastical and secular authorities stemmed, ironically, from the monks' desire to avoid worldly entanglements. If neither prelates nor princes sought to increase their power at the expense of others but instead concentrated on their appointed duties, then monks could live in peace at the center of a united Church.

Unfortunately for the Cistercians, not all prelates and princes possessed such virtues, and even the actions of those whom the Cistercians advised did not always receive the monks' approval. The Cistercians watched the increasing centralization of papal and secular governments and the increasing focus on law and jurisdiction as instruments of political control, and although they opposed neither centralization nor the exercise of justice, their assumptions differed from the lawyers and schoolmen who aided these developments. They were interested not in the definition and expansion of juridical powers but in the exercise of these powers, and they advocated a balance between justice and mercy that depended on the personal virtues of the ruler rather than on more absolute notions of right and wrong.[86] As a result, they viewed with suspicion both papal and secular efforts to extend and centralize their jurisdiction and, through their letters and treatises, sought to encourage leaders to quell their ambitions and focus instead on their spiritual well-being. But such advice could not prevent major conflicts within Christendom, and the Cistercians found that they had to work still more actively for the unity of the Church in order to repair the splits and tears caused by those leaders who ignored the virtues that would have made their rule a ministry, and who desired to dominate instead.

Chapter 8

Repairing a Divided Church

~~~~~

The Cistercians' image of a peaceful and united Church relied on virtuous leaders to provide the spiritual direction that aided Christians in their progress toward the divine. The monks offered advice and created models to demonstrate how secular and ecclesiastical leaders were to exercise their authority, but they also recognized that neither prelates nor princes necessarily possessed the virtues that they advocated. Nor, of course, was twelfth-century society united and peaceful. New monastic groups quarreled over interpretations of the Benedictine Rule, regular canons challenged monastic definitions of the apostolic life, prelates disputed with religious dissenters over interpretations of the Bible, scholars argued among themselves over the proper balance between reason and authority, bishops clashed with townspeople over the establishment of local liberties, kings contended with bishops over the boundaries of their legal authority, and popes fought with emperors over the relation of *imperium* and *sacerdotium*. Not only did Christian society fall far short of heavenly perfection and divine harmony, but the contentiousness of society seemed to demonstrate that neither prelates nor princes could ever unite society in a common movement toward the divine. Until the unlikely event that these leaders learned to exercise their authority virtuously to prevent disputes and schisms, the Cistercians encouraged members of their own order to take a more active role in promoting social reform and uniting Christendom.

Most of the Cistercians' activities outside their monasteries involved mediating disputes and encouraging reform. The schisms that elicited the Cistercians' greatest concerns were those caused by disputed papal and episcopal elections, and those caused by heresy and religious dissent. The Cistercians' response to these divisions stemmed from their vision of a Church linked by caritas, for they argued that the actions of corrupt officials caused such problems, and they relied on character, personality, and personal connections rather than on legal considerations to determine the merits of a case. As long as the Cistercian order and its friends held similar opinions about a schism or dispute, the monks could describe their position as that of the entire Church, summon their opponents to abandon their apparently isolated positions, and welcome them back into Christian unity as men of virtue if they did so. This process worked during the papal schism of the 1130's and in some contested episcopal elections thereafter, but it became less effective as disputes became increasingly based on legal principles and disputants became less willing to compromise. Meanwhile, the Cistercians' networks had spread across Europe, and the monks had developed good relations with people who later opposed one another. By the 1160's, the new papal schism and the Becket controversy demonstrated that the Cistercians could themselves be divided by the conflicts they had hoped to heal.

The attitude of these active and articulate Cistercians toward the institutional Church is a reminder that the creation of abstract institutions in a society long accustomed to face-to-face relations was neither a smooth nor a rapid development. Throughout the twelfth century, people experimented with ways to understand the links between individuals who were separated by distance and perhaps even unknown to one another, and they did not immediately embrace abstract legal definitions of group affiliations. The conception of Christian society formulated by these twelfth-century Cistercians provides one example of an intermediate position. The monks used their idea of caritas to link distant individuals and groups: caritas united not only the disparate abbeys in their order and in the larger monastic world but also the Church and all of Christendom. But the Cistercians' idea of caritas still ultimately depended on assumptions drawn from a face-to-face society and reflected their attempt to extend the relations they had developed in small communities to the world around them. Even as ecclesiastical officials began to define procedures and laws to determine the merits of a case, these Cistercians continued to rely more on personal connections than on abstract principles and arguments; as we will see, such a position gradually became less effective as the disputants became less open to compromise.

I

The Cistercian order was founded as the upheavals of the papal reform movement subsided and the popes and their allies began to create an ecclesiastical institution bound together by rational and legal principles. The papal reformers had based their claims for clerical superiority on the priesthood's sacramental monopoly, and by investigating precedents and church canons, they started to create a hierarchically organized institution that linked local churches to their bishops and bishops to the papacy through a system of legal and financial obligations.[1] One of the issues that twelfth-century monks had to resolve was their relation to this new institutional church; if priests controlled the primary access to salvation, what was the role for monks?

The Cistercians accepted the idea that the secular clergy, with their monopoly over the sacraments, were responsible for the salvation of the laity. As we have seen, they neither challenged the jurisdiction of their bishops nor insisted that their prayers offered the central means for their society's salvation; they assumed that it was the role of the prelates to lead Christian society and hoped to concentrate on their own salvation instead. At the same time, however, they could not ignore the condition of the society around them. Their monasteries were part of the larger Church, their order's unity depended on the unity of Christian society as a whole, and the caritas that linked them with their brothers and with the divine was the same caritas that united the Church with Christ. Although the sacramental hierarchy of the institutional church did not constitute the entire Church, the Cistercians saw these men as its leaders; if their institution could not exist in a unified and harmonious state on earth, how could the rest of Christendom be united?

The schism of 1130 demonstrates the difficulty twelfth-century thinkers had in defining a new, abstract ecclesiological theory that would provide legal support for the already established papal government and resolve the new problems caused when popes and cardinals explored their powers. Recent interpretations of the schism suggest that it resulted from a division in the curia between older Roman cardinals who wished to continue the Gregorian fight for papal supremacy and more recently appointed cardinals, led by the papal chancellor Haimeric, who were allied with northern monastic groups and were more interested in moral reform.[2] In 1124, Haimeric and his supporters had been able to install their candidate as Pope Honorius II, but only with the help of their military allies, the Frangipani; in January 1130, at Honorius's death, they still did not fully dominate the curia. They tried to compensate for their lack of an outright majority by keeping Honorius's death a secret and holding an election for a new pope before their rivals could organize. This ruse resulted instead in a divided curia, two rival elections, and two consecrated popes: Haimeric's candidate, Innocent II, and the candidate of the older faction, Anacletus II, from the family of the Pierleoni. Both popes asked European rulers for support; Innocent II, threatened by the greater military strength of the Pierleoni, left Rome for Pisa and then for France.

It may be possible in retrospect to examine the legal positions of the two popes and determine the relative validity of their claims, but even modern historians have reached opposing conclusions.[3] In the 1130's, the canonical principles that determined the legitimacy of a pope's selection were still imprecise enough to allow two men to claim concurrently that their elections and consecrations had been valid. The people who tried to move beyond this impasse relied more on diplomacy, character, and consensus than they did on legal precedents.[4] Both sides claimed that they were supported by a united Christendom, implying that their opponent was a schismatic outside the Church. Those supporting Anacletus stressed the unanimity of the people of Rome in acclaiming his election, the harmony of the officials administering Rome, and his acceptance by the Sicilians and the entire Church in the east; those supporting Innocent II emphasized the unanimous support of the "catholic" cardinals, the patriarchs in the Holy Land, and the kings and prelates of France, England, and Germany. Both sides' assertions that they were supported by a universal consensus were exaggerated, but in their diplomatic efforts to create this consensus, both sides used synods and general councils to demonstrate this support. Eventually, the precedents set by these practical appeals to synodal judgment became incorporated into fourteenth-century conciliar ideas and political doctrines of assent.[5]

In its lack of certain precedent and legal guidelines, the schism of 1130 demonstrates a central characteristic of the first half of the twelfth century: that, in the words of Karl Morrison, "It was an age brave, or desperate, enough to pose questions that were beyond its power to answer."[6] In such an environment, the Cistercians' image of a Church bound by *caritas* rather than canon law flourished, for it provided a means of both understanding the schism and resolving it. In 1130, Bernard of Clairvaux had not fully articulated his ideas about the relationship of individual moral character and the unity of the Church. But the schism gave him the opportunity to act intuitively on ideas that he and others were later to express more clearly, and his success in helping to resolve the dispute gave him confidence that his vision of Christian society was right.

Innocent's initial supporters in northern France developed out of the connections that Cardinal Haimeric and the papal legate Matthew of Albano had made during a series of ecclesiastical councils in 1128 and 1129. These men included many in Bernard of Clairvaux's web of associates: the archbishop Rainald of Rheims, the bishops Geoffrey of Chartres, Jocelin of Soissons, Stephen of Paris, and Bartholomew of Laon, and the abbots Alvisus of Anchin, Suger of Saint-Denis, Peter the Venerable, and Norbert of Xanten.[7] The Cistercians had established ties with Haimeric by 1126, and at the start of the schism they were predisposed toward Innocent II.[8] Bernard of Clairvaux became one of Innocent's most effective supporters, but despite the picture in the *Vita prima* of Bernard single-handedly working for Innocent's success, Bernard acted as a part of a group of like-minded bishops and abbots. In the late summer of 1130, Bernard joined a large assembly of archbishops, bishops, and abbots at Etampes, where Louis VI agreed to support Innocent, and when he met Henry I of England to elicit this monarch's support, he worked with a familiar group composed of the allies of Haimeric and Innocent, including Suger of Saint-Denis and Geoffrey of Chartres.[9] In Germany, it was Norbert of Xanten, the founder of Premontré and, by 1130, the archbishop of Magdeburg, who solicited Emperor Lothair's initial support for Innocent. Bernard later joined Norbert and other German prelates at Liège in 1131 to negotiate with the emperor about the conditions of his allegiance.[10] In the late fall of 1131, the men most responsible for soliciting Innocent's northern support gathered in council at Rheims; there Innocent received letters of support from the rulers of western Europe. Norbert of Xanten presented a letter from Lothair; Hugh of Rouen, a letter from Henry I; bishops from Spain, letters from the kings of Aragon and Castille; and Hugh of Pontigny, a letter from the Carthusians that was read to the council by Geoffrey, bishop of Chartres.[11] The presence of Hugh of Pontigny at Rheims demonstrates that Bernard was not the only Cistercian supporting Innocent II. Stephen Harding may have been present as well, for while at Rheims, Innocent asked Stephen to mediate in a dispute between the Burgundian religious communities of Saint Stephen and Saint-Seine.[12]

Bernard remained one in a group of men around Innocent, and his travels on Innocent's behalf usually involved Innocent's other allies as well. In the spring of 1131, and again in 1134, Bernard traveled to southern France to negotiate with Count William X of Poitiers, the first time with bishop Jocelin of Soissons, the second time with bishop Geoffrey of Chartres.[13] Between 1132 and 1138, Bernard also made three trips to Italy to assist the pope in negotiating with Italian cities and, eventually, with Roger of Sicily. Again he traveled with friends. When Bernard accompanied Innocent into Rome in 1133, Norbert of Xanten was present as well; when Bernard returned to Italy in 1135 to attend a council at Pisa, he was joined by the archbishops and bishops of Sens, Chartres, Arras, and Bourges as well as the abbots of Cluny and Vézelay.[14] After the council, Bernard, Geoffrey of Chartres, and two cardinals traveled to Milan to settle disturbances in the church there. Only when Bernard traveled to Italy in 1136 to try to convince both the prominent Roman families and Roger of Sicily to abandon Anacletus did he travel without the company of his episcopal friends.[15] But even then he had the companionship of monks from Clairvaux, including his brother Gerard and the Baldwin who had recently become cardinal.[16] By working in such groups, Bernard was able to maintain a community around him that resembled the larger community of his brothers back at Clairvaux.

Bernard of Clairvaux was not Innocent's most virulent propagandist, nor was he the only one of Innocent's supporters to argue that the disputed election be judged more on merit than on legal issues, but his letters and travels and the utter conviction with which he argued made this position the dominant and, ultimately, the victorious one.[17] In fact, Bernard is so associated with the argument for Innocent's personal worthiness that he is often given credit for introducing it as a criterion for Innocent's legitimacy, even though others had made this argument before Bernard entered the discussion at Etampes.[18] Bernard did discuss the legality of Innocent's elections, but that was not his central concern.[19] In fact, he was not always consistent in his legal arguments. He asserted that the priority of Innocent's election made it valid, for instance, but he argued against the election of Philip as archbishop of Tours in 1133, even though Philip had been elected prior to the other candidate.[20] Bernard's support for Innocent was based primarily on character, both Innocent's own and that of those who elected him. As Bernard told Archbishop Hildebert of Tours, "The choice of the better part, the approval of the majority, and what is even more efficacious, the witness of his good character, recommend Innocent to all and confirm him as pontiff."[21] Bernard's letter to Geoffrey of Loreto made a similar point; Innocent's "reputation is found to be more distinguished and his election more sound, and he prevailed in both the numbers and the merits of his electors."[22] Even when Bernard described Innocent's election as "a purer promotion, with more credible reasons, and first in time," he justified this not by canonical precedent but by the "virtues and dignity of the electors."[23]

At the core of Bernard's position was his concern for the unity of the Church. He explained his own actions and travels on behalf of Innocent as necessary efforts to preserve ecclesiastical unity, and he called on others to become active when this unity was threatened.[24] The rhetoric of his letters made it appear as if a unified Church backed Innocent while a small number of dissidents tried to rip this unity apart. Even his arguments about the priority of Innocent's election served this purpose, for he presented Anacletus's election as dividing a Church that had already united around Innocent. Repeatedly, Bernard listed numerous people who recognized Innocent. "The Kings of Germany, France, England, Scotland, Spain, and Jerusalem, with all their clergy and people, support and cling to the lord Innocent, as sons to their father, limbs to their head, and they diligently preserve unity in the bond of peace," Bernard told master Geoffrey of Loreto. "He is rejected by his city but accepted by the world," he told Hildebert of Tours.[25] Once Bernard had framed the issue in terms of Church unity, the dispute became part of a larger cosmic battle between good and evil; Anacletus and his supporters, as the Antichrist and his servants, tore open the side of Christ and displayed the pride, ambition, and desire for dominion that Cistercian authors presented as the root of all evils.[26]

Recent scholarship has suggested that neither Anacletus, nor his ally Gerard of Angoulême, nor the cardinals who supported him, were actually any more ambitious or sinful than Innocent and his supporters. Nor is it any longer certain that Haimeric and Innocent fully embraced the program of moral reform advocated by their monastic allies.[27] But Bernard's argument started with different assumptions than those of the modern historians who have analyzed the schism politically and legally.

Because the schism disrupted the unity of the Church, it was part of Satan's ongoing efforts to disrupt human salvation; because Anacletus and his allies threatened the Church, their characters had to be evil. Their evil characters then further reinforced the argument made by Innocent's allies, that Innocent was the valid pope because of his good character.

Despite Bernard's exaggerated rhetoric, false claims, and circular logic, his argument about character and consensus was not just part of a propaganda campaign nor merely evidence of the paucity of canonical precedents for Innocent's position. Bernard's stance was consistent with a Cistercian conception of Church unity in which caritas rather than legal principles bound the institution together. Bernard's actions and comments during the schism of 1130 parallel his later expressions about the relation of virtue to the unity of the Church. Whether he acted on ideas he had developed but not yet fully articulated, or whether his later writings were influenced by his position during the schism, is impossible to determine. In either case, his argument about Innocent's moral character is inseparable from Cistercian ideas about ecclesiastical unity and virtuous authority. Bernard's letters implied that the caritas uniting the Church also linked consensus with good character: Innocent's character ensured that he had the support of virtuous men united by caritas, and the support of virtuous men demonstrated that Innocent's character must be good and united to them in caritas.

The circularity of the argument did not bother Bernard. That the two propositions reinforced one another only further demonstrated their truth. But this argument showed how the Cistercians' ideas about caritas and moral character intersected with their reliance on an established web of friends and connections. In fact, the backing Innocent received from men Bernard knew and trusted reinforced or perhaps even created Bernard's belief in Innocent's personal worthiness. He himself explained his support for Innocent in these terms. In his letter to the bishops of Aquitaine, he first listed the archbishops and bishops who had already recognized Innocent as pope and then claimed, "the special renown of these men, the excellence of their sanctity, and their authority respected even by their enemies easily persuaded us, who hold a lesser position in both merits and office, to follow them whether right or wrong."[28] Although there may be some false modesty in this statement, many on the list did recognize Innocent before Bernard appeared at the council of Etampes in May, and they may well have influenced Bernard's position.[29] Once Bernard's mind was made up, however, he put his considerable rhetorical and diplomatic talents to work and joined his ecclesiastical friends on Innocent's behalf.

Bernard's activities further reinforced his belief that the Church could be united by the consensus of men of good character. In his travels, he further expanded the Cistercians' network of friends and helped to create a web of Cistercian abbeys across Europe; these friends and abbeys then united in Innocent's support.[30] He established some of these abbeys in territories whose leaders had originally supported Anacletus; William of Aquitaine, Roger of Sicily, and the people of Milan all founded Cistercian houses after they recognized Innocent as pope.[31] The foundations signified that these schismatics had rejoined the Church and seemed to further the possibility of a united Christendom.

The Cistercians' involvement in contested episcopal elections followed a pattern similar to Bernard's actions during the papal schism. Most of the evidence for the monks' attitudes and activities again comes from Bernard of Clairvaux, but Bernard continued to rely on his friends and connections to channel news to Clairvaux and to offer advice, particularly about cases in which he did not know the facts firsthand. Much information must have come from abbots of affiliated monasteries because nearly all the episcopal elections in which Bernard intervened were in dioceses in which the Cistercians had already established an abbey.[32] As with the schism, Bernard judged these disputes primarily on the character, or reputed character, of the claimants, and he again blackened the reputations of his opponents, claiming that they destroyed Church unity. Even when he also mentioned legal issues, his central concern was character. He criticized the episcopal election at Langres, for instance, because it occurred without heeding the mandate of the pope to take Bernard's advice and the advice of other religious men into consideration; he criticized the election at York as having been made under coercion from the king's men. In both cases, the disputants ultimately appealed to the pope. Nonetheless, Bernard's primary objection to both episcopal candidates was character. He had refused to become involved in the Langres election unless the electors "intended to elect a good and suitable person," and he initially criticized the man who was elected as someone "of whom I wished we had heard better and more honorable things."[33] His language soon became more vehement, and his imagery emphasized the damage done to the Church, both by the candidate himself and by those supporting him. "O kindly mother church of Lyons!" he mourned in a letter to the dean and treasurer of the cathedral at Lyons. "You have chosen a monster and not a groom for your daughter."[34] This bishop-elect was a man "whom the good dread and the evil ridicule," he told the papal curia; and he accused the bishop's supporters—the archbishop of Lyons, the bishops of Autun and Mâcon, and even Peter the Venerable of Cluny—of using their wealth and power to attack the rock of the Church.[35]

In the election at Langres, Bernard may have had direct contact with the bishop-elect, but in other elections he relied on information passed to him by his friends and fellow Cistercians. When William Fitzherbert was elected archbishop of York in 1140, Bernard depended on the Cistercians at Fountains and Rievaulx. He told Innocent II, "According to the witness of truthful men, we detect that he [William] is rotten from the soles of his feet to the crown of his head."[36] Repeatedly, he emphasized the religious character of the men opposing William, describing the Cistercians who had traveled to Rome to object to the election as "simple, upright, and God-fearing men, who have undertaken the hard labor of their journey for God's cause and not their own," and he blackened the character of William and his supporters, suggesting that William desired power and wealth and that his patron, Henry of Winchester, was a Philistine.[37] Bernard's attitude toward other episcopal elections also depended on the character of the bishop-elect as reported by men Bernard knew and trusted. When the church of Valence elected a new bishop after the death of the Cistercian bishop, John, Bernard approved of their choice because he trusted the character of the electors.[38] And soon after the monastery of Belloc in the diocese of Rodez became affiliated with Clairvaux, Bernard objected to the character of the new bishop-elect of Rodez and told the pope that he had heard evil things about this man, "according to truthful men."[39]

Bernard's activities demonstrate the way the Cistercians' emphasis on good character and their use of networks of affiliated abbeys and sympathetic churchmen comprised part of their conception of the Church. They understood and supported the idea of a single, hierarchically organized institutional church with a pope who had the authority to repair the problems beneath him, and they even recognized that much of the pope's authority stemmed from his ability to judge the legal merits of a case. They also recognized that the Church was an abstract institution that bound together strangers spread across Europe. However, by stressing the bonds of caritas rather than law and definitions, their idea of the Church still depended on assumptions drawn from a smaller, face-to-face society. They based their decisions on issues of character that could only be determined by knowing the persons in question; and when they did not know a person themselves, they relied on the opinions of their friends. They made two fundamental assumptions: first, that all people of good character were united by caritas and would reach the same divinely sanctioned position on an issue; and second, that all of the people with whom the monks had developed close contacts were people of good character. This mirage seemed real during the 1130's, when most of the Cistercians' connections were Innocent's advocates or people who had abandoned their support for Anacletus, but it began to fade even as the schism ended and Bernard stopped in Lyons to discuss the Langres election on his way north from Rome. But although the Langres election and other ecclesiastical disputes did not always create a consensus among all the people who had supported Innocent II, enough of a core remained that Bernard's emphasis on character and connections could still create the semblance of a united Church. The illusory nature of this Church united in caritas became clear only after Bernard's death, during the schism and disputes of the 1160's.

II

The papal schism of 1159 and the controversy between Thomas Becket and Henry II changed the Cistercians' political landscape. Their pattern of supporting one another and working with a network of allied ecclesiastics continued after the death of Bernard in 1153, for the Cistercian abbots and bishops of the 1150's and 1160's were still linked by the friendships that they had developed in their cloisters over the previous two decades.[40] In the disputes of the 1160's, however, the Cistercians could no longer rely on the unity of their ecclesiastical friends and secular patrons. They had long-standing connections with Roland Bandinelli, who became Pope Alexander III in 1159, but they had also developed good relations with Emperor Frederick Barbarossa; they were sympathetic to Thomas Becket but had long-standing ties with King Henry II. These disputes not only fractured the Cistercians' network of connections but also brought to the fore ideas about the organization of society that differed from the monks' picture of a united Christendom. In both cases, the disputes concerned issues of jurisdiction, and in both cases, the monks' sense that justice depended less on absolute definitions of right than on character and virtue conflicted with the antagonists' interest in clear-cut definitions and solutions.

If the schism of 1130 raised issues about synodal authority that were only resolved with the development of conciliar ideas in the fourteenth century, the schism of 1159 reopened questions about the right relation of *regnum* and sacerdotium that were central to eleventh- and twelfth-century social theory. As Frederick Barbarossa tried to restore the glory of his empire, he developed an interest in Roman law and asserted what he considered to be his imperial rights in Italy. He cooperated with popes Eugenius III, Anastasius IV, and Hadrian IV in suppressing the Roman commune, but his relationship with the papacy soured after the council of Besançon in 1157. There Roland, then papal chancellor, seemed to suggest that the emperor held his crown as a fief (*beneficium*) from the pope, and Frederick and his allied bishops responded with a claim that the imperial position derived, not from the pope, but from election by the German princes. Frederick's unwillingness to help the pope against the Sicilian Normans, his assertion of financial and political rights in northern Italy, and his demand for homage from Italian bishops and the payment of taxes in territory controlled by the pope all further strained imperial-papal relations. Tensions between pro- and anti-imperial factions emerged in the papal curia, and at the death of Hadrian IV in September 1159, the rival groups elected two popes: one the imperial ally Victor IV, the other the former papal chancellor, who took the name Alexander III. Frederick Barbarossa responded to the schism by claiming that his position as advocate of the Roman Church gave him the responsibility to summon a council to judge the election; Alexander III and his allies, in comparison, argued that the pope could be judged by no one. The schism, which endured eighteen years and outlasted the lives of both Victor IV and his successor Paschal III, thus touched on fundamental issues of papal-imperial relations, but it also became inevitably intertwined with the complicated rivalries and alliances current in both Italian and northern European politics.[41]

The Cistercians recognized the legal issues raised by the schism, and they certainly understood the political rivalries underlying the schism because they spent much time negotiating for peace, first between Frederick and the northern Italian cities, and then between kings Henry II and Louis VII. Still, they did not discuss these disputes in legal or political terms but instead described them by using the familiar images of ecclesiastical unity and the familiar tactics of demonizing their opponents. Abbot Gilbert of Hoyland lamented that the emperor and his supporters had plucked out the locks of the bride and torn them to pieces, and he complained that Christians no longer heard the voice of the bride but only that of the emperor.[42] Similarly, Geoffrey of Auxerre, in a sermon given at the council of Tours in 1163, blamed the divisions in the Church not on disputes over ecclesiastical liberties but on the moral failings of the clergy. If only the clergy had developed a balance between their earthly administration and a contemplative life, "the Church would not today be cut asunder, nor would the tunic of Christ appear to be ripped."[43] In another sermon, inspired by a council of Frederick's ecclesiastical allies, Geoffrey lamented the "raving of a Teutonic growl" that compelled attendance at this evil assembly and bound "by detestable sacraments those whom he separated from the body of Christ, so that they would not return from him to unity"; he summoned his monks to wake their divine king with their prayers and to beg the Virgin Mary to intercede on their behalf.[44] The unanimity of the Cistercians' prayers, Geoffrey argued, would encourage God to destroy the evil councils of the schismatics and save the flock of Christians from the ravages of wolves and dragons. These sermons still articulated a vision of the Church based on consensus and character in which ecclesiastical unity stemmed from the virtuous exercise of power by both ecclesiastical and secular authorities.

Much of the Cistercians' support for Alexander III depended on personal connections.[45] Just as the Cistercians had developed close relations with the chancellor Haimeric in the disputed election of 1130, so they had developed ties with the papal chancellor Roland before his election as pope. Pope Eugenius III had made Roland a cardinal in 1150 and appointed him chancellor in the last year of his pontificate.[46] At least two Cistercian cardinals were in the curia at the time of Roland's election as pope: Henry, the titular priest of the church of Saints Nereus and Achilleus, was the former abbot of Trefontane and, like Roland, had been raised to his position by Eugenius III; and William, the titular deacon of Saint Peter-in-Chains, had become cardinal in 1158.[47] Both these men frequently served as delegates on behalf of their new pope.

One of the first letters Alexander III received as pope came from the Cistercian abbot Philip of L'Aumône. Philip praised Alexander's election using the language of friendship and unity:

My heart breathed in joy at your acceptance of the highest dignity, and a joyous serenity flowered in my spirit just like a crown of hope that is decorated in glory. Embracing your position with the arms of true love, I have shown a devoted thanksgiving for you with the generosity of a good spirit. A voice of praise has sounded in unison and we repeat a song to our God about your promotion, threatening 'Woe to the man through whom scandal comes!' (Matt. 18.7).[48]

Philip's actions reinforced his words, for he delivered letters on Alexander's behalf to Henry II of England and Louis VII of France and then worked for a peace treaty between the two kings.[49] Alexander also developed a close relationship with Louis VI's brother, the former Cistercian monk Henry, who by 1159 was bishop of Beauvais. Henry received two early letters from Alexander that deplored the division of the Church and spoke of his hope that Henry would aid his cause: "We are not unmindful of your own friendship from the past and that of your most beloved brothers; we sincerely love you with charity in the heart of Christ, and can willingly hear your requests with God."[50] After Henry became the archbishop of Rheims in 1162, he served as one of Alexander's strongest allies in France and, at times, used a network of Cistercian abbots and bishops as messengers and mediators.[51] Nearly one-quarter of the letters Alexander wrote before Henry's death in 1175 were addressed to Henry, asking him to investigate abuses, mediate disputes, and generally serve as a conduit for Alexander's wishes.[52]

These Cistercian ties to Alexander III did not preclude connections with Frederick Barbarossa. In fact, in the fall of 1159, the abbots of Cîteaux, Clairvaux, and Morimond, along with the Cistercian archbishop Peter of Tarentaise, were present at Frederick's court; they had arrived to negotiate a peace between the emperor and the city of Milan and participated in a council in early October at which Frederick asserted the right to judge the claims of the candidates for the papacy.[53] Adam, the Cistercian abbot of Eberbach, also appeared in the emperor's company in the fall of 1159.[54] It seems that there was sufficient Cistercian sympathy for Frederick that Alexander III worried that the order might support the imperial faction.[55] Concurrently, another group of Cistercians was aiding the peace negotiations between Louis VII and Henry II. Peter, bishop of Pavia and former abbot of the Cistercian abbey of Lucedio, went to France in September at the request of Louis VII to help forge a truce between Louis and Henry, and Philip of L'Aumône was sent north to Henry in October. The negotiations were successful and a truce between the two kings was signed in December.[56]

Alexander III used Cistercian mediators to try to draw all three monarchs to his side. In December 1159, he sent both Cistercian cardinals, William and Henry, along with a third cardinal, Otto of Saint Gregorio, to meet with Frederick; Cardinals Henry and Otto then went north with letters for Louis VII and Henry II in early 1160, where they probably met with Philip of L'Aumône. Cardinal William and the abbot of Clairvaux remained with Frederick and observed the council of Pavia in February 1160 before moving north across the Alps. At Pavia, Frederick's episcopal allies decided in favor of Victor IV, whom Frederick formally recognized; Alexander responded by excommunicating Frederick. By late spring in 1160, Alexander had a large group of Cistercians soliciting support for him in French and English territories: these included the two Cistercian cardinals, the bishop Henry of Beauvais, and the abbots Fastred of Clairvaux and Philip of L'Aumône. It is possible that abbots Guichard of Pontigny and Aelred of Rievaulx also worked on Alexander's behalf, for the only privileges that Alexander issued for monasteries in 1160 were for their communities.[57] Aelred wrote a letter criticizing the bishops who had participated in the council of Pavia, and a chronicler from Peterborough later attributed Henry II's allegiance to Alexander to Aelred's influence.[58] This Cistercian activity bore fruit; in July of 1160, the French and English kings met in Beauvais and agreed to recognize Alexander.[59] In September the Cistercian order formally pledged their support for Alexander, and in October Louis and Henry met at Toulouse with the bishops from their realms and, after an examination of the elections, again declared their support for Alexander.[60]

Neither Henry II nor Louis VII remained strongly committed to Alexander. Not only were the two kings rivals with one another, but both also used the threat of an alliance with the emperor to win concessions from the pope. In 1162, Louis entered into negotiations with Frederick; Alexander used his Cistercian connections to try to keep Louis's allegiance.[61] Aelred of Rievaulx, working with the bishops of Lisieux and Everux, helped to counteract Frederick's overtures to Henry II, and both monarchs met with Alexander in September, probably at Chouzy-sur-

Loire, where they planned a larger council to be held in Tours in May 1163.[62] That winter and spring, Cistercians continued their activities on Alexander's behalf. Henry, no longer bishop of Beauvais but archbishop of Rheims, and the abbots Philip of L'Aumône, Robert of Foigny, and Henry of Hautecombe carried messages for Alexander; the abbots of Cîteaux and Clairvaux met with Alexander in March 1163; and Geoffrey of Auxerre, then abbot of Clairvaux, attended the council at Tours.[63] Probably prior to the council, Abbot William of Morimond presented Alexander with letters from Duke Welf of Bavaria pledging Welf's fidelity.[64] At Tours, Alexander excommunicated Pope Victor and the imperial chancellor Rainald of Dassel, but he did not repeat his earlier excommunication of Frederick.

The council's relatively mild criticisms of Frederick reflected Alexander's hope that he might lure the emperor away from Victor.[65] After Tours, Alexander began to negotiate with Frederick, again with Cistercian help. In August 1163, two Cistercian bishops, Peter of Pavia and Henry of Troyes, were part of a papal delegation that tried to persuade the emperor to renounce Victor and join Alexander, but Frederick continued to insist that the dispute be submitted to arbitration.[66] Alexander sent a second delegation to Frederick a year later, this time consisting of Peter of Pavia and two cardinals, one of whom was the Cistercian William. Peter remained in Italy until after the death of Victor on April 20, 1164, when Frederick recalled Peter to him, possibly to discuss whether he would recognize Alexander or support a new pope.[67]

Although the French and English kings were often at loggerheads and did not always support Alexander with enthusiasm, there was seldom any real possibility that they would join the imperial camp. As a result, during the first four years of the schism, the Cistercians in French and English territories experienced little conflict between their activity on behalf of Alexander and their relations with their rulers. For Cistercian abbeys in the imperial territories, however, this sense of unity was impossible. The abbots of these communities had to reconcile their order's alliance with Alexander with Frederick's support of Victor. The position these abbots took demonstrates the importance of their local connections, for they responded less to Frederick's policies than to the positions of their diocesan bishops and, in some cases, to those of their counts.[68] In Italy, the Milanese abbey of Morimundo sided with the archbishop of Milan in Milan's long-standing dispute with Frederick and in June of 1160 was burned by imperial troops.[69] The Cistercian abbeys around Rome also suffered from the warfare in that territory. Most abbeys in Lombardy and the Papal States cultivated a position of neutrality, neither treating with imperial bishops nor supplying pro-Alexander propaganda until after 1167, when the episcopate of Italy began a gradual defection from Frederick's position. At that point, the Cistercian abbeys in the region began to establish relations with Alexander.[70]

A similar pattern appeared in imperial territory north of the Alps. Many Cistercian abbots remained quiet and continued to accept donations and privileges from imperial bishops and Frederick's secular allies, whereas a few actively supported Alexander, especially those abbots in the archdioceses of Salzburg and Tarentaise, where the metropolitan bishops also endorsed that pope. In general, the security of the Cistercian abbeys in imperial territory depended on their local bishops; in the few cases that Cistercians were expelled from their monasteries, the close relationship between the monks and the local bishop had collapsed. In Burgundy, for instance, once Abbot Guichard of Pontigny was elected archbishop of Lyons in 1165 and joined the Cistercian archbishop Peter of Tarentaise in boosting Alexander's position, many Burgundian bishops began to abandon the imperial side. Cistercian abbots in that region then also became more vocal in Alexander's support. The archbishop of Besançon, however, remained loyal to Frederick, and it is likely that the chronicle accounts of Cistercians expelled from Burgundy around 1166 referred to monks from that diocese.[71] Similarly, in 1165 Archbishop Conrad of Mainz refused to swear at the diet of Würzburg that he would not recognize Alexander, fled his diocese, and was replaced by an imperial archbishop; a Cistercian abbot, Eberhard of Eberbach, was left to choose not only between two popes but also between two archbishops. He sided with Conrad and left his community for refuge at Saint Anastasius near Rome. He was the only German Cistercian exiled for supporting Alexander, although his cause may have been as much that of his archbishop as that of his pope.[72]

Between 1165 and 1167, we find little Cistercian activity concerning the schism, perhaps because many active Cistercians were involved in the dispute between Henry II and Becket, perhaps because Frederick's military offensive against Rome left little room for negotiation, and perhaps because internal divisions within the order left little time for the monks to mediate. After taking Rome in 1167 only to watch his troops die of disease, Frederick seemed willing to negotiate with Alexander. The pope asked Abbot Alexander of Cîteaux, the prior of the Grand Chartreuse, and the Cistercian bishop Peter of Pavia to met with the emperor, but as Frederick's situation improved, he avoided this delegation and returned north.[73] In 1169, Alexander of Cîteaux again served as an intermediary between Frederick and Alexander III, this time accompanied by Abbot Pons of Clairvaux.[74] In the spring of 1171, Pons and his prior Gerard met again with Frederick to arrange a peace between him and Louis VII; subsequently, they met Alexander III, who was not enthusiastic about an agreement.[75]

The same year, tensions erupted again between Louis VII and Henry II as Louis encouraged prince Henry's rebellion against his father. The Cistercian archbishop Peter of Tarentaise led the attempts to end this war; by the summer of 1173, he, Alexander of Cîteaux, and Pons, now bishop of Clermont, worked to reconcile the two kings. The kings finally met on Ash Wednesday in 1174 at the Cistercian abbey of Montmer, where Peter placed ashes on the brows of both monarchs.[76] In 1175, representatives of both Frederick and Alexander met in the Cistercian abbey of Morimundo but fighting in Italy again broke out; after Frederick's defeat at Legnano in May 1176, the Cistercians Hugh of Bonnevaux and Bishop Pons were involved in the drawn-out negotiations between pope and emperor that ended in 1177 with the Peace of Venice.[77] According to both Alexander and Frederick, the responsibility for this peace lay primarily with the two Cistercians.[78]

That the Cistercian order as a whole was able to side with Alexander III while still allowing individual Cistercian abbots to retain ties with the emperor and his allies speaks to the nature of this dispute. Seldom did either antagonist force his supporters to take extreme positions; even the oath Frederick required at the diet of Würzburg asked people to reject Alexander but did not insist that they support the imperial candidate, Paschal III. Similarly, Alexander initially excommunicated Frederick after the council at Pavia, but did not declare him deposed, and at the council of Tours he repeated his excommunication of Victor and Frederick's chancellor but not of Frederick himself. As long as both sides continued to negotiate, the Cistercians' network of friends, bishops, and affiliated monasteries provided Alexander III with a great asset. Nonetheless, the political realities of the schism became increasingly difficult to reconcile with the Cistercians' image of the Church as a universal body that united

all virtuous Christians in caritas. Many of the monasteries in imperial territories still tried to preserve the sense of ecclesiastical unity that encompassed their order, the papacy, and their local episcopal and secular
connections: the abbey of Hautcrêt, for example, obtained from the
bishop of Lausanne the confirmation of a donation that was dated by the
year of the emperor's reign but witnessed by an Alexandrine legate, and
after the schism was resolved, a later bishop of Lausanne confirmed acts
that the monks had obtained from the schismatic archbishop of Besançon.[79]

The papal schism stretched thin the Cistercians' sense of Christian
unity and demonstrated its weaknesses. By the 1160's, the monks' networks crossed so many political rivalries that the cohesion of their order
began to tear. Their negotiations were most successful when they could
use their connections to work out a compromise and develop a consensus that reestablished ecclesiastical unity; they worked less well in
resolving disputes over legal definitions and jurisdiction. The schism of
1159 may have started as a juridical dispute over the right relation of
imperium and sacerdotium, but with the complicated politics of the
1160's, it became a conflict whose antagonists were open to compromise. As a result, the peace that the Cistercian prelates helped to work out
reinstituted a cooperation between pope and emperor, but the monks
achieved this only by ignoring the problems of defining the relation between imperial and papal authority in both the German church and
Italian territory.[80] When the Cistercians were confronted with a dispute
that remained focused on juridical issues, the disjuncture between their
vision of a Christian society united by consensus and good character
and the emerging view of a society bound by law caught the monks in
conflicts that they could neither resolve nor explain.

III

If the schism of 1159 suggested potential flaws in the Cistercians' social
vision, the controversy between Thomas Becket and Henry II and the
concurrent tension between Henry II and Louis VII made these flaws real.
The Cistercians' image of the Church was based on the possibility of concord among all Christians and was reinforced by the seeming agreement among the monasteries in their order, their bishops, and their
friends and supporters. The Becket conflict, however, disrupted this

unity, for it pitted the Cistercians' usual sympathy for episcopal rights against their friendly relations with Henry II, and it exacerbated the tensions between Henry II and Louis VII. Furthermore, both Henry II and Becket viewed their conflict in black-and-white terms that left little room for mediation and compromise. As a result, it became very difficult for the monks to maintain good relations with both sides, and for the first time the order could not present a unified position in the face of a divided Christian society.

In discussions of the Becket controversy, it is easy to forget that Becket's contemporaries did not consider him a saint until after his murder.[81] The Cistercians were not inevitably Becket's allies. They had developed close ties to Henry II, and most Cistercian monasteries in England were established in the north, especially in the archdiocese of York, whose metropolitan had long disputed with the archbishop of Canterbury. In the 1160's, two archbishops of York, Roger of Pont l'Evêche and Thomas, were among Becket's most vehement opponents. Furthermore, Becket's previous position as royal chancellor did not fit the Cistercians' idea of the proper background for a virtuous prelate.[82] Thus, although the Cistercians may have been sympathetic to Becket's defense of ecclesiastical liberties, many of them, like many English bishops and even Alexander III, appear less enamored of his character and methods.

Cistercian activity around the time of Becket's election in 1162 demonstrates their links with Henry II and some suspicions about Becket. The Cistercian cardinals Henry and William had been in contact with Henry II throughout much of 1161; they had provided a dispensation for young Henry to marry Margaret of France, and they had helped King Henry arrange the resignation of the archbishop of Dol. Cardinal Henry had baptized the princess Eleanor in September 1161 and assisted at the translation of the bodies of some dukes of Normandy in early 1162.[83] On his election, Becket solicited prayers from, among others, the monks at Rievaulx; Maurice of Rievaulx responded by telling Becket to correct the abuses in the English church and to reform his own character by renouncing worldly pomp and popularity. The tone of the letter became increasingly critical as it progressed; Maurice ended by advising Becket, "Knowing the will of your Lord, you should not resist his ordination but, mindful of his command, you should be content to enact those limits established by your forefathers."[84] Becket did not heed this advice.[85]

At the same time, there were Cistercians in 1163 who were concerned

about Henry II's interference in ecclesiastical matters and the attempts by
Bishop Gilbert Foliot of London and the monks of Canterbury to escape
the archbishop's jurisdiction. In the late summer of 1163, when Bishop
John of Poitiers wrote to Becket complaining about the king's infringe-
ment on Poitiers' liberties, he mentioned a letter carried by the abbot of
Pontigny on his behalf; he also remarked that he expected to have the support of the abbots of Clairvaux and Fossenova at the papal curia.[86] In the
fall, John again wrote Becket to inform him that Cardinal Henry and Abbot Philip of L'Aumône were working to elicit Gilbert Foliot's profession
of obedience to Canterbury and that the monks at Pontigny and Clairvaux had made commemorations for Becket in their prayers. That winter, Abbot Guichard of Pontigny went on a secret mission to the pope,
where he received help from Cardinal Henry in his attempt to bring
under Becket's control the monks of Saint Augustine's at Canterbury.[87]
In neither case, however, were the Cistercians in direct contact with
Becket. Instead, they worked through John of Poitiers and John of Salisbury, men whom they and their friends knew, and they became involved in issues that had long been among their concerns: a dislike of monastic exemptions and a desire to preserve the hierarchical organization
of the Church.

In the fall of 1163, when Henry and Becket first began to quarrel
about jurisdiction over criminous clerics, Pope Alexander approached the
conflict as one open to compromise and used Cistercians as his envoys.
In November, he sent Philip of L'Aumône to England to meet with the
English clergy and to advise Becket to work out a solution with Henry.
After the council at Clarendon, however, when Henry insisted that the
vague customs of the realm be written down and that the bishops swear
to uphold them, compromise became less possible. In June 1164, the
bishop of Poitiers reminded Becket that he had the support of the monks
at Pontigny and hinted that the abbey would offer him refuge if he was
forced from England.[88] Abbot Guichard of Pontigny, his successor Garin,
and abbots of monasteries affiliated with Pontigny, especially Isaac of Stella
and Urban of Cercamp, appear to have been Becket's strongest supporters among the Cistercians; Archbishop Henry of Rheims also may
have been an advocate for Becket, but his primary allegiance lay with his
brother Louis VII and, like Louis, he may have supported Becket to
embarrass Henry.[89] When Becket did leave England in the fall of 1164, he
went first to the Cistercian house of Clairmarais and by early in 1165

had settled at Pontigny, conveniently close to Alexander III's residence at Sens.

Becket's behavior at Pontigny probably did much to elicit Cistercian support. There he wore a Cistercian habit, spent time in meditation and prayer, and in general took on the role of the Cistercians' ideal monk-bishop.[90] Such behavior may well have given the Cistercians some hope that Becket would work for the good of the Church rather than his own glory, and that a compromise might still be possible. Many of the Cistercians' actions in early 1165 show a continued interest in facilitating negotiations; the Cistercian abbot of Velasse served as the pope's messenger to the empress Matilda, who then arranged a meeting between Louis VII, Alexander III, and Henry II. The rulers met at Gisors in Normandy in April 1165, with Becket positioned nearby at the Cistercian abbey of Notre-Dame-du-Val, but negotiations for Becket to meet Henry II came to naught.[91] Also that spring, probably in March, Cardinal William and Abbot Gilbert of Cîteaux, himself English, met with Henry II at Rouen. There Gilbert promised to preserve peace between Henry and the Cistercians by prohibiting English Cistercians from publicizing Becket's "acerbic" words and positions.[92] This meeting has been described as evidence of Gilbert's "double-dealing"—as demonstrating that Gilbert tried to placate Henry while accepting the benefits that Becket's presence at Pontigny gave to the order.[93] Yet, in the context of spring negotiations and the hope that Becket and Henry II might meet in April, such an agreement may well have stemmed from Gilbert's vain desire to remain on good terms with both antagonists and to support the basic premise of Becket's position, if not his tactics.[94]

For a year, Gilbert's position seemed tenable. At Pontigny, Becket put pressure on the English king by his humble and virtuous behavior, which won him more allies than his extreme pronouncements. By the spring of 1166, however, it became clear that negotiations not only were fruitless but also had trapped the mediators between two powerful and uncompromising men. Gilbert could not prevent monks sympathetic to Becket from working on his behalf. In a letter probably written in 1165 or 1166, Alexander III wrote the abbots of Cîteaux and Pontigny, asking that they not punish a brother who had carried messages for Becket into England; in May and June of 1166, Abbot Urban of Cercamp carried two letters from Becket to Henry II in which Becket set forth his ideas on the relationship between king and Church, warning Henry of divine wrath if he did not make peace on Becket's terms.[95] On June 12, Becket used his recently granted legatine powers to excommunicate his enemies in Henry's court and threatened to excommunicate Henry. In the midst of legal appeals and counterappeals, Henry struck back with the weapon closest at hand—the Cistercians. Perhaps as early as May, he had written Gilbert of Cîteaux, reminding him of his promise and threatening "to seek remedy for his injuries" if Gilbert did not control his monks; over the summer, he publicly threatened the English Cistercians with exile if Becket remained sheltered at Pontigny.[96] At the Cistercian Chapter General in September 1166, the Cistercians bowed to Henry's pressure and asked Becket to leave.[97] By November, Becket had moved to the Benedictine house of Sainte-Columbe at Sens.

The Becket controversy, and the accompanying political tensions between Henry II and Louis VII, divided the Cistercian order as had no previous political crisis. In late March 1165, soon after Gilbert returned from his meeting with Henry II, he received a letter from Alexander III asking him to accompany the Cistercian prelates Henry of Rheims and Alan of Auxerre to Clairvaux to convince Geoffrey of Auxerre to resign as abbot. Alexander explained this move in vague terms that had no relation to the Cistercians' statutory reasons for an abbot's removal: "Since the abbot has watched over the monastery, he has not received the favor and reverence in the eyes of kings and princes that his ancestors knew how to achieve, and not only has this monastery been dishonored, but the entire order has sustained no small inconvenience and harm from this."[98] Within a few days, it became clear that this delegation had met resistance. On April 1, Alexander called for a conference with Henry of Rheims, Cardinal Henry, and Godfrey, the former bishop of Langres, in order to prevent this affair from creating a great disturbance.[99] In late May, negotiations clearly continued, as Alexander refused Henry of Rheims's request to remove Cardinal Henry from the delegation.[100] According to some accounts, Geoffrey abdicated, or was deposed, that summer, but a letter written by John of Salisbury implies that he remained abbot until the following summer, perhaps until after the Chapter General in September 1166.[101]

The Cistercians' success in keeping this matter quiet has left modern historians to speculate about politics within the order. Some have followed a fifteenth-century account and suggested that Geoffrey was deposed because of his "reprehensible behavior."[102] This seems unlikely, especially considering Geoffrey's continued leadership in the order.[103] Another explanation connects Geoffrey's deposition to the Becket controversy, suggesting that he may have led an anti-Becket faction within the order, and that the pope therefore wished to remove him. His future activity on Henry's behalf is cited in support of this theory.[104] However, the theory does not explain why the attack was directed against Geoffrey and not Gilbert of Cîteaux, who had actually met with Henry in the spring of 1165. Nor is it clear why Alexander would start proceedings on such grounds at a time when he still hoped for results from a meeting between Becket and Henry and did not wholeheartedly support Becket himself. Furthermore, it was not until the summer of 1166 that the order confronted Henry's threats and had to decide whether to acquiesce to his demands.

A final explanation offers a variation on this theory. It suggests that the impetus for Geoffrey's removal came from Henry of Rheims, working for his brother Louis VII, rather than from the pope. Alexander mentioned in his letter that Clairvaux "had lost the favor of kings and princes," Henry of Rheims appears to have been more eager to depose Geoffrey than was Alexander, and Louis clearly enjoyed embarrassing his royal rival by supporting Becket at Pontigny. Geoffrey himself was English and had traveled to England in 1164 to meet with the English Cistercians and negotiate a possible association with the congregation at Sepringham; it is possible that his sympathy for Henry II may have clashed with a pro-Becket faction at Clairvaux that had developed under the influence of the former monk Henry of Rheims.[105] Becket's appearance at Clairvaux on Palm Sunday in 1169 while the new abbot Pons was absent in Germany further suggests that some monks there still had sympathy for Becket.[106] If such disagreements and factions existed within the abbey, they may well have given Henry of Rheims the excuse to force Geoffrey's removal and, once Henry II began to negotiate with Frederick Barbarossa in the summer of 1165, Alexander III must have found any Cistercian support for Henry II less acceptable.[107] Gilbert of Cîteaux probably had to acquiesce to Geoffrey's departure because, in many ways, it was an attack on him as well. The lack of solid evidence about the reason for Geoffrey's departure leaves all of these theories in the realm of speculation, but coupled with Becket's subsequent departure from Pontigny, it suggests that, for the first time, the order was seriously divided in its response to ecclesiastical politics.

Even after 1166, the Cistercian order still did not have to choose between a defense of the liberties of the Church on the one hand and an acceptance of royal control over ecclesiastical matters on the other. As the
positions of both the pope and the English bishops demonstrate, it was
possible to distance oneself from Becket without accepting Henry's
claims.[108] Instead, the Cistercians had to decide whether to defend
Becket or work for a negotiated settlement with Henry. In general, their
predisposition toward negotiation prevailed. Henry's threats and Becket's
departure from Pontigny did not end their involvement in the dispute,
but after 1166 most monks worked more closely with Henry and Alexander III than with the archbishop. Although this may look like an alliance with Henry and a capitulation to political pressure, it also suggests
that many Cistercians believed that Henry's gradual concessions demonstrated a willingness to negotiate. Becket, in comparison, may well have
found a principled exile more attractive than a settlement that would have
returned him to live among his enemies in England. His stance often
found little favor either with the pope or with those English ecclesiastics
interested in a functioning English church, and even allies such as Louis
VII and John of Salisbury found his intransigence frustrating. The Cistercians, like many other churchmen at the time, were caught in the
confusion caused by the politics of the Becket controversy. Certainly, their
continued relations with Henry II should not be seen, as some have argued, as a sign that the Cistercian order had abandoned its ideals in order to protect its material well-being.[109]

For over a year after Becket left Pontigny, Cardinal William was the
only Cistercian directly involved in negotiations between Henry II and
Becket. Alexander III appointed William and a second cardinal, Otto, as
papal legates in February 1167, but their attempts at arbitration came to
naught, in part because Becket believed that William was prejudiced
against him.[110] In 1168, the Cistercian abbots Philip of L'Aumône and
Leodegar of La Cour-Dieu negotiated with Becket on behalf of a former
clerk who had fallen from his favor, and in the winter of 1168–69, some
unnamed Cistercians carried messages from one of Becket's staunchest allies, Archbishop William of Sens, to Henry II. Henry claimed to want to
talk to these monks about papal peace proposals, but he remained an-
tagonistic toward Archbishop William and Louis VII.[111] In 1169, Becket
chose his appearance at Clairvaux on Palm Sunday as an opportunity to
excommunicate Gilbert Foliot and the bishop of Salisbury, but unlike his

actions at Vézelay in 1166, this action did not provoke retribution against the Cistercians. In fact, a number of English Cistercian abbots gave Gilbert Foliot testimonials in his appeal to the pope, again hinting at a division within the order.[112] In August, the Cistercian abbots of Montmer, Beaubec, and Rievaulx, along with Geoffrey of Auxerre, attended a council to advise Henry II on how to make peace with Becket, and in early 1170, Geoffrey of Auxerre and Abbot Alexander of Cîteaux were part of a delegation that invited Becket to meet with Henry in Normandy.[113] Again, these negotiations proved fruitless; rather than meet Becket, Henry left Normandy for England, and Becket complained that he had been deceived by the king and by the Cistercian intermediaries.[114]

What made a settlement between these men so difficult is that both seem to have recognized the legal implications of the seemingly trivial phrases and actions that would have smoothed a compromise. Becket insisted on qualifying any statement about the relation of archbishop to king with the phrases *salvo honore dei* and *salvo ordine suo*, whereas Henry sabotaged one potential peace agreement by refusing to give Becket the kiss of peace.[115] Perhaps it was their recognition of the impossibility of ever finding a solution, coupled with the pressure placed on Becket by young Henry's coronation by the archbishop of York, that enabled the two men to be reconciled in July of 1170 without any discussion of the issues about which they had fought for so long. However, once back in England, Becket continued his uncompromising ways and immediately suspended and excommunicated his episcopal enemies. He repeated these actions at Canterbury on Christmas Day. Four days later, he was murdered by Henry's men.

Even Becket's death did not immediately end the divisions in the Cistercian order. Garin, the abbot of Pontigny, demanded vengeance against Henry, whereas in 1171 Richard, the abbot of the Norman abbey of Velasse, served as one of Henry's representatives to a provincial council at Sens and to the papal curia. Alexander then sent Richard back to Henry with a summons that Henry should return from Ireland.[116] Though other Cistercians did not work so closely with Henry, they maintained good relations with him; after the canonization of Bernard of Clairvaux in 1174, Abbot Henry of Clairvaux wrote to the king, lamenting his absence from the celebration of the new saint's feast, and offering him one of Bernard's fingers as a relic.[117] Gradually, the tensions must have faded, for by the late 1170's, Garin, now archbishop of Bourges, joined

Abbot Henry in fighting the Cathars in southern France. Yet some Cistercians' stories about Becket continue to display a certain ambiguity. Whereas one Burgundian abbot dreamed that Becket intended to be present at Garin's consecration as archbishop of Bourges, Caesarius of Heisterbach recounted debates over Becket's sanctity that were only resolved by Becket's posthumous miracles.[118] Becket was, perhaps, a better model bishop once martyred and sanctified than he was while alive.

It has been argued that the Cistercians' activity in the disputes of the 1160's marked the end of a period of idealism and the beginning of a realpolitik that put the order's economic well-being before their advocacy of an ideal Christian society.[119] Gilbert of Cîteaux surfaces as the central architect of this new pragmatism; his agreement with Henry II, his participation in Geoffrey of Auxerre's ouster, and his request that Becket leave Pontigny have suggested to some that he was playing a double game and trying to maintain good relations with all sides so as to protect the property and position of the order. But the argument that their actions after 1166 show a turning away from their idealistic political role assumes that the Cistercians' idea of the proper order of the Church depended on definitions of legal principle rather than on an organic image based on consensus and personal relations. Furthermore, it ignores the confusion that the politics of the Becket controversy caused for many other churchmen of that time. Instead, the Cistercians' actions demonstrate their continued attempts to create consensus and unity, even when the protagonists in the dispute were unwilling to compromise.

Nonetheless, the conflicts of the 1160's do mark a notable change in the character of the Cistercians' activities. Although the Cistercians did not abandon them, their ideals had become less applicable to the society in which they lived. The Cistercians' conception of an ideal Church was not one based on legal definitions of ecclesiastical liberties, but was instead a moral and ethical conception of Christian unity that, for a time, the monks could actually recognize in the concord of their friends and affiliates. But it became ever more difficult to maintain such an appearance of concord in a society increasingly juridical in nature and increasingly contentious in its attempts to make distinctions, establish boundaries, and define principles of social organization. In the 1130's and 1140's, with a set of allegiances established by common support for Innocent II, the Cistercians experienced little conflict between their image of the Church, their political activities, and their economic interests; their patrons, their bishops, and their pope were all in general agreement. By the 1160's and 1170's, the Cistercians had not abandoned their moral and universal image of the Church, but they did begin to experience conflicts stemming from its disjunction with the actual nature of ecclesiastical institutions.

In *De corruptis moribus cleri et populi*, probably written in the 1180's, the Cistercian Baldwin of Ford continued to view ecclesiastical conflicts in moral terms. He blamed the martyrdom of Thomas Becket on the evil behavior of the clergy. Because the clergy did not live virtuously, Baldwin argued, the laity persecuted them instead of looking to them as models of good Christian behavior. Because of their undisciplined and disordered life, they had not acted as Christian ministers and thus had provoked Henry II's hatred. Baldwin certainly did not condone Henry's actions, but he blamed on the immorality of the clergy the ability of secular powers to invade areas of ecclesiastical jurisdiction, to resist Church councils, and to scorn the sacraments and even their religion. Only if the priesthood reformed itself would the proper order of society be restored.[120] Underneath this call for reform lay a vision of the Church still based on the image of the bride as a collection of individual souls united by their efforts to reform their wills and participate in divine love. It was a vision that extended the principles of the Cistercians' monastic communities into the surrounding society, but a vision that, by the late twelfth century, had become increasingly anachronistic.

Chapter 9

"Bulwarks Against the Savage Beasts"

The Threat of Heresy

Twice in the twelfth century, the Cistercians worked to repair a Church divided by schism; twice they found that the restoration of ecclesiastical unity did not create a united Christendom. In the 1140's and again after 1170, the Cistercians fought against heresy. In 1145, Bernard of Clairvaux, accompanied by his secretary Geoffrey of Auxerre, preached in southern France against Henry of Lausanne and his followers; in 1178, Henry of Marcy, the abbot of Clairvaux, returned to southern France to combat the Cathars. The Cistercians' response to heresy, like their response to schism, stemmed from their idea of Christian unity. But they perceived heresy as a different kind of threat than schism: schisms and disputes openly tore the bride's coat or cut her hair, but heresy was a secret canker that ate away the body of the Church and could only occasionally be forced out into the open. Their idea that heretics were stubborn and irrational and thus unsusceptible to reconversion increased the Cistercians' sense of heresy's danger and led them to encourage all virtuous Christians to expel heretics from Christian society. They were not the only twelfth-century Christians to stress repressive measures over reconversion, but their increasingly close relations with ecclesiastical officials meant that their attitudes toward heretics influenced papal policy. Yet their response to heresy again demonstrates that they conceived of a Church united by consensus and good character rather than legal procedures and principles. Urging secular and ecclesiastical authorities to cooperate in the eradication of heresy, the monks presented this challenge as analogous to a crusade: the threat of heresy provided opportunities for people to progress in virtue and further bind the orthodox Church together in caritas.

Historians who have studied the growth of religious dissent in the twelfth century have read beneath the officials' descriptions to try to understand the dissenters' varied concerns and beliefs. They have distinguished between intellectual and popular heretics, Cathars, Waldensians, and various critics—both religious and political—of ecclesiastical wealth and clerical monopoly.[1] The Cistercians who attacked heretics, however, made no such distinctions. Even in comparison to some of their contemporaries, they did not try to define the various positions of the religious dissenters or fashion arguments to refute heretical beliefs. Instead, they presented all heresies as part of an ongoing diabolical battle against the unity of the Church, and they focused more on the dangerous opportunity that heretics offered to the faithful than they did on the heresy itself.

Bernard's two sermons about heresy in his Song of Songs commentary demonstrate this approach. Bernard wrote his sermons in response to a request from the Premonstratensian canon, Eberwin of Steinfeld, who in 1143 or 1144 asked Bernard to interpret the appearance of heretics around Cologne in terms of the biblical passage on the foxes spoiling the fruit on the vine. Eberwin wanted "arguments and authorities from our own faith to destroy them."[2] In his letter, Eberwin carefully distinguished between two groups of dissenters, one that denied the authority and power of all priests because of clerical worldliness, and the other, "found recently," that had an alternative priesthood and its own sacraments. The members of this second group refused to eat meat, rejected marriage, offered to debate their beliefs with Catholic churchmen, and claimed to be the true Church, "which until now had been hidden, ever since the time of the martyrs."[3] It is quite likely that these newer heretics were one of the first groups of Cathars in western Europe.[4]

Bernard's sermons used the information from this letter but transformed the character of the groups Eberwin had described. First, Bernard merged the doctrines that the canon had so carefully distinguished. Although he recognized that some dissenters rejected marriage completely whereas others allowed the marriage of virgins, he otherwise lumped together their different teachings about food, prayer, and the sacraments. More important, he ignored Eberwin's comment that the second group of dissenters was willing to debate its beliefs, and instead focused on the idea that its church had been hidden since the time of the martyrs. Combining this idea with the biblical passage about the foxes spoiling the vines, Bernard articulated an image of heretics who disguised themselves as holy people and refused to preach openly at all. This was a new and especially pernicious threat, Bernard argued, for unlike earlier generations of heretics who had proclaimed their beliefs openly and thus were caught and refuted, these new heretics fought a guerrilla battle, preferring "to injure than to conquer, and to creep rather than be seen."[5] Elaborating on Eberwin's suggestion, Bernard described the new heretics as foxes who pillaged the vineyard of the Christian Church without being seen; their faith seemed orthodox, their life without reproach, their deeds even matched their words, and their presence was only known by the destruction they left behind them.[6]

Bernard stressed the secretive character of heresy even when it was clear that the heretics criticized were preaching openly. Predisposed by biblical passages suggesting that hypocrisy was to characterize the last age before the Second Coming, Bernard found deceit and secrecy everywhere.[7] Modern scholars carefully distinguish between Abelard's heretical doctrines, Henry of Lausanne's popular heresy, and Arnold of Brescia's political critiques, but to Bernard they posed the same threat. Although all proclaimed their ideas publicly, Bernard argued that they hid their true character under a guise of holiness. Bernard wrote that Abelard and Arnold of Brescia "had the appearance of religion in their food and clothing, but denied its strength, and deceived people by transforming themselves into angels of light, even though they were Satan," and Henry of Lausanne appeared as "a greedy wolf in the clothes of a sheep," a "cunning serpent" who again "had the appearance of religion, but denied its strength."[8] Bernard's emphasis on the secret and hypocritical nature of heretics added a new tone to current descriptions of religious dissenters. Although other ecclesiastics had described heretics' "secret conventicles," most prelates before the middle of the twelfth century worried more about heresy's open threat and condemned dissenters because of their public proselytizing.[9] This forceful characterization of all heretics, however open, as secretive contributed greatly to the developing idea that heresy was an underground threat to the stability and unity of Christian society.

Other Cistercian authors used similar imagery to emphasize the hypocrisy and secrecy of dissenters who actually preached openly. Henry of Lausanne preached and debated his ideas in public, but Geoffrey of Auxerre's account of him stressed the way he went into hiding when Bernard appeared around Toulouse.[10] Similarly, Peter Waldo was condemned for preaching without approval, but Geoffrey's description of him pointed to his ability to hide his heretical disease under a veneer of sanctity.[11] According to Henry of Marcy, the Cathars he combated "have no known approach but follow circular paths, and their newest abominations are concealed in the labyrinth of their deception. They scatter from the hand like little deer, and, like twisting snakes, the more tightly they are held, the more easily they slip away."[12] Henry filled his account of his expedition against the Cathars with images of metamorphosis: the heretics were foxes who became moles and gnawed at the roots of plants they dared not destroy from above, or they were leopards who ducked into the ground "like vile reptiles" so they would not be betrayed by the pattern of their spots. This stress on the slippery character of heretics and the difficulties of catching them influenced the Cistercians' ideas on how they should be fought.

Although these Cistercians portrayed all twelfth-century heretics as hypocrites who hid their pernicious teaching under the appearance of a holy life, they nonetheless recognized that some publicized their ideas and, because of this public presence, could be found, trapped, and refuted.[13] Abelard, for example, may have hid the error of his ideas under a veneer of truth and disguised an evil life under a habit of sanctity, but he did not hide the ideas themselves. "The twisting snake has come out of his cave," Bernard warned; "I wish that his poisonous writings still lurked in boxes and were not read in public places!"[14] In fact, part of Bernard's complaint about Abelard's ideas concerned the publicity his teaching received. Matters of faith, which Bernard believed should be reserved for contemplation, were instead discussed "in the streets and the squares" where they could "corrupt the faith of simple people"; Abelard's books, Bernard complained, would "pour his poison into succeeding generations, and harm all generations that are to come."[15] Similarly, when Geoffrey of Auxerre sought to point out and correct the supposed errors in the arguments of the scholar-bishop Gilbert de la Porrée, he did so because he worried that Gilbert's students were "young souls who praise novelties, rush to read sacred pages without the rudder that is Christ, and pry into the depths of God without the spirit that alone comprehends them."[16] Both Cistercians criticized the methodology used by these scholars and the ideas they produced, but the heart of their criticism paralleled their more general criticism of the emerging scholastic culture—just as the schools generally encouraged ambitious young men to seek ecclesiastical offices without teaching the requisite virtues for their proper administration, so these masters encouraged curious young men to investigate Christian mysteries without first stressing the need for spiritual progress. The spiritual pride of Abelard and Gilbert led them into error, but it also gave them the confidence to publicize their ideas, and thus they could be caught and refuted.

If educated heretics could be located and fought, the heresy that appeared outside of the schools seemed to the Cistercians to be harder to find and more difficult to combat. Late-eleventh- and early-twelfth-century descriptions of heretics tended to reflect the scorn of learned churchmen toward the expression of religious ideas by unschooled common people, but the church authorities who encountered these dissenters generally thought they could impress or bully them back into orthodoxy.[17] Bernard, in comparison, portrayed these new and secret heretics not only as "stupid and foolish" but also as incorrigible: their followers "are not to be convinced by logical reasoning which they do not understand, nor corrected by authorities which they do not accept, nor won over by persuasion, because they are completely ruined."[18] The ultimate proof of their irrationality was their preference for death over conversion; they died not as martyrs whose piety had endowed them with a contempt for death, but as apostates whose heresy had hardened their hearts.

The idea of heretics as stupid and irrational and the conception of heresy as a hidden animal eating at the heart of the Church both may have been fantasies, but their influence on ecclesiastical policy toward religious dissent was real. Heresy provoked an increasingly centralized, rational, and legal response from churchmen who developed means of defining, classifying, and combating its threat. Over the course of the twelfth century, heresy became less of a local concern and instead received attention from the papacy; churchmen stopped reacting to individual cases of dissent and started to search actively for an underground heretical movement; scholars sought to define the differences between heretical and orthodox doctrine; and ecclesiastical officials gradually abandoned efforts at conversion for coercion and punishment.[19] The Cistercians aided some of these developments: their emphasis on the secretive character of heresy suggested that churchmen needed to take the initiative in searching for religious deviance, and their sense that heretics were irrational and obstinate influenced the increasing emphasis on coercion. But, as was the case during the schisms, the Cistercians' perspective remained rooted in their own conceptions of Christian unity. They were less concerned with defining a legal inquisitorial procedure or distinguishing orthodox from heretical teachings than they were with encouraging ecclesiastical and secular leaders to work together to combat and expel this threat to the unity of the Church.

Both Bernard and the other Cistercians involved in combating heresy supported papal efforts to fight the threat from Rome rather than at a local level. Despite Bernard's criticisms of the growing legal apparatus of the papacy, and his arguments for settling disputes at a local level, he attended papal councils about heresy, participated in papal delegations to fight heretics, and appealed to the pope himself to judge heretical errors. Henry of Lausanne had provoked a purely local reaction when he preached in Le Mans in 1116, but in 1135 he was captured by the bishop of Arles and brought before Pope Innocent II at the council at Pisa, making him the first heretic to receive papal attention.[20] There he was condemned and, according to Geoffrey of Auxerre, turned over to Bernard with the idea that he would become a monk, although it is not clear he ever entered Clairvaux.[21] Henry emerged in southern France about a decade later and again provoked a papal response that involved Bernard: the abbot participated in a papal delegation sent to Toulouse to counteract Henry's influence. Abelard's appeal to Rome after the council at Sens provoked letters from Bernard to Innocent on his responsibility to combat heresy, and eight years later at the council at Rheims, Bernard tried unsuccessfully to convince Eugenius III to condemn what he and Geoffrey of Auxerre perceived to be the errors of Gilbert de la Porrée.[22] The same council also brought Eon de L'Etoile to judgment and condemned his followers to be released to the secular authorities to be burned. This was the first time that the papacy consciously participated in the death of a heretic.[23] Bernard's position on this sentence is not known, but, as we will see, his ideas did influence the council's canons against heresy. Later Cistercians were even more closely allied with the papacy. In 1178, Abbot Henry of Marcy, Garin, the former abbot of Pontigny and now archbishop of Bourges, the bishops of Bath and Poitiers, and the cardinal Peter of Saint Chrysogonus composed a papal delegation against the Cathars; in 1181, as papal legate, Henry again returned to southern France. As legate he also joined the Cistercians Archbishop Guichard of Lyons and Geoffrey of Auxerre at a council in Lyons in 1180 to hear Peter Waldo's profession of faith.[24]

Although these Cistercians were willing to work on behalf of the pope, their approach to heresy's threat was rooted in their own monastic culture and their vision of Christian unity. Bernard, for instance, encouraged churchmen to investigate rumors of heresy in their territories, but the proposal for finding heretics that he outlined in his first sermon about the foxes in the vineyard demonstrates how far he was from advocating a procedure of legal *inquisitio*. He suggested a test based on the presumption that a person who defied Church teachings in one matter remained defiant in other matters as well, and thus was a heretic. He offered a scenario in which churchmen questioned a man who lived a seemingly holy life in the company of a woman. If the man admitted that the woman was neither his wife nor a relative, he was to be reminded that the Church forbade the cohabitation of men and women vowed to celibacy. "If you do not wish to disrupt the Church," Bernard imagined saying to the man, "send the woman away. Otherwise from this one suspicion will come others, which are not now detected, but will without a doubt become credible."[25] Bernard insisted that churchmen separate men and women who claimed to be leading chaste lives in one another's company; if they refused to enter religious communities, church authorities were then justified in expelling them from their congregations as heretics.

Bernard's logic was specious, but his reasoning was based on certain fundamental Cistercian assumptions about the process of spiritual development and the indispensable lessons learned by living in a community. When Bernard described both Henry of Lausanne and Abelard, he linked their independence from the constraints of a community with their association with women. Henry was "an apostate who had abandoned the monastic habit" and who could be found after a day of preaching "with prostitutes and sometimes even with wives," whereas Abelard was "a monk without a rule, a prelate without responsibility, an abbot without discipline, who argues with boys and associates with women."[26] This independence blatantly contradicted one of the central assumptions of the Cistercians' culture, that one could only control one's will by living in a community in which one learned obedience by obeying commands and learned humility by responding to the needs of others. Henry and Abelard, in comparison, trusted too much in their own abilities. They used their unaided reason to comprehend divine mysteries or to interpret the Scriptures, and they believed that they could control their wills and their desires by themselves. For Bernard, contact with women made this presumption most apparent, because he believed it was impossible for a man and a women to live chastely together.[27] As a result, men and women who claimed to live together in celibacy were not only proud but also hypocritical and thus probably heretics. By putting their own understanding before divine knowledge, they had willfully rejected divine caritas, had separated themselves from God, and without divine aid were inevitably mistaken in their understanding of their religion.

Bernard's activities during his preaching mission against Henry of Lausanne in 1145 also demonstrates his lack of interest in defining Church doctrine and developing legal procedures to find and judge heretics. Geoffrey of Auxerre's account of this trip makes clear that Bernard's success had more to do with his ability to make others recognize divine power than it did with any exposition of orthodox doctrine.[28] As Bernard traveled through southern France, he touched the sick, the crippled, and the blind, listened to the troubled and the possessed, negotiated with feuding factions, administered sacraments, and left in his wake accounts of miraculous cures and peaceful reconciliations.[29] Only after Geoffrey described Bernard's entrance into the city of Albi, where his audience greatly outnumbered that of the papal legate, did he mention that Bernard had explained the sacrament of the Eucharist and the differences between orthodox and heretical positions on the subject; this clearly was much less important to Geoffrey than the abbot's other actions. R. I. Moore has argued that Bernard and Henry were similar figures: both used their diplomatic and negotiating skills to convince people that they could relieve the distress and disease common in their lives.[30] If Geoffrey's account is to be believed, Bernard was even more successful at this than was Henry. Geoffrey's account of his preaching suggests that Bernard was able to make the spiritual power of orthodox Christianity manifest to the people of the south. This was something that was not done again with any degree of success until Dominic's activity in the early thirteenth century.

Bernard did, however, advocate two responses to heresy that had important ramifications for ecclesiastical policy toward religious dissent. The first was the idea that heretics were to be ostracized both religiously and politically. In concluding his sermon on the seemingly chaste couples who were actually heretics, Bernard argued that any such couple that refused to live apart was to be separated from the community of Christians because they had already separated themselves from the Church "by their proven cohabitation."[31] He made this position plain on his mission to the south, for there he announced that heretics and their supporters could not give evidence or seek redress in the courts and were to be avoided both socially and politically.[32] Bernard's second influential idea was his suggestion that secular and ecclesiastical authorities cooperate in fighting heresy. Before he left Clairvaux for the south, Bernard asked the count of Toulouse to support his mission "with the power of your right hand," and, once he returned north, he sent the Cistercian abbot of Grandselve to Toulouse with a message that the people of the city were to pursue and capture the heretics in their community.[33] Three years later, Bernard's arguments that heretics were to be shunned as well as excommunicated, and that the secular powers were to help enforce this exclusion, received official sanction at the council at Rheims. There Canon 18 ruled that anyone defending or supporting heretics be excommunicated, with their lands placed under an interdict.[34]

Bernard's ideas about excluding heretics from the community of Christians and his hope that secular and ecclesiastical officials would cooperate in this fight had their roots in his conception of a Church unified by caritas. In his 50th sermon on the Song of Songs, Bernard discussed the love of one's neighbors and enemies. One loved one's neighbors, Bernard argued, because they too loved God, and it was possible to love in an enemy that part of him which might learn to love the divine. As a result, a person was always to have some feeling of love toward others, even toward enemies. However, Bernard did admit one exception:

When it is known that a person will not return to the love of God, it is unavoidable that you consider him, not as almost nothing, but as totally nothing, because he is nothing for eternity. Not only is he not to be loved, but even more, he should be treated with hatred, according to the psalm, "Lord, do I not hate those who hate you, and loathe those who rise up against you?" (Ps. 138.21).[35]

Although Bernard never stated it explicitly, his attitude toward heretics suggested that he placed them among those to be hated because they had made clear, by their hypocrisy and pride, that they did not accept divine love. Once they were outside the Church and the caritas that united it, Bernard was no longer concerned about their spiritual well-being but only about their effect on others.

Bernard not only wished to see secular and ecclesiastical officials co-operate in ostracizing and expelling heretics from Christian society but also suggested that such actions had spiritual benefits for the actors. "There must be heresies and schisms," Bernard told both Innocent II and an anonymous Cistercian abbot, paraphrasing I Corinthians 11, "so that those who are righteous may be revealed."[36] Schisms and heresies were a part of the challenge of earthly existence, and although Bernard lamented the continual need to combat their "thorns and thistles," he also encouraged Innocent to live up to the example of his predecessors and to use the threat of Abelard's ideas to perfect his own virtue.[37] Such was the case not only for prelates but for all good Christians. When Eberwin described the heretics around Cologne, he mentioned that some had been burned by enthusiastic people in the region. Bernard commented that he approved of their zeal, but not the action itself, because he did not think belief could be coerced. Yet he continued, "No doubt it is better for them to be compelled by the sword of someone who carries the sword in a good cause than to be allowed to draw other people into error. For a righteous avenger against those who do evil is a servant of God."[38]

Bernard was not the only monk to condone, or even advocate, the use of secular force against heresy. Peter the Venerable, in his *Tractatus contra Petrobrusianos* (c. 1140), called on his audience of churchmen to root out heresy, both by preaching and, "if necessary, by force of arms with the help of the laity."[39] Like Bernard, he had some difficulty reconciling this call to arms with the idea that conversion was better than extermination, but, also like Bernard, he focused more on heresy's threat to orthodox Christians than on the need to save the heretic. But the differences between the two monks are also interesting. Concerned that heresy would trigger Christians' hidden doubts about their religion, Peter wrote to "soothe the secret thoughts of some Catholics, by healing their minds of a weakness of faith not apparent to men, or by fortifying them against those whose tongue the prophet called a sharp sword."[40] Peter's treatise contained expositions and rebuttals of the Petrobrusians' ideas. Bernard, in comparison, considered not people's doubts but their inner motivations and their progress in virtue. He held out to secular lords the idea that, if they used their swords as "righteous avengers" to cleanse the Church of heresy, they performed a virtuous act. Just as he considered Abelard a test sent to help Innocent II to increase his virtue, so Bernard implied that heresy could test the virtue of those with secular authority if they used their swords in the service of the Church. Such an attitude contributed, eventually, to the thirteenth-century crusade against the Cathars.

Over thirty years later, Henry of Marcy's expedition to southern France and his subsequent participation in the Third Lateran Council demonstrate that Cistercians concerned about heresy continued to stress cooperation between secular and ecclesiastical authorities and the meritorious zeal with which they were to act. The papal mission to southern France in 1178 combined a legal procedure for finding, classifying, and combating heresy with the Cistercians' idea that a joint action of secular and ecclesiastical authorities could protect Church unity by forcibly excluding those who consciously seemed to place themselves outside of Church boundaries. The delegation itself stemmed from the cooperation of secular and ecclesiastical authorities. Henry claimed to travel south only at the command of the pope and at the request of both Henry II and Louis VII.[41] The initial impetus for the delegation was a letter that Count Raymond V of Toulouse had written to Henry of Marcy a year earlier in which he asked for Henry's assistance, mentioned that he had already resolved to use coercive measures against the heretics, and said he expected Louis VII's support.[42] By the time the delegation arrived in the south, Raymond had already issued an edict expelling heretics from his lands. The papal representatives hoped to rescue the bishop of Albi, who was a prisoner in the castle of Roger of Béziers; although they failed at that, they staged the confession of two Cathar bishops, established a procedure by which prominent and orthodox men in Toulouse gave depositions about suspected heretics, and with the help of the count of Toulouse, caught and punished one Cathar, a prominent citizen of Toulouse, Peter Maurand.[43]

The two letters describing the expedition, one written by the cardinal Peter of Saint Chrysogonus and the other by Henry of Marcy, differ in significant ways. Peter's account describes the legal procedures used by the expedition: the safe conduct offered to two suspected Cathars, their confrontation with orthodox churchmen, the testimony by witnesses who heard the suspects express heretical ideas, the refusal of the Cathars to uphold their orthodox statements with an oath, and their excommunication.[44] Henry's letter, by comparison, focuses on the apprehension and punishment of Peter Maurand, who was caught with the help of the count of Toulouse, and evinces more interest in reinforcing the faith of the good Christians in the city than in catching the bad.[45] Unlike the Cathars in Peter's letter, who disputed the tenets of the faith with the churchmen, Henry described Peter Maurand as vanquished by the power of relics and the performance of religious rituals. According to Henry, the procession of relics into the church moved the faithful to tears and inspired the heretics present to hide; during the chant, Peter turned pale and looked frightened. Henry continued: "When the Holy Ghost approached, how could any spirit remain among its enemies? You could see the man destroyed as though by some paralytic disease, and although everyone said he was so eloquent that he usually bested everyone in speech, he retained neither his language nor his sense."[46] When the Bible on which Peter had sworn his oath of orthodoxy was opened, the clerics found the passage "What have we to do with you, Jesus, Son of God? Have you come to destroy us before the time?" (Mark 1.24). With this passage confirming that he had separated himself from Jesus, Peter could no longer hide his heretical ideas. To the great horror of the congregation, he admitted that he denied the Real Presence in the Eucharist, was immediately judged to be a heretic and a criminal, and was led away in chains. Only his willingness to reconvert to Christianity saved him from death; he performed a public penance in which he was led barefoot, naked, and beaten around the churches of the city; his possessions were confiscated and a castle razed; and he was ordered to spend three years in service to the poor in Jerusalem.

Henry's account, like Geoffrey of Auxerre's description of Bernard's expedition thirty years earlier, stressed that divine power fought heresy more effectively than intellectual arguments or legal witnesses. Unlike Bernard, Henry did not work miracles, but he did gather together traditional symbols of the divine presence on earth: relics, the Bible, the Eucharist. Like Bernard, he understood the importance of community pressure; Peter, who had sworn an oath that he did not hold heretical ideas before a crowd of people who knew he did, could not then withstand the rituals that confirmed the community's harmony with the divine and proclaimed his own exclusion.[47] This community pressure not only effected

Peter Maurand's confession but also reunited the Catholics in the city. As Henry described it, as the news of Peter's confession and conviction spread,

the mouths of the faithful opened, O Christ, and the lips of Catholic people were unsealed in your praise. The glory of the faith burst forth as if for the first time in that city, and the citizens, who until now had despaired, breathed again in the hope of eternal salvation. From that moment the word of faith grew and multiplied and the face of the whole city seemed brighter as it escaped from the darkness of error into the shining light of virtue.[48]

Heresy had again served as a goad to bring good Christians to God.

Henry's optimism was premature. After he and his companions left the region, Peter Maurand and his family returned to their position of power and influence in Toulouse, and Maurand's sons and descendants, if not Peter himself, remained Cathars.[49] Furthermore, the second half of Henry's letter, which describes Henry's trip to the castle of Roger of Béziers to advise the lord and his wife to release the bishop of Albi, demonstrates the limits of ecclesiastical action in cases in which prelates did not have the cooperation of secular lords. According to Henry, the territory was a "great cesspool of evil" filled with heretics and their supporters; unable to rescue the bishop, the best he could do was excommunicate Roger before returning to the north. Equally unsuccessful was a council that Henry, the Cistercian archbishop Guichard of Lyons, and Geoffrey of Auxerre attended at Lyons two years later. There they heard Peter Waldo give a profession of faith that, according to Geoffrey, merely provided another example of Waldo's hypocrisy; he "returned to his vomit," and soon went back to his unauthorized preaching.[50]

At the Third Lateran Council in 1179, Henry's ideas about combating heresy became incorporated into ecclesiastical policy.[51] The council's 27th canon, the only one that touched on the Church's response to religious dissent, made no mention of an inquisitorial procedure to seek out heretics but instead demanded that ecclesiastical and secular authorities fight together to suppress heresy. It asked secular princes to dissolve all bonds of loyalty and obedience owed to heretics and their supporters, and it called for a crusade against the heretics of southern France in which the participants were to receive a remission of penance and a promise of eternal reward.[52] At this council, Alexander III made Henry cardinal-bishop of Albano and asked him to return as papal legate to southern France to initiate this crusade. In 1181, Henry led an army against Roger of Béziers's castle and captured the two Cathar leaders to whom Peter of Saint Chrysogonus had given a safe conduct three years before.[53] This expedition set the precedent for the use of force against lords who did not themselves take action against the heretics in their territory, and it established Henry as the precursor of Arnold Amaury, the abbot of Clairvaux who led the later Albigensian Crusade.

Henry's letter describing his first expedition to Toulouse also served as a call to all faithful Christians to join his new expedition against the Cathars. He drew language and ideas from Bernard's call for the Second Crusade thirty years before.[54] Bernard had presented the expedition to Jerusalem as a means for the laity to increase in virtue by sacrificing themselves to protect the unity the Church.[55] Henry presented a crusade against the Cathars in much the same terms. The Cathars threatened Christian unity and thus human salvation; to fight against them was a vir-

Figure 6. David slays Goliath and cuts off his head with his sword. *The Bible of Stephen Harding* (1109–11). Dijon, Bibliothèque municipale, MS 14, f. 13 (detail). Photograph courtesy Bibliothèque municipale, Dijon, France.

tuous act that also reinforced the Church's unity and its defenses against its enemies. Henry began by lamenting the afflictions of the faith, calling on faithful Christians to "deplore the damage to human salvation," and ended by calling on Christian princes to "avenge the wounds of Christ and bring to this desert the garden of the Lord, and to the wilderness the sweetness of paradise."[56] He compared the Christians' battle against the Cathars to the battle of David and Goliath, an image that Bernard had used to describe the fight against Abelard, and one that further reinforced the idea of heresy's gigantic threat.[57] The fight against these Goliath Cathars avenged Christ's wounds but also reinforced the Christians' own faith.

Why do you waver, David? Why are you anxious, man of faith? Take up your sling and stone, strike the brow of the blasphemer, and raise his evil head, which he lifts so impudently, on the point of your sword. If Christ's supporters are vanquished in this battle, if the mother Church is in the least degree maltreated, we know that our cause lacks advocates but not merit. We know that victory will not be denied to our champion if he who is about to fight makes war in the love of Christ.[58]

Such a battle united its soldiers into a unified Church; it made them a "bulwark against the savage beasts" of heresy and established a firm boundary between those linked by caritas within the Church and those who, by stubbornly remaining outside, lost their humanity as they lost all participation in divine love, and became no better than animals.

The Cistercians approached heresy in much the same way that they approached schisms: as a threat to the unity of the Church and therefore to human salvation. They explained both threats in organic and physical terms, as a danger to the body of the Church that was the bride of Christ. In a society in which the advisers of princes and prelates thought increasingly in terms of legal procedures, the Cistercians continued to present this unity as a matter of individual virtue and moral reform. Their response to heresy drew on many of the themes that they had established as they articulated their vision of a Church bound by charity: the need for individuals to grow in virtue, the cooperation of secular and ecclesiastical authorities, and especially an aggressive conception of caritas. Although their moral reaction to ecclesiastical schisms and disputes became increasingly anachronistic, their approach to heresy remained influential and was incorporated into ecclesiastical policy. Not only were the monks' ideas about the secular isolation of heretics and their supporters included in the canons of church councils, but the abbots' efforts to make the spiritual power of the orthodox church real to the people of southern France anticipated the thirteenth-century preaching missions of Dominic and his companions, and their ideas about the virtuous use of the sword set the groundwork for the later Albigensian Crusade.

Conclusion

The opposition of monastery and school is a favorite image for historians of twelfth-century Europe. Monasteries, embedded in a rural landscape of peasants and feudal lords and dependent on patterns of thought that relied on authority, symbolize an older society, whereas the schools stand for a new world of towns and markets, lawyers and bureaucrats, logic and experimentation. The Cistercians often appear as conservatives who opposed the new schools and all that they stood for. Indeed, twelfth-century authors themselves contrasted the Cistercians and the schools. Cistercian preachers portrayed schools as centers of ambition and intellectual presumption that produced unworthy churchmen; scholars saw their monastic opponents as logically inept and more powerful than holy; and only a few observers such as John of Salisbury more temperately distinguished between logical and rhetorical talents.[1]

The urban schools and the Cistercian monasteries were not as different as either twelfth-century polemics or many modern historical studies suggest. In fact, their heated opposition stemmed partially from the natural competition of institutions that served similar social roles and thus made a great effort to assert their differences. They recruited from the same pool of young men, often the younger sons of a military elite who had already received a rudimentary education, and they prepared these men for positions in the ecclesiastical hierarchy. Where they differed, and of course differed fundamentally, was in the nature of this education. Nonetheless, that monasteries within the Cistercian order actually, if not intentionally, functioned as schools to educate a virtuous clergy suggests that their position in society was more complicated than that of dyed-in-the-wool conservatives.[2] They gradually developed a role that responded to the social and conceptual upheavals of the eleventh and twelfth centuries and combined monastic traditions with the new attitudes toward self, nature, and reform that were characteristic of the new society of the twelfth century.

The Investiture Controversy and church reform movement changed the locus of sacred power in European society. Whereas before 1050 such power had been diffuse and connections with the divine were effected through relics, saints' shrines, royal decisions, and monastic prayers, by the twelfth century these local and diverse receptacles for the holy were being overlaid by a centralized hierarchy of priests whose position was based on their monopoly of the sacraments and the importance of these sacraments as the primary means for contact with the divine. Monasteries did not lose all responsibility for human salvation; monks continued to pray for the well-being of society and to offer spiritual benefits to their benefactors, but such benefits began to be tied to monk-priests' performance of sacraments rather than to their prayers or less tangible offers to share in the benefits of the community.[3] As a result, many twelfth-century monasteries modified their cultures to reflect the transformations in these links between the sacred and the profane.

The diversity of religious movements in the twelfth century reflects the various responses to these changes. Many older Benedictine monasteries became communities of monk-priests and continued to channel salvation to the laity; Abbot Rupert of Deutz portrayed the mass as the central means of contact with the divine, and the monks of Marmoutier developed histories that reinforced their sense of community at the same time that individual private masses predominated over their communal rituals.[4] Some new religious orders such as the Carthusians greatly reduced their communal rituals and increased the time spent in solitary prayer.[5] Still other religious figures, such as the hermits in Craon who lived on the honey and nuts they found in the forest, shifted away from the gift and countergift economy on which the exchange of spiritual benefits for land was based and instead provided for the laity through their preaching and example.[6]

As the Cistercians gradually created their monastic culture, they had to determine the relation between the individual monk, his community, and his society and establish a connection between the monastery and the sacramental hierarchy. They curtailed but did not eliminate their obligations to their benefactors, they established close ties with their bishops, and they created an internal organization that emphasized the possibility of individual spiritual growth within a communal setting. Furthermore, they developed a shared sense of identity that depended on participation in communal rituals within each abbey yet also linked monasteries spread across great distances and men separated by different tasks and functions.

The Cistercians' understanding of Christian caritas was central to many aspects of this culture. It linked an individual's search for salvation with his responsibilities to his brothers, it bound men of diverse ability and different functions into a unified community, and it united monks and abbeys separated by physical distances into a single order. The Cistercians then offered their communities as models for the unity that could be created out of the diversity of Christian society if individual Christians grew in virtue by disciplining their wills in communal life. The Cistercians did not try to incorporate the entire world into their monastery. They did, however, present the contemplative virtues as essential for people of all social orders, suggesting that only through a life modeled on that of a Cistercian community could people really progress toward virtue and divine love.

The Cistercians did not merely serve as a passive example for a unified Church. Their use and understanding of caritas also reflected their desire to reform and transform their surroundings, to find the divine harmonies in the natural world and the goodness in human nature. But they could not limit this transformation to the land within their monastic boundaries and the men within their communities. It accomplished nothing to reform themselves, they argued, if the rest of the Church remained in disarray. As a result, their monasteries became a source of advice, especially for those whose positions gave them the responsibility and authority to work for the reordering and reunification of Christian society. Yet, as much as the monks worked for the moral reform of their leaders, especially ecclesiastical officials, they also believed that monks were not to sit back and watch the Church be torn by division, schism, and heresy. In such cases, they not only offered advice but also left their monasteries to preach, negotiate, and try to repair the scandals that so threatened ecclesiastical unity.

The Cistercians were by no means alone in their conception of the Church as a moral institution and their calls for the reform of the clergy. Scholars such as John of Salisbury and Gilbert Foliot, despite taking opposite sides in the Becket controversy, both also advocated an organic and moral conception of the Church; Parisian moral theologians expressed criticisms of clerical immorality and scholarly ambition similar to those of the Cistercians.[7] But underlying the similarities between the monks' and the masters' calls for moral reform were fundamental differences stemming from different assumptions about their society and the Church. The Cistercians' vision of the Church was rooted in their own conception of individual, interior reform; late-twelfth-century scholars looked outward to the duties and responsibilities of different social orders rather than inward to the soul's progress toward the divine.[8] Although not all of these masters were lawyers, most understood issues in legal terms. John of Salisbury and Gilbert Foliot discussed the relationship of regnum to sacerdotium, and the Parisian moral theologians around Peter the Chanter elaborated the doctrine and practice of the sacrament of penance, which they viewed in legal terms as a matter of restitution for improper acts.

For a brief period between about 1130 and 1160, the Cistercians' vision of a society bound by the moral growth and virtuous qualities of its members had a semblance of reality, and it provided a means of understanding the bonds that held together the abstract Church. By the 1160's, in a Church increasingly dominated by lawyers and defined by legal principles, the Cistercians' view of a Christian society united by love and virtue became increasingly disassociated from the political reality, although it did remain as an important ideal that periodically reemerged as a critique of the growing worldly power of the ecclesiastical hierarchy.[9] The Cistercians' network of friends and allies, which had provided the unified community of virtuous men during the schism of 1130, both grew and began to fragment, and it became harder to heal the divisions in Christian society by advocating moral reform. Only in the battle against heresy did the Cistercians' vision of the Church continue to make an impact, for the boundaries of their charity helped to define the enemy, and their stress on the cooperation between secular and religious authority and the spiritual rewards of fighting heresy influenced the Church's increasingly violent response to religious dissent. The Cistercians' concept of caritas, and the crusading ideology it engendered, had become incorporated into an ecclesiastical policy of religious coercion.

Cistercian caritas had never been a gentle virtue. In the sermons and stories delivered within their communities, charity developed an aggressive and military character—it was a powerful duke who slew his enemies by the thousand, or a sword to be lifted in battle—and when invoked outside their monasteries, it could sanction just such violent activity. Walter Map, the secular cleric who described, and satirized, the world he saw around him from his vantage point at the English court, lambasted the harshness of Cistercian caritas:

> There is no one, I take it, who does not enjoy benefit from some person: no one therefore who has not a neighbour. So, however far off they [the Cistercians] keep those who have taken them in, they are still their neighbours; and if they hate them, how do they love God? Oh! they say, they love them in the Lord; and loving them in the Lord they define as wishing for the salvation of the soul of their neighbour—every aid to his body they exclude. Well, after that fashion I am sure I love all my enemies: I desire that they may depart and be with Christ.[10]

Just as Walter disliked the Cistercians for economic practices that had been present from the early years of the order, so also he pinpointed an aspect of Cistercian charity that had long been a part of their culture. The Cistercians combined in their understanding of caritas both their aggressive confidence and their fraternal love. The bond of affection between the monks expressed the companionship of an elite group of men who believed they shared an especially difficult life and sought to encourage one another in it. Their descriptions of the mutual love between God and humanity expressed their belief that they were to strive to control and transform their carnal natures and their conviction that they would be saved. But they also recognized that this process of transformation would never be complete on earth. Earthly existence was a constant struggle—to live without comforts, to control the will, to coax a living from the land, to balance one's own needs with those of one's brothers and neighbors—and these necessary tensions and conflicts that helped a monk to progress toward the divine were only resolved once he found rest in heaven.

The Cistercians' distinction between an ideal society in which physical needs and the human will were fully controlled and a distorted society in which humans always had to struggle influenced the monks' attitude toward their own political behavior. They did not hesitate to write letters of advice to prelates and princes, to provide models for the behavior of figures with authority, and to criticize these authorities when they abused their power, but they were more defensive about the mediation and negotiations that took them out of their monasteries. Their ambivalence about this behavior showed that they continued to long for the perfection of Christian society that they knew was possible only in heaven.

The monks expressed a disquiet with their political behavior, especially when faced with real or imagined criticisms of their activities. In 1129, stung by attacks emanating from the papal curia, Bernard of Clairvaux wrote Cardinal Haimeric to claim that he had helped the papal legate, the archbishop of Rheims, and the bishop of Laon to reform monasteries and remove a corrupt bishop only because he had been "summoned and dragged" into their presence.[11] Bernard wanted to remain within his monastic community; he resolved not to leave for anything other than his order's business unless bidden by his bishop or papal authority, and he asked that others stop demanding his participation. Yet the sarcastic tone of his letter makes clear that he knew this was impossible. He told Haimeric:

I am delighted to know that your Prudence is displeased at our involvement in such matters. This is most just and friendly of you. Act if you so wish, for you recognize and discern what is advantageous for your friend and suitable for a monk; pay attention, I beg, so that both our desires are quickly fulfilled. This satisfies your sense of justice and takes into consideration my salvation. May it please you to enjoin those noisy and inconvenient frogs not to leave their hollows and to remain content with their marshes. They are not to be heard any more in councils nor found in palaces; no necessity and no authority can draw them into disputes and negotiations.[12]

But as Bernard himself admitted, it was not only the demands of authority that dragged this frog from his pond; necessity pulled him out as well. He ended his letter by stating that, even if he kept silent, the troubles of the Church would not cease.

Bernard did not keep silent. A year later, the cardinals elected two popes, and Bernard began his Europe-wide travels on behalf of Innocent II. Toward the end of his life, when again faced with criticisms, he again lamented activities unsuited to the monastic life. In a letter to Bernard, the prior of the Carthusian house of Portes, he first defended himself from accusations that he had influenced Pope Eugenius III's decision to reject a Carthusian monk as bishop of Geneva. Then, at the end of the letter, he appended the famous passage in which he asked the Carthusians to pity his "monstrous life, his bitter conscience." Bernard lamented: "I am a kind of chimera of my age, neither cleric nor layman. For I have long abandoned the society of monks, although not the habit. I do not wish to write of the things I expect you have heard about me from others: what I do, what I desire, what crises bend me down in the world, or rather, throw me from precipices. If you have not heard, I beg that you ask and, according to what you hear, offer your advice and the assistance of your prayers."[13] Amid his complaints, however, Bernard made two points. First, his description of himself as a chimera may have served to remind the Carthusians that there were drawbacks as well as advantages for monks who took on ecclesiastical responsibilities and that they were not to be so eager to see their monk consecrated. Second, although bewailing his activities, he nonetheless involved the Carthusians in them by asking for their advice and for the "assistance" of their prayers. As with his first letter, Bernard gave no indication that he could abandon his activity to remain full-time at Clairvaux.[14]

Bernard was not the only active Cistercian who longed for a life of prayer and contemplation. The large number of Cistercian bishops who retired to their former monasteries speaks of the continued attraction of the peace and order of monastic life.[15] After becoming cardinal-bishop of Albano, Henry of Marcy dedicated his *Tractatus de peregrinante civitate dei* to the monks at Clairvaux and expressed in the prologue a yearning for his former community and his interior debate as he struggled to reconcile his longing for a monastic life with the demands of his position. He contrasted the stability of monastic life with the storms that now buffeted him, exhausting and chastening him. Uncertain whether to resign his position, he could not even find solace in the Bible, for conflicting scriptural passages warned him not to soil his feet once he had purified them, yet reminded him that he had to act at the bidding of one greater than himself.[16] Caught between biblical precepts, Henry finally realized that he could not abandon the mission God had given him.

Once Henry resolved to retain his position, his response was twofold. On the one hand, he continued to look to Clairvaux and to praise the support and comfort he received from the monks. On the other hand, he directed his attention and that of his monks toward the condition of the Church and the hope for a heavenly Jerusalem. As members of this city, he and his monks would again be united, but only if they worked to ensure its existence. He told the community at Clairvaux:

In this city I have currently met my brothers and sons from Clairvaux, whose absence I deplore; in this city I find inscribed as citizens all good people who are on pilgrimage in this world. So what else now remains but that we should eagerly sow fields, plant vineyards, and make a fruitful yield so that, after the many and various disturbances described above, the city with dwelling places is finally found?[17]

Henry recognized that Clairvaux's community could not exist in isolation and that the life he so longed for could only be realized in heaven. He and his monks could not simply tend to the fields at Clairvaux, for the Cistercians were part of a larger Christian society, and their own unity in the heavenly Church depended on the continued reform of the Church while on pilgrimage on earth.

Bernard wrote of the "necessities" as well as the "authorities" that drew him from his monastery; Henry of Marcy comforted himself and his former monks by explaining his absence as a transitory affair that was to be rectified in heaven. Geoffrey of Auxerre was even more explicit in explaining the Cistercians' activities as compelled by the condition of the Church. When he preached at the council at Tours in 1163, he not only rebuked the presumption and ambition of the clergy and called for their moral reform but also articulated a vision of ecclesiastical unity drawn from the prophet Ezechiel. Each prelate, he suggested, should draw his church alongside him just as the four-faced beasts of Ezechiel's vision each drew a wheel; but just as Ezechiel saw the wheels become united into a wheel within a wheel, so "it seems that a single border should contain all the Catholic churches at the same time."[18] Geoffrey then used this image to explain to his audience the Cistercians' activities on behalf of Alexander III. The Cistercians too were a wheel to be united in a single border, and their political actions stemmed "not from human presumption but from the fear of God, because the small wheel of the Cistercian order can produce nothing more for us if there is not a wheel in the middle of the wheels." Geoffrey then made his point even more explicit. "Monastic society," he told his audience, "by which we live for God and vow to keep the hard ways, produces nothing for the eternal salvation of souls if there is not ecclesiastical unity. Without a doubt, it is impossible for a limb to be part of a body if it does not wish to be under a head."[19] In another sermon, this time to a monastic audience, Geoffrey made the point again, arguing that neither the monastic religion, however perfect and separated from worldly cares it might be, nor the honest life of the faithful could please God if they existed outside the unity of the Church.[20]

No matter how defensive about their activity and how sorrowful to see some of their members accept ecclesiastical positions, the Cistercians felt compelled to work for ecclesiastical unity. Their order existed only as a part of the larger Church and could not ignore the Church's problems. Earthly society could never be perfectly united, but it also could never stop striving to be so. If the Church went astray, monastic prayer and contemplation, which benefited a monk's own salvation, would be of no avail. As long as Christian society continued to exist in pilgrimage on earth, the Cistercians extended their charity outside the boundaries of their monasteries.

Appendix

Cistercian Prelates, 1126–80

The following chronological list is derived from Willi, "Päpste, Kardinäle und Bischöfe," with corrections as noted. I have cited references to these prelates where they appear in Cistercian texts.

POPES

Eugenius III. Pope, 1145–53. Formerly Peter Bernard Paganelli of Pisa. Former monk at Clairvaux; first abbot of Trefontane, 1140–45. He received numerous letters, as well as the treatise *De consideratione* from Bernard of Clairvaux; see especially Letter 238. *Vita prima* 2.8.50, 4.7.41. For his letters and bulls, see JL 2: 20–89 and *PL* 180.

CARDINALS

Martin Cibo. Cardinal-priest of Saint Stephen in Monte Celio, 1130–44. From Genoa; former monk at Clairvaux. See *De consideratione* 4.14.

Baldwin. According to Migne, Innocent II made Baldwin a cardinal at the council at Clermont in 1130; Baldwin then became archbishop of Pisa in 1137 (*PL* 182: 301). But these cannot be the same Baldwins, because a cardinal-priest Baldwin appears on papal bulls the very year Baldwin became archbishop of Pisa. This is possibly the same Baldwin mentioned in Bernard of Clairvaux, Letter 144.

Stephen. Cardinal-bishop of Palestrina, 1141–44. Former monk at Clairvaux; possibly from Châlons. See *Vita prima* 2.8.49; Bernard of Clairvaux, Letter 224.

Henry Moricotti. Cardinal-priest of Saints Nereus and Achilleus, 1151–67. Abbot of Trefontane, 1148–50. Willi gives his dates as 1150–79, but JL gives them as above. See *Vita prima* 2.8.49.

Hugh of Châlons. Cardinal-priest of Ostia, 1150–58. Former monk at Clairvaux;

abbot of Trois-Fontaines c. 1147–50. Announced Eugenius III's death to the Cistercian order; *PL* 182: 694. See *Vita prima* 2.8.49. Bernard of Clairvaux, Letters 290, 296.

Roland of Pisa. Cardinal-deacon of Saints Cosmas and Damian, 1150. Willi gives his dates as 1150–54, but Jaffé identifies him as cardinal for two months, 23 October to 17 December 1150.

Bernard. Cardinal-deacon of Saints Cosmas and Damian, 1150–54. Willi places another Cistercian, Roland, as cardinal–deacon of Saints Cosmas and Damian during this period, and dates Bernard's tenure as 1153–1170. But according to JL, there was another cardinal in this church by 1157. Bernard is mentioned in John of Salisbury, *Policraticus* 5.15, as a cardinal during the pontificate of Eugenius III. See also *Vita prima* 2.8.49.

William of Pavia. Cardinal-priest of St. Peter-in-Chains, 1158–76. Cardinal-bishop of Porto and Saint Rufina, 1176–77. Former monk of Chiaravalle.

Odo of Soissons. Cardinal-bishop of Tusculum, 1170–c.1171. Abbot of Ourscamp, 1167–70. Chancellor of the cathedral school at Notre-Dame, Paris, 1153–c.1165; entered Ourscamp, c.1165. See Leclercq, "Lettres d'Odon d'Ourscamp."

Henry of Marcy. Cardinal-bishop of Albano, 1179–89. Abbot of Hautecombe, 1160–76, and abbot of Clairvaux, 1176–79. Buried at Clairvaux. See *Exordium magnum* 2.30; *Chronicon Clarevallense* 1179. His letters and treatises are in *PL* 204. See Congar, "Henri de Marcy."

BISHOPS

Peter I. Archbishop of Tarentaise, 1126–40. Abbot of La Ferté, 1121–26. Both Dimier, *Bibliographie générale*, and Crozet, "L'épiscopat de France," claim he was elected in 1124, but he appears on a charter of 1126 as abbot of La Ferté; *GC* 4: 238, Instrumenta 21. Gams gives his dates as 1132–40.

Hugh of Mâcon. Bishop of Auxerre, 1136–51. Entered Cîteaux with Bernard in 1113. First abbot of Pontigny, 1114–36. Buried at Pontigny. See Bernard of Clairvaux, Letter 276; *Vita prima* 1.3.14; Bouchard, *Spirituality and Administration*.

Garin. Bishop of Sitten, 1138–50. Abbot of Aulps, 1113–38. (Aulps became a Cistercian house in 1136.) Buried at Aulps. See *Vita prima* 2.8.49.

Otto of Freising. Bishop of Freising, 1138–58. Entered Morimond in 1128. Abbot of Morimond, 1131–38. Buried at Morimond. Author of the *Deeds of Frederick Barbarossa* and *Chronicle of Two Cities*.

Baldwin. Archbishop of Pisa, 1137–45. Sometimes confused with the cardinal Baldwin. See Bernard of Clairvaux, Letter 245; *Vita prima* 2.8.49; *Exordium magnum* 3.26.

Godfrey of la Roche. Bishop of Langres, 1139–63. Resigned and returned to Clairvaux. Died in 1164. Entered Cîteaux with Bernard in 1113 and moved to Clairvaux in 1115. First abbot of Fontenay, 1118–27. Prior of Clairvaux, 1127–39. See Bernard of Clairvaux, Letter 170. *Vita prima* 2.5.29, 2.8.49; *Chronicon Clarevallense* 1161, 1164; and Constable, "Disputed Election."

Nehemiah O'Moriertach. Bishop of Cloyne, Ireland, 1140–49.

John. Bishop of Valence, 1141–46. First abbot of Bonnevaux, 1118–41. *Exordium magnum* 1.35. *Vita* in *Thesaurus novus anecdotorum*, 3: 1693–1702.

Peter II. Archbishop of Tarentaise, 1141–74. Canonized in 1199. Entered Bonnevaux in 1122. First abbot of Tamie, 1132–41. *Vita* composed by Geoffrey of Auxerre, *AASS* Mai 2: 320–35, *Chronicon clarevallense* 1174. See also Dimier, *Bibliographie générale.*

Henry. Bishop of Comaccio, 1141–?.

Fredrick. Bishop of Ungarn, 1142–?. Former abbot of Baumgarten.

Rotauld. Bishop of Vannes, 1143–77. First abbot of Lanvaux. Buried at Lanvaux.

John of Châtillon. Bishop of Aleth and Saint Malo, 1144–63. Former monk at Clairvaux. First abbot of Bégard and of Buzay.

Amadeus of Clermont. Bishop of Lausanne, 1145–59. Entered Clairvaux in 1125. Abbot of Hautecombe, 1135–45. See *Vita prima* 2.8.49. For his homilies in praise of the Virgin Mary, see *SC* 72.

Henry von Kärnten. Bishop of Troyes, 1145–69. Former monk at Morimond. First abbot of Villers-Betnach, 1132–45. Buried at Boulancourt.

Bernard. Bishop of Nantes, 1147–1169. Former monk at Clairvaux. *Vita prima* 2.8.49.

Henry Murdac. Archbishop of York, 1147–53. Former monk at Clairvaux. First abbot of Vauclair, 1134–38. Abbot of Fountains, 1138–47. See Bernard of Clairvaux, Letters 321 and 535; *Vita prima* 2.8.49; and Baker, "*Viri religiosi.*"

John. Bishop of Piacenza, 1147–55. First abbot of Columba, 1137–47. Died at Columba.

Dodo. Possibly bishop of Rieti, 1137–81.

Peter of Pavia. Bishop of Pavia, 1148–80. Abbot of Locedio.

Conrad of Austria. Bishop of Passau, 1148–64; Archbishop of Salzburg, 1164–69. Brother of Otto of Freising, and abbot of Heiligenkreuz.

Gerard. Bishop of Tournai, 1149–66. Former monk at Clairvaux, and abbot of Villers. See *Vita prima* 2.8.49.

Henry of France. Bishop of Beauvais, 1149–62; Archbishop of Rheims, 1162–75. Brother of Louis VII of France. Former monk at Clairvaux. *Vita prima* 2.8.49. For Henry's letters, see *PL* 196.

Christian O'Conarchy. Bishop of Lismore and Waterford, 1150–71. Died in 1186. First abbot of Mellifont, 1142–50. See *Vita prima* 2.8.49.

Humbert. Bishop of Nepi, 1150–70?. Former monk at Clairvaux. See *Vita prima* 2.8.49.

Algott. Bishop of Chur, 1151–60. Former monk at Clairvaux. See *Vita prima* 2.8.49.

Alan of Flanders. Bishop of Auxerre. 1152–67. Resigned and returned to L'Arrivour; died in 1185. Former monk at Clairvaux; abbot of L'Arrivour, 1140–52. See Bernard of Clairvaux, Letters 274–76, 280, 282; *De consideratione* 3.2.11; *Vita prima* 2.8.49; *Chronicon Clarevallense* 1165. See also Bouchard, *Spirituality and Administration*, pp. 389–90.

Finnus. Bishop of Kildare, Ireland, 1152–60. Former abbot of Newry.

Bernard. Bishop of Saint Jean of Maurienne, 1153–58. Former abbot of Hautecombe.

Amaury. Bishop of Senlis, 1154–67. Former monk at Chaalis. Buried in Chaalis.

Berno. Bishop of Schwerin, 1155–91. Former monk at Amelunxborn.

Rainald. Bishop of Meaux, 1158–61?. Former abbot of Jouy. Buried at Jouy.

Faramund. Bishop of Veroli, 1160–81. Former monk at Casamari. Buried at Casamari.

Ordonius. Bishop of Salamanca, Spain, 1160–64?.

Andreas of Paris. Bishop of Arras, 1161–1173. Abbot of Vaux-de-Cernay, 1156–61.

Rodolf. Bishop of Ferentino, 1161–91. Former monk at Casamari.

Stephen. Archbishop of Uppsala, 1162–15. Former monk and abbot of Alavastra; buried at Alavastra.

Conrad. Bishop of Lübeck, 1164–72. Former abbot of Riddaghausen.

Guichard. Archbishop of Lyons, 1165–80. Monk at Cîteaux. Abbot of Pontigny, 1136–65. Buried at Pontigny. See *Chronicon Clarevallense* 1174.

Stephen of San Martino. Bishop of Huesca, 1165–80. Former abbot of Poblet.

Horislav. Bishop of Prague, 1167. First abbot of Sedlec, Bohemia, 1143–67. Buried at Sedlec.

Pons of Polignac. Bishop of Clermont-Ferrand, 1170–89. Former abbot of Grandselve, 1158–65, and abbot of Clairvaux, 1165–70. See *Exordium magnum* 2.26; *Chronicon Clarevallense* 1165, 1170.

Gerard. Archbishop of Ravenna, 1170–90. Possibly a Cistercian.

Godfrey of Melna. Bishop of Sorra, Sardinia, 1171–78. Buried at Clairvaux. See *Exordium magnum* 3.23; *Chronicon Clarevallense* 1178.

Simon. Bishop of Moray, Scotland, 1171–84. Former monk of Melrose. Abbot of Coggeshale.

Stephan. Bishop of Ripen, Denmark, 1171–77. Former monk and abbot of Herrevad.

Fulk. Bishop of Fréjus, 1174–92. Former abbot of Thoronet, 1170–74.

Garin. Archbishop of Bourges, 1174–80/81. Former abbot of Pontigny, 1165–74.

Jocelin. Bishop of Glasgow, 1174–99. Consecrated at Clairvaux by Bishop Eskil of Lund, 1175. Former abbot of Melrose, 1170–74. Buried at Melrose.

Leonard. Bishop of Cesena, Italy, 1175–85?.

Ancher. Bishop of Sorra, 1178?–1180?; Archbishop of Torres/Sassari, Sardinia, 1180–?. Former monk of Clairvaux. According to the *Chronicon Clarevallense* 1178, Ancher became the bishop of Sorra after the death of the Cistercian bishop Godfrey and became archbishop of Torres after the death of the Cistercian archbishop Herbert. Former monk of Clairvaux. *PL* 185: 1248.

Felix O'Dullany. Bishop of Ossory, Ireland, 1178–1202. Former abbot of Geripont.

Herbert. Archbishop of Torres/Sassari, Sardinia, 1178–80. Former monk at Clairvaux, abbot of Mores. See *Chronicon Clarevallense* 1178. Author of the *De miraculis, PL* 185.

Phillip. Bishop of Rennes, 1179–81. Abbot of Clairmont.

Odanus O'Heda. Bishop of Lismore and Waterford, 1179?–?. Possibly a Cistercian.

Baldwin of Ford. Bishop of Worcester, 1180–84. Archbishop of Canterbury, 1184–93. Monk and abbot of Ford. Author of *Spiritual Tractates, PL* 204.

Henry von Homburg. Bishop of Basel, 1180–91. Monk of Lützel.

Reference Matter

Abbreviations

AASS   *Acta sanctorum quotquot toto orbe coluntur.* Ed. Society of Bolandists. New ed. Vols. 1–. Paris, 1863–.

ASOC   *Analecta sacri ordinis cisterciensis.*

CCCM   *Corpus Christianorum continuatio mediaevalis.* Turnhout, 1971–.

CFS   Cistercian Fathers Series. 1970–.

Cîteaux   *Chartes et documents concernant l'abbaye de Cîteaux, 1098–1182.* Ed. J. Marlier. Rome, 1969.

Clairvaux   *Recueil des chartes de l'abbaye de Clairvaux.* Ed. Jean Waquet. Troyes, 1950.

COCR   *Collectanea ordinis cisterciensium reformatorum.*

CSS   Cistercian Studies Series. 1970–.

GC   *Gallia Christiana in provincias ecclesiasticas distributa.* Ed. Dionysus Sammarthan. Paris, 1715–1865; Reprint, Farnsborough, Eng., 1970.

James   *The Letters of St. Bernard of Clairvaux.* Trans. Bruno Scott James. Chicago, 1953.

JL   Jaffé, Philip. *Regesta pontificum Romanorum.* Ed. S. Löwenfeld, R. Kaltenbrunner, and P. Ewald. Leipzig, 1885–88.

Molesme   *Cartulaires de l'abbaye de Molesme: 916–1250.* Ed. Jacques Laurent. Paris, 1907.

PL   *Patrologia cursus completus, series latina.* Ed. J. P. Migne. 221 vols. Paris, 1844–64.

Pontigny   *Le premier cartulaire de l'abbaye cistercienne de Pontigny (XIIe–XIIIe s.).* Ed. Martine Garrigues. Collection de documents inédits sur l'histoire de France 14. Paris, 1981.

RB   *Regula Benedicti.* In Timothy Fry, ed. *RB 80: The Rule of Saint Benedict in Latin and English.* Collegeville, Minn. 1981.

RHGF	*Recueil des historiens des Gaules et de la France.* Ed. M. Bouquet et al. 24 vols. Paris, 1738–1904.
La Ferté	*Recueil des pancartes de l'abbaye de la Ferté-sur-Grosne (1113–1178).* Ed. Georges Duby. Annales de la Faculté des Lettres, n.s. 3. Aix-en-Provence, 1953.
SBO	*Sancti Bernardi opera.* Ed. Jean Leclercq, C. H. Talbot, and H. M. Rochais. 8 vols. Rome, 1957–77.
SC	*Sources Chrétiennes.* Paris, 1942–.
Ser. sup. cant.	Bernard of Clairvaux, *Sermones super cantica canticorum.* In *SBO* 1–2.
Statuta	Canivez, Joseph Marie. *1116–1220.* Vol. 1 of *Statuta capitulorum generalium ordinis cisterciensis ab anno 1116 ad annum 1786.* Louvain, 1933.

Notes

⸻

INTRODUCTION

1. The documents describing the early history of the Cistercian order include the *Exordium parvum*, the *Exordium cistercii*, the *Carta caritatis prior*, and the *Summa cartae caritatis*. They are no longer considered unambiguous accounts of the foundation of the order. The first versions of the *Carta caritatis* and the *Exordium parvum* probably were started in the years following the foundation of La Ferté in 1113, modified in 1119, and further expanded the following decade. The *Exordium cistercii* and the *Summa cartae caritatis* probably were not composed until after Stephen Harding's death in 1134. For recent interpretations of these documents, see Auberger, *L'unanimité cistercienne primitive*; C. Waddell, "The *Exordium cistercii*." For a summary of the older studies, see Knowles, "Primitive Cistercian Documents"; for the documents themselves, see Bouton and Van Damme, eds., *Les plus anciens textes de Cîteaux*. All future citations of these documents refer to this edition.

2. René Locatelli, "L'expansion de l'ordre cistercien"; Southern, *Western Society and the Church*, p. 254.

3. See Appendix; see also Willi, "Päpste, Kardinäle und Bischöfe"; Lipkin, "Entrance of the Cistercians into the Church Hierarchy."

4. See Southern, *Making of the Middle Ages*, esp. pp. 219–57; Morris, *Discovery of the Individual*; Bynum, *Jesus as Mother*.

5. Stock, *Implications of Literacy*, pp. 405–8, 451–54.

6. For economic developments, see Gimpel, *Medieval Machine*; for the Cistercians' influence on the development of the medieval university, see Ferruolo, *Origins of the University*.

7. Rosenwein, *Rhinoceros Bound* and *To Be the Neighbor of St. Peter*; Little, *Religious Poverty*. For other studies that examine the relationship between religious communities and their society, see Brown, "Rise and Function of the

Holy Man"; Farmer, *Communities of St. Martin*; S. White, *Custom, Kinship, and Gifts to Saints*; Head, *Hagiography and the Cult of Saints;* Bouchard, *Sword, Miter, and Cloister*; and the discussion of Columbanus and Boniface in Geary, *Before France and Germany*.

8. See, e.g., Leclercq, *Saint Bernard and the Cistercian Spirit*, and the collection of articles in Elder and Sommerfeldt, eds., *Chimaera of His Age*. One of the most recent attempts to unravel some of Bernard's contradictions is Evans, *Mind of St. Bernard*. The two standard modern biographies of Bernard are Vacandard, *Vie de Saint Bernard,* and W. Williams, *Saint Bernard of Clairvaux*. Bernard's earliest biographers tried to instill the sense of his uniqueness. For studies on the hagiographical accounts of Bernard, see the articles by Bredero, including "Etudes sur la *Vita prima*," "The Canonization of Bernard of Clairvaux," and "Saint Bernard and the Historians." See also Goodrich, "Reliability of the *Vita prima.*"

9. McGuire, *Difficult Saint*, p. 23.

10. For studies emphasizing the dichotomy between the Cistercians' ideals and the reality of their behavior, see Lekai, *Cistercians: Ideals and Reality*, and the collection of essays in Sommerfeldt, ed., *Cistercian Ideals and Reality*. For other discussions of a Cistercian decline, see Hill, *English Cistercian Monasteries*; Preiss, *Die politische Tätigkeit*. The idea of a Cistercian decline is also implied by the standard biographies of Bernard. See Vacandard, *Vie de Saint Bernard*; W. Williams, *Saint Bernard of Clairvaux*.

11. For a discussion of this historiographical tradition, see Constable, "Study of Monastic History Today." Even Van Engen, who criticizes the picture of decadent twelfth-century Benedictines, accepts the "commonsense applicability" of a cycle of "charismatic foundation, mature institutionalization, and decadent stagnation" to religious orders and "other collective human enterprises"; see Van Engen, " 'Crisis of Cenobitism' Reconsidered," p. 274.

12. Initial questions about the early Cistercian documents were raised by Lefèvre in a series of articles including "La véritable *Carta Caritatis* primitive," "Le vrai récit?" and "Que savons-nous du Cîteaux primitif?" See also n. 1.

13. Auberger argues that an early version of the *Exordium parvum*, which he calls the *Exordium primitif,* was composed between 1119 and 1123 and was rewritten between 1140 and 1150. The *Exordium cistercii* was initially composed around 1123 but was later revised. Auberger, *L'unanimité cistercienne primitive*, pp. 42–60. For the regulations "called those of 1134," see pp. 61–62.

14. Auberger, *L'unanimité cistercienne primitive*, pp. 132, 253, 318–22. As I explain in Chapter 2, I find these distinctions overblown. For a study that explores continuities between the Cistercian and other eleventh-century monastic reforms, see Lackner, *Eleventh-Century Background of Cîteaux*.

15. See, e.g., Roehl, "Plan and Reality in a Medieval Monastic Economy";

Chauvin, "Réalités et évolution de l'économie cistercienne," pp. 17–18. For a different approach to the problem, see Bouchard, "Cistercian Ideals versus Reality." For the idea that "local conditions" contributed to the Cistercians' inability to maintain the order's ideals, see Berman, *Medieval Agriculture.*

16. For the argument about the Cistercian grange system, see Berman, *Medieval Agriculture*; for the argument about the Cistercians' entrepreneurial attitude, see Bouchard, *Holy Entrepreneurs.*

17. Leclercq, *Love of Learning.*

18. See the works of Bynum, especially *Jesus as Mother*, and her more general discussions of the interpretation of religious symbols in *Holy Feast and Holy Fast* and *Fragmentation and Redemption.* See also the works cited in n. 7. McGuire, in *Friendship and Community*, does not explicitly use interpretations drawn from cultural anthropology, but he nonetheless provides an analysis of an important aspect of monastic culture.

19. McGuire, "Structure and Consciousness," and "The First Cistercian Renewal and a Changing Image of Saint Bernard," in *Difficult Saint*, pp. 153–87.

20. Bynum, "Jesus as Mother, and Abbot as Mother: Some Themes in Twelfth-Century Cistercian Writing" and "The Cistercian Conception of Community," in *Jesus as Mother*, pp. 110–69; McGuire, *Friendship and Community.*

21. Markus, in *End of Ancient Christianity*, esp. pp. 157–212, has explored how early Christian thinkers understood the relations between "desert," "city," and "monastery" to demonstrate the different ways in which monasteries served as models for Christian society.

22. The inadequacy of a person's own beliefs as a sufficient historical explanation becomes especially clear when analyzing religious warfare and persecution. See Langmuir, *History, Religion and Antisemitism*, p. 9; his view that the religious explanations given by medieval Christians and Jews for their conduct toward one another did not suffice as historical explanations for that conduct echoes that of one of the first religious theorists, Jean Bodin, who found similar problems in the explanations given during the sixteenth-century religious wars and European explorations of non-Christian societies. See Preus, *Explaining Religion*, pp. 3–20.

23. See Goodenough, "Toward an Anthropologically Useful Definition of Religion," p. 165.

24. Preus, *Explaining Religion*, pp. 157–64; see also Momigliano, *On Pagans, Jews, and Christians*, pp. 159–77.

25. Langmuir, *History, Religion and Antisemitism*, pp. 163–68. Langmuir's position is not far from that of James, who also distinguished between "personal religion" and "institutional religion" but who generally downplayed religion as a social phenomenon and stressed the psychological side of religious experiences; see James, *Varieties of Religious Experience*, pp. 28–31.

26. Langmuir, *History, Religion and Antisemitism*, pp. 160–61; see also Goodenough, "Toward an Anthropologically Useful Definition," pp. 166–69.

27. Langmuir, *History, Religion and Antisemitism*, p. 136.

28. Ibid., p. 173.

29. At times, however, it is tempting to try. See, e.g., Benton, *Self and Society*, introduction; Leclercq, *Second Look*. For a study of an individual's religious mentality that does not rely on psychohistory, see Brown, *Augustine of Hippo*.

30. Biersack, "Local Knowledge, Local History." See also Ricoeur, "Structure, Word, Event," pp. 79–96.

31. Geertz, *Interpretation of Cultures*, p. 5. See also Darnton, "Symbolic Element in History," esp. his discussion of the advertisement "Fiji $499" that appeared on a graduate student's door in the depths of winter. He explains that, as a member of Princeton's academic culture, he could find meanings in this sign, although not exactly the same meanings as the graduate student who put it up.

32. See Hobsbawm and Ranger, eds., *Invention of Tradition*.

33. Stock, *Implications of Literacy*, p. 405.

34. Along with the works cited in n. 8, see Leclercq, *Second Look*; McGuire, *Difficult Saint*. See also the collections of articles in *Bernard de Clairvaux: Histoire, mentalités, spiritualité*; *Mélanges Saint Bernard*; *Bernard of Clairvaux: Studies Presented to Dom Jean Leclercq*; Pennington, ed., *Saint Bernard of Clairvaux*; Sommerfeldt, ed., *Bernardus Magister*. See also the bibliographies listing the historiography of Bernard: Bouton, *Bibliographie Bernardine 1891–1957*; Rochais and Manning, *Bibliographie de Saint Bernard*.

35. Thus, identity within the family is not the same as identity at work, which differs again from identity in church or synagogue.

36. A very different explanation for the authority of religious figures follows the work of Turner and relies on his concept of liminality. Turner suggests that, by withdrawing from the "structural relations of the world," religious figures entered a marginal state marked by a lack of social differentiation and an egalitarian brotherhood. From this liminal state, however, they reentered society on a new level, with a new understanding of the structural relations within it, and thus possessed a new authority. See especially his discussion of Francis of Assisi in *Ritual Process*, pp. 140–53. One problem with this interpretation relates to the issue discussed above: a liminal state cannot be a complete withdrawal, or even an antistructure to society's structure; a monastery incorporated much of its society's structures into its own organization and culture.

37. Understanding the religious mentality of the monks' lay benefactors is especially problematic. The best documents we have for the benefactors' motivations are the charters recording land transactions, but the initial phrases noting the benefactors' reasons are heavily formulaic and were often composed

by the monks. For studies of monastic benefactors and their possible motivations, see Rosenwein, *Rhinoceros Bound* and *To Be the Neighbor of Saint Peter*; S. White, *Custom, Kinship, and Gifts*; Bouchard, *Sword, Miter, and Cloister*.

38. See especially Peter the Venerable, *Letters*, no. 28.

39. The best-known critics of the Cistercians are the Welshmen Gerald of Wales, who criticized all forms of monasticism in his *Speculum ecclesiae*, and Walter Map, who was particularly hostile to the Cistercians in his *De nugis curialium*. For a discussion of these men, see Knowles, *Monastic Order in England*, pp. 670–77.

PART I

1. Mahn, *L'ordre cistercien*, p. 41.

2. Auberger, *L'unanimité cistercienne primitive*, pp. 42–62.

3. For attempts to understand the ideas of these earliest Cistercians, see Auberger, *L'unanimité cistercienne primitive*; Cowdrey, " 'Quidem frater Stephanus nomine.' " Cowdrey, however, admits his interpretation is speculative.

4. Words and translations pose serious problems for the study of the history of a concept such as charity. As an idea is translated from one language to another, it is labeled with a word. This word is seldom coined for the occasion but is usually already in use for expressing ideas close to, but not identical with, the one in translation. Thus, as a concept moves between languages, it picks up new connotations. Such was the case as biblical ideas about charitable love moved from Hebrew to Greek and Latin and eventually to modern languages such as English. In New Testament Greek, God's love for humanity (as shown in the sacrifice of Jesus), human love for God, and the ethical love between people were usually encompassed by the noun "agape" and its accompanying verb. Occasionally, it was interchanged with "philia," which originally described ties of family or fellowship; but "eros," with its associations of longing and sexual love, seldom appeared in the New Testament. See D. D. Williams, *Spirit and the Forms of Love*, pp. 44–45; Moffatt, *Love in the New Testament*, pp. 46–47. For the Vulgate, Jerome had two Latin verbs at his disposal, "amare" and "diligere," and three nouns, "amor," "dilectio," and "caritas." Usually he translated "agapan" as "diligere," and "philein" as "amare"; "agape," however, was less likely to be "dilectio" than "caritas"; Prat, "Charité." The connotations and the complexity of the ideas associated with these terms continued to change with time.

Modern writers who translate these medieval works into modern European languages are faced with new problems. English and French, at least, have lost the concern for these distinctions, and lump a craving for chocolate, a passion for a lover, a desire for God, and God's benevolence toward humanity under one word: *aimer*, or "to love." Both languages do possess a variation of "caritas"—in English "charity"; in French *charité*—but the common usage of both tends to describe the giving of alms or gifts, occasionally with a sense of condescension, rather than a more abstract selfless love. For want of a better word, however, I am continuing to use the more archaic meaning of the word "charity" to express the concept of good or Christian love that Augustine, Bernard, and other medieval authors usually meant when they used the word "caritas," sometimes meant when they used "diligere" and "dilectio," and occasionally even meant by "amare."

5. Burnaby, *Amor Dei*, p. 115.

6. In his texts, they could mean the love of one person for another, the love of a person for God, and the love of God for humanity. E.g., in *De diligendo deo*, Bernard alternately used "amare" and "diligere" when discussing how God should be loved. He followed the usage of the Vulgate and wrote "diligere" when discussing the commandment to love God or neighbor, but often switched in midparagraph to the verb "amare." See *De diligendo deo* 15–17, *SBO* 3: 131–34.

7. Burnaby, *Amor Dei*, p. 263.

8. For an early example of this emphasis on the love of the incarnate Jesus, see Peter Damian, *Vita beati Romualdi*. See also Southern, *Making of the Middle Ages*, pp. 231–40.

9. For the new religious movements of the eleventh and twelfth centuries, see, among others, Little, *Religious Poverty*; Chenu, "Monks, Canons and Laymen in Search of the Apostolic Life" and "The Evangelical Awakening," in *Nature, Man and Society*, pp. 202–38; Vicaire, *L'imitation des apôtres*; Grundmann, *Religiöse Bewegungen im Mittelalter*; Lawrence, *Medieval Monasticism*; Leyser, *Hermits and the New Monasticism*.

10. Stock, *Implications of Literacy*, pp. 90, 329, 405.

11. These men include Guerric of Igny, Aelred of Rievaulx, Isaac of Stella, Gilbert of Hoyland, and Geoffrey of Auxerre. Auberger divides these men into three generations. He suggests that Guerric, like Bernard of Clairvaux, was a second-generation Cistercian; he places Aelred sometimes in the second generation and sometimes in the third; he locates Isaac of Stella firmly in the third generation; and he considers Gilbert of Hoyland a fourth-generation Cistercian. (He does not consider the writings of Geoffrey of Auxerre.) To consider Bernard, who became abbot of Clairvaux in 1115 and died in 1153, and Guerric—who probably entered Clairvaux in the mid-1120's, became abbot of Igny in 1138, and died in 1157—the same generation may take their chronological ages into consideration, but it ignores the fact that Bernard was Guerric's monastic father for over a decade. Similarly, it makes no sense to place Aelred, Isaac, and Gilbert in different generations when the milestones in their lives occurred at about the same times: Gilbert probably entered Clairvaux around 1132, became abbot of

Hoyland between 1147 and 1150, and died in 1172; Aelred entered Rievaulx in 1134, became abbot in 1147, and died five years before Gilbert, in 1167; Isaac entered Stella around 1140, was abbot there between 1147 and 1167, when he left for the Ile de Ré, and died shortly thereafter. Geoffrey of Auxerre was probably younger than the others; he entered Clairvaux around 1140 and died in 1188 after serving as abbot at Igny, Clairvaux, and Hautecombe. I consider these men members of the same monastic generation; their abbacies straddled the last decades of Bernard's life and the first decades after his death, and they transmitted, often with modifications, ideas learned from Bernard to the generation of monks who entered the order after Bernard's death. Even Geoffrey of Auxerre, who did not leave Clairvaux until after 1153, fits this pattern; the one man who does not is Isaac of Stella, whose direct contact with Bernard may have been minimal. To see these men as members of three different generations is to separate men who were near contemporaries. For Guerric's life, see Morson and Costello, "Introduction," in Guerric of Igny, *Liturgical Sermons.* For Gilbert of Hoyland, see Mikkers, "De vita et operibus Gilberti." For Isaac of Stella, see the two different interpretations by Raciti, "Isaac de l'Etoile et son siècle" and "Isaac de l'Etoile"; Salet, "L'homme" in Isaac of Stella, *Sermons, SC* 130: 7–25; McGinn, *Golden Chain,* pp. 1–23. For Aelred, see Squire, *Aelred of Rievaulx.*

12. See Leclercq, "S. Bernard et ses secrétaires" and "Les Sermons sur les Cantiques ont-ils été prononcés?" in *Recueil d'études sur Saint Bernard,* 1: 3–27, 193–213.

13. Whereas Talbot, in Aelred of Rievaulx, *Sermones inediti,* pp. 8–9, suggests that Aelred wrote out his sermons from his own notes in his own hand, Squire argues that Aelred revised and published his sermons over a number of years and that, like Bernard, either he or his disciples created literary sermons from the simpler materials Aelred had used while preaching; Squire, "Literary Evidence." Raciti, in his edition of Aelred's sermons, *Opera omnia, CCCM* 2a: v–vi, points out that, with the exception of the sermons on Isaiah, Aelred did not publish "official" versions of his sermons. Instead, one finds both simpler and more elaborate sermons on the same themes, sermons that develop the same subjects in the same ways but have no common phrases, and sermons on dissimilar topics that nonetheless have common passages. Raciti concludes that there is no one "authentic" recension, but he does not exclude the possibility that these variations may have resulted from Aelred's reworking of these sermons, probably with the aid of secretaries.

CHAPTER 1

1. *RB* Prol. 45. Benedict borrowed this phrase, as he had so much else in his Rule, from the Rule of the Master.

2. De Vogüé, *Rule of Saint Benedict*, pp. 25–33.
3. *RB* 5.12.
4. *RB* Prol. 49; de Vogüé, *Rule of Saint Benedict*, pp. 33.
5. *RB* 7.67.
6. For the "individualism" of the twelfth century, see Morris, *Discovery of the Individual*. Bynum, in "Did the Twelfth-century Discover the Individual?" *Jesus as Mother*, pp. 82–109, criticizes his undefined assumptions about the nature of individualism. She prefers to substitute "self" for "individual" and argues that the twelfth century was also a period of group definition. For a discussion of the differences between medieval and modern conceptions of individuality, see Benton, "Consciousness of Self."
7. Many of the stories told by Guibert of Nogent, e.g., express his sense of disquiet that monks who appeared holy had secret failings that were revealed at their deaths or by the manner of their deaths; see Benton, *Self and Society*. Cistercian sermons are filled with complaints about hypocrisy, sometimes about the preacher's own hypocrisy. See, e.g., Guerric of Igny, *De epiphania, sermo quartus* 3, *SC* 166: 292, CFS, 8: 93, in which he comments on the disjunction between his outward appearance of piety and the condition of his soul. For the most famous twelfth-century example of such self-criticism, see the letters from Heloise to Abelard; Radice, trans., *Letters of Abelard and Heloise*.
8. The Italians Romuald of Ravenna, John Gualbert, and Peter Damian are early examples of men who experienced conflicts in ethical standards and eventually developed new religious communities that they hoped would better reconcile behavior with intention. Both Romuald and John felt torn between their families' feuding ethics and the need for Christian compassion; both entered traditional monasteries to try to resolve their conflicts, only to discover a disjunction between the monks' behaviors and the rules they followed; both eventually founded new communities that claimed to follow the intent of the early monastic fathers. Peter Damian's ethical conflict was somewhat different: he was torn between the traditions of gift-giving and his sense that religious men should be poor. For the lives of Romuald, John Gualbert, and Peter Damian, see Peter Damian, *Vita beati Romualdi*; *S. Joannis Gualberti Vita*; John of Lodi, *Vita Petri Damiani*. For brief descriptions of the lives of many of the eleventh- and twelfth-century religious reformers, see Little, *Religious Poverty*. Although Little emphasizes money itself as a causal force, rather than the new social relations engendered by both the increased use of money and urbanization, he moved the discussion of religious change away from both the Marxist arguments that attributed the rise of religious dissent to class formation, and the more religious arguments that attributed religious change to intellectual factors such as reading the Gospels. For another argument that associates religious change with the dislocations of a changing society, see Moore, *Origins of European Dissent*.

9. Morris, *Discovery of the Individual*, esp. pp. 65–138. For monks at Marmoutier interested in motivation, see Farmer's discussion of John of Marmoutier's "Deeds of the Counts of Anjou" in *Communities of St. Martin*, pp. 88–95. See also Gold's discussion of the conflicts in twelfth-century epics and romances in *Lady and the Virgin*.

10. For developments in the sacrament of penance, see Anciaux, *La théologie du sacrement de pénitence*. These changes appeared in religious life before they were institutionalized in the sacrament of penance. See, e.g., Romuald of Ravenna or John Gualbert, both of whom developed an inner compunction to replace penitential acts that seemed insufficient.

11. For a discussion of the changing relationship between monasteries and their benefactors, see McLaughlin, *Consorting with Saints*. For the intercessory role played by the monks at Cluny, see Le Goff, *Birth of Purgatory*, pp. 124–27; Heath, *Crux Imperatorum Philosophia*; Wollasch, "Ein cluniacensisches Totenbuch." For Marmoutier, see Farmer, *Communities of St. Martin*, p. 123.

12. Peter the Venerable, *Letters*, no. 28, 1: 81–82. For the separate place for contemplation, see Peter the Venerable, *Statuta Petri Venerabilis*, no. 53; for the elimination of pauses between the psalms, see no. 1. A number of Peter's statutes sought to ensure that the words of the liturgy corresponded to both the liturgical calendar and the world he saw around him. E.g., he changed the hymn for the night of the Nativity from *Nota tuba* to *Caeleste organum* because *Nota tuba* was a "series of words in disarray in which nothing pertained to the Nativity of the Savior"; he changed the hour for prime in the winter so that the monks would not sing *Iam lucis orto sidere* until the sun had risen, and he suggested that the crosses used during extreme unction be made of wood as the monks did not sing "Behold the gold or the silver of the cross" but "Behold the wood of the cross on which the salvation of the world hangs." *Statuta* nos. 9, 61, 62. See also Knowles, "Reforming Decrees of Peter the Venerable"; Constable, "Monastic Policy of Peter the Venerable"; Folz, "Pierre le Vénérable et la liturgie."

13. Van Engen, *Rupert of Deutz*, pp. 299–334, esp. pp. 303–4.

14. Farmer, *Communities of St. Martin*, pp. 124–25.

15. Guido I, prior of La Chartreuse, *Consuetudines cartusiae* 7, 14, 41, SC 313: 176–77, 296–97, 244–46.

16. *Statuta*, 1: 31 (1134, no. 78). In 1157, they raised the age from sixteen to nineteen; 1: 62 (1157, no. 28).

17. William of Saint-Thierry, *Vita prima* 1.3.17, *PL* 185: 236. William died in 1148.

18. Dimier, "Un témoin tardif peu connu," p. 91; Lynch, "Cistercians and Underage Novices," p. 285.

19. Guido I, *Consuetudines cartusiae* 27, SC 313: 220.

20. Bouchard, *Sword, Miter, and Cloister*, pp. 136–38. She argues that these families used such donations to enhance their social status.

21. For a donation that specifies that a son may enter Cîteaux when he comes of age if he wishes, see *Cîteaux*, pp. 125–26 (no. 157). For other charters noting the relationship of donor to monks, see *Cîteaux*, pp. 93–94 (no. 91); *Clairvaux*, pp. 11 (no. 6), 37 (no. 17), 45–46 (no. 19), 74 (no. 62), 19 (no. 71); *Pontigny*, pp. 134 (no. 73), 182–83 (no. 116); *La Ferté*, pp. 52–53 (no. 17).

22. For the letters, see Leclercq, "Lettres de S. Bernard." For a discussion of the way one collection of Cistercian miracle tales reflected the monks' sense of their history, see McGuire, "Structure and Consciousness."

23. She points out that maternal language in monastic sermons tells us more about the monks' ideas about the feminine than it does about their actual experience of mothers; Bynum, "Jesus as Mother and Abbot as Mother," in *Jesus as Mother*, p. 167.

24. Duby, "Youth in Aristocratic Society," in *Chivalrous Society*, pp. 112–16.

25. Baldwin, "Masters at Paris," pp. 138–72; Murray, *Reason and Society*, pp. 214–33. See also Ferruolo, *Origins of the University*.

26. Abelard is the classic example of the scholar who gave up his sword for the weapons of disputation. See also Duby, "Culture of the Knightly Class," pp. 256–57.

27. Le Goff, *Intellectuals in the Middle Ages*, pp. 24–34; H. Waddell, *Wandering Scholars*.

28. Even the date of this conversion was important to the Cistercians' conception of their history. Traditionally, 1112 has been given as the date when Bernard entered Cîteaux. According to the *Exordium parvum*, it was this influx of new monks that rescued Cîteaux from extinction. However, not only has the reliability of the *Exordium parvum* been questioned, but Bredero has shown that the *Vita prima* of Bernard was modified by later Cistercians to emphasize the importance of his arrival. The earliest recensions of the manuscripts give the date of 1113, implying that Cîteaux had already received enough new monks to arrange for the foundation of La Ferté before Bernard arrived. It is unclear who these earliest arrivals were. See Bredero, "Etudes sur la *Vita prima*." However, historians' acceptance of the traditional date of 1112 has died hard. See, e.g., Evans, *Mind of St. Bernard*, who gives the date as 1113 in her chronological table (p. xi), but still uses 1112 in the body of the text (p. 2).

29. Geoffrey of Auxerre's "Fragmenta" 1, p. 89–90, on which William of Saint-Thierry based his book of the *Vita prima*, describes Bernard's father Tescelin Sorus as "native of Châtillon, but lord of a minor castle called Fontaines" (Erat quidem indigena Castellionis sed dominus minoris castri cui Fontane nomen est). For efforts to connect Bernard of Clairvaux to noble families, especially the lords of Châtillon, see Jobin, *Saint Bernard et sa famille*; Richard, "Le milieu familial," pp. 9–10; Chaume, "Les origines familiales." Bouchard, recognizing that the labeling of Bernard's father as "de Châtillon" did

not necessarily make him related to the lords of Châtillon, concludes that Josbert's family was unrelated to Bernard; see *Sword, Miter, and Cloister,* pp. 237–38. But she has ignored evidence from Geoffrey of Auxerre and William of Saint-Thierry, both of whom described Josbert Rufus of Châtillon, viscount of Dijon, as "ipsius abbatis propinquus secundum carnem." Geoffrey of Auxerre, "Fragmenta" 19, p. 99; William of Saint-Thierry, *Vita prima* 1.9.43, *PL* 185: 252. Exactly what this relationship was, however, remains unspecified.

Bernard's mother's family is easier to trace. Aleth came from the family of the lords of Montbard; her brother Gaudry was lord of Touillon and entered Cîteaux along with Bernard; through marriage, she was related to the lords of La Roche. Godfrey, the brother of Rayner of La Roche, entered Cîteaux with Bernard and later became bishop of Langres. See Bouchard, *Sword, Miter, and Cloister,* pp. 334–38, 396. William of Saint-Thierry described Godfrey as "propinquus sanguine" to Bernard; *Vita prima* 1.9.45, *PL* 185: 253. This may imply a closer relationship than being both the brother of Bernard's aunt's second husband and the brother-in-law of Bernard's cousin, as Bouchard argues. Fossier suggests that the lords of La Roche were related to Tescelin; "La fondation de Clairvaux."

30. "Verbum fratris difficilius admittebat"; "ut mos est sapientiae saecularis, levitatem reputans, obstinato animo salubre consilium et fratris monita repellebat." William of Saint-Thierry, *Vita prima* 1.3.10–11, *PL* 185: 232–33.

31. "Spirituali militiae dextras dederunt." William of Saint-Thierry, *Vita prima* 1.9.55, *PL* 185: 257.

32. *RB* 60.

33. For a discussion of the men Bernard attracted to Clairvaux, see Dimier, "Saint Bernard et le recrutement." Of the men Dimier named, 28 were scholars, 21 were clerics or cathedral canons, 15 were monks or hermits, and 18 were knights.

34. Historians have given various dates for the institution of the Cistercian lay brotherhood. From his reading of Pontigny's foundation charter, Dubois believes it unlikely that the lay brotherhood was established before 1115; see "L'institution des convers." Hallinger suggested that the lay brotherhood began before 1119; "Woher kommen die Laienbrüder?"p. 10. The earliest statutes regulating the lay brothers' activities are in the *Summa cartae caritatis.*

35. For the origins of eleventh- and twelfth-century lay brotherhoods, see Hallinger, "Woher kommen die Laienbrüder?"; Constable, "*Famuli* and *Conversi* at Cluny." For the possible influence of eleventh-century religious foundations on the Cistercians, see Duvernay, "Cîteaux, Vallombreuse, et Etienne Harding." Mahn, in *L'ordre cistercien,* pp. 38–39, makes a similar suggestion.

36. For the spiritual motivations of the lay brothers, see Hallinger, "Woher kommen die Laienbrüder?" pp. 84–95; for the idea that the lay brotherhood con-

tinued the class divisions of feudalism, see Werner, "Bemerken zu einer neuen These," and, more recently, Alfonso, "Cistercians and Feudalism." For a summary of the historiographical debates concerning the lay brothers, see Lescher, "Laybrothers."

37. For a possible example of this at Cîteaux, see *Cîteaux*, pp. 143–45 (no. 177). Berman has found evidence of this in southern France; see her *Medieval Agriculture*, pp. 55–57. It is unclear what happened to the wives and families of these men.

38. *Statuta*, 1: 108 (1188, no. 8).

39. For Bernard's uncle, see *PL* 185: 1461. For others, see Othon, "De l'institution et des us des convers," p. 161 n. 2. It is possible that, at least in the early years of the order, illiterate aristocrats became lay brothers rather than monks. For priests who became lay brothers, see Caesarius of Heisterbach, *Dialogue on Miracles* 1.39, pp. 50–51.

40. For these stories, see Herbert of Clairvaux, *De miraculis* 1.15–16, 18, 29, 32, *PL* 185: 1291–92, 1293, 1301, 1304.

41. Such stories began to be collected in the third quarter of the twelfth century, at a time when lay brother unrest began to be noticeable, and it is possible that they were an attempt by the choir monks to quell the lay brothers' discontent. See Chapter 4.

42. Rosenwein, "Feudal War and Monastic Peace" and *Rhinoceros Bound*.

43. "Nonne uidetis homines saeculi nobiles, ad conuersionem uenientes, lanceas et gladios suos dimittere et quasi rusticos manibus suis cibum suum operari?" Aelred of Rievaulx, *Sermo 3: In nativitate domini* 11, *CCCM* 2a: 29.

44. "Fossa profundae humilitatis castra cingebat; super quam fortissimus et pulcherrimus murus oboedientiae aedificatus caelos penetrabat, quem bonorum exemplorum historiae undique depictae mirabiliter decorabant. Aedificatus autem erat cum propugnaculis; mille clypei ex eo pendebant, omnis armatura fortium. Porta professionis omnibus patens; ianitor in limine, dignos inducens et indignos abiciens." Bernard of Clairvaux, *De filio regis* 5, *SBO* 6.2: 264.

45. "Postremo providus, et eruditus, et perfectus in regno caritatis." *De filio regis* 7, *SBO*, 6.2: 266–67.

46. "Interim Caritas morae impatiens, ordinari exercitum, aperiri portas, et persequi inimicos praecipit, aperte denuntians: 'Vadam ad portas inferi.' Sicque uno impetu universus Caritatis procedit exercitus, quos Babylonici non ferentes fugiunt, sed non effugiunt. Cadunt mille a latere Temperantiae et decem millia a dextris Prudentiae. Occidit Timor mille et Caritas decem millia." Bernard of Clairvaux, *De conflictu duorum regum* 7, *SBO* 6.2: 273.

47. Leclerq, "Aggressiveness or Repression in St. Bernard and in his Monks," in *Monks and Love*, esp. p. 90. The argument that follows owes much to Leclercq's essay. But whereas Leclercq is primarily interested in showing how the

use of martial and courtly themes and images helped the monks to discharge and sublimate their aggressive impulses, I am more concerned with the way the use of such imagery affected the monks' understanding of their religious life. We cannot tell if these stories helped monks to control their desire for violence or for sex; we can, however, see how the abbots' use of these images influenced what they taught their monks about the purpose and goals of monastic life.

48. Duby, "Youth in Aristocratic Society," in *Chivalrous Society*, pp. 112–16.

49. Orderic Vitalis, *Ecclesiastical History* 5.10, 3: 97–114.

50. For the use of imagery in learning and memorizing information, see Spence, *Memory Palace of Matteo Ricci*, pp. 1–23.

51. Aelred of Rievaulx, *Sermo 19: In assumptione sanctae Mariae* 7–16, CCCM 2a: 148–50.

52. "Tria sunt quibus servatur unitas: patientia, humilitas, et caritas. His armari debet miles Christi, patientiam habens quasi scutum, quod ferat et circumferat contra omnia adversa; humilitatem quasi loricam, quae conservet interiora praecordia; caritatem quasi lanceam, per quam, sicut dicit Apostolus, omnes impetens in provocatione caritatis et omnibus omnia se faciens, belligeratur bellum Domini. Oportet etiam ut habeat galeam salutis, quae est spes, caput, id est principale mentis, muniens et conservans. Habeat etiam gladium verbi Dei, et equum boni desiderii." Bernard of Clairvaux, *Sententiarum series prima* 32, *SBO* 6.2: 18.

53. "Indutos lorica justitiae et galea salutis, habentes scutum fidei et gladium spiritus, quod est verbum Dei." Nicholas of Clairvaux, Letter 45, *PL* 196: 1645.

54. Rosenwein, "Feudal War and Monastic Peace" and *Rhinoceros Bound*. See also Rosenwein and Little, "Social Meaning in the Monastic and Mendicant Spiritualities."

55. Nicholas of Clairvaux, Letter 45, *PL* 196: 1645.

56. It is possible that they even eliminated the entire Office of the Dead for a time. William of Malmesbury mentions that they performed vigils for the dead, but a Benedictine monk who replied to Bernard's *Apologia* in 1127 or 1128 specifies that there is no such office in the Cistercians' daily liturgy. William of Malmesbury, *De gestis regum Anglorum* 4.336, RS 90.2.383. Wilmart, "Une riposte de l'ancien monachisme." By the time the customary was composed, around 1134, there was an office for the dead; Griesser, "*Ecclesiastica officia*," p. 214. See C. Waddell, "Early Cistercian Experience of Liturgy," p. 87.

57. Griesser, "*Ecclesiastica officia*," pp. 216–17, 261–62.

58. Ibid., p. 235.

59. "Pro anima uxoris meae, Elisabeth, eo videlicet pacto ut fratres ibi commorantes, singulis annis in anniversario die sui obitus, memoriam ejus in suis orationibus habeant, que obiit in vigilia sancti Georgii matris." *Pontigny*, pp. 165–66 (no. 95).

60. A charter from La Ferté suggests that this might have been more common than the statutes of the Chapter General suggest: around 1140, Bernard de Vers, his sons, and his daughter-in-law gave La Ferté a mill near the abbey. In return, if they died without excommunication and were carried to the door of the monastery, they were to be buried there and commemorated by the entire order like monks. *La Ferté*, p. 46 (no. 8). In 1155, the monks at La Ferté offered a benefactor an anniversary feast; *La Ferté*, p. 54 (no. 18). This occurred at Cîteaux as well. See *Cîteaux*, pp. 122–23 (no. 150), and the numerous occasions in the 1170's when their benefactors shared in the prayers and benefits of the order.

61. These family members received a full office, a private mass from each priest, 50 psalms or prayers from the other monks, and a yearly commemoration in chapter. Griesser, *"Ecclesiastica officia,"* p. 296.

62. *Summa cartae caritatis* 24, p. 124; *Statuta*, 1: 19 (1134, no. 27).

63. *Statuta*, 1: 47, 68 (1152, no. 10; 1157, no. 63).

64. Nor was Cistercian life entirely free of violence. See Dimier, "Violences, rixes et homicides."

65. Leclercq, "Aggressiveness or Repression in St. Bernard and in his Monks," in *Monks and Love*, pp. 92–93.

66. "Quid enim aliud debuit dici poenitentia peccatorum nisi violentia in regnum coelorum? An non violentia est rapere virtute quod non erat concessum naturae"; "Virtute igitur dilectionis armatus sis, quicumque es ille pius invasor qui rapere contendis regnum coelorum? . . . ut vires exercitet, constantiam probet multiplicet victorias, augeatque coronas." Guerric of Igny, *In nativitate sancti Ioannis Baptistae, sermo secundus* 1–3, *SC* 202: 327–32, CFS, 32: 129–32.

67. "Sed et attrahendus quadam violentia precis vehementiaque fervoris"; "Pia violentia qua regnum coeleste rapitur." Guerric of Igny, *In prima dominica adventus Domini, sermo tertius* 3, *SC* 166: 128, CFS, 8: 18–19.

68. See also Nicholas of Clairvaux, who, in Letter 35 to Walter, speaks of the labor and prayers of community "qui vim faciunt regno coelorum et violenter rapiunt illud"; *PL* 196: 1627.

69. See Bynum, *Docere verbo et exemplo*, for the idea of the monastery as a school and monks as learners.

70. See Leclercq, *Love of Learning*.

71. For monastic criticism of the schools, see Ferruolo, *Origins of the University*, esp. pp. 47–92.

72. Bernard of Clairvaux, Letter 106, *SBO* 7: 266 (James, no. 107).

73. "Sub illo magistro cujus scola in terris est, et cathedra in coelis." Nicholas of Clairvaux, Letter 38, *PL* 196: 1633. See also Letter 16, *PL* 196: 1612.

74. "Tota die, ut audio, philosophos, rhetores, et poetas legis; putasne in-

telligis, quae legis? Crede mihi, plus invenies apud nos in securi et ascia, quam apud vos in scripto et pagina." Nicholas of Clairvaux, Letter 38, *PL* 196: 1636. See Bernard of Clairvaux, Letter 106, *SBO* 7: 267.

75. Bernard of Clairvaux, Letters 104, 108, *SBO* 7: 261, 278 (James, nos. 105, 110).

76. "Quam salubrius disceres Iesum, et hunc cruxifixum, quam utique scientiam haud facile, nisi qui mundo crucifixus erit, apprehendit." Bernard of Clairvaux, Letter 108, *SBO* 7: 278 (James, no. 110).

77. "Conversi ab inanibus studiis ad verae sapientiae cultum." Geoffrey of Auxerre, *Vita prima* 4.2.10, *PL* 185: 327.

78. Cited in Leclercq, "Les souvenirs inédits de Geoffroy d'Auxerre sur Saint Bernard," *Etudes sur saint Bernard*, p. 153. See also Bernard of Clairvaux, *Ser. sup. cant.* 20.3–4, *SBO* 1: 115–16.

79. See, e.g., Feiss, "Bernardus Scholasticus," pp. 349–78; and Vergier, "Le cloître et les écoles."

80. See McGinn, *Golden Chain*, pp. 234–38. For Isaac's biography, see pp. 7–23. Isaac, however, became marginalized in the order; he left Stella for the Atlantic island of Ré in 1167, perhaps because of a desire for greater solitude and poverty, perhaps because of his unpopular support for Thomas Becket, and perhaps because of controversy over the scholastic terminology in his preaching.

81. "Quo utendum sit ad superiora quaedam et sanctiora et magis intima arcana sapientiae." Gilbert of Hoyland, Letter 2.2, *PL* 184: 291, CFS, 34: 94.

82. "Delectat te vehementer, animum amoremque arripuit attraxitque ad se tuum exigua haec et ambigua naturarum rationumque notitia, ad quam vix longo circuitu et sinuosis anfractibus pervenitur." Gilbert of Hoyland, Letter 2.2, *PL* 184: 292, CFS, 34: 95.

83. "Tunc profusius explicantem, et expedientem copiosius quae senseris de venia, gratia, gloria, de his quae vel dedit, vel reddidit, vel addidit, et universis quae pro nobis pertulit et contulit nobis Dominus." Letter 2.3, *PL* 184: 292.

84. See, e.g., Bernard of Clairvaux, *Ser. sup. cant.* 33.14–16, 77.1–2, *SBO* 7: 243–44, 8: 262; Gilbert of Hoyland, *Sermones in canticum* 30.6–8, 38.4, *PL* 184: 158–59, 201.

85. Leclercq, "Lettres d'Odon d'Ourscamp," p. 151.

86. "Saeculares et saecularibus conjunctae, religionis nomen in contemptum et opprobrium adduxerunt; et mundum, et quae mundi sunt, nostri penitus respuerunt et expuerunt a cogitationibus et operibus suis." Nicholas of Clairvaux, Letter 36, *PL* 196: 1632.

87. See, e.g., Rupert of Deutz's defense of black monks, as discussed by Van Engen, *Rupert of Deutz*, pp. 314–34.

CHAPTER 2

1. Gilson, *Mystical Theology*; Delfgaauw, "La nature et les degrés de l'amour"; Dumont, "Seeking God in Community According to St. Aelred"; Casey, *Athirst for God*; Sommerfeldt, *Spiritual Teachings of Bernard of Clairvaux*.

2. See Bynum, *Docere verbo et exemplo*; Bynum, "The Cistercian Conception of Community," in *Jesus as Mother*, pp. 59–81.

3. This has been called a "crisis in cenobitism." The phrase was first used by Morin in "Rainaud l'ermite et Ives de Chartres"; see also Dereine, "Odon de Tournai et la crise du cénobitisme"; and the more general treatments in Leclercq, "Monastic Crisis of the Eleventh and Twelfth Centuries"; Cantor, "Crisis of Western Monasticism"; Knowles, *Christian Monasticism*, pp. 69–71. The causes of the "crisis" were variously given as the increased wealth of the eleventh-century Benedictine communities, their overmodification of the Benedictine Rule, and the failure of the alliance of monks and Gregorian reformers to reshape Christian society; its results were depicted as a movement of men away from communal organizations toward a more eremitical life. Recently, historians have modified this explanation of both causes and effects. They have criticized the view that twelfth-century Benedictine monasticism was "decadent" and have suggested that the new twelfth-century monks emphasized a different form of community from their predecessors. See especially Bynum's essays in *Jesus as Mother*; Van Engen, "'Crisis of Cenobitism' Reconsidered"; Farmer, *Communities of St. Martin*, pp. 117–50.

4. Peter Damian, *De fuga dignitatum ecclesiasticarum*, PL 145: 457; *Vita beati Bernardi*, PL 172: 1380; Little, *Religious Poverty*, p. 77.

5. Peter the Venerable, *De miraculis libri duo* 1.9, CCCM 83: 35–36. Peter was trying to hold together these great communal rituals at a time when the increasing number of priests among his monks led men to skip conventual prayers for their own performance of the mass. Peter the Venerable, *Statuta Petri Venerabilis*, nos. 6, 72.

6. Constable, "Eremitical Forms of Monastic Life"; Farmer, *Communities of St. Martin*, pp. 129–32.

7. For one monastery's solution, see Farmer, *Communities of St. Martin*, pp. 135–50.

8. Auberger, *L'unanimité cistercienne primitive*, esp. pp. 22, 83, 317–20. Auberger has performed a very careful analysis of the early Cistercian documents, but there is much in his argument with which I disagree. Most importantly, he argues for distinctions that I find a matter more of degree than of kind. I do not deny that there are variations in the ideas of Cistercian authors, but whereas Auberger focuses on individual differences, I focus on similarities. For a more general comparison between the Cistercians' legislation and their language of friendship, see Southern, *Western Society and the Church*, p. 257.

9. For arguments concerning the "intent" of the first Cistercians, see Pennington, ed., *Cistercian Spirit*; Leclercq, "Intentions of the Founders." For discussions of the Cistercians' interpretations of the Benedictine Rule, see Lekai, "The Rule and the Early Cistercians"; Leclercq, "St. Bernard and the Rule"; Goodrich, "Cistercian Founders and the Rule."

10. For Robert's life, see Spahr, *Das Leben des hl. Robert von Molesme*; C. Waddell, "Pre-Cistercian Background of Cîteaux and the Cistercian Liturgy," pp. 119–21. Some historians have suggested that Robert was born into a noble Burgundian family with connections with many of the important benefactors of Molesme; for this, see Lackner, *Eleventh-Century Background of Cîteaux*, p. 218, who follows the work of Chaume. Bouchard, however, believes Robert came from the petty aristocracy of Champagne; *Sword, Miter, and Cloister*, p. 78. She gives no evidence for this statement. Given the paucity of contemporary evidence for Robert's life, it is unlikely that his family background can ever be established.

11. According to Laurent in *Molesme*, 1: 147, Robert became abbot of Saint-Michel of Tonnerre in 1068; Godefrey, in "L'histoire du prieuré de Saint-Ayoul," suggests that Robert was prior at Saint-Ayoul between 1072 and 1074. See also Spahr, *Das Leben des hl. Robert von Molesme*, pp. xliii–xlv; Lackner, *Eleventh-Century Background of Cîteaux*, pp. 218–20.

12. For Robert's "solita levitate," see *Exordium parvum* 7, p. 65. For his movement and his various monastic offices, see Spahr, *Das Leben des hl. Robert von Molesme*, pp. 8–16, and Spahr's analysis of the corroborating evidence, pp. xli–xlvii. The author of Robert's *Vita* had no reason to present Robert as more mobile than he was. If anything, he tried to counter the criticism of Robert's instability by suggesting that Robert received papal approval before he left Saint-Ayoul to direct the hermits at Collan; Spahr, *Das Leben des hl. Robert von Molesme*, p. 10.

13. *Molesme*, 2: 12 (no. 6), 19 (no. 11), 31 (no. 21). Other prominent benefactors included the duke and duchess of Lorraine and the counts of Bar-sur-Aube, Brienne, Bar-sur-Seine, and Tonnerre.

14. These first ten years are often seen as an "heroic" period during which the monks lived the life of self-denial that they desired, and they are often compared to the later "corrupt" years of the monastery's wealth. The monks, however, saw less virtue in this poverty; in 1083, Raynard, bishop of Langres, issued a plea for donations, undoubtedly with the knowledge of Abbot Robert. Lackner, *Eleventh-Century Background of Cîteaux*, pp. 224, 244–45.

15. *Molesme*, 1: 135–37; 2: 58–59 (no. 46), 68 (no. 57), 108 (no. 104), 161 (no. 177), 177 (no. 197), 164 (no. 181), 178 (no. 198).

16. *Molesme*, 2: 12 (no. 6).

17. Lackner, *Eleventh-Century Background of Cîteaux*, p. 230.

18. Spahr, *Das Leben des hl. Robert von Molesme*, pp. 13–15. Robert supposedly

joined a group of hermits at Aux, and Alberic, Stephen, and two other monks may have lived for a time as hermits at Vivicus. Auberger, in *L'unanimité cistercienne primitive*, p. 79, invokes Orderic Vitalis to suggest that the two monks who accompanied Stephen and Alberic to Vivicus were John and Hildebod; Orderic, however, does not mention the retreat at Vivicus and only locates John and Hildebod at Cîteaux. Orderic Vitalis, *Ecclesiastical History* 8.26, 4: 312–25.

19. It was not unusual for abbots to take eremitical retreats. See Constable, "Eremitical Forms of Monastic Life." For Robert's supposed frustration about the behavior of the monks at Molesme, see Spahr, *Das Leben des hl. Robert von Molesme*, pp. 13–14. Around 1135, Orderic Vitalis painted a vivid picture of Robert's attempts to reform his monks; *Ecclesiastical History* 8.26, 4: 312–17.

20. "Regulae beatissimi Benedicti quam illuc huc usque tepide ac negligenter in eodem monasterio tenueratis, artius deinceps atque perfectius inhaerere velle professos fuisse"; "ibique salubrius atque quietius domino famulari." *Exordium parvum* 2, p. 58.

21. *Cîteaux*, p. 98 (no. 101).

22. Odo negotiated with Rainard of Beaune to obtain for the monks certain lands around Cîteaux that Rainard would have preferred to retain; he gave the monks a vineyard near Meursault; and according to the *Exordium parvum*, helped to fund the construction of the buildings and supplied the monks with necessities, land, and livestock. But he made his donation of the vineyard on Christmas Day 1098, "coram procerum suorum copiosa multitudine." *Cîteaux*, pp. 49–51 (no. 23), 52–53 (no. 26).

23. "Quidam monachi cum eo qui heremum non diligebant"; *Exordium parvum* 7, pp. 64–65. The primitive kernel of the *Exordium parvum* probably included the decree of the papal legate, Archbishop Hugh of Lyons, about the relation between Cîteaux and Molesme; Auberger, *L'unanimité cistercienne primitive*, p. 50. The comment about Robert's return to Molesme follows the text of the decree. It is unclear whether Robert left Cîteaux because he disliked the austerities of Cîteaux and longed for the comforts of Molesme, as the late-twelfth-century *Exordium magnum* claims, or whether he could not withstand the pressures of a council of ecclesiastical dignitaries who had assembled to consider the complaints about Robert's desertion made by the monks of Molesme; Conrad of Eberbach, *Exordium magnum* 1.15, p. 68. Certainly, Robert's former predilection for the poor and harsh years of a religious foundation suggests that Cîteaux should have pleased him, but by 1099 he was at least 70 years old and may have found the life too difficult.

24. *RB* 2.2, 5.4.

25. *RB* 2.34.

26. *RB* 18.22–23, 39–41, 55.1–3. Benedict was aware that an abbot might err;

his Rule, unlike that of the Master he used as a model, traces out the abbot's duties with some specificity and emphasizes his obligation to follow it. See de Vogüé, *Rule of Saint Benedict*, p. 73.

27. *RB* 34.1–2, 55.20–21.

28. According to Gregory the Great, Benedict administered his distant communities through an often miraculous discretion by which he could be present to all his monks in spirit, if not in body: he sensed when his monks ate or drank outside their communities, he knew when they had accepted gifts, and he told one group where to build their new chapel by appearing to them in a dream. *Dialogues* 2.12–13, 19, 22, *SC* 290: 174–78, 194–96, 200–204.

29. Peter Damian, *De fuga dignitatum ecclesiasticarum*, *PL* 145: 455–64, esp. col. 457.

30. The *Carta caritatis* evolved gradually: the copy of the charter recording Pontigny's foundation in 1114 mentioned a no-longer-extant primitive version that probably comprised the first four chapters of the existing *Carta caritatis prior*; in 1119, Pope Calixtus II confirmed this *Carta caritatis prior*, which added to the primitive charter some of the abbots' decisions in the years between 1115 and 1119; between 1165 and 1173, the monks modified the charter again, creating the *Carta caritatis posterior*; Auberger, *L'unanimité cistercienne primitive*, pp. 26–34.

31. Auberger suggests that he did this under compulsion from the other abbots. But even the first four chapters of the *Carta caritatis prior* curtail the abbot's discretionary authority. Auberger may be right, however, that the later chapters, concerning the relationship of other abbots to the abbot of Cîteaux, were added because of these abbots' concern about their independence.

32. *Carta caritatis prior* 1, 4, pp. 91, 93.

33. "Quo pacto, quove modo, immo qua caritate monachi eorum per abbatias in diversis mundi partibus corporibus divisi animis indissolubiliter conglutinarentur." *Carta caritatis prior* 1, p. 89.

34. "Non alium inducant sensum in lectione sanctae regulae, [sed] sicut antecessores nostri, sancti patres, monachi scilicet novi monasterii, intellexerunt et tenuerunt, et nos hodie intelligimus et tenemus, ita ipsi intelligant et teneant." *Carta caritatis prior* 2, p. 92.

35. "Si quando a sancto proposito et observantia sanctae regulae paululum, quod absit, declinare temptaverint, per nostram sollicitudinem ad rectitudinem vitae redire possint." *Carta caritatis prior* 1, p. 91.

36. "Secundum formam morum et librorum novi monasterii possideant, quatinus in actibus nostris nulla sit discordia, sed una caritate, una regula similibusque vivamus moribus." *Carta caritatis prior* 3, p. 92.

37. These statutes, often called the "Statutes of 1134," pose difficulties in dating. It seems likely, however, that those statutes also included in the *Summa*

cartae caritatis (the *Capitula*) were composed before it was assembled in 1123–24. See Auberger, *L'unanimité cistercienne primitive*, pp. 61–62. For a discussion of the problems with Canivez's edition of the statutes, and notice of the preparation of a new edition, see C. Waddell, "Toward a New Provisional Edition of the Statutes," pp. 384–419.

38. *Statuta*, 1: 13, 16 (1134, nos. 4, 15); see also *Summa cartae caritatis* 11, p. 121.

39. *Statuta*, 1: 16 (1134, no. 14); see also *Summa cartae caritatis* 12, p. 121.

40. *RB* 39–40, 55.

41. Griesser, in "*Ecclesiastica officia*," dates the manuscript between 1130 and 1134.

42. For Cluny, see Ulrich, *Antiquiores consuetudines Cluniacensis monasterii* 3.2, *PL* 149: 733–34. For Cîteaux, see Griesser, "*Ecclesiastica officia*," p. 270.

43. "Domno abbati, in omni loco, ut dignum est, singularis reverentia defertur." Ulrich, *Antiquiores consuetudines Cluniacensis monasterii* 3.2, *PL* 149: 733–34; cf. Griesser, "*Ecclesiastica officia*," pp. 270–71.

44. Lanfranc, *Monastic Constitutions*, p. 73.

45. Griesser, "*Ecclesiastica officia*," p. 234.

46. Ibid., pp. 238, 243.

47. *Statuta*, 1: 23 (1134, no. 37).

48. "Ita regulae incubantes ut nec iota unum nec apicem praetereundum putent"; "Abbas nihil sibi, nisi quod aliis, licere permittit; ubique praesens, ubique gregis sui curam circumferens: solummodo edentibus non adest, quia mensa ejus cum peregrinis et pauperibus est semper." William of Malmesbury, *De gestis regum Anglorum* 4.336, RS 90.2: 383.

49. Duby, "Youth in Aristocratic Society," in *Chivalrous Society*, pp. 112–16.

50. Marie de France, *Lays*, pp. 28–55, esp. pp. 31–33 (lines 45–122); Chrétien de Troyes, *Knight with the Lion, or Yvain*.

51. *L'Histoire de Guillaume le Maréchal* 15884, 1: 208, quoted in Duby, "Youth in Aristocratic Society," in *Chivalrous Society*, p. 114; Duby, *William Marshal*, p. 53.

52. McGuire, *Friendship and Community*, esp. p. 251.

53. McGuire, "Was Bernard a Friend?" in *Difficult Saint*, pp. 43–73.

54. William of Saint-Thierry, *Vita prima*, 1.3.15, *PL* 185: 235. William described this band in religious terms, as modeled on the community of apostles in Acts. Still, beneath the language lay similarities between the youths at Châtillon and those seeking their knightly fortune. Both groups were in transition, whether between childhood and recognition as full adults or between the life of a knight and that of a monk, and they ignored many societal structures and roles, stressing instead the egalitarian relations between their members. For a discussion of such liminal communities, see Turner, *Dramas, Fields, and Metaphors*, pp. 231–71.

55. "Sequenti nocte pariter accubuerunt in angustissimo strato ita ut vix ca-

peret alterum"; "Ibi confirmato ex integro sodalicio spirituali, redierunt manu sese tenentes alterutrum." Geoffrey of Auxerre, "Fragmenta" 11, pp. 94–95. These were used, but modified, by William of Saint-Thierry in creating the *Vita prima*. McGuire suggests that William toned down the highly emotional and physical relationship between Hugh and Bernard; *Friendship and Community*, p. 252.

56. Bernard of Clairvaux, Letter 109, *SBO* 7: 280–81 (James, no. 111). For the conversion of the group of knights, see William of Saint-Thierry, *Vita prima* 1.11.55, *PL* 185: 257.

57. McGuire, *Friendship and Community*, pp. 279–91.

58. *Vita s. Petri prioris Juliacensis* 2, *PL* 185: 1259; see also William of Malmesbury, *De gestis regum Anglorum* 4.334, RS 90.2: 381.

59. Guido, *Consuetudines cartusiae* 15, *SC* 313: 196–201.

60. Farmer, *Communities of St. Martin*, pp. 127–50.

61. Leyser, *Hermits and the New Monasticism*, considers the early Cistercians to be hermits. But for Cistercian criticisms of the eremitical life, see Bynum, "The Cistercian Conception of Community," in *Jesus as Mother*, p. 63; Bernard of Clairvaux, *Contra vitam heremiticam*, in Leclercq, *Etudes sur saint Bernard*, pp. 138–39; Aelred of Rievaulx, *In natali sancti Benedicti* 18–20, *CCCM* 2a: 56–57.

62. Gilbert of Hoyland, *Sermones in canticum* 23.3, *PL* 184: 120, CFS, 20: 287, stresses not only the discipline of the body during the offices but also the discipline of the mind: the monks are exhorted to concentrate on the meaning of the words. See also Guerric of Igny, *Sermo ad excitandam devotionem in psalmodia* 5, *SC* 202: 526–28, CFS, 32: 217–18.

63. Griesser, "*Ecclesiastica officia*," pp. 226–27.

64. *Summa cartae caritatis* 16, p. 123; *Statuta*, 1: 24–25 (1134, no. 51).

65. The more abstract bonds linking the choir monks to the lay brothers and each Cistercian abbey to the others are discussed in Chapter 4.

66. "In his desertis nostris et quietem habeamus solitudinis, nec tamen consolatione careamus gratae ac sanctae societatis. Licet cuique sedere solitarium et tacere . . . nec tamen 'vae soli,' eo quod non habeat confoventem, aut si ceciderit sublevantem." Guerric of Igny, *In prima dominica adventus Domini, sermo quartus* 2, *SC* 166: 136–38, CFS, 8: 23–24.

67. Some Cistercians, most notably William of Saint-Thierry and Isaac of Stella, wrote abstract analyses of the soul, but even these speculative works were based in monastic experience; most other authors used a theological anthropology to understand how human reform and divine contact were possible rather than to speculate on the nature of the soul and its powers. For both groups, speculative self-analysis was useless without the practical; there was no reason to understand the nature of the soul unless this knowledge aided the soul's movement toward God. See the distinction between moral-ascetical analyses and speculative-systematic approaches in McGinn, *Three Treatises on Man*, pp.

81–83. This emphasis on the practical, experiential, and moral was a common trait of many monastic theologians; Leclercq, *Love of Learning*, pp. 277–81.

68. Along with the works cited in the notes below, this section is indebted to the analyses of Bernard of Clairvaux's ideas presented in Casey, *Athirst for God*, and Sommerfeldt, *Spiritual Teachings of Saint Bernard of Clairvaux*.

69. Bernard of Clairvaux, *De gratia et libero arbitrio* 9.28, *SBO* 3: 185, CFS, 19: 84; William of Saint-Thierry, *De natura corporis et animae* 2.5, *PL* 180: 717, CFS, 24: 132–35; Aelred of Rievaulx, *De speculo caritatis* 1.3.9, 1.9.27, *CCCM* 1: 16, 23, CFS, 17: 90–91; Isaac of Stella, *Sermo secundus* (for the Feast of All Saints) 13, *SC* 13: 106, CFS, 11: 14, Isaac of Stella, *Sermo decimussextus:* (first sermon for Septuagesima Sunday) 15, *SC* 130: 304–6, CFS, 11: 134. See also Javelet, *Image et ressemblance*, 1: 198–99.

70. See, e.g., Bernard of Clairvaux, *Ser. sup. cant.* 1.9, *SBO*, 1: 6: "Furthermore, if you look back on your own experience . . ."

71. Even their analyses of the rational soul varied; William of Saint-Thierry, e.g., believed that the three parts of the soul corresponded to the three parts of the Trinity; Isaac of Stella equated the soul's power of understanding (*sensus*) with the divine image and the power of desire (*affectus*) with the divine likeness; and Aelred divided the soul into the Augustinian triad of memory, intellect, and will. Bernard of Clairvaux, *De gratia et libero arbitrio* 9.30, 10.32–35, *SBO*, 3: 187, 188–91, CFS, 19: 85–86, 88–90; William of Saint-Thierry, *De natura corporis et animae* 2.11, 13, *PL* 180: 714, CFS, 24: 142–45; Isaac of Stella, *Letter on the Soul* 7, CFS, 24: 189; Aelred of Rievaulx, *Dialogus de anima* 2, *CCCM* 1: 706–31. See also McGinn, *Three Treatises on Man,* p. 83.

72. Bynum, "The Cistercian Conception of Community," in *Jesus as Mother*, pp. 62–66.

73. Isaac of Stella, *Sermo quintus* (for the Feast of All Saints) 21, *SC* 130: 158, CFS, 11: 44. Translation by Hugh McCaffery.

74. Bernard of Clairvaux, *De diligendo deo* 9.29, *SBO* 3: 144, CFS, 13: 118.

75. William of Saint-Thierry, *Golden Epistle* 2.8.227–2.9.233, CFS, 12: 86–87.

76. Aelred of Rievaulx, *De speculo caritatis* 1.27.78–1.30.86, *CCCM* 1: 46–51.

77. Bernard of Clairvaux, *De diligendo deo* 10.27–28, *SBO* 3: 142–43, CFS, 13: 119–20. For a discussion of how Bernard differed from Augustine in his analysis of the soul, see Gilson, *Spirit of Mediaeval Philosophy*, pp. 210–13. For a discussion of how Bernard's analysis differed from that of other Cistercians, see McGinn, *Three Treatises on Man*, p. 80. See also Casey, *Athirst for God*, esp. ch. 4.

78. William of Saint-Thierry, *Exposition on the Song of Songs* 1.26, 1.30, CFS, 6: 21, 25.

79. William of Saint-Thierry, *Golden Epistle* 2.14.251, CFS, 12: 93.

80. Bernard of Clairvaux, *De diligendo deo* 10.27, *SBO* 3: 142, CFS, 13: 119; William of Saint-Thierry, *Golden Epistle* 2.10.235, CFS, 12: 88.

81. "Is per se sufficit, is per se placet, et propter se. Ipse meritum, ipse praemium est sibi. Amor praeter se non requirit causam, non fructum: fructus eius, usus eius. Amo, quia amo; amo, ut amem. Magna res amor, si tamen ad suum recurrat principium, si suae origini redditus, si refusus suo fonti, semper ex eo sumat unde iugiter fluat. Solus est amor ex omnibus animae motibus, sensibus atque affectibus, in quo potest creatura, etsi non ex aequo, respondere Auctori, vel de simili mutuam rependere vicem. . . . Nam cum amat Deus, non aliud vult, quam amari: quippe non ad aliud amat, nisi ut ametur, sciens ipso amore beatos, qui se amaverint." Bernard of Clairvaux, *Ser. sup. cant.* 83.4, *SBO* 2: 300–1, CFS, 40: 184.

82. Bernard of Clairvaux, *Ser. sup. cant.* 5.1, *SBO* 1: 21, CFS, 4: 25.

83. Bernard of Clairvaux, *Ser. sup. cant.* 24.6, *SBO* 1: 157, CFS, 7: 46–47.

84. As Bernard asked, "Nec praecepto indicitur, sed naturae inseritur. Quis nempe carnem suam odio habuit?" *De diligendo deo* 7.23, *SBO* 3: 138, CFS, 13: 115.

85. Bernard of Clairvaux, *De diligendo deo* 11.30, *SBO* 3: 145, CFS, 13: 122.

86. "Quod si gravatur homo fraternis, non dico necessitatibus subvenire, sed et voluptatibus deservire, castiget ipse suas, si non vult esse transgressor. Quantum vult, sibi indulgeat, dum aeque et proximo tantumdem meminerit exhibendum." Bernard of Clairvaux, *De diligendo deo* 8.23, *SBO* 3: 138–39, CFS, 13: 116.

87. Guerric of Igny makes a similar argument in discussing the obligation of giving alms in his *In purificatione, sermo quartus* 6, *SC* 166: 366–68, CFS, 8: 125.

88. This love is closely related to, but not the same as, friendship. Friendship did not always require someone's physical presence; in fact, we know about most friendships because of the survival of letters written between men who were separated. I wonder if it might not have been easier for monks to share their thoughts and concerns with men who were not members of their own communities. Still, it was possible to express the sense of community, solace, and aid offered by the physical presence of fellow monks without such feelings leading to particular and individualized friendships. See, e.g., Guerric of Igny's celebration of community; *In prima dominica adventus Domini, sermo quartus* 2, *SC* 166: 136–38.

89. Aelred of Rievaulx, *De speculo caritatis* 3.27.65, *CCCM* 1: 136, CFS, 17: 265.

90. Baldwin of Ford, *De vita coenobitica, seu communi, PL* 204: 559, CFS, 41: 180.

91. "Humanum, inquam, et necesse affici erga caros, sive delectabiliter, cum praesto sunt, sive, cum absunt, moleste. Non erit otiosa socialis conversatio, praesertim inter amicos; et quid effecerit mutuus amor in sibi praesentibus, horror indicat separationis, et dolor de invicem in separatis." Bernard of Clairvaux, *Ser. sup. cant.* 26.10, *SBO* 1: 178, CFS, 7: 69.

92. Bernard of Clairvaux, Letters 144–45, *SBO* 7: 344–47 (James, no. 144–45); Henry of Marcy, *Tractatus de peregrinante civitate dei, PL* 204: 251–52.

93. This is another area in which friendship and the physical presence of a community become interwoven; one definition McGuire gives for friendship is that friends are the guardians of the soul; *Friendship and Community*, p. xv.

94. Bernard of Clairvaux, *De gradibus humilitatis et superbiae* 14.42, 19.48, 20.50, *SBO* 3: 49, 53–54, CFS, 13: 70, 75–76.

95. Guerric of Igny, *In sollemnitate apostolorum Petri et Pauli, sermo secundus,* 45.4, *SC* 202: 390, CFS, 32: 157; "Ut qui juxta sedent, si forte ex se frigidi sint, vicinis possint scintillis accendi"; Gilbert of Hoyland, *Sermones in canticum* 23.3, *PL* 184: 121, CFS, 20: 288.

96. See esp. Aelred of Rievaulx, *De speculo caritatis* 3.24, *CCCM* 1: 131. This is a very different conception of interpersonal relationships than that assumed in the Benedictine Rule. Benedict was suspicious of relations between monks, assuming that they would lead to faction and jealousy. Although it is not clear that Aelred managed to solve the problems of jealousy that special friendships caused, he assumed that such relationships would enhance people's good qualities rather than encourage their baser instincts. See McGuire, *Friendship and Community*, esp. pp. 333–38.

97. "Ad omnes autem pertinet ut providentes bona non solum coram Deo sed et coram hominibus, nec conscientiam negligant amore famae, nec famam fiducia conscientiae. Nam et de ipsa conscientia quomodo tibi blandiri potes nisi sine querela sis inter fratres. . . . Putas enim satis esse si non scandalizas? Immo scandalizas si non aedificas, si non testimonium habens bonum intus et foris, quantum ad gradum tuum attinet Deum ubique glorificas." Guerric of Igny, *In festivitate sancti Benedicti, sermo tertius* 24.5, *SC* 202: 86, CFS, 32: 22.

98. "Bonum pacis et caritatis inter se reforment"; "ibi caritative clametur." *Carta caritatis prior* 7, p. 95.

99. Griesser, "*Ecclesiastica officia,*" p. 237.

100. "Omnes inclinato capite debent esse, et pio et fraterno affectu compassionem super eum habere." Lanfranc, *Monastic Constitutions*, pp. 112–13.

101. "Dictum namque est quod ex consideratione suiipsius cuique veniat mansuetum esse ad omnes, dum homo, consilio sapientissimi Pauli, ut pie condescendere sciat praeoccupatis in peccato, considerat seipsum, ne et ipse tentetur. Annon hinc denique amor proximi radicem trahit . . . ? Ex intimis sane humanis affectibus primordia ducit sui ortus fraterna dilectio, et de insita homini ad seipsum naturali quadam dulcedine, tamquam de humore terreno, sumit procul dubio vegatationem et vim, per quam, spirante quidem gratia desuper, fructus parturit pietatis"; Bernard of Clairvaux, *Ser. sup. cant.* 44.4, *SBO* 2: 46, CFS, 7: 227–28.

102. Bernard of Clairvaux, *De gradibus humilitatis et superbiae* 3, *SBO* 3:

20–21; Aelred of Rievaulx, *De speculo caritatis* 3.3, *CCCM* 1: 106, CFS, 17: 223; see also Guerric of Igny, *In purificatione, sermo quartus* 5, *SC* 166: 364–66; *In festivitate sancti Benedicti, sermo tertius* 4, *SC* 202: 82–84.

103. Aelred of Rievaulx, *De speculo caritatis* 3.2.3–5, *CCCM* 1: 106–7, CFS, 17: 224.

104. See, e.g., Aelred of Rievaulx, *De speculo caritatis* 3.5.15, *CCCM* 1: 112, CFS, 17: 231.

105. "Exemplo scilicet Salvatoris nostri, qui pati voluit ut compati sciret, miser fieri ut misereri disceret. . . . Non quod ante misereri nesciret, cuius misericordia ab aeterno et usque in aeternum; sed quod natura sciebat ab aeterno, temporali didicit experimento." Bernard of Clairvaux, *De gradibus humilitatis et superbiae* 3.6, *SBO* 3: 21, CFS, 13: 35.

106. Bernard of Clairvaux, *Ser. sup. cant.* 20.6, *SBO* 1: 118, CFS, 1: 153.

107. "Bonus tamen amor iste carnalis, per quem vita carnalis excluditur, contemnitur et vincitur mundus." Bernard of Clairvaux, *Ser. sup. cant.* 20.9, *SBO* 1: 120, CFS, 1: 54.

108. Guerric of Igny, *In nativitate Domini, sermo quintus* 1, *SC* 166: 222, CFS, 8: 61.

109. "Ea quae est proximi reducitur ad charitatem Dei, cum proximus non sit diligendus, nisi secundum Deum, in Deo, vel propter Deum." Baldwin of Ford, *Tractatus* 14, *PL* 204: 541, CFS, 41: 146. See also Bernard of Clairvaux, *De diligendo deo* 10.28, *SBO* 3: 143, CFS, 13: 120; Bernard of Clairvaux, *Ser. sup. cant.* 50.6–7, 57.11.

110. Aelred of Rievaulx, *De speculo caritatis* 3.9–10, *CCCM* 1: 109–10, CFS, 17: 226–27; Bernard of Clairvaux, *Ser. sup. cant.* 50.7, *SBO* 2: 82, CFS, 31: 35–36.

111. Bernard of Clairvaux, *Ser. sup. cant.* 50.7, *SBO* 2: 82, CFS, 31: 36.

112. Bernard of Clairvaux, *De diligendo deo* 10.27, *SBO* 3: 142–44, CFS, 13: 119–21.

113. "Subito invidet saeculum nequam, perturbat diei malitia, corpus mortis aggravat, sollicitat carnis necessitas, defectus corruptionis non sustinet, quodque his violentius est, fraterna revocat caritas." Bernard of Clairvaux, *De diligendo deo* 10.27, *SBO* 3: 142, CFS, 13: 119–20. As he wrote in another context, "In this life there is not an abundance of contemplation nor long-lasting leisure, because the benefits of service and work press more compellingly and more urgently." Bernard of Clairvaux, *Ser. sup. cant.* 58.1, *SBO* 2: 127, CFS, 31: 108. Gilbert of Hoyland also spoke of the obligation of caring for others, but noted that the reasons for such fraternal charity were disturbing. Compassion for others was good, but the wretchedness and neediness that compelled this compassion were not. Gilbert of Hoyland, *Sermones in canticum* 10.2, *PL* 184: 55, CFS, 14: 135.

114. "Tanto interdum repleat zelo et desiderio acquirendi Deo qui eum similiter diligant." Bernard of Clairvaux, *Ser. sup. cant.* 57.9, *SBO* 2: 124, CFS, 31: 103.

115. "Et paci terrae magis quam caeli gloriae, iure humanitatis et ipsa necessitate intendimus." Bernard of Clairvaux, *Ser. sup. cant.* 50.5, *SBO* 2: 81, CFS, 31: 34.

116. Bernard of Clairvaux, *Ser. sup. cant.* 50.5, *SBO* 2: 81, CFS, 31: 34–35.

117. Leclercq, "Les sermons sur les Cantiques ont-ils été prononcés?" in *Recueil d'études sur Saint Bernard*, pp. 193–212.

118. Augustine, *Confessions*, pp. 4, 7–9. Even Anselm of Bec, who was described by his biographer as mourning the death of his friend Osbern, wrote of his tears in terms of a desire for salvation, not as an expression of his longing for the physical presence of the deceased. See McGuire, "Monks and Tears: A Twelfth-Century Change," in *Difficult Saint*, pp. 137–39.

119. McGuire, "Monks and Tears: A Twelfth-Century Change," in *Difficult Saint*, pp. 141–42. For Bernard's new category, see *In epiphania sermo* 3.8, *SBO* 4: 30. Both Bernard and Aelred mentioned that even Jesus had wept at the death of Lazarus, tears the abbots insisted displayed Jesus' humanity: they were not a sign of his lack of faith, but a witness to his human nature. See Bernard of Clairvaux, *Ser. sup. cant.* 26.12, *SBO* 1: 179, CFS, 7: 73; Aelred of Rievaulx, *De speculo caritatis* 1.34.112, *CCCM* 1: 63, CFS, 17: 157.

120. Bynum, in "Jesus as Mother, Abbot as Mother," in *Jesus as Mother*, p. 168, suggests that the Cistercians' use of maternal imagery stems from this ambivalence.

121. Bernard of Clairvaux, *Ser. sup. cant.* 52.7, *SBO* 2:95, CFS, 31: 56; Gilbert of Hoyland, *Sermones in canticum* 10.2, *PL* 184: 56, CFS, 14: 135.

CHAPTER 3

1. See, e.g., Southern, *Western Society and the Church*, pp. 254–59; Gimpel, *Medieval Machine*, pp. 46–47.

2. See Duby, *Rural Economy and Country Life*, pp. 70–71, for general doubts about the role of monks in reclaiming land; for the Cistercians specifically, see esp. Berman, *Medieval Agriculture*, pp. 10, 11–30; Berman, "Development of Cistercian Economic Practice"; Bouchard, "Twelfth-Century Burgundy."

3. See the collection of essays in *L'économie cistercienne*, esp. Chauvin, "Réalités et évolution de l'économie cistercienne"; Fossier, "L'économie cistercienne"; Higounet, "Essai sur les granges cisterciennes." See also Berman, *Medieval Agriculture*; Bouchard, *Holy Entrepreneurs*. See also the critique of the assumption that the Cistercian economy was independent of manorial and "feu-

dal" structures in Alfonso, "Cistercians and Feudalism." Unmentioned by Alfonso is a second assumption in this literature: that the labor of celibate men was more efficient than family labor. None of these historians consider female contributions to household production, or address what happened to women and children when men became lay brothers. In fact, Berman considers women and children only as increasing labor costs; see *Medieval Agriculture*, p. 79. For a discussion of female contributions to the household economy, see Hanawalt, *Ties That Bound*.

4. See, e.g., Roehl, "Plan and Reality in a Medieval Monastic Economy"; Lekai, "Ideals and Reality." In *Medieval Agriculture*, Berman expresses an intent to move beyond this paradigm, but she still makes distinctions between the Cistercians' ideals and the reality of their practice.

5. Bouchard, *Holy Entrepreneurs*, esp. pp. 185–98.

6. *Exordium parvum* 3, pp. 59–60; *Exordium cistercii* 1, p. III; William of Saint-Thierry, *Vita prima* 1.5.25, *PL* 185: 241. See Deut. 32.10.

7. Auberger, *L'unanimité cistercienne primitive*, pp. 120–24. See also below, Chapter 3, pp. 94–95.

8. Bouchard assumes the locations on the edges of dioceses demonstrate the monks' desire to distance themselves from cities; this assumption only holds where the bishop's city lies in the center of the diocese. But Pontigny lies seven kilometers from Auxerre, and La Ferté is about the same distance from Chalon-sur-Saône. Cîteaux was about ten kilometers from both Dijon and Beaune, although much farther from the bishop's seat at Chalon. Nor did a location on the edge of a diocese serve to limit episcopal control; instead, the monks established close ties not only with their diocesan bishop but with the neighboring bishops as well. See Chapter 5. For the abbeys' proximity to settled lands, see discussion below and the maps in Auberger, *L'unanimité cistercienne primitive*, docs. II/II-1 through II/II-4, pp. 438–41.

9. See Auberger, *L'unanimité cistercienne primitive*, p. 62, who dates the *Summa cartae caritatis* to 1123–24 and assumes that the capitula attached to it reflect decisions made before then. Thus, Bouchard's comment that most of the "unquestionably authentic" legislation about Cistercian property dates from the second half of the twelfth century seems overstated; *Holy Entrepreneurs*, p. 189.

10. "In civitatibus castellis villis nulla construenda esse coenobia." *Summa cartae caritatis* 9, p. 121. Bouchard asserts that the central characteristic of the Cistercians' "solitude" was their distance from the distractions of an urban environment rather than their "isolation from certain forms of exchange or economic activity"; *Holy Entrepreneurs*, pp. 193–94. Although distance from towns may have distinguished Cistercian communities from older abbeys such as Saint-Bénigne, Vézelay, or Cluny, which had been constructed in towns or had watched towns

grow up around them, it does not distinguish them from communities such as Molesme.

11. "Ecclesias, altaria, sepulturas, decimas alieni laboris vel nutrimenti, villas, villanos, terrarum census, furnorum vel molendinorum redditus et caetera his similia monasticae puritati adversantia nostri et nominis et ordinis excludit institutio." *Summa cartae caritatis* 23, p. 124.

12. *Cîteaux*, p. 79 (no. 66).

13. "Nobis nostra professio et antiquorum monachorum exempla victum ex propriis praescribunt laboribus, et non ex sanctuario Dei." Bernard of Clairvaux, Letter 397, *SBO* 8: 374 (James, no. 429). This was written before Hugh of Pontigny became bishop of Auxerre in 1136. The *Exordium parvum* contains similar language but is even more specific. According to the church fathers, it states, tithes were to be divided into four parts: one part for the bishop, one part for priests, one part to support widows, paupers, and guests, and a final part for the upkeep of the churches. "And because in this reckoning they did not find mention of a role for the monk who possesses his own land and lives through his labor and that of his livestock, they therefore avoided handling these revenues as an unjust usurpation of the rights of others." *Exordium parvum* 15, p. 77.

14. For arguments justifying the monastic possession of tithes, see Constable, *Monastic Tithes*, pp. 165–85.

15. Molesme's cartulary, e.g., lists the churches and manors given to the community, and even records the names of the families attached to the donated property. See *Molesme*, 2: 19–20 (no. 12), 33 (no. 23), for two of the many examples.

16. For the debates over the Cistercian lay brotherhood, see Chapter 1.

17. Higounet, "Essai sur les granges cisterciennes," pp. 157–80. See also Berman, *Medieval Agriculture*, esp. p. 10.

18. For hired labor, see *Summa cartae caritatis* 20, 24, pp. 123, 124; *Exordium parvum* 15, p. 78.

19. *Cîteaux*, pp. 58 (no. 37), 76 (no. 61); *Clairvaux*, pp. 14–15 (no. 7).

20. Bouchard notes that accepting donations was one of the central functions of all twelfth-century monasteries, and Van Engen has demonstrated that abbots tended to be judged on their ability to protect and increase their abbeys' property. Bouchard, "Cistercian Ideals versus Reality"; Van Engen, " 'Crisis of Cenobitism' Reconsidered."

21. Hutchison, *Hermit Monks of Grandmont*, pp. 16–20. The Carthusians also limited the amount of land they obtained to a carefully defined domain fully separated from the secular society around them. See Bligny, *Recueil des plus anciens actes de la Grande-Chartreuse*, pp. xvii–xx.

22. For specific examples, see below, nn. 29, 36, 38, 49–51, 54–55, 57. Both Berman and Bouchard find these methods of land acquisition among the

abbeys they study; the two historians disagree, however, about whether there is a clear distinction between sales and gift/countergift transactions. Bouchard wishes to separate sales, in which the "property being bought or sold and the price were clear and concrete," from gifts, which were more complex transactions that established long-term relationships between the donors, the monks, and their heavenly patrons; *Holy Entrepreneurs*, pp. 56–65 (esp. 64), 75–79. Berman, in comparison, argues that the scribal language of gift-giving often overlay more contractual exchanges between the Cistercians and their benefactors; see *Medieval Agriculture*, pp. 36–54, and her review of Bouchard's book, forthcoming in *Cîteaux*. (I thank her for sending me an advance copy of this work.) In her criticism of Bouchard, Berman blurs the distinction between use of the verb *donare* and the more precise *donare in elemosina* or gifts "for good of my soul and those of my ancestors." In my reading of the land transactions from Cîteaux, Clairvaux, Pontigny, and La Ferté, the Cistercian (or episcopal) scribes tended to use "donare" and "dono" as all-purpose words, but transactions specifically described as sales were not given pious motives. Thus, in a record of an exchange between Pontigny and Garnier of Ligny, the scribe, writing with the donor's voice, wishes to distinguish between gifts, exchanges, and sales: "Opere precium est ac salubre datoribus, quecumque elemosina pauperibus Christi nodaverint seu commutaverint vel vendiderint, ea distinctione declarare, testibus confirmare, posteriorum memorie commendare ne presentium incuria litigare cogantur futuri." But he then uses the verb "donare" to describe all the transactions; *Pontigny*, p.177 (no. 108). Yet, although I think the monks, the donors, and their scribes did try (sometimes unsuccessfully) to separate sales from other forms of property conveyance, I agree with Berman that the Cistercians' contracts with their neighbors did not recreate the gift/countergift relationships that existed between older monasteries and their benefactors. As the preamble to the charter from Pontigny suggests, the Cistercians' care in distinguishing types of transactions, as well as their care in giving compensation to all the possible claimants to a piece of property, was to prevent future disputes and ensure that the monks held the property free and clear from all obligations to their neighbors.

23. Rosenwein, *To Be the Neighbor of St. Peter*, p. 141.

24. Here I disagree with Bouchard, who, in *Holy Entrepreneurs*, has tried to use Rosenwein's model for tenth- and eleventh-century Cluny to understand the relations of the twelfth-century Cistercians with their patrons. Regardless of the problems of dating the Cistercian statutes, one cannot assume the Cistercians exploited their land in the same manner as the monks of Cluny, and the Cistercians' form of exploitation made it more difficult for benefactors to view the donated property as unchanged. Furthermore, other studies have suggested that, by the mid–twelfth century, the relationship between benefactor and

monastery began to change, the transfer of property and rights took on more importance, sales became more frequent, and there was less effort to preserve an ongoing relationship between benefactor and monastery. Even the exhange of land for spiritual benefits took on a more commercial character as charters began to specify the prayers and services given in return for property of a defined value. See Rosenwein, *To Be the Neighbor of St. Peter*, pp. 202–5; White, *Custom, Kinship, and Gifts to Saints*, pp. 191–92; McLaughlin, *Consorting with Saints*, pp. 255–56.

25. Bedos-Rezak, "Diplomatic Sources." I am grateful to the author for sending me an advance copy of this article.

26. See, e.g., Berman, "Origins of the Filiation of Morimond in Southern France."

27. It is possible that the monks carefully described their negotiations for these properties so that they could demonstrate their rights should they ever have been challenged, but it is unclear that such documents were actually used to settle legal disputes. See Bedos-Rezak, "Diplomatic Sources"; Tabuteau, *Transfers of Property*, p. 212.

28. *Cîteaux*, pp. 19–20. Presumably, most of the notices were destroyed after they were copied, although there is one extant twelfth-century notice recording the monks' rights to a vineyard at Meursault (Arch. Côte d'Or, 11 H 881). Marlier suggests that these notices were assembled from original charters that were probably destroyed once the notice was made. Assuming the thirteenth-century scribes copied correctly and did not distort what had previously been recorded, these notices reflect the twelfth-century efforts of the monks to organize their property. One sign that these notices were not distorted is that the cartulary records a number of different notices for the same piece of property, suggesting that the scribes made no effort to consolidate duplicate notices.

29. Arch. Côte d'Or, 11 H 64 (cartulary 166), ff. 35r–36v; printed in *Cîteaux*, pp. 72–75 (no. 58). The document itself has few chronological markers, but Marlier estimated the approximate dates for the notices. At the end of the notice, the scribe commented, "Here are collected in one place the acts of various times."

30. *Cîteaux*, pp. 73 (no. 58).

31. "Quas terras et prata seu quicquid aliud inibi habebant antedictis monachis se daturos promiserunt, si monachi illi eis adquirerent terras et prata ac silvas quas domnus Wido de Troens et Ogerius de Basshei et fratres ejus tunc temporis tenebant, quia juris Busceranorum fratrum erant, sed milites predicti eis reddere nolebant." *Cîteaux*, pp. 73–74 (no. 58).

32. "Hoc pratum totum nunc est monachorum." *Cîteaux*, p. 75 (no. 58).

33. "Ac terminus illarum ex una parte usque in rivulum qui appellatur vetus Musana descenderit, sicuti homines senes et illarum terrarum periti, Radulfus scilicet et Geofridus ac Humbertus fusorius, in villa mirri[ni]acensi degentes, et

Arnulfus Cenlitta de Viliaco et multi alii vicini monachis cisterciensibus testificabantur, quique etiam has terras omnes et terras domni Bernardi de Ruele coram multis hominibus qui in vicino habitabant, monachis determinaverunt." *Cîteaux*, p. 75 (no. 58).

34. Arch. Côte d'Or, 11 H 64 (cartulary 166), ff. 36v–37v; printed in *Cîteaux*, pp. 76–77 (no. 62–63).

35. The Cistercians did not always get an outright grant of the tithe. Often it was commuted to a cens taken from the produce of the land. The cens appears to have been less than the tithe, for a number of notices record that, if the land did not produce, the Cistercians would pay the traditional tithe (a proportional amount) rather than the fixed measure. See, e.g., *Cîteaux*, p. 64 (no. 41iv). Berman, in her review of Bouchard's *Holy Entrepreneurs*, argues that this notice, describing lands at Gilly, was "a convoluted form of a *medium vestum* contract" in which the Cistercians, as Saint-Germain's tenants, eventually divided ownership rights to the property as compensation for their improvements to it. However, I view this cens more as a countergift in compensation for the gift of the tithe rather than the establishment of an owner-tenant relationship, especially because the monks from Saint-Germain specified that the Cistercians were to again pay the tithe if the land did not produce.

36. *Cîteaux*, pp. 52–53 (no. 26), 63–65 (no. 41), 68–70 (no. 51).

37. *Pontigny*, pp. 33–59, esp. 55–57.

38. Ibid., pp. 152–88, (nos. 84–124).

39. For these paths, see ibid., pp. 161 (no. 89), 177 (no. 108), 15 (no. 86). For the settlement of Ligny, see ibid., pp. 172–73 (no. 102), 159 (no. 87), 162 (no. 91).

40. Ibid., pp. 153–54 (no. 84). This notice may well have been a compilation of earlier charters: it calls Stephen Harding the abbot of the *novi monasterii*, a usage that had disappeared by 1119.

41. If these peasants ever gave land to the monastery, the gifts were not recorded. In 1118, John of the Mill and his family granted the monks more land between Sainte-Procaire and Venouse and received in return eight pounds of pennies; ibid., pp. 160–63 (no. 89). Bouchard suggests that John must have been a knight because he held the property "in fief" from one Bartholomew (Bartholomeus, de cujus beneficio nos hec habere recognoscimus); *Holy Entrepreneurs*, p. 174.

42. Ibid., pp. 154–57 (no. 85). Charters 86–116, for the most part, record transactions that occurred before 1156; the exceptions are 93, 100, 103, 113, which record families approving donations made by their relatives. The last group contains charters (nos. 117–24) dated between the 1160's and the 1180's that primarily record settlements of disputes.

43. Ibid.

44. The grange at Lorant was the furthest grange from Pontigny; its donation was not recorded in the cartulary. See Ibid., p. 26. The charter recording the donation of land for this grange is edited in Quantin, *Cartulaire général de l'Yonne*, 2: 48 (no. 43).

45. "Sed quoniam fratribus Pontiniacensibus nimis durum videbatur ut propter se habitatores villae illius a suis possessionibus excluderentur, placitam illis hominibus feci recompensationem ita ut sponte discederent et in pace monachis locum dimitterent." *Pontigny*, p. 156 (no. 85).

46. "Quod terram ipsam ab habitatione hominum suorum immunem et incultam facerent et domos ipsorum cum pace eorumdem a toto territorio auferrent"; ibid., p. 160 (no. 88). That this depopulation could occur at Pontigny without the direct negotiations with peasant proprietors apparent at both Cîteaux and La Ferté suggests there was a more entrenched manorial structure around Pontigny in which the peasantry had fewer rights to the land. See also ibid., p. 158 (no. 86).

47. Ibid., pp. 164, 169–72, 173–74, 178, 180–82, 185–88 (nos. 93, 99–101, 103, 109, 112–14, 120–23).

48. Most of La Ferté's pancartes received seals from two bishops of Chalon: Walter (1126–58) sealed eight, and his successor Peter (1158–78) sealed nine. Unlike most Burgundian Cistercian pancartes, La Ferté's come close to being a form of cartulary. Perhaps this is a result of their production at the monastery rather than the episcopal chancery. Except for the two earliest charters, the rest present the acts set apart from one another by rubrics that summarize their contents. The pancartes do not begin with invocations but acts themselves often begin with an elaborate invocation. The bishop only appears at the end, where he condemns anyone who disturbs the monks and their property. There were no witnesses to the episcopal confirmations. For a discussion of the production of these pancartes, see *La Ferté*, pp. 23–29. The only pancartes likely to have been produced in an episcopal chancery were the first two (nos. 21, 23), which were sealed by the bishop of Autun and the archbishop of Besançon, and the pancarte for Clux (no. 26), which was produced at Besançon by the vice chancellor of the archbishop. Duby speculates that the reception of lands outside their immediate diocese may have initially prompted the monks to present their records to a bishop for confirmation; *La Ferté*, p. 26.

49. See, e.g., ibid., p. 65 (no. 31, pancarte no. 5), which notes the hierarchy of tenants who had rights to the land, from the donor's wife to the bishop of Chalon. See also pp. 169–70 (no. 206, pancarte 21) in which a Lord Anseric "before he took a wife" and the *rustici* from Boeris gave land for the grange at Chavals.

50. Ibid., pp. 90–97 (nos. 82–95, pancarte 6); for the list of rents, see p. 93

(no. 87). Pancarte 15 also begins by describing the process of marking the monks' land in the presence of a village community.

51. Ibid., p. 93 (no. 87, pancarte 6).

52. These pancartes do not give as clear an indication that they were initially composed by the monks as the ones from La Ferté, but they do occasionally refer to land with first-person possessive adjectives ("our divisions"), suggesting that the monks had a voice in their composition. In *Holy Entrepreneurs*, pp. 91–92, Bouchard suggests that the brief record of each transaction in these pancartes, and especially the lack of any record of countergifts, reflects the scribal practice at the episcopal chancery, and does not record the full extent of the transactions between Clairvaux and its patrons. The bishop, she suggests, "may well not have considered the countergift an integral or even important part of the transfer of property *to* the monastery" (p. 92). But Godfrey, the bishop of Langres who issued the great majority of the pancartes for Clairvaux, had been the abbot of Fontenay and the prior of Clairvaux before becoming bishop. If he did not find the countergifts important enough to record, I assume that this reflected the attitude of the monks themselves. Thus, if the monks of Clairvaux gave countergifts to a donor or his family, they did not establish a relationship that the monks considered worth recording.

53. "Quidquid de feodo ejus vel jam adquisisse vel in furturum adquirere possent ab his qui ab ispo tenere videbantur." *Clairvaux*, pp. 8 (no. 6: 1), 9 (no. 6: 7); see also pp. 20 (no. 13), 36 (no. 17). From this wording it is clear these acts were not placed in chronological order.

54. Ibid., pp. 20–25 (no. 13). Of the remaining three acts, one was the gift of an allod; another was a son's concession of a donation made by his father.

55. "Quicquid habebant infra divisiones terrarum nostrarum que sunt ultra Albam"; "intra divisiones terrarum nostrarum." Ibid., pp. 40–41 (no. 18).

56. Dodo of Mundeville gave the monks half a vineyard in the *finagio* of Perrecin; his sons later donated the other half. ("Postea duo filii . . . dederunt eidem monasterio aliam medietatem predicte vinee.") Ibid., pp. 37 (no. 17).

57. Ibid., pp. 46–47 (no. 20).

58. For exchanges of property, see ibid., pp. 38–39 (no. 17: 14, 17: 21), in which the monks offered Ansulf son of Aaloz land at Aconville for his property in the finagio of Fraville, and gave Albert of Mundeville seven *jugera* of land in the finagio of Mundeville for seven jugera of land next to fields the monks already controlled. See also p. 80 (no. 73). For offers of material compensation, usually in the form of an annual cens, see pp. 25 (no. 13: 24), 30 (no. 14: 40), 43 (no. 18: 39), 67 (no. 50), 69 (no. 53), 87–88 (no. 85). For a sale, see pp. 100–101 (no. 95). See also pp. 36 (no. 17: 4), and 37 (no. 17: 10), in which the monks give one Henry land at Lesperoier with three sous and six *nummis* for land at Aure-

font. As mentioned above, we do not see the monks offering countergifts to donors and their families. On p. 22 (no. 13: 10), Count Theobald agreed to preserve the peace between his vassals and the monks by granting a new fief to anyone who disputed the gifts made to Clairvaux.

59. "Pro anima mariti sui"; "pro anima ipsius dedit." Ibid., pp. 63 (no. 42), 94 (no. 90). These two donors were Theca, a woman from Angente, and Renaud of Grancey. Again, it is possible that the monks or the bishop did not generally consider such spiritual benefits worth recording, but such an attitude itself is significant, for it suggests a shift away from the idea that one of the fundamental roles of a monastic community was to offer spiritual benefits to its patrons.

60. Ibid., pp. 16 (no. 9), 48 (no. 22), 49 (no. 23), 52 (no. 26), 53 (no. 28), 54 (no. 30), 56 (no. 32), 57 (no. 33). None of these charters was issued by the bishop of Langres. The only others were the two donors mentioned above. The status of these donors raises interesting questions about the extent to which Clairvaux really supported the religiosity and growing self-identity of an emerging knightly class. Bouchard, in *Sword, Miter, and Cloister*, pp. 131–49, argues that, in Burgundy, the Cistercians' primary donors were lesser knights who had not patronized monastic communities before. She suggests that their gifts to Cistercian houses contributed to their emerging identity as aristocrats. It is possible, however, that these families show up on Cistercian charters not because of their great devotion to Cistercian monks but because it was only the Cistercians who insisted on gaining their rights to their property rather than allowing them to hold lands in fief from the monks.

61. This may have been why they so relied on the bishop of Langres to confirm donations.

62. The monks at Clairvaux settled at least 30 quarrels with their neighbors in the years before 1174. *Clairvaux*, pp. 18 (no. 11), 22 (no. 13: 10), 44 (no. 18: 35), 44 (no. 18: 38), 45–46 (no. 19), 46–47 (no. 20), 59 (no. 36), 61 (no. 39), 65 (no. 46), 65 (no. 47), 66 (no. 49), 74 (no. 63), 79 (no. 71), 91 (no. 89: 4), 99 (no. 94), 101 (no. 96), 116 (no. 105), 118 (no. 106), 120 (no. 108), 126 (no. 119: 1), 128 (no. 119: 15), 128 (no. 119: 17), 133 (no. 122), 135 (no. 124), 141 (no. 132), 147 (no. 135), 152 (no. 141), 154 (no. 144), 156 (no. 146), 157 (no. 148).

63. See, e.g., the long dispute over Cîteaux's lands at Gergeuil. Cîteaux had first received property at Gergeuil around 1110, when Elisabeth of Vergy, her husband, and Odo the Green gave the monks land there to establish a grange. Sometime after 1115, however, the brothers Humbert, Hugh, and Ulrich, as well as Pons from the castle of Blaisy, claimed rights on that land, but then relinquished their claims to the monks without compensation: "terram illam in terris, in silvis et partis liberrimam eis dimiserunt." Pons of Vergy, however, challenged Elisabeth's right to donate the land; in 1125, after receiving other land and revenue from both Elisabeth and Hugh the White of Vergy, he finally dropped

his claim to Gergueil. Even then Cîteaux's problems were not over, for Pons's son Josbert contested the settlement, claiming he had not agreed to it. At the same time, he and his parents together contested yet another grant given to Cîteaux. Finally, the monks of Cîteaux gave them twenty sous "propter quos clamores," and were thereafter left in peace. *Cîteaux*, pp. 57 (no. 36), 71 (no. 55), 85–87 (no. 78).

64. See, e.g., *La Ferté*, pp. 126–28 (no. 145), 139–41 (no. 163); *Pontigny*, pp. 166 (no. 96), 134–35 (no. 73); *Cîteaux*, pp. 131–32 (no. 166), 146–47 (no. 179); *Clairvaux*, pp. 101–2 (no. 96), 119–20 (no. 108), 156 (no. 146).

65. It is possible that this dispute with Rainard of Beaune, as well as Molesme's demand that Robert return, may have been responsible for Alberic seeking the privilege of papal protection for Cîteaux.

66. *Cîteaux*, p. 51 (no. 23). Bouchard uses this transaction to suggest that the monks implemented lease arrangements to cultivate the friendship of their neighbors. Although leasing may have established close ties with some bene-factors, in this transaction the relationship between the viscount of Beaune and the Cistercians seems anything but friendly. Furthermore, the viscount did not give any more land to the monastery. Bouchard, *Holy Entrepreneurs*, p. 48.

67. *Cîteaux*, pp. 52–53 (no. 26), 63 (no. 39), 69 (no. 51), 86 (no. 78).

68. Cîteaux, e.g., held rights in the salt pits at Salins that included an annual rent of 20 sous and a man called "Martin the German." The monks clearly kept their rights over this man, as he witnessed a later donation of salt. Ibid., pp. 110–11, 125 (no. 122ii, 122iv, 156). Cîteaux also accepted rents from a house and tavern in Dijon; ibid., pp. 93–94 (no. 91), 97 (no. 99).

69. *La Ferté*, p. 93 (no. 87); *Pontigny*, pp. 133–34 (no. 61), 139 (no. 67). Do-nations of rents, like the donations of tithes, are ambiguous because they usu-ally allowed the monks to retain revenues formerly owed to the donor. For ex-amples of such concessions, see *Clairvaux*, p. 30 (no. 14: 38, 40, 41), 39–40 (no. 18: 7); *La Ferté*, p. 142 (nos. 165, 166).

70. Gerald of Wales, *Speculum ecclesiae* 2.12, RS 21.4: 54; Letter from Abbot Stephen of Sainte-Geneviève to Archbishop William of Rheims, dated 1177–92, *PL* 211: 351. "Credo, Pater, quia Cisterciensis de numero sunt eorum qui violenti diripiunt coelum sed utrum violenter eis terram rapere liceat, nondum lege."

71. Walter Map, *De nugis curialium* 1.25, p. 93.

72. Smalley, *Study of the Bible*, pp. 1–36; Chenu, "The Symbolist Mentality," in *Nature, Man and Society*, pp. 119–23.

73. See esp. Smalley's discussion of the Victorines in *Study of the Bible*. See also Chenu, "Nature and Man—The Renaissance of the Twelfth Century," in *Na-ture, Man and Society*, pp. 1–48; Stock, *Implications of Literacy*, pp. 315–25, and his discussion of Bernard of Clairvaux, pp. 403–54.

74. Chenu, "The Symbolist Mentality," in *Nature, Man and Society*, pp. 124–26.

75. Bernard of Clairvaux, *Ser. sup. cant.* 1.2, 1.12, *SBO* 1: 3, 8, CFS, 4: 1, 7.

76. "Mei similis anima onerata peccatis, suaeque adhuc carnis obnoxia passionibus." Bernard of Clairvaux, *Ser. sup. cant.* 3.1, *SBO* 1: 14, CFS, 4: 16.

77. See Augustine, *Literal Meaning of Genesis* 11.32, 2: 165.

78. Leclercq, "Aggressiveness or Repression in St. Bernard and in his Monks," in *Monks and Love*, p. 90.

79. William of Saint-Thierry, *Vita prima* 1.3.6–7, *PL* 185: 230–31; Aelred of Rievaulx, *De institutione inclusarum* 18, 32, *CCCM* 1: 653–54, 674. See also his *Speculum caritatis* 1.79, *CCCM* 1: 47.

80. William of Saint-Thierry, *Vita prima* 1.3.10–11, *PL* 185: 232–33.

81. Griesser, "*Ecclesiastica officia*," pp. 263–64.

82. Herbert of Clairvaux's *De miraculis* contains four stories about sexual temptation. Peter the Venerable's *De miraculis*, in comparison, contains no such stories.

83. Herbert of Clairvaux, *De miraculis* 1.3, *PL* 185: 1278–79.

84. Herbert of Clairvaux, *De miraculis* 1.4, *PL* 185: 1284–85. For others with a similar lesson, see 1.9, 1.26, *PL* 185: 1294–96, 1300.

85. "Si quis in se unquam talem expertus est vel dilectionis vel desiderii sensum, proprii aestimare potest conjectura exempli, quam querulo sponsa corde protulerit: 'Non inveni illum.' " Gilbert of Hoyland, *Sermones in canticum* 3.1, *PL* 184: 22, CFS, 14: 66.

86. For a discussion of how Bernard of Clairvaux incorporated into his mysticism his experience of both the world and the words of a text, see Stock, *Implications of Literacy*, pp. 417–54.

87. "Felix osculum, ac stupenda dignatione mirabile, in quo non os ori imprimitur, sed Deus homini unitur. Et ibi quidem contactus labiorum complexum significat animorum, hic autem confoederatio naturarum divinis humana componit." Bernard of Clairvaux, *Ser. sup. cant.* 2.3, *SBO* 1: 10, CFS, 4: 10.

88. "Nonne denique ita invicem loquimur: 'Osculare me,' vel: 'Da mihi osculum?' . . . Alterutrum osculari parantes, non versus invicem ora tendimus, quae tamen ab invicem non requirimus nominatim?" Bernard of Clairvaux, *Ser. sup. cant.* 4.1, *SBO* 1: 18, CFS, 4: 21–22.

89. "Aut ipsius etiam indultoris et benefactoris sui praesentiam, eo quidem modo quo in corpore fragili possibile est, obtinet intueri." Bernard of Clairvaux, *Ser. sup. cant.* 4.1, *SBO* 1: 19, CFS, 4: 22.

90. "Ne auditu quidem dignum quod foris sonat, si non intus adiuvet Spiritus infirmitatem intelligentiae nostrae." Bernard of Clairvaux, *Ser. sup. cant.* 61.2, *SBO* 2: 149, CFS, 31: 141–42.

91. "Nec sane 'foramina petrae' aut 'cavernas maceriae' latebras putetis op-

erantium iniquitatem, ne qua prorsus suspicio subeat de operibus tenebrarum." Bernard of Clairvaux, *Ser. sup. cant.* 61.2, *SBO* 2: 150, CFS, 31: 141–42.

92. Bernard of Clairvaux, *Ser. sup. cant.* 61.3, 62.1,2,6, *SBO* 2: 150, 148–49, 152, CFS, 31: 142, 149–50, 151, 157.

93. "Vox resonat gratiarum actionis, vox admirationis et laudis." Bernard of Clairvaux, *Ser. sup. cant.* 62.2, *SBO* 2: 156, CFS, 31: 152.

94. "Foderunt manus eius et pedes, latusque lancea foraverunt, et per has rimas licet mihi sugere mel de petra, oleumque de saxo durissimo. . . . Patet arcanum cordis per foramina corporis." Bernard of Clairvaux, *Ser. sup. cant.* 61.4, *SBO* 2: 150–51, CFS, 31: 143–44.

95. "Submittitur enim sensus, non amittitur. Nec deest dolor, sed contemnitur." Bernard of Clairvaux, *Ser. sup. cant.* 61.8, *SBO* 2: 153, CFS, 31: 147.

96. "Sponsi amoris exagitata incendio ebullit, et excrescit effusa et effluens." Gilbert of Hoyland, *Sermones in canticum* 2.4, *PL* 184: 19, CFS, 14: 59.

97. "Suavissimum mihi cervical, bone Jesu, spinea illa capitis tui corona. Dulcis lectulus illud crucis tuae lignum." Gilbert of Hoyland, *Sermones in canticum* 2.7, *PL* 184: 21, CFS, 14: 62.

98. "Nam etsi novimus Christum secundum carnem, secundum carnis concupiscentiam tamen non novimus. Communis quidem carnis natura, sed non est communis illi carnis illecebra. Non refutavit lectum doloris nostri, sed non se reclinavit usque ad sensum delectationis nostrae." Gilbert of Hoyland, *Sermones in canticum* 2.5, *PL* 184: 20, CFS, 14: 59.

99. See, e.g., Leclercq, *Second Look*, pp. 103–27; the carefully nuanced arguments of Matter, *Voice of My Beloved*; and the more general discussion in Bynum, "The Body of Christ in the Later Middle Ages," in *Fragmentation and Redemption*, pp. 85–86.

100. Bynum's work, both in *Holy Feast and Holy Fast*, and *Fragmentation and Redemption*, has shattered the idea that medieval religious people hated their bodies and all aspects of physicality.

101. See Foucault, *History of Sexuality*, for an insightful analysis of our modern preoccupation with sex; see Brown, *Body and Society*, esp. Chapter 1, for a discussion of elite Roman society in which anger, and not sexuality, was perceived as the most disruptive human passion and the one least susceptible to control. Although it is impossible to know what the monks thought while reading the Song of Songs and hearing sermons on its meanings, I suspect they may have enjoyed the sensuality of the natural images more than those concerning the human body and sexual desire. It is also important to note that images we moderns might consider as erotic, such as long discussions of the beauty of the bride's breasts, were images that the Cistercians associated with maternity instead. See Bynum's discussion of breasts symbolizing food in "The Body of Christ in the Later Middle Ages," in *Fragmentation and Redemption*, p. 86, and Guerric

of Igny, *In sollemnitate apostolorum Petri et Pauli, sermo secundus*, SC 202: 380–94.

102. See esp. Constable, "Renewal and Reform," pp. 48–67; Farmer, *Communities of St. Martin*, pp. 185–86. See also Williams, *Wilderness and Paradise*, pp. 28–46; Ward, "Desert Myth," pp. 183–99.

103. Bernard of Clairvaux, *Ser. sup. cant.* 30.6, *SBO* 2: 213, CFS, 7: 117–18. See also Sermon 58.10.

104. Gilbert of Hoyland, *Sermones in canticum* 35–36, *PL* 184: 183–192, CFS, 26: 425–43, esp. 426. See also Sermon 40.5, in which the bride's garden figures either the state of the soul or the Church.

105. Chenu, "Nature and Man—The Renaissance of the Twelfth Century," in *Nature, Man and Society*, pp. 37–48. But see the insightful comments of Stiegmann, "Tradition of Aesthetics," pp. 129–47.

106. Leclercq, *Love of Learning*, pp. 164–66. He has modified a similar stance concerning the monks' use of sexual imagery, but there is still a tendency to see natural images solely in terms of a spiritual rebirth, and not in terms of the Cistercians' activities on their property. See Auberger, *L'unanimité cistercienne primitive*, pp. 166–82. But for an interpretation that connects the Cistercians' "mythological" writings with their actual activites, see McGuire, *Difficult Saint*, pp. 286–87.

107. "Si non advertisti, adverte de medio floris huius quasi aureas virgulas prodeuntes, cinctas candissimo flore, pulchre ac decenter disposito in coronam." Bernard of Clairvaux, *Ser. sup. cant.* 70.5, *SBO* 2: 210, CFS, 40: 41.

108. Isaac of Stella, *Sermo vigesimusquartus* (seventh sermon for Sexagesima) 1–4, *SC* 207: 98–102, CFS, 11: 197–98.

109. Gilbert of Hoyland, *Sermones in canticum* 36.2, *PL* 184: 188–89, CFS, 26: 436.

110. See, e.g., Isaac of Stella, Sermons 5, 7, 9, 17, 18, *SC* 130: 160, 190, 220, 310–28, 207: 8, CFS 11: 45, 62, 80, 139–47, 149. See also the sermon of Hugh, abbot of Pontigny, "Homo nascitur ad laborem," B.N. lat. 3301c, ff. 11r–12v.

111. Aelred of Rievaulx, *De quadragesimali ieiunio*, in *Sermones inediti*, p. 55; see also *De adventu Domini*, in *Sermones inediti*, p. 32. Guerric of Igny, *De resurrectione Domini, sermo tertius* 4, *SC* 202: 254.

112. Nicholas of Clairvaux, Letter 38, *PL* 196: 1636; Bernard of Clairvaux, Letter 106, *SBO* 7: 267.

113. Farmer, *Communities of St. Martin*, p. 185.

114. *Exordium cistercii* 1, p. 111. See also William of Saint-Thierry, *Vita prima* 1.5.25, *PL* 185: 241. The Cistercians' use of this passage also established an implicit comparison to Molesme, for it goes on to describe how the Israelites became fat and sleek and forsook their God.

115. "Pinguescent speciosa deserti et florebit solitudo. . . . Tunc erit desertum

quasi deliciae paradisi et solitudo quasi hortus Domini." Guerric of Igny, *In na-vitate sancti Ioannis Baptistae, sermo quartus* 1, *SC* 202: 352, CFS, 32: 141.

116. "Locus horroris et vastae solitudinis." Guerric of Igny, *In pentecostem, sermo primus* 4, *SC* 202: 320–22, CFS, 32: 113–14; *Sermo ad excitandam devotionem in psalmodia* 1, *SC* 202: 516, CFS, 32: 213.

117. Guerric of Igny, *In sollemnitate omnium sanctorum sermo* 3, *SC* 202: 502–4; Gilbert of Hoyland, *Sermones in canticum* 4.5, *PL* 184: 29; CFS, 14: 79.

118. "Possit emortuum recreare spiritum, delicati animi detergere fastidia, in-devotae mentis emollire duritiam." Gilbert of Hoyland, *Tractatus VII ad Roger abbatem* 4, *PL* 184: 283, CFS, 34: 70; see Constable, "Renewal and Reform," p. 55.

119. Walter Daniel, *Life of Ailred*, p. 12.

CHAPTER 4

1. See Duby, *Three Orders*.

2. Unfortunately, this is what Duby does in *Three Orders*, pp. 222–27. A close reading of the one passage he analyzes shows more contradictions in Bernard's view of society than Duby admits.

3. Acts 4.32; Ps. 132. See, e.g., Gilbert of Hoyland, *Sermones in canticum* 11.2, 35.7, *PL* 184: 59, 187, CFS, 14: 142, 26: 433. See also Bernard of Clairvaux, *Sermo de diversis*, 42, *SBO* 6.1: 258.

4. *Summa cartae caritatis* 16, p. 123; *Statuta*, 1: 24–25 (1134, no. 51); Griesser, "*Ecclesiastica officia*," pp. 226–27.

5. "Discordes ad communionem revocant unitatis, concordes in vinculo pacis continent et conservant." Geoffrey of Auxerre, *Expositio in cantica canticorum*, 2: 449.

6. "Videas illum peccata sua flentem, alium in Dei laudibus exsultantem, hunc omnibus ministrantem, illum alios erudientem, hunc orantem, illum legentem; hunc miserentem, illum peccata punientem; hunc caritate flagrantem, illum humilitate pollentem; hunc in prosperis humilem, illum in adversitate sub-limem; hunc in activa laborantem, illum in contemplativa quiescentem. . . . Quae prius habitabas in regione umbrae mortis, transi ad regionem vitae et veri-tatis." Bernard of Clairvaux, *Sermo de diversis* 42.4, *SBO* 6.1: 258.

7. Bernard of Clairvaux, Letter 143, *SBO* 7: 343 (James, no. 144).

8. "Quo pacto quove modo, immo qua caritate monachi eorum per abbatias in diversis mundi partibus corporibus divisi animis indissolubiliter cong-lutinarentur." *Carta caritatis prior* 1, p. 89.

9. For a discussion of the importance of uniformity for the Cistercians, see Goodrich, "Caritas and Cistercian Uniformity."

10. "Quatinus in actibus nostris nulla sit discordia, sed una caritate, una regula similibusque vivamus moribus." *Carta cartitatis prior* 3, p. 92.

11. *Carta caritatis prior* 1, 4, pp. 91, 93.

12. *Carta caritatis prior* 7, p. 95.

13. "Ibique de salute animarum suarum tractent, in observatione sanctae regulae vel ordinis, si quid emendandum est vel augendum ordinent, bonum pacis et caritatis inter se reforment." Ibid.

14. For Innocent II's bull in 1132 describing "conversos vestros, qui monachi non sunt," see *Cîteaux*, pp. 92–93. "Et coadjutores nostros sub cura nostra sicut et monachos suscipimus, fratres et participes nostrorum tam spiritualium quam temporalium bonorum aeque ut monachos habemus." *Summa cartae caritatis* 20, pp. 123–24.

15. *Summa cartae caritatis* 22, p. 124; *Statuta*, 1: 108 (1188, no. 8).

16. For a dating of the customary, see Auberger, *L'unanimité cistercienne primitive*, pp. 63–65. He suggests a date after 1134 and before 1145 for the composition of the *Usus conversorum* as established in Trente MS. 1711. For other work on dating the manuscripts, see Lefèvre, "L'évolution des *Usus conversorum.*" It is possible there was a "noyau primitif" of the *Usus* established earlier, but there is no way to determine its contents from the existing manuscripts. Auberger, *L'unanimité cistercienne primitive*, p. 64.

17. "Cum constet super animas fratrum laicorum eque ut monachorum curam nos suscepisse ab episcopis. miror quosdam abbates nostro monachis quidem discipline debitam impendere diligentiam. conversis vero aut nullam aut minimam. . . . Proinde sicut monachorum usus necessarie quidem. conscripsimus ut ubicumque in moribus nostris unitas conservetur, ita et conversis qualiter et in temporalibus et in spiritualibus. providendum sit"; Auberger, *L'unanimité cistercienne primitive*, pp. 379–80. The text is from Trente MS. 1711. See also Auberger, *L'unanimité cistercienne primitive*, pp. 64–65.

18. See the *Usus conversorum* in Auberger, *L'unanimité cistercienne primitive*, pp. 379–90. See also Othon, "De l'institution et des us de convers," who relied on a customary from the end of the twelfth century.

19. Griesser, "*Ecclesiastica officia*," p. 199.

20. Ibid., pp. 200, 195, 212.

21. Ibid., pp. 185, 194, 197–98, 100.

22. See, e.g., Geoffrey of Auxerre, *Expositio in cantica canticorum*, 2: 337–38; Gilbert of Hoyland, *Sermones in canticum* 43.5, 45.6, *PL* 184: 228, 240, CFS, 26: 520–21, 545.

23. "Quasi popularibus negotiis occupantur." *Sermo de diversis* 9.4, *SBO* 6.1: 120. Bernard made a similar association between Martha and monastic officials in Sermon 57 on the Song of Songs, in which he advocated the presence of Martha, Mary, and Lazarus within each individual, but then recognized

that at least they could be found within a single community—the contemplative monks were Mary, the novices were Lazarus, and those who administered the external concerns of the monastery were Martha; *SBO* 2: 126.

24. Aelred of Rievaulx, *In natali sanctorum apostolorum Petri et Pauli* 14–19, *CCCM* 2a: 135–38.

25. Geoffrey of Auxerre, *Expositio in cantica canticorum*, 2: 449–55.

26. "Martham accipite conversos laborantes; Mariam, monachos contemplantes, Lazarum, novitios plorantes, qui nuper sunt a mortuis resuscitati." Nicholas of Clairvaux, Letter 36, *PL* 196: 1632.

27. "Pares constat esse in gratia redemptionis." Auberger, *L'unanimité cistercienne primitive*, p. 380.

28. "Regnum Dei non carnis nobilitate, non terrenis divitiis possidetur, sed sola obedientiae virtute acquiritur." Herbert of Clairvaux, *De miraculis* 1.29, *PL* 185: 1302.

29. Herbert of Clairvaux, *De miraculis* 1.18, *PL* 185: 1293–94.

30. Herbert of Clairvaux, *De miraculis* 1.15, 2.30, *PL* 185: 1291–92, 1340–42. These are called *bubalos*; perhaps they were water buffalo?

31. Herbert of Clairvaux, *De miraculis* 1.16, *PL* 185: 1292.

32. Herbert of Clairvaux, *De miraculis* 1.31, *PL* 185: 1304.

33. "Et, dum ista fierent, viro cuidam spirituali demonstratum est in visione quod duo pulcherrima templa fabricarentur in Claravalle; unum in infirmitorio monachorum, alterum in infirmitorio conversorum. Sed primum illud hoc altero longe nobilius erat atque venustius. Constat igitur quia in gemina constructione templorum . . . designata sit evidenter pretiosa in conspectu Domini mors amborum. Templorum autem differentia meritorum distantiam indicat, quia, quamvis utrumque sanctum, tamen alterum altero sanctiorem existere credimus apud Deum." Herbert of Clairvaux, *De miraculis* 1.1, *PL* 185: 1276.

34. "Nam etsi fulgebunt iusti sicut sol in regno Patris eorum, alii tamen aliis amplius, pro diversitate meritorum." Bernard of Clairvaux, *Apologia* 4.9, *SBO* 3: 89, CFS, 1: 44.

35. The first recorded revolt of the lay brothers occurred around 1168 at the monastery of Schönau in the diocese of Worms; there were then none until the last decade of the twelfth century. Between 1190 and 1215 there were 29, including one at La Ferté in 1201. There were two at Pontigny, one in 1230 and 1238, but none at Cîteaux or Clairvaux between 1168 and 1308. Donnelly, *Decline*, pp. 71–80.

36. Conrad of Eberbach, *Exordium magnum* 5.10, pp. 292–98.

37. "Ut arduos durissimosque labores . . . intolerabiles iudicarent." Ibid., p. 293.

38. Geoffrey of Auxerre, *Expositio in cantica canticorum*, 2: 369–81. See also Gilbert of Hoyland, *Sermones in canticum* 23.1, 30.5, *PL* 184: 118, 157, CFS, 20:

284, 377; Gilbert associated the bride's eyes with teachers or prelates and her hair with disciples or the faithful people.

39. "Lectulus est ecclesiae quies coenobitarum, domus conventus popolorum; tigna principes utriusque ordinis, qui iustis legibus fortiter stringunt, laquearia bene instituti cleri mores ornantes ecclesiasm." Geoffrey of Auxerre, *Expositio in cantica canticorum*, 1: 48. See also Bernard of Clairvaux, *Ser. sup. cant.* 46.2, *SBO* 2: 56–57, CFS, 7: 242; and Hugh of Pontigny, who constructed Solomon's temple out of the stone of prelates, the wood of active people, and the gold of contemplatives. Cited in Talbot, "Sermons of Hugh of Pontigny," p. 21.

40. Bernard of Clairvaux, *Apologia* 3.6, *SBO* 3: 86, CFS, 1: 41.

41. "Simulque expressit sanctae desiderium animae, et epithalamii carmen." Bernard of Clairvaux, *Ser. sup. cant.* 1.8, *SBO* 1: 6, CFS, 4: 5.

42. Matter, *Voice of My Beloved*, pp. 87–111, 123.

43. Congar, "L'ecclésiologie de S. Bernard," pp. 140–41.

44. Gilbert of Hoyland, *Sermones in canticum* 5.4, *PL* 184: 34, CFS, 14: 88; Geoffrey of Auxerre, *Expositio in cantica canticorum*, 2: 305.

45. "Non tantum vicos districte viventium habet civitas Ierusalem, sed plateas, humiliora et planiora diligentium." Geoffrey of Auxerre, *Expositio in cantica canticorum*, 2: 305.

46. See, e.g., Bernard of Clairvaux: "Although we are obliged by our religion to extend the warmth of our charity to all the faithful, nonetheless our devotion is greater toward those whom the profession of a common life makes almost one." Letter 544, *SBO* 8: 511 (James, no. 396).

47. Gilbert of Hoyland, *Sermones in canticum* 10.2, *PL* 184: 56, CFS, 14: 134.

48. Hugh of Pontigny, "Homo nascitur ad laborem," B.N. lat. 3301c, ff. 11r–12v; see also "Maria virgo assumpta est," B.N. lat. 3301c, f. 38r–v. Henry of Marcy, *Tractatus de peregrinante civitate dei*, *PL* 204: 261–62.

49. "Ultimus hic contemplationis modus simplicium est; secundus, eruditorum; primus, purissimorum." Gilbert of Hoyland, *Sermones in canticum* 43.6, *PL* 184: 229, CFS, 26: 522.

50. Geoffrey of Auxerre, *Expositio in cantica canticorum*, 2: 409. See also pp. 499–500.

51. Duby, *Three Orders*, p. 81.

52. Gregory the Great, *Homélies sur Ezéchiel* 1.8–10, *SC* 327: 290–91.

53. Bernard of Clairvaux, *Sermo de diversis* 9.3, *SBO* 6.1: 119; Bernard of Clairvaux, *Sermo ad abbates*, *SBO* 5: 289.

54. Henry of Marcy, *Tractatus de peregrinante civitate dei*, *PL* 204: 315. The *De peregrinante civitate dei*, replete with triads that express, among other things, virtues and intellectual qualities, sacraments, stages of history and spiritual development, and social orders, was generally loath to distinguish the monastic life

from the secular. Henry also used the apostles Peter, James, and John to exemplify teaching and pastoral care, the spiritual life, and contemplation, whereas Noah, Daniel, and Job figured doctrine, understanding (*intelligentiae*), and faith; *PL* 204: 315, 342.

55. "Nos tamen in his verbis tria solemus hominum intelligere genera, quibus solis loquitur Deus pacem, sicut et Propheta alius tres tantum praevidit salvandos, Noe, Danielem et Iob, contrario quidem ordine, sed eosdem ordines exprimens, continentium scilicet, praelatorum et coniugatorum, si tamen continentes a carnalibus illecebris ad ea quae cordis sunt, id est ad spiritualia desideria convertantur—unde et Daniel vir desideriorum ab Angelo nominatur—et praelati prodesse magis studeant quam praeesse, quoniam ipsos maxime decet sanctitudo—unde et in psalmo sancti spiritualiter appellantur—et coniugati mandata non transgrediantur, ut merito plebs Dei et oves pascuae eius debeant nominari." Bernard of Clairvaux, *Sermo de diversis* 9.3, *SBO* 6.1: 119.

56. Bernard of Clairvaux, *Sermo ad abbates*, *SBO* 5: 289.

57. Geoffrey of Auxerre, *Expositio in cantica canticorum*, 2: 238.

58. "Oritur in prelatis, floret in contemplatiuis, fructificat in actiuis. . . . Ex primo assimilatur bonis auditoribus, ex secundo ueris doctoribus, ex tercio actioni pie insistentibus. De certo, loquente Ihesu, sedente Maria, sola Martha parat conuiuia, quia prelatis doctrine, contemplatiuis Deo uacantibus, soli actiui uite presentis utriusque ministrant necessaria. Et quia pro carnalibus spiritualia sibi iure debentur, iuste Martha postulat ut ei Maria suffragetur. Vtique actiuus contemplatiui meritis et precibus tutius innitatur, conuenienter subiungitur, quia Maria optimam partem elegit. Tres sunt partes; una bona, alia melior, tercia optima." Hugh of Pontigny, quoted in Talbot, "Sermons of Hugh of Pontigny," p. 20. Talbot suggests that these are divisions in the monastery; but, as Hugh clearly states, they are also the three orders in the Church.

59. See, e.g., Bernard of Clairvaux, *Ser. sup. cant.* 12.9, *SBO* 1: 66; Gilbert of Hoyland, *Sermones in canticum* 16, 30, *PL* 184: 83, 158–60.

60. Bernard of Clairvaux, *Apologia* 4.8, *SBO* 3: 88, CFS, 1: 43–44.

61. Markus, *End of Ancient Christianity*, esp. pp. 181–97, 201–2, 223–28.

62. Gregory the Great, *Regulae pastoralis*, esp. 1.2, 1.10, 4.1.

63. For Abbo of Fleury's understanding of Noah, Daniel, and Job, see Mostert, *Political Theology of Abbo of Fleury*, pp. 88–89. For Cluny, see Iogna-Prat, *Agni immaculati*, pp. 344–50; Duby, *Three Orders*, pp. 192–205. For Rupert of Deutz, see Van Engen, *Rupert of Deutz*, pp. 265–66.

64. For monastic exemptions, see Lemarignier, *Etude sur les privilèges d'exemption*; Lemarignier, "L'exemption monastique." For a study of the patronage, protection, and hope for salvation that Fleury offered its benefactors and neighbors, see Head, *Hagiography and the Cult of Saints*.

PART II

1. Bynum, "Did the Twelfth Century Discover the Individual?" in *Jesus as Mother*, pp. 82–109.

2. Robinson, *Authority and Resistance*, pp. 39–49; Gilchrist, "Canon Law Aspects of the Gregorian Reform Progamme," *Journal of Ecclesiastical History* 13 (1962): 21–38.

3. Reynolds, *Kingdoms and Communities*, esp. pp. 38–66.

4. "For as in one body we have many members and all the members do not have the same function, so we, though many, are one body in Christ, and individually members one of another" (Rom. 12.4–5). See Wallace-Hadrill, *Early Germanic Kingship*, p. 107, who discusses the idea of the emperor as the *corrector* of a community of believers that he was to unite in peace and concord. See also Nelson, "Kingship and Empire," pp. 213–29, esp. p. 221. For an example of the Carolingian language used to stress the cooperation of an emperor and his churchmen, see Alcuin, *Synodus quae facta est in Anglorum Saxonia* (786) cap. 14, as cited in Burns, ed., *Cambridge History*, p. 291: "Let there be harmony everywhere and agreement between kings and bishops, churchmen and laymen and all the Christian people, so that there may be unity everywhere in the churches of God and lasting peace in one Church, one faith, hope and charity, having one head who is Christ, whose members must help each other and love each other in mutual charity." For the use of such imagery by the eleventh-century imperial apologists, see Robinson, *Authority and Resistance*, pp. 89–95.

5. Koziol, *Begging Pardon and Favor*, pp. 254–58; Poly and Bournazel, *Feudal Transformation*, pp. 151–62. For recent work on the Peace of God, see Head and Landes, eds., *Essays on the Peace of God*.

6. Jacqueline argues that Bernard of Clairvaux was more knowledgeable about canon law than is usually recognized, that the library at Clairvaux possessed manuscripts of the pseudo-Isidorian decretals and Gregory VII's *Registrum*, and that Bernard not only had access to the works of Ivo of Chartres but quoted from them and used Ivo's ideas in helping to settle the papal schism of the 1130's. See Jacqueline, "Yves de Chartres" and *Episcopat et papauté*, esp. pp. 23–40, 72–73. But however much Bernard was willing to use canon law to aid in the settlement of disputes, he did not view Christian society as did most canonists, as a body held together by its obedience to the pope and the laws that the popes instituted. See Ullmann, *Growth of Papal Government*, as well as the criticisms of Ullmann's earlier arguments by Stickler, "Concerning the Political Theories of the Medieval Canonists," and Tierney, "Some Recent Works on the Political Theories of the Medieval Canonists." Ivo's ideas might have appealed to Bernard more than those of the Italian scholars because Ivo did not try to resolve all contractions in the law with an appeal to the fixed principles of natural

law but instead appealed to the moral character of the ruler, who was to use discretion to interpret each *decretum* as best suited the situation. See Kuttner, "Forgotten Definition of Justice"; Koziol, *Begging Pardon and Favor*, pp. 214–15.

7. Gregory the Great, *Regulae pastoralis* 1.10, 2.6, *SC* 381: 160–64, 202–19. Pope Gregory VII certainly used Gregory the Great as a model, but he appears to have been more interested in Gregory's life and letters than in the *Regulae pastoralis*; see Robinson, *Authority and Resistance*, pp. 31–39. For two twelfth-century authors whose language and concerns were close to those of the Cistercians, but who nonetheless defined a much clearer relationship between secular and ecclesiastical authority, see Hugh of Saint Victor and John of Salisbury. In his *De sacramentis christianae fidei* 2.2.2–4, *PL* 176: 416–18, Hugh describes the two orders within the one body of Christ. He not only ranks the spiritual order superior but considers this superiority in juridical terms, for the spiritual power both establishes secular power and has the right to judge it. John of Salisbury, in *Policraticus* 4.3, calls the prince a *minister*, but he is a *sacerdotii minister*, implying the precedence of spiritual powers over his authority. See also Smalley, *Becket Conflict*, p. 99. The Cistercians, following Gregory the Great and Augustine, described both secular and ecclesiastical authorities as the ministers of those that they ruled and thus made much less of a distinction between the virtuous exercise of secular and ecclesiastical authority.

8. Augustine, *City of God* 19.15–20; see also the works by Markus: *Saeculum*, esp. pp. 163–65; "Sacred and the Secular"; "Gregory the Great's *Rector*, pp. 137–46; "The Latin Fathers," pp. 121–22.

9. For analysis of the oppositions and balances in Gregory's thought, see Straw, *Gregory the Great*.

CHAPTER 5

1. For the hermits at Pontigny and Morimond, see *Pontigny*, pp. 152–54 (no. 84); *GC* 4: 159, Instrumenta 36. For the aid the first Cistercian houses received from other monks, see *Cîteaux*, pp. 60–61, 63, 64, 74 (nos. 39, 41, 58); *Clairvaux*, 4, 7 (nos. 3, 5).

2. See, e.g., Letter 382, *SBO* 8: 348 (James, no. 41).

3. Letters 14–16 to Pope Honorius and Cardinal Haimeric for Saint-Bénigne of Dijon; Letter 39 to Theobald of Champagne, for canons of Larzicourt; Letters 43–44 to Archbishop Henry of Sens for monks of Molesme; Letter 54 to Haimeric, on behalf of the abbot of Hautecombe; Letter 58 to Bishop Ebal of Châlons, for canons regular at Châlons-sur-Marne; Letter 59 to Bishop Willenc of Langres, for canons of Saint Stephen at Dijon; Letter 60 to Bishop Willenc of Langres, for Molesme; Letter 158 to Innocent II, about the murder of the prior of Saint Victor; Letter 510 to the archbishop of Trèves, about the convent

of Saint Maur at Verdun; Letter 516 to the count of Nevers, asking protection for Molesme; letter 513 to Count Ebal of Flore, on behalf of monks at Liessies; Letter 200 about a quarrel between Fontevrault and the bishop of Angers; Letter 263 to the bishop of Soissons for the abbot of Chézy; Letters 231 and 232 to the cardinal-bishops of Ostia, Tusculum, and Palestrina for the abbots of Lagny and Saint Theofred; Letter 251 to Pope Eugenius, about punishing the monks of Beaune; Letter 261 to Eugenius, for the abbot of Saint-Urban; Letter 262 to Eugenius, for the abbey of Sainte-Marie-sur-Meuse; Letter 309 to Eugenius, for the abbot of Saint-Denis; Letter 270 to Eugenius, for the prior of La Chartreuse; Letter 277 to Eugenius, for Peter the Venerable; Letter 279 to Count Henry of Champagne, about pigs stolen from the abbot of Châtillon; Letter 291 to Eugenius, for the church of Saint Eugendus in Jura: Letter 315 to Matilda, queen of England, about the tithe for La Chapelle; Letters 285–87 to Eugenius and the bishop of Ostia on behalf of Abbot Odo of Saint-Denis; Letter 375 to Countess Ida of Nevers, about merchants' access to Vézelay; Letter 394 to Archbishop Peter of Lyons, on behalf of the abbot of Ainay; Letter 423 to a bishop, on behalf of Saint Martin. For these letters, see *SBO* 7–8. Interventions in disputes include: Stephen Harding and Bernard of Clairvaux settled a dispute between Saint Stephen of Dijon and Saint-Seine; Bourrier, *Chartes de l'abbaye de Saint-Etienne*, no. 23. Rainald Bar, abbot of Cîteaux, settled a dispute between Saint Peter of Chalon and Bishop Walter of Chalon over cemetery rights; *GC* 4.240–41, Instrumenta 24. Bernard of Clairvaux and Bishops Henry of Troyes and Godfrey of Langres settled a tithe dispute concerning Saint Peter of Troyes; Lalore, *Collection*, 3: 260. Bishops Hugh of Auxerre, Godfrey of Langres, Alan of Auxerre, and Henry of Troyes and Bernard of Clairvaux intervened in a long dispute concerning the monastery of Vézelay; *PL* 180: 1178, 1424, 1502–3, 1537, 1551, 1556. Bernard of Clairvaux settled a dispute for All Saints of Châlons; Lalore, *Collection*, 4: 245. Goswin of Cîteaux settled a dispute between the nuns of Vaubans and the dean and chapter of the cathedral of Langres; B.N. lat. 17100, p. 93.

4. McGuire, *Friendship and Community*, esp. pp. 231–95.

5. Aelred of Rievaulx, *Speculum caritatis* 1.107, *CCCM* 1: 60; Aelred of Rievaulx, *Amicitia spiritalis*, esp. Book 3; Nicholas of Clairvaux, Letters 15, 31, 35, *PL* 196: 1609, 1622, 1626–27. It is noteworthy that, with the exception of Nicholas of Clairvaux, McGuire's best examples of epistolary friendships come from letters written by non-Cistercians, such as Peter of Celle and Peter the Venerable, to Cistercians; McGuire, *Friendship and Community*, esp. pp. 251–91. Is this perhaps evidence of an effort by these monks to experience, through letters, the fraternal love and support that Cistercian monks received in person?

6. C. Waddell, "Notes Towards the Exegesis of a Letter," pp. 10–39. McGuire

argues that Stephen had mastered the traditional Benedictine language of friendship; *Friendship and Community*, p. 252.

7. William of Saint-Thierry, *Vita prima* 1.7.33, *PL* 185: 246–47.

8. "Et licet nos ordo divisus dividat, charitas ligat, quia non color vestium, sed amor cordium hanc effecit unitatem, imo unanimitatem, amantissime pater." Gerard of Perona, in Peter of Celles, Letter 59, *PL* 202: 474. For an analysis of Nicholas's letters of friendship, see *Friendship and Community*, pp. 279–91.

9. See Cowdrey, "Legal Problems," who also argues that the Cistercians' *Carta caritatis* owed a debt to the older confraternities' ideas of concord and love, but that it surpassed the gift-exchange nature of confraternities by giving its rules legal force. See also Berlière, "Les fraternités monastiques."

10. Griesser, "*Ecclesiastica officia*," p. 171. See also Talbot, "Associations."

11. This agreement gave the monks of Saint Waast full participation in the spiritual benefits of Cîteaux's prayers; *Cîteaux*, p. 84 (no. 75).

12. *Statuta*, 1: 35–37. The monks of La Ferté and Saint Martin also ended a dispute over lands and rents by agreeing to hold "a brief office for the dead" in both churches when a monk from either community died; Bulliot, *Essai historique*, pp. 35–36.

13. "In conventu Cisterciensi, vestri, tamquam specialis domini, et patris, et amici carissimi, et vestrorum, tam vivorum quam mortuorum, memoria facta est." Bernard of Clairvaux, Letter 389, *SBO* 8: 357 (James, no. 309).

14. Nicholas of Clairvaux, Letters 10, 27, 43, 46, *PL* 196: 1606–7, 1619–20, 1643–44, 1647–48. See also Bernard of Clairvaux, Letters 91, 147, 154, 204, 228, 387, *SBO* 7: 239, 350, 8: 63, 98, 355.

15. "Ita regulae incubantes ut nec unum nec apicem praetereundum putent." William of Malmesbury, *De gestis regum Anglorum* 4.336, RS 90.2: 383. "Studiosos scrutatores Regulae beati Benedicti." Rupert of Deutz, *Super quaedam capitula regulae divi Benedicti abbatis* 2.13, *PL* 170: 509.

16. See above, Chapter 3, pp. 69–70.

17. For Abelard's criticism of the Cistercians' break with the traditional Roman chant, see his Letter 10, *PL* 178: 399–40.

18. "Propter dissimilitudinem." *Statuta*, 1: 27 (1134, no. 41).

19. Even if we accept Auberger's argument that the polemical language of the *Exordium parvum* was not added until sometime between 1130 and 1150, the original dossier of documents incorporated into the *Exordium parvum* expresses implicit critiques of Molesme; Auberger, *L'unanimité cistercienne primitive*, p. 52.

20. The *Exordium cistercii* is usually seen as less "polemical" than the *Exordium parvum*; see Auberger, *L'unanimité cistercienne primitive*, p. 53.

21. "Ceterum quia possesssionibus virtutibusque diuturna non solet esse societas, hoc quidam ex illa sancta congregatione viri nimirum sapientes, altius

intelligentes, elegerunt potius studiis coelestibus occupari quam terrenis implicare negotiis." *Exordium cistercii* I, p. III.

22. This was further reinforced by using the passage from Deuteronomy, "a place of horror and vast solitude," to describe Cîteaux, for the biblical passage goes on to describe how the Israelites became fat and sleek and forsook God; Deut. 32.10–18.

23. For the Cistercians' economic aid to Molesme, see *Molesme*, pp. 243–45, 374–75; Bernard of Clairvaux, Letters 43, 44, 60, 516, *SBO* 7: 131, 132, 153, 8: 475, *GC* 12: III, Instrumenta 17. Other Cistercians continued to aid Molesme: Guichard of Pontigny and Bishop Godfrey of Langres settled a dispute between Molesme and Lord Herbert of Merry, *Molesme*, p. 316; and Godfrey, as former bishop of Langres, witnessed an agreement between Molesme and the archdeacon of Tonnerre, *Molesme*, p. 307.

24. *Molesme*, pp. 243–44. See also *Molesme*, p. 482: in 1126, Hugh of Pontigny and Bernard of Clairvaux witnessed a charter issued by the bishop of Auxerre confirming Molesme's possession of churches and tithes.

25. For a discussion of the debates over the apostolic life, see Chenu, "Monks, Canons and Laymen in Search of the Apostolic Life," in *Nature, Man and Society*, pp. 202–38. See also Constable, *Monastic Tithes*, pp. 136–85; Van Engen, *Rupert of Deutz*, pp. 299–334.

26. This letter is undated, but was written before Hugh became bishop of Auxerre in 1136.

27. "Qua audacia, o monachi, praesumitis, seu vinum de vinea quam non plantastis, seu lac de grege quem non pascitis? Quo pacto ibi exigitis, ubi nihil exhibetis? Certe si ita vultis, baptizate nascentes, sepelite morientes, visitate iacentes, copulate nubentes, instruite rudes, corripite delinquentes, excommunicate contemnentes, absolvite resipiscentes, reconciliate paenitentes, et in medio denique ecclesiae aperiat os suum monachus, cuius officium est sedere et tacere. Sic fortasse dignum se probabit mercenarius mercede sua. Alioquin invidiosum admodum est, velle metere ubi non seminaveris; sed et colligere quod alius sparserit, etiam iniuriosum." Bernard of Clairvaux, Letter 397, *SBO* 8: 374–75 (James, no. 429).

28. See, e.g., *Molesme*, p. 482 (no. 641), pp. 243–44 (no. 262); Quantin, *Cartulaire général de l'Yonne*, 1: 332; Lalore, *Cartulaire de l'abbaye de Montiéramey*, in *Collection des principaux cartulaires*, 7: 63, 65–66.

29. They appear to have adopted a position similar to that expressed by the author of the *Libellus de diuersis ordinibus*. This author differentiated between monks who lived close to people and took on the burdens of priests, and those who lived at a distance. Those monks who accepted priestly responsibilities, this author argued, could also accept tithes. *Libellus de diuersis ordinibus et professionibus qui sunt in aecclesia*, p. 27.

30. Constable, *Monastic Tithes*, p. 286.

31. The first Cistercian house to receive a privilege from Alexander, reversing Hadrian's policy, was Rievaulx, in 1160; *PL* 200: 92–95. For other privileges to Cistercian houses, see *PL* 200: 155, 255, 267, 295, 343, 356, 359, 386, 423, 734.

32. "Interim autem propter scandalum gravius, quod super retentione decimarum undique crescit in dies. . . . " *Statuta*, 1: 86–87 (1180, no. 1).

33. For a fuller discussion of Rupert's criticisms, see van Engen, *Rupert of Deutz*, pp. 314–23.

34. Rupert of Deutz, *Super quaedam capitula regulae divi Benedicti abbatis* 3.13, 14, *PL* 170: 521–22.

35. Rupert of Deutz, *Super quaedam capitula regulae divi Benedicti abbatis* 3.10, *PL* 170: 517–18.

36. In fact, the only time Rupert discussed caritas in his defense of his traditions and his attack on the new monks was in his discussion of the mass. Rupert of Deutz, *Super quaedam capitula regulae divi Benedicti abbatis* 3.10, *PL* 170: 518.

37. *RB* 61.

38. For Cluny's privilege of 931, see *PL* 132: 1057, and its later expansion, *PL* 151: 487. For Fleury, see *PL* 132: 1074. For the eleventh-century canonists, see Fournier and Le Bras, *Histoire des collections canoniques*, 1: 366ff.

39. Bernard of Clairvaux, Letters 408, 417, 442, *SBO* 8: 389, 401, 420 (James, nos. 440, 448, 461).

40. Bernard of Clairvaux, Letter 34, *SBO* 7: 90–91 (James, no. 35).

41. Bernard of Clairvaux, Letter 32, *SBO* 7: 87 (James, no. 33). "Nec ignoro quin possint apud Sanctum Bertinum fratres suam ipsorum operari salutem; sed quos illuc vocaverit Deus." Letter 395, *SBO* 8: 370–71 (James, no. 420).

42. "Diligam vos semper, carissimi fratres, in Domino, et cum omni amore serviam vobis in eo, cuius servi estis: immo Christum, cuius membra estis, semper in vobis honorabo. . . . Quem ergo Dominus vocavit, vide ne revoces; quem Deus erexit, tu inclinare noli; nec ponas ei offendiculum, cui Deus manum porrigit ascendenti." Bernard of Clairvaux, Letter 382, *SBO* 8: 347–48 (James, no. 419).

43. Bernard of Clairvaux, Letters 397, 81, *SBO* 8: 373, 7: 214 (James, nos. 429, 83). See also Bernard of Clairvaux, Letters 78, 91, *SBO* 7: 205, 239 (James, nos. 80, 94).

44. *GC* 10: 191–92, Instrumenta 6; *Statuta*, 1: 35–37; Bernard of Clairvaux, Letters 79, 253, *SBO* 7: 210–12, 8: 149–55 (James, nos. 81, 328).

45. "Quid peccavi? An quod vestram personam semper amavi, vestrum Ordinem fovi et promovi semper, quod in me fuit?" Bernard of Clairvaux, Letter 253, *SBO* 8: 149 (James, no. 328).

46. "Reliquum est, ut diligentes vos diligatis, praesertim solliciti servare

unitatem spiritus in vinculo pacis: illo, inquam, vinculo, quod inter nos et vos causa pacis caritatisque firmatum est, utiliter quidem, et non minus forsitan vobis quam nobis. . . . Olim me alligavi forti vinculo, caritate non ficta, illa quae numquam excidit. Cum turbatis ero pacificus, conturbantibus quoque dabo locum irae, ne diabolo dem." Bernard of Clairvaux, Letter 253, *SBO* 8: 154–55 (James, no. 328).

47. Bernard of Clairvaux, Letter 85, *SBO* 7: 220–22 (James, no. 87).

48. See, e.g., the letters between Nicholas of Clairvaux and Peter of Celles, as discussed in McGuire, *Friendship and Community*, pp. 280–84.

49. Ibid., pp. 253–88; Lang, "Friendship between Peter the Venerable and Bernard of Clairvaux." But see the recent article by Bredero, "Saint Bernard in His Relations with Peter the Venerable."

50. "Sed haec infirmantium sunt fomenta, non arma pugnantium. Ecce enim qui mollibus vestiuntur in domibus regum sunt." Matt. 11.8. Bernard of Clairvaux, Letter 1, *SBO* 7: 9 (James, no. 1).

51. Bernard of Clairvaux, *Apologia* 11.27, *SBO* 3: 103, CFS, 1: 62.

52. *PL* 179: 122.

53. For the grant from Cluny, see *Clairvaux*, pp. 7–8 (no. 5); for other examples, see Chapter 3.

54. Innocent II cited a letter from Pope Gregory the Great in which he determined that people who lived a communal life and gave all they could in alms need not divide their income; *Cîteaux*, 92–93 (no. 90). For the Cistercians' account of Innocent's visit to Clairvaux in 1131, and his reaction to these "poor of Christ," see Arnold of Bonneval, *Vita prima* 2.1.6, *PL* 185: 272.

55. Peter the Venerable, *Letters* no. 33, 1: 108; for Cluny's financial straits, see Duby, "Economie domainale."

56. Constable, "Cluniac Tithes."

57. Constable, *Monastic Tithes*, pp. 275, 290; Henry of Marcy, Letter 9, *PL* 204: 222; Mahn, *L'ordre cistercien*, p. 110.

58. Constable, "Disputed Election at Langres."

59. See Peter the Venerable, *Letters* nos. 29, 64, 72, 1: 101–4, 193–94, 206; Bernard of Clairvaux, Letters 164–70, *SBO* 7: 372–85.

60. The bishops claimed they had the right to consecrate the abbot of Saint-Germain of Auxerre and receive his profession of obedience, but Peter claimed that Saint-Germain's association with Cluny exempted the abbot from the bishop's control. The conflict finally ended in 1154 when Pope Anastasius IV sent Alan of Auxerre a detailed bull that established the same relations between the monastery of Saint-Germain and the bishop of Auxerre that Cistercian abbeys had developed with their bishops. The abbot of Saint-Germain was to be elected with the advice of the abbot of Cluny, but the bishop of Auxerre had the right to approve or reject the candidate, to bless the abbot-elect, and to re-

ceive his obedience. The bishop could not punish the monks in the monastery, but he did maintain the right to bless the holy oil, consecrate altars, and ordain monks into the priesthood. See *PL* 179: 616–17; *PL* 188: 1348; *GC* 12: 112–13, Instrumenta 20. The Cistercians generally were opposed to monastic exemptions. See also the complaint made by Abbot Rainald of Cîteaux and the entire Chapter General about the scandal caused by the monastery of Vézelay's efforts to escape the jurisdiction of the bishop of Autun; *PL* 179: 671. For further complaints about monastic exemptions, see Bernard of Clairvaux, *De consideratione* 3.14, *SBO* 3: 442; Bernard of Clairvaux, *De moribus et officio episcoporum* 33–36, *SBO* 7: 127–30.

61. Hugh of Pontigny became bishop of Auxerre in 1136; his predecessor had been Hugh of Montiagu, a monk of Cluny and the first Cluniac abbot of Saint-Germain; see Bouchard, *Sword, Miter, and Cloister*, p. 389.

62. Traditionally, scholars assumed that Letter 28 was written before Bernard's *Apologia*, in 1124–25. Constable, however, argues that Peter wrote the letter after the trial and condemnation of Pons in 1126; Peter the Venerable, *Letters*, 2: 271–74. Rudolph, in *"Things of Greater Importance,"* pp. 209–26, returns to the older argument of Letter 28's precedence.

63. In so doing, Peter was following a long-standing Cluniac conception of the relation of the Benedictine Rule to divine law. See Rosenwein, "Rules and the 'Rule.'" The eleventh-century customary of Ulrich of Cluny reflects this idea of the abbot as interpreter of divine law: "If there is doubt about any custom, whatever [the abbot] should decide about it is to be held by the other monks as if law." Ulrich, *Antiquiores consuetudines Cluniacensis monasterii* 3.2, *PL* 149: 734.

64. "Non eum ad ferendum incongruum et noxium laborem uiolenter impellam." Peter the Venerable, *Letters* no. 28, 1: 101. For the articulation of the Cistercian idea about pushing monks to the furthest extent of their ability, see Bernard of Clairvaux, Letter 1, *SBO* 7: 9–11.

65. "Ista caritas destruit caritatem, haec discretio discretionem confundit. Talis misericordia crudelitate plena est, qua videlicet ita corpori servitur, ut anima iuguletur." Bernard of Clairvaux, *Apologia* 8.16, *SBO* 3: 95.

66. Iogna-Prat, *Agni immaculati*; Duby, *Three Orders*, pp. 201–3. Peter the Venerable justified Cluny's possession of tithes by invoking the superior efficacy of its prayers; *Letters* no. 28, 1: 81–82.

67. "Ibi omnium professionum, dignitatum et ordinum persone fastum luxumque saecularem, in humilem et pauperem monachorum uitam commutauerunt." Peter the Venerable, *De miraculis* 1.9, *CCCM* 83: 35–36.

68. Cluny, at the time of Peter the Venerable, probably held between 300 and 400 monks; Constable, "Monastic Policy of Peter the Venerable," p. 128. For Peter's efforts to hold this community together, see Chapter 2.

69. "At uos sancti, uos singulares, uos in uniuerso orbe uere monachi, aliis omnibus falsis et perditis, secundum nominis interpretationem solos uos inter omnes constituitis, unde et habitum insoliti coloris praetenditis, et ad distinctionem cunctorum totius fere mundi monachorum, inter nigros uos candidos ostentatis." Peter the Venerable, *Letters* no. 28, 1: 57.

70. "Iecit inter nos pomum discordiae, ut recedente una et sola caritate, uniuersa uirtutum genera minore labore ualeat effugare, et praeciso bonorum omnium capite, membra simul omnia cogantur interire." Peter the Venerable, *Letters* nos. 34, 35, 1: 112, 114.

71. "Per eam quae nos in domo dei unanimes fecit"; "quia cum dolet unum membrum, condolent omnia membra." Peter the Venerable, *Letters* no. 29, 1: 103.

72. "Nichil distinguendum diuersis usibus, inter hos et illos monachos, quos eadem fides et caritas uere facere debet germanos." Peter the Venerable, *Letters* no. 150, 1: 371.

73. McGuire, *Friendship and Community*, pp. 253–54; Peter the Venerable, *Letters* no. 65, 1: 194–95; Bernard of Clairvaux, Letter 147, *SBO* 7: 350–51 (James, no. 147).

74. Peter the Venerable, *Letters* no. 111, 1: 274–99. "Melleam inter nos caritatis dulcedinem iocundis" is from page 276. McGuire, *Friendship and Community*, pp. 257–58, makes the excellent point that this opening section is not a mere "rhetorical flourish" and argues that Peter then places the disagreements between the two orders within the context of this personal bond. I see it slightly differently: that Peter used his discussion of friendship, as well as his plea for harmony between the two groups, to assert his view of monastic charity and equality.

75. "Non tam vivere secundum Regulam quam ipsam ex integro pure ad litteram, uti se sane professos esse putant." Bernard of Clairvaux, *De praecepto et dispensatione* 16.49, *SBO* 3: 286.

76. "Altiora seu artiora"; "consuetudinibus magis Regulae puritatem." Bernard of Clairvaux, *De praecepto et dispensatione* 16.45, 46, *SBO* 3: 284, 285, CSS, 1: 139, 140.

77. "Sed a summa unitate deriuata, corrupta reparans, discissa redintegrans, diuisa unificans uniuersa uniat caritas. Sic plane, sic decet, ut quibus est unus dominus, una fides, unum baptisma, quos continet una aecclesia, quos manet una perennis et beata uita, eis quoque iuxta scripturam, sit cor unum et anima una." Peter the Venerable, *Letters* no. 111, 1: 294.

78. "Diversitas autem hic quidem in ordinum vel operationum multifaria divisione, illic vero in quadam meritorum notissima, sed ordinatissima distinctione. . . . Nam etsi fulgebunt iusti sicut sol in regno patris eorum, alii tamen aliis amplius, pro diversitate meritorum." Bernard of Clairvaux, *Apologia* 4.8–9, *SBO* 3: 88–89, CFS, 1: 43–44.

79. *Libellus de diuersis ordinibus*, pp. 27, 55.

80. Peter the Venerable, *Letters* nos. 158, 186, 1: 378, 434–35.

81. *Libellus de diuersis ordinibus*, pp. 54–55.

82. See, e.g., the Benedictine response to Bernard's *Apologia* in Wilmart, "Une riposte de l'ancien monachisme."

83. "Mixti bonis hipochritae procedunt, candidis seu uariis indumentis amiciti homines illudunt, et populis ingens spectaculum efficiunt. Veris Dei cultoribus scemate non uirtute assimilari plerique gestiunt, suique multitudine intuentibus fastidium ingerunt, et probatos cenobitas quantum ad fallaces hominum obtutus attinet despicabiliores faciunt." Orderic Vitalis, *Historia aecclesiastica* 8.27, 4: 326–27. Translation by Marjorie Chibnall.

CHAPTER 6

1. Bouchard estimates that the majority of charters and pancartes for Burgundian houses, as many as 90 percent in some cases, were issued by the diocesan bishop or a neighboring bishop; *Holy Entrepreneurs*, p. 18. In many cases, the bishop's pancarte supplies the only record of a group of donations; see Chapter 3.

2. Mahn, *L'ordre cistercien*, p. 97.

3. Ibid., p. 76.

4. *Carta caritatis prior* 8, pp. 97–98. By the later versions, however, the bishop had lost this right of intervention, and the abbots could remove another abbot themselves.

5. Mahn, *L'ordre cistercien*, pp. 89–91. Only in the thirteenth century did this liberty lead to conflicts, for Cistercians then began to seek these rights for bishops who had resigned their sees and retired to Cistercian abbeys. In the 1230's, a cardinal, once a Cistercian monk, claimed that retired bishops had performed consecrations since the time of Bernard, or "time immemorial," but this seems to be an argumentative device rather than a statement of fact. Mahn finds it surprising that the Cistercians were so late in seeking this liberty from their bishops, especially because they had received other more important liberties earlier; ibid., pp. 89–93, 267.

6. "Non quod debitam obedientiam praelatis nostris denegemus, sed quod in ordine nostro tenere statuimus, observare debemus." *Statuta*, 1: 22 (1134, no. 36).

7. *Cîteaux*, pp. 76–77 (no. 61), 83 (no. 70); *Clairvaux*, pp. 1–2 (no. 1); *Pontigny*, pp. 295 (no. 267), 296 (no. 269).

8. The bishops of Langres, Chalon-sur-Saône, Châlons-sur-Marne, Troyes, Auxerre, Sens, Autun, Mâcon, Toul, and Besançon.

9. *Cîteaux*, p. 53 (no. 27); *La Ferté*, pp. 41–42 (no. 1). According to the copy

of La Ferté's foundation charter in this pancarte, the bishop heard of Stephen Harding's desire to expand his community in 1113 and, together with the two counts of Chalon, established the new monastery in a forest donated by the counts.

10. "Si antistes in cujus diocesi locus ille situs erat, hoc amplectaretur." *Pontigny*, p. 153 (no. 84).

11. Arch. Haute-Marne 8 H 1. See also *GC* 4: 159, Instrumenta 36.

12. William of Saint-Thierry, *Vita prima* 1.7.32, *PL* 185: 246. William performed the ordination because of the absence of Joceran of Langres. Clairvaux did not establish an affiliate in the diocese of Langres until Auberive in 1127.

13. Cîteaux's affiliates, Preuilly (founded 1118) and Vauluisant (1128), and Pontigny's affiliates, Fontaine-Jean and Jouy (both 1124). Janauschek, *Originum*, pp. 5–6, 10, 12–13, 16.

14. Bernard of Clairvaux, *De moribus et officio episcoporum*, *SBO* 7: 100–31.

15. As was often the case, the Cistercians had established good relations with both parties to the dispute, having associated Louis VI with their prayers sometime before 1129. See Bernard of Clairvaux, Letter 45, *SBO* 7: 133–34.

16. Bernard of Clairvaux, Letter 49, *SBO* 7: 140–41 (James, no. 52).

17. Bernard of Clairvaux, Letter 51, *SBO* 7: 143 (James, no. 54).

18. *GC* 10: 161–62, Instrumenta 17; William of Saint-Thierry, *Vita prima* 1.7.32, *PL* 185: 246.

19. "Ex illa die et ex illa hora facti sunt eo unum et anima una in Domino, in tantum ut saepe alter alterum hospitem deinceps haberet, et propria esset domus Episcopi Clarae-Vallis; Clarae-Vallensium vero efficeretur non sola domus Episcopi, sed et per ipsum tota civitas Catalaunensis." William of Saint-Thierry, *Vita prima* 1.7.31, *PL* 185: 246. See also William of Saint-Thierry, *Vita prima* 1.13.65, *PL* 185: 263, for Bernard's frequent visits to Châlons.

20. Bernard of Clairvaux, Letter 13, *SBO* 7: 62–63 (James, no. 14).

21. Bernard of Clairvaux, Letter 58, *SBO* 7: 150–51 (James, no. 61).

22. Bernard of Clairvaux, Letter 48, *SBO* 7: 137 (James, no. 51).

23. Clerval, *Les écoles de Chartres*, p. 153.

24. *GC* 8: 419–20, Instrumenta 7; *Molesme*, p. 482 (no. 641); Bernard of Clairvaux, Letters 55–57, *SBO* 7: 147–49 (James, nos. 58–60). The canons of Saint Karlephi of Blois donated the land for the community, Theobald of Champagne compensated the canons for their gift, and Geoffrey approved the transaction.

25. In *De consideratione* 4.13, Bernard recalled his friendship with Geoffrey, describing him as a man "who at his own expense vigorously administered the legation to Aquitaine for so many years!" *SBO* 3: 459, CFS, 37: 127. For Geoffrey's activities during the schism, see *Chronicon Mauriniacensi*, *RHGF* 12: 81–81, and Arnold of Bonneval, *Vita prima* 2.6.34, *PL* 185: 287. For his participation in the preaching campaign against the heretics in Languedoc, see Geof-

frey of Auxerre, *Vita prima* 3.6.18, *PL,* 185: 313–14. For his participation at the council of Sens, see the joint letter to Innocent II by the bishops of Rheims, Soissons, Arras, and Chartres, *PL* 182: 337–38.

26. In the *Vita prima* 1.7.32, William of Saint-Thierry mentions that he started to visit Bernard around the same time that Bishop William appeared at Clairvaux and ordered Bernard to moderate his ascetic practices; *PL* 185: 246.

27. According to a charter reproduced in the *Gallia christiana,* the foundation of this house was complicated by the fact that Bartholomew, who clearly was attracted to the new religious movements, offered the same piece of land to Norbert of Xanten, for a house of regular canons, and to Bernard. Bernard refused the gift and soon after established Foigny on a piece of land that he received from the Benedictine abbey of Saint-Michel-en-Thiérache; *GC* 10: 191–92, Instrumenta 6. As a result, the foundation of Foigny not only created a tie between the Cistercians and Bartholomew of Laon but also helped to establish good relations between the Cistercians and the Premonstratensians. See Chapter 5.

28. Janauschek, *Originum,* p. 14.

29. *GC* 10: 378–79, Instrumenta 35.

30. Clairvaux, however, was not in the archdiocese of Rheims. One wonders, again, whether Bernard's presence was due to his relation with William of Saint-Thierry. It is also interesting that none of the three charters concerning this reform mentions Bernard or lists him as a witness. Bernard's modern biographers, in contrast, impute the impetus for reform to him; W. Williams, *Saint Bernard,* pp. 196–97. This is one of many examples of the way Bernard's influence has been exaggerated over the centuries.

31. Bernard of Clairvaux, Letter 48, *SBO* 7: 137–38 (James, no. 51).

32. For the foundation of Ourscamp, see *GC* 10: 375–77, Instrumenta 14; the initial gifts came from Simon, bishop of Noyon and Tournai, and the monks of Mont Saint-Eloi. For Longpont, see *GC* 10: 111–12, Instrumenta 22; the initial donation came from Jocelin, bishop of Soissons, and his chapter. For Vaucelles, see *GC* 3: 32–33, Instrumenta 35; the bishop of Cambrai issued the foundation charter. Even before Bernard traveled to Arras in 1128, the Cistercians had established connections in the north. In 1124, Stephen Harding traveled in Flanders and established a prayer association with the monks at Saint Waast in Arras. It is possible that Stephen's connections in Flanders originated with Molesme because, in 1095, Robert of Molesme had traveled in Flanders, but it does not appear that Robert's secretary, Stephen Harding, accompanied him. By the mid-1120's, Clairvaux at least had received recruits from the north; one was Guerric, who became the abbot of Igny in 1128. See Morson and Costello, "Introduction," pp. x–xviii; Bernard of Clairvaux, Letters 87–90, *SBO* 7: 224–38. The installation of monks from Molesme into the priory of Lucheaux

in 1095 had been witnessed by John, abbot of Mont Saint-Eloi in Arras; it is possible that the Cistercians' connection with Mont Saint-Eloi began with this contact. *Molesme,* 1: 89–90 (no. 84).

33. For Bernard's response to Hugh's letter, see Bernard of Clairvaux, Letter 77, *SBO* 7: 184–200.

34. Bernard of Clairvaux, Letter 45, *SBO* 7: 133–34.

35. Bernard of Clairvaux, Letter 46, *SBO* 7: 135 (James, no. 49).

36. Suger of Saint-Denis, *Vie de Louis VI le Gros,* pp. 282–84.

37. *PL* 173: 1412–13.

38. Bernard of Clairvaux, Letter 158, *SBO* 7: 365–67 (James, no. 164). For more letters about this dispute, see d'Archery, *Spicilegium,* 3: 491.

39. *Gesta concilio Trencensi, RHGF* 14: 231–32.

40. Also present were the bishops of Soissons, Troyes, Orléans, Melun, and Beauvais, in many of whose dioceses the Cistercians soon established new monasteries, and the abbot of Vézelay, whom the Cistercians later supported in a long dispute with the duke of Burgundy and the bishop of Autun.

41. There are three men called Peter of Tarentaise, two Cistercian archbishops and a thirteenth-century Dominican. Peter I was archbishop from 1126 to 1140; Peter II was archbishop from 1141 to 1174.

42. JL 1: 558 lists Innocent's cardinals. According to Mabillon's annotations of Bernard's letters, a Baldwin was the first Cistercian cardinal, created by Innocent at the council of Clermont in 1130, and afterward elected archbishop of Pisa. *PL* 182: 301n. 394. Arnold of Bonneval, *Vita prima,* 2.8.49, *PL* 185: 297, mentions a Baldwin from Pisa who "filled the Church with great light," but does not list him as a cardinal. Nor, however, does he mention Martin. In Letter 144, written in 1137, Bernard mentions a "dear brother Baldwin" who acted as his secretary while Bernard was in Italy in 1136–38 and who had been called by the Church to another position; he does not give Baldwin a title. *SBO* 7: 346 (James, no. 146). In Letter 245, written to Eugenius around 1147, Bernard recalls a Baldwin, archbishop of Pisa, who had died. It seems unlikely that these are the same men because the cardinal Baldwin appears on papal bulls the very year a Baldwin became archbishop of Pisa. Martin Cibo, in contrast, is described by Bernard in *De consideratione* 4.13, as "our beloved Martin of blessed memory," who was a cardinal-priest and a legate in Dacia. He appears on papal charters between 1133 and 1143; JL 1: 558.

43. See Appendix. See also Lipkin, "Entrance of the Cistercians into the Church Hierarchy." His graphs show the aggregate number of Cistercian bishops each year.

44. For an account of the election at Langres, see Constable, "Disputed Election at Langres." For York, see Baker, "'*Viri religiosi*' and the York Election Dispute"; for Auxerre, see Bouchard, *Spirituality and Administration,* pp. 69–71.

45. John of Châtillon, abbot of Buzay, elected bishop of Aleth in 1144; Amadeus of Clermont, abbot of Hautecombe, elected bishop of Lausanne in 1145; Henry Murdac, abbot of Fountains, elected archbishop of York in 1147; John, abbot of Colombia, elected bishop of Piacenza in 1147; Gerard, abbot of Villers, elected bishop of Tournai in 1149; Christian O'Conarchy, abbot of Mellifont, elected bishop of Lismore in 1150; Alan of Flanders, abbot of L'Arrivour, elected bishop of Auxerre in 1152; Hugh, abbot of Trois-Fontaines, appointed cardinal bishop of Ostia in 1150. I have included Godfrey, elected bishop of Langres in 1139, who was abbot of Fontenay before returning to Clairvaux as prior. The pattern continues later in the century as well. Five of Clairvaux's bishops elected between 1150 and 1215 had been abbots of affiliated houses before becoming bishop. However, a second pattern also developed: abbots of affiliated houses moved back to Cîteaux, Clairvaux, or Pontigny as abbots there, and then were elected bishop. For example, Pons of Polignac was abbot of Grandselve and then Clairvaux before becoming bishop of Clermont in 1170; Henry of Marcy was abbot of Hautecombe and then Clairvaux before becoming cardinal-bishop of Albano in 1179; Guy of Paré was abbot of Notre-Dame-du-Val and then Cîteaux before being appointed cardinal-bishop of Palestrina in 1199; Walter was abbot of Preuilly, Fontaine-Jean, and Pontigny before becoming bishop of Chartres in 1219. See Appendix.

46. Willi, "Päpste, Kardinäle und Bischöfe," p. 355. See also Conrad of Eberbach, *Exordium magnum* 1.35, pp. 96–97; *Vita S. Johannis Valentinensis Episcopi*, 3: 1693–1702.

47. Hugh of Mâcon, abbot 1114–36, bishop of Auxerre 1136–51; Guichard, abbot 1137–65, archbishop of Lyons 1165–80; Garin, abbot 1165–74, archbishop of Bourges 1174–80; Garmund, dates uncertain, elected bishop of Auxerre in 1181 in a disputed election, but died before his consecration; Peter, abbot 1177–80, bishop of Arras 1184–1203; Mainard, abbot 1184–88, appointed cardinal-bishop of Palestrina but died that year; Gerard, appointed cardinal deacon in 1198; and Walter, abbot 1212–19, bishop of Chartres 1219–34.

48. In 1170, Pons of Polignac was elected bishop of Clermont-Ferrand; in 1179, Henry of Marcy was elected cardinal-bishop of Albano; and, in 1193, Garnier of Rochefort became bishop of Langres. Abbot Peter of Cîteaux, who had been abbot of Pontigny, became bishop of Arras in 1184; Guy of Paré, abbot of Cîteaux, became cardinal-bishop of Palestrina in 1199; and Arnold Amaury became archbishop of Narbonne in 1212.

49. The very legitimacy of monks becoming bishops had been questioned during the reform movement of the late eleventh century. Peter Damian, for one, argued that a monk who became a bishop had renounced his regular life and was no longer a monk, and the council at Clermont in 1096 forbade the simultaneous administration of both an abbey and a bishopric. By the mid–twelfth cen-

tury, the election of a monk to an episcopal see was generally accepted. Gratian, in his *Decretum*, argued that it was possible to reconcile monastic status with episcopal functions as long as a monk-bishop received permission from his superior. Later decretists, more concerned with the personal status of the monk-bishops, argued that such a bishop was released from his monastic vow of obedience but not from those of poverty and continence. See Oliger, *Les évêques réguliers*, pp. 92–110.

50. *Statuta*, 1: 22 (1134, no. 34).

51. "Episcopi assumpti de ordine nostro consuetudinem nostram tenebunt in qualitate ciborum, in forma indumentorum, in observantia ieiuniorum, in officio Horarum regularium, excepto quod mantellum de vili panno et pelle ovina, et pileum similem aut simplicem de lana habere poterunt qui voluerint. Cum quibus tamen rebus claustra nostra minime intrabunt, nec conventibus nostris intererunt, propter dissimilitudinem. Solatia poterunt unicuique dari de domibus nostris usque ad duos monachos et tres conversos si tot necessarii fuerint, ita tamen ut nemini illorum saecularia negotia vel curae imponantur." *Statuta*, 1: 27 (1134, no. 61).

52. Geoffrey of Auxerre, *Vita sancti Petri archiepiscopi Tarentasiensi, AASS* Mai 2: 326.

53. Conrad of Eberbach, *Exordium magnum* 1.35, 2.26. 2.31, 3.25, 3.26, pp. 96–97, 129, 141, 205, 207. For another account of the life of a Cistercian bishop, see *Vita S. Johannis Valentinensis episcopi*, 3: 1693–1702.

54. *Gesta pontificium Autissiodorensium*, 1: 419.

55. Mainard and Nargaud witnessed a grant of lands at Ligny to Pontigny in 1135–36; in a second, undated charter, they are explicitly labeled as the bishop's monks. A monk named Garin appeared in charters issued between 1146 and 1151, in one case accompanied by the abbot and other monks of Pontigny, and in another accompanied by the fourth of Hugh's monk-companions, Gelinus; *Pontigny*, pp. 162 (no. 91), 179–80 (no. 111), 189 (no. 120), 166–67 (no. 96), 141 (no. 69).

56. "Stephanus et Willermus monachi lausannensis episcopi." *Cîteaux*, p. 112 (no. 126).

57. Rainald, called the "bishop's monk," witnessed a donation of forest rights to the church of Saint Laurent of Champigny; designated only as "monk," he also witnessed a donation to Pontigny of land at Sainte-Procaire made by William III, count of Nevers, and his vassals. *Clairvaux*, p. 62 (no. 41); *Pontigny*, pp. 164–65 (no. 94).

58. He is called "frater Gillebertus monachus et capellanus noster" in a charter of 1162 in which Godfrey exempted Clairvaux from paying any tithes in his diocese; *Clairvaux*, p. 58 (no. 34). Gilbert also witnessed two charters issued in 1157, one in which Godfrey donated two churches to the abbot of Saint-Michel

of Tonnerre, and another in which Godfrey granted Cîteaux the tithes at Rosey, and he witnessed a charter of 1160 in which Godfrey granted to the monastery of Saint-Seine the revenues from two churches that it administered; Quantin, *Cartulaire général de l'Yonne*, 2: 89–90 (no. 82); *Cîteaux*, p. 123 (no. 152); B.N. lat. 12824, p. 323; also B.N. lat. 9874, p. 8.

59. *Cîteaux*, pp. 143–44 (no. 177).

60. Willi, "Päpste, Kardinäle und Bischöfe," pp. 269, 331.

61. Fossier argues that, during the abbacy of Geoffrey of Auxerre, Clairvaux developed a policy of land acquisition in which it actively solicited rights and donations. He suggests that the impetus for this policy came from Godfrey of Langres, who had recently retired to Clairvaux, and that Geoffrey's resignation in 1163 was due to pressure from other Cistercians, especially Alan, bishop of Auxerre, and Alexander, abbot of Cîteaux, who believed Clairvaux had abandoned Bernard's ideals, and who were especially upset with Clairvaux's possession of a mill. Fossier, "La vie économique de Clairvaux," pp. 107–9. For other theories concerning Geoffrey's deposition or resignation, see Lenssen, "L'abdication du bienheureux Geoffroy."

62. Crozet, "L'épiscopat de France de l'ordre de Cîteaux," pp. 265–66; Dimier, "Mourir à Clairvaux!" For Boulancourt, see *GC* 12: 268, Instrumenta 26. This pattern is also true for Cistercian bishops from other houses. Amaury, bishop of Senlis, was buried at Chaalis, where he had been abbot, and Rotauld, bishop of Vannes, was buried at his former house of Lanvaux. Crozet, "L'épiscopat de France," pp. 265–66. Abbots of affiliated monasteries often wished to be buried in the houses of their profession; see Dimier, "Mourir à Clairvaux!" pp. 274–77.

63. "Praedictus papa venerabilis adfuit, non tam auctoritate apostolica praesidens, quam fraterna charitate residens inter eos, quasi unus ex eis." Geoffrey of Auxerre, *Vita prima* 4.7.40, *PL* 185: 344.

64. "Vos autem, de quorum collegio ipse est electus, ut sederet super principes terrae et solium gloriae teneret, orate pro eo, constituite perpetua beneficia, ut Dominus sibi indulgeat et coronam gloriae sibi augeat. Pro magistro et fratre nostro similiter orate; pro nobis vero qui in hac valle miseriae, in hanc regionem dissimilitudinis et in medio pravae nationis remansimus et pro Ecclesia romana, quae et tam alto gradu tam brevi spatio usque in profundum abyssi fere cecidit, nihilominus rogamus oretis, ne demergatur in profundum huius magni maris, in quo sunt reptilia quorum non est numerus." *Diversorum ad S. Bernardum et alios*, *PL* 182: 694.

65. Heathcote, "Letter Collections," p. 43.

66. "Argumentum naturale quo dicitur, si mater est diligit, si uobis patri reuerentissime placet attendere, perspicuum apud uos esse confidimus, quam dulcis quam amica erga uos sit, omnium nostorum et singularum affectio, quam

ex eo magis accendi cognouimus quod unice diligentibus uos semper increscit uestre uisionis cupiditas dum renititur desideriis nostris immensa elongionis nostre ab inuicem difficultis." Troyes B.M. lat. 893, f. 37r; also B.N. lat. 11867, f. 3v.

67. "Inhumanum uestre Clareuallis uidetur omnimodis quod si a pio pectore vestro necdum eius memoriam abdiscatis, ex qua Deus in sacro pontificio gloria et honore uos induit excursum, iam multitudine temporum et annorum non apposuistis adhuc reuisare matrem uestram dulcissimam Clareuallem et eius ubera quae suxistis, de quorum quidem dulcedine, uobis si recte sapitis infusum recolitis. Unde nunc fructus honoris et honestatis in populo dei uerbo pariter et exemplo profertis. Noscitis autem desiderabile nobis esse uestre uisitationis auspicium, ut uestra Clareuallis in uobis cum exultatione materna fructum uteri sui respiciens, ad aspectum sui Joseph et osculum uirtute quodammodo exhileranti spiritus reuiuiscat, et de benedictione filii roborata, non quasi iam mortuum seu perditum lamentetur." Troyes B.M. lat. 893, f. 33r; B.N. lat. 11867, f. 1v.

68. "Ceterum et si minus affectio materna fuit ad hoc hactenus penes uos ualida, tamen reuerentia ordinis, a qua uos nullatenus arbitrari debetis exemptum." Troyes B.M. lat. 893, f. 33r.

69. "Tamen ad omnimodam gratiarum actionem, eo magis in Deum pro uobis sumus solliciti et deuoti, quo glorie sui nominis et honori." Troyes B.M. lat. 893, f. 37r. "Hoc anno uos excusatione remota presentis Cisterciensis capitulo si declinare intenditis honorificentie uestre periculum et permanere in gratia uniuersitatis nostrae uel ordinis unitate." Troyes B.M. lat. 893, f. 33r–v.

70. *Pontigny*, p. 118 (no. 45); Quantin, *Cartulaire général de l'Yonne*, 2: 85, 146.

71. *Pontigny*, pp. 133 (no. 60), 126 (no. 53). There are other examples. In the 1140's, Hugh of Auxerre witnessed a settlement of the dispute between Clairvaux and the relatives of Agnon of Bar; in the 1150's, Alan and Godfrey witnessed Henry of Troyes's settlement of a dispute over Pontigny's grange at Boeurs, and Alan and Henry settled a dispute between Pontigny and Montier-la-Celle over tithes. *Clairvaux*, pp. 45–46 (no. 19); *Pontigny*, pp. 98, 126, 127 (nos. 20, 53, 54). One charter of a land donation issued by Henry of Troyes to the Cistercian house of Vauluisant was witnessed by Hugh of Auxerre, Rainald of Cîteaux, and the abbot of Pontigny; another was witnessed by monks of Pontigny. B.N. lat. 5468, p. 201; B.N. lat. 9901, f. 82. Alan of Auxerre granted tithes to the Cistercian house of Reigny with Henry of Troyes as witness, and confirmed a donation to Reigny with Geoffrey, abbot of Clairvaux, as witness. Quantin, *Cartulaire général de l'Yonne*, 2: 141, 151.

72. Using monastic cartularies to determine how many of their disputes the monks won is not entirely reliable, for they did not necessarily have any reason to preserve a record of land they no longer possessed. Nonetheless, of Clairvaux's nine land disputes between 1140 and 1165, eight were mediated by

Godfrey of Langres and all were settled in Clairvaux's favor; *Clairvaux*, pp. 17–19 (no. 11), 45–46 (no. 19), 46–47 (no. 20), 59 (no. 36), 59–60 (no. 37), 61–61 (no. 39), 62 (no. 41), 66 (no. 49), 68–69 (no. 63). Of Pontigny's ten disputes between 1138 and 1166, seven were settled by Cistercian bishops, again in Pontigny's favor; *Pontigny*, pp. 96–97 (no. 18), 98–99 (no. 20), 108 (no. 33), 108–9 (no. 34), 117 (no. 44), 118 (no. 45), 122 (no. 49), 126 (no. 53), 127 (no. 54), 134–36 (no. 62), 169 (no. 99). Cîteaux, the house that, among the first five, produced the fewest bishops, also had the fewest disputes settled by Cistercians. Only two of Cîteaux's six disputes between 1134 and 1162 were settled by Cistercian bishops; the bishops of Autun and Besançon negotiated two other agreements, and the final two were settled by the participants. *Cîteaux*, pp. 100 (no. 105), 103–4 (no. 112), 108 (no. 120), 109–10 (no. 123), 114–15 (no. 132), 127–28 (no. 160), 129–30 (no. 163).

73. Markus, *End of Ancient Christianity*, pp. 157–212, explores the ways in which monasteries served as models of social organization in early medieval society.

74. See Iogna-Prat, *Agni immaculati*; Tellenbach, *Church, State and Christian Society*; Laudage, *Priesterbild und Reformpapsttum*.

75. See, e.g., Humbert of Moyenmoutier, *Adversus simoniacos libri tres*; Peter Damian, *Liber Gomorrhianus*; and *S. Joannis Gualberti vita*. See Morris, *Papal Monarchy*, pp. 89–101. For the debate over Cluny's influence on the papal reform movement, see esp. Cowdrey, *Cluniacs and the Gregorian Reform*, and the overview of Cluniac historiography provided in Rosenwein, *Rhinoceros Bound*, pp. 3–29. See also Cowdrey, *Age of Abbot Desiderius*, for a monastery with a strong influence on the Gregorian reform, but one less concerned with moral issues than with political power.

76. Geoffrey of Auxerre, *Sermo ad praelatos*, *PL* 184: 1100.

77. Gregory the Great, *Regula pastoralis*, esp. 1.2, 1.8, 1.10, *SC* 381: 133–37, 155–57, 161–65.

78. For these theologians and their ideas about reform, see Smalley, *Becket Conflict*; Ferruolo, *Origins of the University*; Baldwin, *Masters, Princes and Merchants*.

79. For Bernard's descriptions of a prelate as steward, see *De consideratione* 2.12, 3.2, *SBO* 3: 419, 432, CFS, 37: 60, 80. For descriptions of prelates as brothers, see *De consideratione* 4.23, *SBO* 3: 466, CFS, 37: 137. For descriptions of prelates as shepherds, see *De consideratione* 1.5, 2.15, *SBO* 3: 389–90, 423, CFS, 37: 32, 66–67. See also Bernard of Clairvaux, *Ser. sup. cant.* 25.2; 76.9, *SBO* 1: 163, 2: 259. For comments about ministering rather than dominating, see Bernard of Clairvaux, *De consideratione* 2.9, *SBO* 3: 416, CFS, 37: 56; Bernard of Clairvaux, *De moribus et officio episcoporum* 3, *SBO* 7: 103.

80. The comparisons of prelates to shepherds, hirelings, and thieves come

from John 10.1–18. These are favorite images, used by Bernard in his sermon to the clerics in Paris, by Aelred of Rievaulx in a sermon to a synod of clerics, and by Geoffrey of Auxerre at the council at Tours. Bernard of Clairvaux, *Ad clericos de conversione* 22.39, *SBO* 4: 115, CFS, 25: 77–78; Aelred of Rievaulx, "*Sermo in synodo de pastore et mercenario et fure et lupo,*" in *Sermones inediti,* pp. 150–56; Geoffrey of Auxerre, *Sermo ad praelatos, PL* 184: 1095–1102. See also B.N. n.a. lat. 1476, f. 85r–87v.

81. Aelred of Rievaulx, "*Sermo in synodo de pastore et mercenario et fure et lupo,*" in *Sermones inediti,* p. 155; Bernard of Clairvaux, *De moribus et officio episcoporum,* esp. 3, 4, 19, 27, *SBO* 7: 103–4, 114–16, 122; Geoffrey of Auxerre, *Sermo ad praelatos, PL* 184: 1098–99.

82. Geoffrey of Auxerre, *Sermo ad praelatos, PL* 184: 1099.

83. Geoffrey of Auxerre, *Sermo ad praelatos, PL* 184: 1097. Bernard of Clairvaux, *Ad clericos de conversione* 32, *SBO* 4: 109, CFS, 25: 69.

84. "Non est vobis securum, curam animarum habere, et animas non curare; de Christi patrimonio vivere, et Christo non servire." Nicholas of Clairvaux, Letter 36, *PL* 196: 1632.

85. Bernard of Clairvaux, *De moribus et officio episcoporum* 28, *SBO* 7: 123.

86. "Rogo, quae haec tam odiosa praesumptio, quis hic tantus ardor dominandi super terram, quae principandi tam effrenis cupiditas?" Ibid.

87. "Habent haec infima et terrena iudices suos, reges et principes terrae. Quid fines alienos invaditis?" Bernard of Clairvaux, *De consideratione* 1.7, *SBO* 3: 402, CFS, 37: 36.

88. Bernard of Clairvaux, *De moribus et officio episcoporum* 7.25–30, *SBO* 7: 121–25.

89. "Vacat prebenda, vacat archidiaconatus, vacat episcopatus. Venit cum funiculo ambitionis Philisteus, suggerit ut petatur, suggerit ut extorqueatur, postremo suggerit ut ematur." Aelred of Rievaulx, "*Sermo in synodo de pastore et mercenario et fure et lupo,*" in *Sermones inediti,* p. 155.

90. Bernard of Clairvaux, *De consideratione* 3.20, *SBO* 3: 447–48, CFS, 37: 106; Bernard of Clairvaux, *De moribus et officio episcoporum* 2.4–6, *SBO* 7: 104–5.

91. "Plus calcaria fulgent quam altaria." Bernard of Clairvaux, *Ser. sup. cant.* 33.15, *SBO* 1: 244, CFS, 7: 158.

92. Aelred of Rievaulx, "*Sermo in synodo de pastore et mercenario et fure et lupo,*" in *Sermones inediti,* pp. 154–55; Bernard of Clairvaux, *Ser. sup. cant.* 23.12, *SBO* 1: 146, CFS, 7: 36.

93. Holtzmann, *Papsturkunden in England,* p. 231 (no. 66). See also Bernard of Clairvaux, *De consideratione* 3.17–18, *SBO* 3: 444–45, CFS, 37: 101–3.

94. "Tunc denique tibi licitum censeas, suis ecclesias mutilare membris, confundere ordinem perturbare terminos, quos posuerunt patres tui?" Ber-

nard of Clairvaux, *De consideratione* 3.17, *SBO* 3: 444, CFS, 37: 101. See also *De consideratione* 3.14, *SBO* 3: 442, CFS, 37: 97–98; and *De moribus et officio episcoporum* 33–36, *SBO* 7: 127–30.

95. *Variorum ad Innocentium, PL* 179: 671.

96. Bernard of Clairvaux, *De consideratione* 2.7, 3.11, *SBO* 3: 435–36, 438, CFS, 37: 87, 91–92.

97. Bernard of Clairvaux, Letter 46, *SBO* 7: 134 (James, no. 49).

98. "Iustitiam in Ecclesia deperire, annullari Ecclesiae claves, episcopalem omnino vilescere auctoritatem, cum nemo episcoporum in promptu habeat ulcisci iniurias Dei, nulli liceat illicita quaevis in propria quidem parochia, castigare." Bernard of Clairvaux, Letter 178, *SBO* 7: 398 (James, no. 218).

99. See Kennan, " '*De consideratione*' of Saint Bernard," pp. 75, 112. Saltman, in *Theobald, Archbishop of Canterbury*, argues that, starting in the 1130's, the primatial power of the archbishop of Canterbury became "practically nonexistent, and his ordinary metropolitan power seriously limited," p. 133. Under Innocent II, Theobald's power was eclipsed by the appointment of Henry of Winchester as papal legate. Under Eugenius III, he regained much power, but this was due to his own appointment as legate rather than to any increase in his metropolitan authority. The policy of all of the midcentury popes was to reduce bishops and archbishops alike to a dependence on the papacy and, in England, to assert the independence of the archbishop of York from any claims of primacy by Canterbury. See also Haller, *Das Papsttum*, 3: 4, who shows that the popes of the 1130's and 1140's continued the pattern set by Urban II and Pascal II and granted over 50 exemptions apiece to monasteries.

100. Bernard of Clairvaux, *De consideratione* 5.19, *SBO* 3: 446–47, CFS, 37: 104–5.

101. Bernard of Clairvaux, *De consideratione* 2.16, 3.6, 3.10, *SBO* 3: 424, 435, 437–38, CFS, 37: 67–68, 85–86, 90–91. See also *De consideratione* 1.13, *SBO* 3: 408–9, CFS, 37: 43–44.

102. In 1131, e.g., Innocent II delegated to Stephen Harding a dispute between the monastery of Saint-Seine and the canons of Saint Stephen in Dijon; between 1145 and 1147, Bernard of Clairvaux and the Cistercian bishops Hugh of Auxerre and Godfrey of Langres accepted from Eugenius III the authority to settle a dispute between the count of Nevers and the monastery of Vézelay; Innocent II, *Epistolae, PL* 179: 112; Eugenius III, *Epistolae et privilegia, PL* 180: 1178, 1424–25, 1502–3. In 1151, Eugenius asked Hugh of Auxerre and Bernard to settle a dispute between Louis VII and his brother Henry, the Cistercian bishop of Beauvais, and in 1155–56 Hadrian IV ordered the Cistercian bishops Amadeus of Lausanne and Peter II of Tarentaise to resolve a dispute between the abbeys of Saint-Claude and Lac-de-Joux; Eugenius III, *Epistolae et privilegia, PL* 180: 1456–57; Dimier, *Amédée de Lausanne*, p. 367 (no. 37).

103. For historians who argue that Bernard was a Gregorian, see Fliche, "L'influence de Grégoire VII"; W. Williams, *Saint Bernard of Clairvaux*, pp. 243–51, 257–61; Ullmann, *Growth of Papal Government*, pp. 262–72, 426–37. Pacaut, *La théocratie*, pp. 111–14, agrees that Bernard was a Gregorian, but suggests that by the mid–twelfth century, Gregorian ideas were anachronistic. According to Pacaut, Bernard was confused because he could not reconcile his underlying theory with the practical needs of the period. In comparison, Vacandard, in his *Vie de Saint Bernard*, argues that Bernard was no Gregorian but a dualist who separated the functions of the two swords. White, in "Gregorian Ideal," agrees that Bernard was no Gregorian but instead a supporter of a new reforming party around Cardinal Haimeric that opposed the older Gregorians. For a synopsis of this historiography, see Kennan, "'*De consideratione*' of St. Bernard."

104. Kennan sensibly concludes that "the question, whether or not Bernard was a Gregorian, is not the right one to ask of his theory of the papacy," "'*De consideratione*' of St. Bernard," p. 106. See also Jacqueline, *Episcopat et papauté*, who agrees that the argument about whether Bernard was a Gregorian takes specific passages out of the overall context of Bernard's work.

105. "Sed et ordinis exigit ratio, ut qui ad sui mensuram proximum iubetur diligere, prius seipsum diligere norit." Bernard of Clairvaux, *De moribus et officio episcoporum* 4.13, *SBO* 7: 110.

106. "Sane deriventur aquae tuae in plateas: homines et iumenta et pecora bibant ex eis . . . sed inter ceteros bibe et tu de fonte putei tui." Bernard of Clairvaux, *De consideratione* 1.6, *SBO* 3: 400, CFS, 37: 33–34. See also *De consideratione* 2.6.

107. "Qui enim sibi nequam est, cui bonus erit?" Aelred of Rievaulx, "*Sermo in synodo de pastore et mercenario et fure et lupo*," in *Sermones inediti*, p. 155.

108. Bernard of Clairvaux, *Ser. sup. cant.* 18.3, *SBO* 1: 104, for the image about reservoirs.

109. Aelred of Rievaulx, *Sermo in synodo de Aaron et filiis eius*, in *Sermones inediti*, pp. 156–61. "Vincula enim Philistei quamdiu non fuerint consuetudine vitiosa durata, compunctione lentescunt, solvuntur confessione, ieiuniis ac vigiliis in misericordie operibus dissolvuntur." "*Sermo in synodo de pastore et mercenario et fure et lupo*," in *Sermones inediti*, p. 155.

110. Bernard of Clairvaux, *De moribus et officio episcoporum* 2.4–6, 3.8, *SBO* 7: 104–5, 107.

111. "In quaerenda gloria Dei et utilitate proximi, ut in omnibus videlicet actis vel dictis suis nihil suum quaerat episcopus, sed tantum aut Dei honorem, aut salutem proximorum, aut utrumque. Hoc enim agens implebit non solum pontificis officium, sed et etymologiam nominis, pontem utique seipsum faciens

inter Deum et proximum." Bernard of Clairvaux, *De moribus et officio episco-porum* 10, *SBO* 7: 108.

112. "Genus, aetas, scientia, cathedra et, quod maius est, primatus praerog-ativa, cui non essent insolentiae fomes, elationis occasio?" Bernard of Clairvaux, *De moribus et officio episcoporum* 7.25, *SBO* 7: 121.

113. Bernard of Clairvaux, *De moribus et officio episcoporum* 5.19–20, 6.23, *SBO* 7: 114–15, 118–19. See also his *De gradibus humilitatis et superbiae.*

114. "Salubris copula, ut cogitans te Summum Pontificem, attendas pariter vilissimum cinerem non fuisse, sed esse." Bernard of Clairvaux, *De consideratione* 2.18, *SBO* 3: 426, CFS, 37: 71.

115. Bernard of Clairvaux, *De consideratione* 1: 8–11, *SBO* 3: 402–7, CFS, 37: 39–42; and *De moribus et officio episcoporum* 4.22–23, *SBO* 7: 117–18.

116. Bernard of Clairvaux, *De consideratione* 1.7, *SBO* 3: 401–2, CFS, 37: 36–37; and Letter 46, *SBO* 7: 135 (James, no. 49). See also his *De consideratione* 2.4, *SBO* 3: 413, CFS, 37: 51.

117. "Bonos in consilio, bonos in obsequio, bonos habeas contubernales, qui vitae et honestatis tuae et custodes sint, et testes." Bernard of Clairvaux, Let-ter 28, *SBO* 7: 82 (James, no. 29).

118. "Quid me beatius quidve securius, cum eiusmodi circa me vitae meae et custodes spectarem, simul et testes? Quibus omnia mea secreta secure com-mitterem, communicarem consilia, quibus me totum refunderem, tamquam al-teri mihi. Qui, si vellem aliquatenus deviare, non sinerent, frenarent praecipitem, dormitantem suscitarent; quorum me reverentia et libertas extollentem reprimeret, excedentem corrigeret; quorum me constantia et fortitudo nutan-tem firmaret, erigeret diffidentem; quorum me fides et sanctitas ad quaeque sancta, ad quaeque honesta, ad quaeque pudica, ad quaeque amabilia et bonae famae provocaret." Bernard of Clairvaux, *De consideratione* 4.15, *SBO* 3: 460, CFS, 37: 128.

119. Bernard of Clairvaux, *De consideratione* 1.8–11, *SBO* 3: 402–7, CFS, 37: 39–42.

120. Aelred of Rievaulx, *Sermo in synodo de Aaron et filiis eius*, in *Sermones inediti*, p. 160.

121. "*Sermo in synodo de pastore et mercenario et fure et lupo*," in *Sermones inediti*, p. 155.

122. "Ita ut summi sacerdotii dignitas monasticae humilitatis puritatem commendabiliorem redderet, et rursum religionis vigor pontifici auctoritatem tribueret, sicque verbo et exemplo populum, cui episcopus datus fuerat, pascens et instruens inter antistites sui temporis spectabilis apparuit demumque cursu vitae suae laudabiliter peracto laboris sui praemium a Domino percepturus re-quievit in pace." Conrad of Eberbach, *Exordium magnum* 2.26, p. 129.

123. "Quam septem annorum curriculo strenue regens et suam ipsius vitam in omni puritate custodiens ministerium suum magnifice honoravit dignumque sanctitatis exemplum posteris dereliquit." Conrad of Eberbach, *Exordium magnum* 3.25, p. 205.

124. Conrad of Eberbach, *Exordium magnum* 2.30–31, 3.26, pp. 138–41, 207–8.

125. *Vita sancti Malachiae* 1.2–3.7, 7.16, 10.21, *SBO* 3: 311–16, 325–26, 331–2, CFS, 10: 16–23, 33–34, 39–40.

126. *In transitu sancti Malachiae episcopi* 6, *SBO* 5: 421, CFS, 10: 102; *Vita sancti Malachiae* 10.21, 14.31–32, *SBO* 3: 332, 338–40, CFS, 10: 40, 47–48.

127. *Vita sancti Malachiae* 7.21, 19.43, *SBO* 3: 331–32, 348–49, CFS, 10: 39–40, 57–58.

128. Despite such oscillation, the two offices remained distinct: Renna has shown that Bernard distorted the chronology of Malachy's life so as to separate his tenure as abbot from his tenure as archbishop. Renna, "St. Bernard's View of the Episcopacy," pp. 43–44.

129. *Vita sancti Petri, AASS*, Mai 2: 326.

130. "Sed parum motus a forma vitae in qua fuerat conversatus." Ibid.

131. Ibid.

132. "Linguae sarculo." "Nunc aspere, nunc lenter convenire, prout cuique expedire videbat." *Vita sancti Malachiae* 3.6, 8.16, *SBO* 3: 315, 325–26, CFS, 10: 22, 34.

133. *Vita sancti Malachiae* 8.17, *SBO* 3: 326, CFS, 10: 34.

134. *Vita sancti Petri, AASS* Mai 2: 327.

135. Ibid., 326–27.

136. Ibid., 327, 329.

137. Ibid., 330, 333.

138. Baldwin, *Masters, Princes and Merchants*, esp. pp. 47–59.

139. Ferruolo, *Origins of the University*, p. 185.

140. *Vita sancti Petri, AASS*, Mai 2: 323.

141. Robson, *Maurice of Sully*, pp. 55–56; Ferruolo, *Origins of the University*, pp. 218–21.

142. Peter the Chanter, cited in Chenu, "The Evangelical Awakening," in *Nature, Man and Society*, p. 244.

143. Renna agrees that Bernard continued to differentiate episcopal from monastic functions. However, he argues that Bernard believed that bishops needed monasteries for their spiritual renewal—that occasional retreats would inspire them with greater reforming zeal. He calls Bernard's ideal papal curia a "quasi-monastery." See "St. Bernard's View of the Episcopacy," pp. 45–46, and n. 24. I believe instead that Bernard advocated the communal, but not necessarily the monastic, life for bishops. As we will see in the following chapter, he

also advocated a communal life for knights. Through such communities, a person of any order could best progress in the virtues necessary for his or her salvation.

144. Ibid., pp. 43–44, n. 15; Bernard of Clairvaux, *De moribus et officio episcoporum* 37, *SBO* 7: 130–31.

145. Bernard of Clairvaux, *De consideratione* 1.8, *SBO* 3: 403, CFS, 37: 38.

146. "Nec delectet molles et femineos humeros virorum supponere sarcinis"; Bernard of Clairvaux, *Ser. sup. cant.* 12.9, *SBO* 1: 66, CFS, 4: 84–85; Gilbert of Hoyland, *Sermones in canticum* 16.4, *PL* 184: 83, CFS, 20: 208–9.

CHAPTER 7

1. Of Bernard's 62 letters to lay persons, 48 (i.e., 77.4 percent) were to people with titles. This phenomenon may, of course, have been an artifact of differences in literacy. English kings, at least, from Henry I on, were educated in Latin and surrounded by clerics; English barons and knights gradually learned enough Latin to cope with the growing number of written documents issuing from the royal chancery. It is less clear, however, that the lesser knights of twelfth-century France were as attuned to written culture. See Clanchy, *From Memory to Written Record*, pp. 186–201; and Stock, *Implications of Literacy*, pp. 13–87. The Cistercians showed little interest in establishing ongoing relations with their knightly patrons; nor did Bernard become a patron saint for the local knights, as had previous monastic saints. Stories of his miracles either present him as a saint who worked throughout Christendom or one who specifically protected his monks. See McGuire, "The First Cistercian Renewal and a Changing Image of St. Bernard," in *Difficult Saint*, pp. 153–87. For cases in which monastic saints did protect local families, see Head, *Hagiography and the Cult of Saints*, pp. 135–87.

2. Barber, "Origins of the Order of the Temple." Aelred wrote his *Genealogia* after Henry's marriage to Eleanor of Aquitaine but before his coronation as king of England. This is not the only genealogical work that Henry received. John of Marmoutier dedicated to him his revised and expanded version of *Deeds of the Counts of Anjou*. See Farmer, *Communities of St. Martin*, pp. 89–95.

3. See Chapter 1, pp. 34–35; Chapter 3, p. 77.

4. *Pontigny*, pp. 152–54 (no. 84).

5. Hugh's connections with the Cistercians, and especially with Pontigny, did not end with this donation. Sometime between 1142 and 1146, he again appeared with William of Nevers when they witnessed the settlement of a dispute between Clairvaux and the lords of Grancey. In 1147, Bishop Hugh of Auxerre, who had been the abbot of Pontigny, issued a charter witnessed by the Cistercian abbots of Bouras, Reigny, and Les Roches, which confirmed Hugh of

Tilio's possessions; *Clairvaux*, pp. 17–19 (no. 11), *PL* 181: 1743–44. This charter also confirms the relation between Hugh of Tilio and the count of Nevers, as it states that William of Nevers gave Hugh a fief (*potestatem*) and castle "as much in compensation for his love and service as for the land of Forgy and the money he gave for it." Hugh appears as well as a witness for a series of early-twelfth-century donations to Molesme; on one he is identified as the seneschal of William II, count of Nevers, and on others he appears as a member of William's court. *Molesme*, 1: 49–50 (no. 34), 2: 276 (no. 41); 2: 321–22 (no. 173a). For Milo of Courtenay, see *GC* 12: 110, Instrumenta 15; Janauschek, *Originum*, p. 10. See also *Molesme*, 1: 49–50 (no. 34).

6. *Exordium parvum* 3, p. 60. For Hugh of Champagne's "antiqui amoris et beneficiorum," see Bernard of Clairvaux, Letter 31, *SBO* 7: 85–86 (James, no. 32). If Hugh made donations to Clairvaux, they do not appear in the pancartes, but Clairvaux's first affiliate, Trois-Fontaines, was constructed on land that Hugh had donated; *GC* 10: 161–62, Instrumenta 17.

7. For the foundation of L'Aumône, see *GC* 8, 419–20, Instrumenta 7. Theobald compensated the canons of Saint Karlephi of Blois for their gift of land to the new monastic community. For the rebuilding of Clairvaux, see Arnold of Bonneval, *Vita prima* 2.5.31, *PL* 185: 285. Traditionally, the date given for the construction of Pontigny has been 1150, but recently Kinder has argued that building probably began as early as 1136 and ended in 1150. See Kinder, "Construction at Pontigny."

8. "Obsecro vos per Dominum Iesum et per illam fraternitatem quam in capitulo nostro suscepistis." Bernard of Clairvaux, Letter 517, *SBO* 8: 476 (James, no. 44).

9. In 1127, when the abbot of the canons of Saint Martin at Epernay wished to leave his position and enter Clairvaux, Theobald acted on Bernard's advice, relinquished his claim to choose a new abbot, and allowed the canons to elect their superior themselves; d'Archery, *Spicilegium*, 13: 305–6, reprinted as 3: 480. For Bernard's letters to Theobald, see Letters 37–39, 72, *SBO* 7: 94–98, 175–78 (James, nos. 39–41, 44).

10. For the Cistercian view of Theobald, see below, p. 182. For writers who maintain this portrayal, see Gerald of Wales, *De principis instructione*, RS 21.8: 135–37. For Suger of Saint-Denis, see *Vie de Louis VI le Gros*, pp. 11, 19, 21.

11. *Clairvaux*, pp. 50, 51, 52–53, 140 (nos. 25, 26, 28, 130); Henry of Albano, Letter 1, *PL* 204: 213–14.

12. Stephen Harding was an Englishman; Hugh of Pontigny probably came from a castellan family in Mâcon, far south of Auxerre; Arnold of Morimond came from a Saxon family. Duby suggests that the lack of family ties between Philbert of La Ferté and the surrounding aristocracy may have been partially responsible for La Ferté's initial poverty; *La Ferté*, p. 6. It is possible that Stephen

Harding developed a conscious policy of appointing abbots who did not have strong family ties with the local nobility. Locatelli, "L'implantation cistercienne dans le comté Bourgogne," argues that no Cistercian house in the county of Burgundy was founded for a family member.

13. *Clairvaux*, pp. 8–15 (no. 6). Not only is there debate over the relationship of Josbert and Bernard (see Chapter 1, n. 29), but there are differing interpretations about the importance of Josbert's family in the establishment of Clairvaux. For those that argue for Josbert's importance, see Fossier, "La fondation de Clairvaux," and especially Auberger, *L'unanimité cistercienne primitive*, p. 94, who constructs an elaborate scenario concerning the foundation of Clairvaux and Josbert's family aspirations. Bouchard, in *Sword, Miter, and Cloister*, pp. 237–38, by contrast, argues that his importance has been overestimated. However, Josbert gave to the monks not only his own land but also whatever they could acquire of land held from him in fief, and many of the transactions on the pancarte of 1135 cited above are donations related to Josbert's gifts.

14. Janauschek, *Originum*, p. 8. Godfrey's brother, Walter of La Roche, constable of the duke of Burgundy, had married Rainard of Montbard's widow Aanold; his brother Rayner married Rainard and Aanold's daughter. For these families, see Chapter 1, n. 29. Godfrey's sister Agnes became the first abbess of the neighboring house of Cistercian nuns at Puits d'Orbe; *Molesme*, 1: 244 (no. 263); Bouchard, *Sword, Miter, and Cloister*, pp. 335–37.

15. The pancarte recording the foundation of Auberive is Arch. Haute Marne, 1 H 7 bis; the charter is printed in *GC* 4: 165–68, Instrumenta 42. For Bernard and the Montbard family, see *Molesme*, pp. 244–45 (no. 263).

16. William of Saint-Thierry, *Vita prima*, 1.9.43, *PL* 185: 252.

17. "Rex caeli et terrae regnum vobis in terra donavit, donaturus et in caelo, si id quod accepistis iuste et sapienter administrare studueritis. Hoc est quod vobis optamus et pro vobis oramus, ut et hic fideliter, et illic feliciter regnetis. Ceterum vos quonam consilio eisdem nostris pro vobis orationibus, quas, si recolitis, olim tam humiliter requisistis, modo tam acriter repugnatis? Qua enim iam fiducia manus pro vobis levare praesumimus ad Sponsum Ecclesiae, quam ita, et sine causa, ut putamus, ausu inconsulto contristatis? . . . Haec ita vobis et pro vobis, audacter quidem, sed amanter, intimare curavimus, monentes et rogantes per illam invicem amicitiam nostram et fraternitatem, cui vos satis dignanter sociastis, sed nunc ipsam graviter laesistis, quatenus a tanto malo citius desistatis." Bernard of Clairvaux, Letter 45, *SBO* 7: 133–34.

18. For Louis's privileges, see *Pontigny*, p. 85 (no. 1); *Cîteaux*, p. 102 (no. 109). For Bernard's letter, see Letter 255, *SBO* 8: 161–62 (James, no. 133).

19. Bernard of Clairvaux, Letters 170, 220–21, *SBO* 7: 283–85, 8: 82–86 (James, nos. 186, 296–97).

20. C. Waddell, "Notes Towards the Exegesis of a Letter," pp. 10–39.

21. Knowles, *Monastic Order in England*, pp. 228–31.

22. For the meeting at Rouen, see Innocent II, *Epistolae et privilegia*, *PL* 179: 96–97; for the grant to Pontigny, see *Pontigny*, p. 86 (no. 3).

23. Bernard of Clairvaux, Letters 238, 520, 531, 533, *SBO* 8: 115, 480, 496 (James, nos. 195, 197, 204–5). For Theobald's own lack of interest in the English throne, see Dunbabin, *France in the Making*, p. 314.

24. For the suspicion of English ecclesiastics and Pope Eugenius III toward Stephen, see Poole, *From Domesday Book to Magna Carta*, pp. 194–95.

25. Walter Daniel, *Life of Ailred*, p. 3.

26. Henry of Albano, Letters 5–6, *PL* 204: 219–20.

27. See Dunbabin, *France in the Making*, pp. 305–10.

28. Rosenwein, *Rhinoceros Bound*, pp. 57–83.

29. See Duby, *Three Orders*; Mostert, *Political Theology of Abbo of Fleury*; Koziol, *Begging Pardon and Favor*; Poly and Bournazel, *Feudal Transformation*, pp. 141–85.

30. See Farmer, *Communities of St. Martin*, pp. 78–95; Dunbabin, *France in the Making*, pp. 246–50.

31. The gradual self-identification of knights and the merging of *miles* and *nobilis* took place at different times in different regions of France. It now appears that Duby's pioneering work on the emergence of the title of knight to apply to all warriors in the eleventh-century Mâconnais described a precocious development in a region influenced by Cluny and its interpretation of the peace movement; only in the south have historians found analagous developments. In Flanders, neighboring imperial territories, and perhaps Normandy, twelfth-century miles were semiservile *ministeriales* clearly defined as not noble; in a region from Poitou to Chartres, miles and nobilis merged, but miles was reserved for the lesser nobility. See Poly and Bournazel, *Feudal Transformation*, pp. 98–107. For Duby's studies of knighthood, see *La société aux XIe et XIIe siècles* and his essays in *Chivalrous Society*.

32. Wallace-Hadrill, *Early Germanic Kingship*, pp. 101–7, 138–40. See also his discussion of King Alfred and Gregory the Great's *Regulae pastoralis*, pp. 143–45. See also Part 2 introduction, n. 4.

33. "Hic in regno terreno semper meditabatur coeleste, ut manifeste daretur intelligi eum non victum cupiditate, sed charitate provocatum, alienae necessitati regnando consulere, non suae voluntati dominando satisfacere." Aelred of Rievaulx, *Genealogia regum Anglorum*, *PL* 195: 718.

34. "Eum non tam in dominum et regem quam in patrem cum omni devotione eligerent." Ibid., *PL* 195: 720, 723.

35. "Patre magis quam rege." Ibid., *PL* 195: 724, 725.

36. "Docere non solum verbo sed etiam exemplo." Ibid., *PL* 195: 727.

37. "Laboriosissime sed strenuissime regnasset"; "homo mansuetus et pius, magis pace quam armis regnum protegens." Ibid., *PL* 195: 730, 734.

38. "Eum regnum non appetivisse sed horruisse, magisque illud ob alienam necessitatem suscepisse quam dominandi libidine victum avide invasisse." Ibid., *PL* 195: 713–14.

39. "Ne pauperes a potentibus praejudicium passi opprimerentur." Ibid., *PL* 195: 727.

40. Bernard of Clairvaux, Letters 220, 303, 511, *SBO* 8: 82–83, 220, 470 (James, nos. 296, 369, 122).

41. "Ad hoc te constituit principem super terram princeps regum terrae." Stephen's letter is collected in Bernard of Clairvaux, *Epistolae*, *PL* 182: 150; Bernard of Clairvaux, Letter 279, *SBO* 8: 191 (James, no. 351).

42. Bernard of Clairvaux, Letters 72, 37, 38, *SBO* 7: 175–78, 94–97 (James, nos. 44, 39, 40).

43. Bernard of Clairvaux, Letter 39, *SBO* 7: 97–98 (James, no. 41).

44. Conrad of Eberbach, *Exordium magnum* 2.15, p. 109. See also Kuttner, "Forgotten Definition of Justice."

45. Koziol, *Begging Pardon and Favor*, pp. 229–34.

46. Bernard of Clairvaux, Letter 39, *SBO* 7:97–98 (James, no. 41).

47. "Et quidem in talibus, ubi culpa tam aperta atque inexcusabilis esse videtur, quatenus nulla nisi cum iustitiae periculo misericordiae occasio relinquatur, etiam tunc tremens et dolens vindicem vos exhibere debetis, magis videlicet officii compulsus necessitate quam vindicandi libidine. Ubi autem obiectum crimen, aut minus certum esse cognoscitur, aut excusandum suscipitur, hoc non solum non renuere, sed et libentissime debetis amplecti, laetus nimirum quod, salva iustitia, pietas vestra locum invenerit." Bernard of Clairvaux, Letter 37, *SBO* 7: 95 (James, no. 39).

48. "Pie iustum ac iuste pium." Bernard of Clairvaux, Letter 38, *SBO* 7: 97 (James, no. 40).

49. In this, their position on the nature of the Church and the cooperation of secular and ecclesiastical authorities was similar to that of Hugh of Saint Victor. In the words of J. A. Watt, Hugh "revealed much of how dualism could be tempered by being situated with the unitary context of the congregation of all the faithful." "Spiritual and Temporal Powers," p. 369. But Hugh more clearly determined that spiritual power both instituted secular power and had the right to judge it; *De sacramentis* 2.2.4, *PL*, 176: 417–18.

50. "Uterque ergo Ecclesiae, et spiritualis scilicet gladius, et materialis, sed is quidem pro Ecclesia, ille vero et ab Ecclesia exserendus: ille sacerdotis, is militis manu, sed sane ad nutum sacerdotis et iussum imperatoris." Bernard of Clairvaux, *De consideratione*, 4.3.7, *SBO* 3: 454.

51. Bernard repeats the figure in Letter 256, *SBO* 8: 163 (James, no. 399). For the pope's spiritual ministry, see Bernard of Clairvaux, *De consideratione* 1.7.

52. "Postremo ad operandum etiam nunc salutem in medio terrae." Bernard of Clairvaux, Letter 139, *SBO* 7: 335 (James, no. 142).

53. "Ergo quae Deus coniunxit, homo non separet. Magis autem quod divina sanxit auctoritas, humana studeat adimplere voluntas, et iungant se animis, qui iuncti sunt institutis." Bernard of Clairvaux, Letter 244, *SBO* 8: 134 (James, no. 320).

54. "Illam maximam regis credidit dignitatem, nullam in ecclesiis Christi habere postestatem." Aelred of Rievaulx, *Genealogia*, *PL* 195: 719.

55. "Tanta enim in verbis, in vultu, in moribus, interioris suavitatis indicia praeferebat." Aelred of Rievaulx, *Genealogia*, *PL* 195: 726. "Lucebat in ipso etiam corpore interioris spiritus sanctitatis, cum singularis quaedam suavitas appareret in vultu, gravitas in incessu, simplicitas in affectu." *Vita sancti Edwardi regis*, *PL* 195: 745.

56. "Jam in hortulo cordis ejus germina laeta repullulant." Henry of Marcy, Letter 1, *PL* 204: 213.

57. "Quoniam igitur animae rationali naturaliter inest amor virtutum, odium vitiorum, quicunque bonis moribus virtutique studuerit, facile sibi omniam illicit et inclinat affectum." Aelred of Rievaulx, *Genealogia regum Anglorum*, *PL* 195: 712–13.

58. In the introduction, Aelred told Henry that he proposed to impress on Henry's mind the virtuous renown of past kings so that he would not be any less loved and admired. Aelred of Rievaulx, *Genealogia regum Anglorum*, *PL* 195: 713.

59. Bernard of Clairvaux, Letters 289, 92, *SBO* 8: 206, 7: 241 (James, nos. 274, 95).

60. "Se inter servos Dei conservum exhibens, non dominum." Arnold of Bonneval, *Vita prima* 2.8.52; *PL* 185: 299.

61. *Vita prima* 2.8.52, 4.3.12, *PL* 185: 299, 328.

62. "Sed et viri illi timentes Deum, et tam ei placere, quam Comiti cupientes." Arnold of Bonneval, *Vita prima* 2.8.53, *PL* 185: 300.

63. Head, *Hagiography and the Cult of Saints*; Rosenwein, *Rhinoceros Bound*.

64. Head and Landes, eds., *Essays on the Peace of God*; Cowdrey, "Peace of God"; Erdmann, *Origin of the Idea of Crusade*.

65. "Malitia fuit, non militia, quod hactenus Christianorum caedibus et rapinis et execrabilibus intenti ignem inexstinguibilem et immortalium cruciatus vermium meruerunt." Henry of Marcy, Letter 32, *PL* 204: 250.

66. "Habes nunc, fortis miles, habes, vir bellicose, ubi dimices absque periculo, ubi et vincere gloria, et mori lucrum." Bernard of Clairvaux, Letter 363, *SBO* 8: 315. This profit was not only for knights; in the same letter, Bernard told

the merchants that the crusade was a market they should not miss, because "that stuff you buy costs little, but if you take it up on a devout shoulder, it will without doubt be worth the kingdom of God."

67. For the development of the idea of "crusade" out of a combination of pilgrimage and holy war, see Erdmann, *Origin of the Idea of Crusade*; Riley-Smith, *First Crusade*; Blake, "Formation of the 'Crusade Idea.'"

68. "Ut militantibus sibi stipendia reddat, indulgentiam delictorum et gloriam sempiternam." Bernard of Clairvaux, Letter 363, *SBO* 8: 314.

69. This point is made especially clear in an addendum to Bernard's Letter 363, *SBO* 8: 315, n. 14, in which he appealed not only to knights and merchants but to people of all ages and both sexes. Not all were to fight—the weak and the poor were to support the warriors with goods and prayers—but the project involved everyone in some way. For Bernard's exclusion of monks, see Letter 511, *SBO* 8: 511 (James, no. 396). See also Nicholas of Clairvaux, Letter 21, written for the monk Walter to his brother W., telling him that it was safer to enter a monastery than to go to Jerusalem. *PL* 196: 1622.

70. "Ecce, te operante, salutem in medio terrae videmus jam perditissimos homines emundari, currare ad confessionem, poenitentiam agere, satisfacere pro praeteritis peccatis, de futuris quaerere et promittere emendationem. Nec mediocri, ut assolent, contenti poenitentia, undique convolant ad perfectionem, mittentes manum ad fortia, crucem sibi bajulant, et relicitis omnibus sequuntur Christum." Henry of Marcy, *Tractatus varii de peregrinante civitate Dei*, 13, *PL* 204: 357.

71. "Intus fide, foris ferro . . . hostibus metum incutiant." Bernard of Clairvaux, *De laude novae militiae* 2.3, 4.8, *SBO* 3: 216, 220, CFS, 19: 123, 139.

72. "Miles, inquam, Christi securus interimit, interit securior. Sibi praestat cum interit, Christo cum interimit." Bernard of Clairvaux, *De laude novae militiae* 3.4, *SBO* 3: 217; CFS, 19: 133–34.

73. "Ut pene dubitem quid potius censeam appellandos, monachos videlicet an milites, nisi quod utrumque forsan congruentius nominarium." Bernard of Clairvaux, *De laude novae militiae* 4.8, *SBO* 3: 221, CFS, 19: 140.

74. "Invenimus hominem secundum cor nostrum, qui in saeculo quaerit Deum, qui sub militari singulo monachum profitetur. . . . videmus tamen te oculis cordis in visceribus Jesu Christi"; Nicholas of Clairvaux, Letter 47, *PL* 196: 1648–49.

75. "Et ne quid desit ex evangelica perfectione, absque omni proprio habitant unius moris in domo una, solliciti servare unitatem spiritus in vinculo pacis. Dicas universae multitudinis esse cor unum et animam unam: ita quisque non omnino propriam sequi voluntatem, sed magis obsequi satagit imperanti. . . . Persona inter eos minime accipitur: defertur meliori, non nobiliori.

Honore se invicem praeveniunt; alterutrum onera portant, ut sic adimpleant legem Christi." Bernard of Clairvaux, *De laude novae militiae* 4.7, *SBO* 3: 220, CFS, 19: 138–39. For William's description, see *Vita prima* 1.3.15, *PL* 185: 235.

76. Bernard of Clairvaux, *De laude novae militiae* 6–13, *SBO* 3: 224–39, CFS, 19: 146–67. See also Nicholas of Clairvaux, Letter 18, to a Knight Templar in the name of Brother Gaucher, in which he mentions that the knight "traverses the stations of our redemption." *PL* 196: 1617.

77. "Puto quod illa austerior, haec dulcior videatur, magisque infirmitati blandiatur humanae quies dormitionis quam labor conversationis, mortis securitas quam vitae rectitudo." Bernard of Clairvaux, *De laude novae militiae* 11, *SBO* 3: 229, CFS, 19: 154.

78. In fact, the Cistercians demonstrated little of the interest in protecting the poor and the powerless that monks of previous generations had shown. The most dramatic evidence of this is, of course, their willingness to remove inhabitants from land acquired by their monasteries. See Chapter 3. See also Poly and Bournazel, *Feudal Transformation*, pp. 174–80, who follow the twelfth-century author of the *Libellus de diuersis ordinibus* in distinguishing between traditional monks, who accepted seigneurial power but exercised it with moderation to protect the peasants from the more rapacious knights, and the new apostolic groups, whose disdain for the material world led them to criticize the comforts that the traditional monks obtained from their seigneury but who did not really notice the peasants at all. For an expression of the traditional, Cluniac attitude toward labor, seigneurial power, and the peasantry, see Peter the Venerable, *Letters* no. 28, 1: 86–87.

79. The sermon was later translated into Latin by Alan of Lille. The text is in B.N. lat. 14859, ff. 233r–34r. The rubric, written in a later hand, states, "Sermo quem composuit abbas cisterciensis romanis verbis apud montem pessulanum in ecclesia beati Firmini, quem postea magister alanus transtulit in latinum." See Alverny, *Alain de Lille*, pp. 13–15. The most likely candidate for the preacher is Arnold Amaury, abbot of Cîteaux from 1202 to 1212 and leader of the Albigensian Crusade. Although he was the only abbot of Cîteaux in the late twelfth and early thirteenth centuries with a southern French background, "abbas cisterciensis" could refer to an abbot from the Cistercian order in general, in which case there are any number of possible abbots from southern French houses.

80. "Surgamus ad sollicitandum rei familiaris. Res familiares hominis sunt proprie cogitiones, proprie voluntates, ipsem et actiones: ad hanc familiam ordinandam surgere debemus ut ordinemus cogitiones ad bene cogitandum, voluntates ad bene volendum, actiones ad bene agendum." B.N. lat. 14859, f. 233ra.

81. B.N. lat. 14859, ff. 233vb–34ra.

82. B.N. lat. 14859, f. 233r.

83. See, e.g., Bernard's criticisms of Henry of Lausanne; Chapter 8, p. 221.

84. B.N. lat. 14859, f. 233va–b.

85. "Aspiremus igitur ad id regnum ubi rex est Christus, ubi regina matri eius, ubi angeli milites, ubi sancti cives." B.N. lat. 14859, f. 234ra.

86. Kuttner, "Forgotten Definition of Justice."

CHAPTER 8

1. For an overview of these developments, see Morris, *Papal Monarchy*, pp. 101–8, 205–34. See also Tellenbach, *Church, State and Christian Society.*

2. For the recent historiography on the schism of 1130, see Chodorow, *Christian Political Theory*, pp. 18–42; Stroll, *Jewish Pope.*

3. For an argument that Innocent was the legally elected pope, see Amélineau, "Saint Bernard et le schisme," and for the canonical arguments in support of Innocent, see Jacqueline, *Épiscopat et papauté*, pp. 72–73. For an argument for Anacletus, see Bernhardi, *Lothar von Supplinburg*, p. 310. For the most widespread argument, that neither election was wholly canonical, but Anacletus's was more valid than Innocent's, see Klewitz, "Das Ende des Reformpapsttums," p. 212.

4. This is especially true of Innocent's supporters, because Innocent's legal position appeared weaker than that of Anacletus. See Stroll, *Jewish Pope*, esp. pp. 91–101. However, Anacletus's claim to have a unified Christendom behind him was considerably weaker than that of Innocent; he may have continued to make his argument for legal validity because other arguments were not working. Looking at the dispute from a modern perspective, it is tempting to give primacy to legal arguments, but it is not clear that people at the time did so.

5. See Morrison, *Tradition and Authority*, pp. 336–40.

6. Ibid., p. 344.

7. Many of Innocent's initial bulls and letters were addressed to these men. See Innocent II, *Epistolae et privilegia*, PL 179: 70–76, 87–88, 162. See also Stroll, *Jewish Pope*, p. 176.

8. Bernard of Clairvaux and Hugh of Pontigny, Letter 311, *SBO* 8: 241 (James, no. 374)

9. It is interesting that two non-Cistercian accounts of the council, Suger's *Vie de Louis VI le Gros* and the chronicle from Maurigny, do not even mention Bernard's presence. Suger, *Vie de Louis VI le Gros*, pp. 258–61; *Chronicon Mauriniacensi*, RHGF 12: 79. For the *Vita prima*, see PL 185: 270; see also Stroll, *Jewish Pope*, p. 175. Bernard's *Vita* also attributes Henry I of England's support for Innocent to Bernard's persuasion. Arnold of Bonneval, *Vita prima* 2.1.4, PL 185: 271. But see William of Malmesbury, *Historia novella* 1.5, PL 179: 1399.

See also Innocent II, *Epistolae et privilegia*, *PL* 179: 96–97. In 1131, at the council at Rheims, Archbishop Hugh of Rouen presented a letter promising Henry's allegiance, suggesting that much of Henry's support might have been due to his activity. The chronicle of Maurigny, showing a French bias, suggests that Henry was convinced by the example of Louis. *Chronicon Mauriniacensi, RHGF* 12: 79.

10. Otto of Freising, *Two Cities* 7.19, pp. 425–26. See, however, Arnold of Bonneval, *Vita prima* 2.5, *PL* 185: 271.

11. *Chronicon Mauriniacensi, RHGF* 12: 82.

12. The other letters Innocent issued at Rheims were addressed to Suger and Peter the Venerable, who were definitely present. Innocent II, *Epistolae et privilegia*, *PL* 179: 112.

13. Neither this first delegation nor that of Peter the Venerable in 1133 met with success. Only in 1134, after the other southern French bishops had made clear their desire to support Innocent, did William inform Bernard and Geoffrey of Chartres that he would abandon Anacletus and Gerard. For these delegations, see Peter the Venerable, *Letters* no. 58, 1: 179, 2: 336–38. See also Bernard's Letter 126 to the bishops of Aquitaine, *SBO* 7: 309–19 (James, no. 129), and his Letter 128 to William, *SBO* 7: 321–22 (James, no. 130).

14. Mansi, *Sacrorum conciliorum*, pp. 487–92. See also Bernard's Letter 255 to Louis VI, criticizing his reluctance to let the French bishops attend the council.

15. Arnold of Bonneval, *Vita prima* 2.7.45, *PL* 185: 294–95.

16. See Bernard of Clairvaux, Letter 144, *SBO* 7: 344–46 (James, no. 146).

17. See Stroll, *Jewish Pope*, p. 160 n. 9, in which she cites Palumbo, *Lo Scisma del MCXXX*, pp. 21–22, as granting "Manfred and Arnulf the dubious honor of writing the most violent pages of all of the Innocentian propaganda." See also Bloch's discussion of Arnulf's *Invectiva* in "Schism of Anacletus II," pp. 166–67.

18. Before the council, Louis VI wrote to Haimeric and the other cardinals who supported Innocent to tell them that, after consulting with his clerical advisers and the archbishop of Rheims, he had decided to recognize Innocent, whom he called "an honest man personally worthy of such an office," and to call a council to affirm this decision. For this letter, see Stroll, *Jewish Pope*, pp. 174–75; the text of the letter is in n. 15. Stroll still suggests that Bernard was responsible for this argument and implies that Suger's advice to Louis took into consideration Bernard's "preternatural persuasive talents" (p. 176). She also argues that Haimeric and Bernard developed a "strategy" to secure Innocent's election, although there is no evidence that Bernard was involved in the dispute until the council at Etampes (p. 96).

19. For a study that argues that Bernard did base his decision on canonical principles, see Jacqueline, *Épiscopat et papauté*, esp. pp. 72–80. See also Part 2 introduction, n. 6.

20. Bernard of Clairvaux, Letter 431, *SBO* 8: 411–13 (James, no. 156). See also Grotz, who in "Kriterien auf dem Prüfstand" argues that Bernard started with a preconceived position and used legal arguments in whatever ways were necessary to support his position.

21. "Electio meliorum, approbatio plurium et, quod his efficacius est, morum attestatio. Innocentium apud omnes commendant, summum confirmant Pontificem." Bernard of Clairvaux, Letter 124, *SBO* 7: 306 (James, no. 127).

22. "Cuius et opinio clarior, et electio sanior inventa est, nimirum eligentium et numero vincens, et merito." Bernard of Clairvaux, Letter 125, *SBO* 7: 308 (James, no. 128). This is not strictly true, as Anacletus received support from a majority of the cardinals. See Stroll, *Jewish Pope*, p. 97.

23. "Promotione purior, et ratione probabilior, et prior tempore"; "merita probant, et dignitas eligentium." Bernard of Clairvaux, Letter 126, *SBO* 7: 318 (James, no. 129).

24. Bernard of Clairvaux, Letter 125, *SBO* 7: 307–8 (James, no. 128).

25. "Alemanniae, Franciae, Angliae, Scotiae, Hispaniarum et Ierosolymorum reges, cum universo clero et populis, favent et adhaerent domino Innocentio, tamquam filii patri, tamquam capiti membra, solliciti servare unitatem spiritus in vinculo pacis." Bernard of Clairvaux, Letter 125, *SBO* 7: 308 (James, no. 128). "Pulsus urbe, ab orbe suscipitur." Letter 124, *SBO* 7: 306 (James, no. 127). See also the long list of prelates and monks in Letter 126.

26. Bernard of Clairvaux, Letter 126, *SBO* 7: 312 (James, no. 129). Although Bernard did not greatly emphasize Anacletus's Jewish background, the invective that did emphasize it served to demonize Anacletus further.

27. Stroll, *Jewish Pope*, pp. 9, 154–55. See also Maleczek, "Kardinal Kollegium."

28. "Horum gloria specialis et praecipua sanctitas, et auctoritas etiam hostibus reverenda, facile nobis, qui minorem et meriti et officii tenemus locum, aut errare secum, aut sapere persuasit." Bernard of Clairvaux, Letter 126, *SBO* 7: 316 (James, no. 129). The ecclesiastics whom Bernard named were archbishops Walter of Ravenna, Hildegard of Tarragona, Norbert of Magdeburg, Conrad of Salzburg, and bishops Equipert of Münster, Hildebrand of Pistoia, Bernard of Pavia, Bernard of Parma, Landulf of Asti, and Hugh of Grenoble.

29. Walter of Ravenna, e.g., wrote to Norbert of Magdeburg (both on Bernard's list) in March or April of 1130, alerting him to Anacletus's Jewish background, and Hugh of Grenoble was also an early supporter of Innocent. Stroll, *Jewish Pope*, pp. 88, 161.

30. In 1131, after Bernard had accompanied Innocent to Liège, the archbishop of Mainz, who was present at Liège, asked the monks of Clairvaux to receive the community of Benedictine monks at Eberbach into their filiation; Janauschek, *Originum*, pp. 21–22. In 1132, after Bernard's trip to Aquitaine

with Jocelin, bishop of Soissons, the monks of Clairvaux founded the house of Longpont in the diocese of Soissons (p. 22). In August 1132, they founded the abbey of Vaucelles in the diocese of Cambrai, which Bernard had passed through the year before on his way to Liège (p. 24; *GC* 10: 111–12, Instrumenta 22).

31. William donated the land for Grace-Dieu in 1134, the Milanese established Chiaravalle in 1135, and Bernard sent a group of monks to Sicily in 1140, at Roger's request. See Janauschek, *Originum*, pp. 34–35, 39, 45; *GC* 2: 387, Instrumenta 8; Bernard of Clairvaux, Letters 134, 208–9, *SBO* 7: 330, 8: 67–69 (James, nos. 135, 277–78).

32. Trois-Fontaines in Châlons-sur-Marne, Clairvaux and Auberive in Langres, Igny in Rheims, Preuilly in Sens, Rievaulx and Fountains in York, Belloc in Rodez, Le Miroir and Bénissons-Dieu in Lyons, Chaalis in Beauvais, Pontigny and Reigny in Auxerre, Longpont in Soissons, Noirlac in Bourges, Val Richer in Lisieux, and La Trappe (Savigniac) in Séez.

33. "Bonam idoneamque personam intendatis eligere"; "de quo utinam meliora atque honestiora audivissemus." Bernard of Clairvaux, Letter 164, *SBO* 7: 372–73 (James, no. 179).

34. "O Lugdunensis pia mater ecclesia! Cuiuscemodi non sponsum, sed monstrum tuae filiae procurasti nunc." Bernard of Clairvaux, Letter 165, *SBO* 7: 376 (James, no. 180).

35. "Et boni horrent, et mali redent." Bernard of Clairvaux, Letters 168, 166, *SBO* 7: 381, 377–78 (James, nos. 183, 181).

36. "Sicut virorum veracium attestatione deprehendimus, a planta pedis usque ad verticem non est in ea sanitas." Bernard of Clairvaux, Letter 346, *SBO* 8: 288 (James, no. 187).

37. "Simplices et recti ac timentes Deum, non suam, sed Dei causam acturi, gravem tanti itineris suscepere laborem." Bernard of Clairvaux, Letters 545, 520, *SBO* 8: 491–92, 480–82 (James, nos. 189, 204).

38. Bernard of Clairvaux, Letter 249, *SBO* 8: 144 (James, no. 325).

39. "Sicut virorum veracium relatione discitur." Bernard of Clairvaux, Letter 328, *SBO* 8: 264–65 (James, no. 381).

40. Even if the monks had not lived within the same community, the Chapters General in the 1140's, when these men were all abbots, had been small enough to allow the development of close relationships.

41. For accounts of the schism, see Pacaut, *Alexandre III*; Somerville, *Pope Alexander III*; Beck et al., *Handbook of Church History* 4.

42. Gilbert of Hoyland, *Sermones in canticum* 30.6, *PL* 184: 158, CFS, 20: 366–67.

43. "Non hodie scinderetur Ecclesia, imo non videretur scindi tunica

Christi." Geoffrey of Auxerre, *Sermo ad praelatos in concilio convocatos*, *PL* 184: 1100; see also B.N. n.a. lat. 1476, ff. 89r–90v.

44. "Fremit Teutonichus furor colligit et cogit"; "ut quos semel a Christi corpore separaverit, execrabilibus obliget sacramentis ne ad eius aliquando redeant unitatem." Geoffrey of Auxerre, *Sermo in concilio de scismate*, B.N. n.a. lat. 1476, ff. 89r–90v.

45. See Mahn, *L'ordre cistercien*, pp. 139–47.

46. Pacaut, *Alexandre III*, pp. 62, 83.

47. Alexander III, Letter 8, *PL* 200: 82. See Willi, "Päpste, Kardinäle und Bischöfe," pp. 26–27, 272.

48. "Susceptis vestrae dignationis apicibus respiravit in gaudio cor meum, et tanquam corona spei quae ornata est gloria, refloruit in spiritu meo jucunda serenitas, et cathedratum vestrum ulnis verae dilectionis amplectens, supplicationem pro vobis exhibui devotam bonorum omnium largitori, sonuitque in commune actio, et vox laudis, et de vestra promotione carmen referimus Deo nostro, voe denuntiamus homini per quem scandalum venit!" Philip L'Aumône, *Variorum epistolae ad Alexandrum III* 1, *PL* 200: 1359–60.

49. Ibid., *PL* 200: 1361.

50. "Nos enim personam tuam, sicut charissimi fratris tui, praeteritae quidem amicitiae non immemores, sincera in Christi visceribus charitate diligere, et postulationes tuas quantum cum Deo possumus libentius exaudire." Alexander III, Letter 6, *PL* 200: 80; also Letter 8, *PL* 200: 81–82.

51. Henry's election was announced to Pope Alexander III by the Cistercian bishop Godfrey of Langres, the Cistercian cardinal Henry of Saints Nereus and Achilleus, and Geoffrey, the abbot of Clairvaux; Alexander then sent Pons, the abbot of Grandselve, back to Archbishop Henry with the pallium; Alexander III, Letter 66, *PL* 200: 137. Not only did Cistercian bishops and abbots serve as messengers between Henry and the pope, but Henry helped to place other Cistercian abbots in episcopal positions and accepted the Cistercians as mediators during his disputes. When the bishop of Arras resigned in the spring of 1161, Henry recommended that Andreas, the Cistercian abbot of Vaux-de-Cernay, be elected to the see, and he later accepted the mediation of Abbot Philip of L'Aumône when he and Bishop Andreas came into conflict; Preiss, *Die politische Tätigkeit*, pp. 56, 72–73.

52. Of 1,167 letters written by Alexander before Henry's death, 270 (or 23 percent) were addressed to Henry.

53. Preiss, *Die politische Tätigkeit*, pp. 30–32. Preiss provides an indispensable guide to the actions of the Cistercians during the schism. Although I sometimes differ with his interpretations, I have relied on his research.

54. Preiss, *Die politische Tätigkeit*, p. 25.

55. Cluniac houses, e.g., supported the Victorines, whereas the Premonstratensian canons were divided. For Alexander's concern about the Cistercians, see Leclercq, "Epîtres d'Alexandre III." The passage in this letter expressing Alexander's doubts about Cistercian support disappeared from most copies of the letter. Because the complete letter appears to have been attached to a copy of the papal bull *Aeterna et incommutabilis* that was sent to England, Leclercq has assumed that some English Cistercians might have opposed Alexander. However, it is possible that Alexander was referring instead to the Cistercian presence at Frederick's court.

56. Preiss, *Die politische Tätigkeit*, pp. 30, 34; *RHGF* 15: 753.

57. Preiss, *Die politische Tätigkeit*, pp. 38, 41; *PL* 200: 85, 92.

58. Unfortunately, Aelred's letter is lost. See Leclercq, "Epîtres d'Alexandre III," p. 69, n. 3. The chronicle of Peterborough is cited in Mahn, *L'ordre cistercien*, p. 141.

59. Somerville, *Pope Alexander III*, p. 2; Cheney, "Recognition of Pope Alexander III." The site of the meeting suggests the important role played by Henry of Beauvais in these negotiations.

60. Preiss, *Die politische Tätigkeit*, p. 42, esp. n. 27; Beck et al., *Handbook of Church History*, 4: 58.

61. In April, Henry, now archbishop of Rheims, Bishop Godfrey of Langres, Bishop Amaury of Senlis, and Abbot Pons of Grandselve, all of whom were Cistercians, negotiated with Louis for Alexander, and later that year Cistercian abbots appear to have been instrumental in convincing Louis to abandon Frederick's plan to submit the papal claimants to arbitration; *PL* 200: 137–40, 158; Preiss, *Die politische Tätigkeit*, pp. 50–52, esp. n. 76.

62. Somerville, *Pope Alexander III*, p. 3; Preiss, *Die politische Tätigkeit*, pp. 53–54.

63. Preiss, *Die politische Tätigkeit*, pp. 55–59.

64. *PL* 220: 256–57; for the possible dating, see Preiss, *Die politische Tätigkeit*, p. 63.

65. Somerville, *Pope Alexander III*, p. 64–65.

66. Preiss, *Die politische Tätigkeit*, p. 64.

67. Ibid., p. 65.

68. Ibid., pp. 156–57.

69. Ibid., p. 157. It is possible that Frederick's action further helped the Cistercians to decide in favor of Alexander III.

70. Ibid., pp. 164–68. Interestingly, it was Morimundo who continued to treat with Frederick the longest, receiving charters in 1174 and again in 1179 (p. 166).

71. For Cistercian persecution by Victorine allies, see *Chronicon Clarevallense*, *PL* 185: 1248; later letters from Alexander III to Cistercian bishops and abbots,

PL 200: 336; *Statuta,* 1: 77. In a sermon, Geoffrey of Auxerre mentioned that monasteries were emptied and injured, and celebrated these "happy monks who sustain the rapine of their goods with joy." Geoffrey of Auxerre, *Sermo in concilio de scismate,* B.N. n.a. lat. 1476, f. 89r. It is not clear to which "schismatic council" Geoffrey referred, for between 1159 and 1163 the Victorines held five papal councils, including one held around Saint-Jean-de-Losne in early September 1163, just before the council at Tours, where Geoffrey is known to have preached a second sermon about the schism; Somerville, *Pope Alexander III,* pp. 4–5. See also Mahn, *L'ordre cistercien,* pp. 146–47; Preiss, *Die politische Tätigkeit,* pp. 178–87.

72. Preiss, *Die politische Tätigkeit,* pp. 221–27. Preiss's comment (p. 222) that Eberhard was the only German Cistercian who willingly undertook the "martyrdom" of exile seems a bit extreme.

73. Robertson, *Materials,* 6: 401–3 (Letter 409). Abbot Alexander was sick and sent Geoffrey of Auxerre in his place; Geoffrey's participation speaks to his rapid rehabilitation after his deposition as abbot of Clairvaux.

74. Ibid., 6: 513, 7: 2 (Letters 461, 532).

75. Letter 792, *PL* 200: 729–30; Preiss, *Die politische Tätigkeit,* pp. 125–26. From Alexander's letter to Henry of Rheims, it seems that Abbot Garin of Pontigny participated in these negotiations as well. Preiss (p. 155) suggests that Cistercians had now taken a middle position between Church and empire.

76. *Vita s. Petri, AASS,* Mai, 2: 334; Alexander III, Letters 1102, 1107, *PL* 200: 962–63, 965–66.

77. Preiss, *Die politische Tätigkeit,* pp. 146–54.

78. Frederick's letter is printed in *RHGF* 16: 698–99; Alexander III, Letter 1308, *PL* 200: 1132–33.

79. Mahn, *L'ordre cistercien,* pp. 145–46; *GC* 15: 151, Instrumenta 48.

80. Morris, *Papal Monarchy,* p. 197; Beck et al., *Handbook of Church History,* 4: 63.

81. There is an enormous amount of historical work on the Becket conflict. See, e.g., Barlow, *Thomas Becket*; Knowles, *Thomas Becket*; Smalley, *Becket Conflict*; Morey, *Gilbert Foliot and His Letters.*

82. See, e.g., Bernard's criticisms of Stephen of Garland, who was a deacon, archdeacon of Notre Dame, and dean of Orléans as well as being Louis VI's seneschal. Bernard of Clairvaux, Letter 78, *SBO* 7: 208–9 (James, no. 80). After Becket's election, Gilbert Foliot joked that Henry II had worked a miracle by transforming a layman and a knight into an archbishop; Barlow, *Thomas Becket,* p. 71.

83. Barlow, *Thomas Becket,* p. 66–67.

84. "Superest igitur ut uolentatem domini tui sciens eius ordinationi non resistas, sed, memor mandatorum eius, ad faciendum ea terminis contentus sis

quos posuerunt patres tui." Powicke, who edited and translated Walter Daniel's *Life of Ailred of Rievaulx*, believed it may have been Aelred who responded to the archbishop's letter (p. xlix–li). For the letter, see Powicke, "Maurice of Rievaulx," p. 29.

85. He did eventually renounce some of his worldliness and pomp but probably not until he began to solicit support for his battle against the king. E.g., Barlow, *Thomas Becket*, pp. 75–76, points out that he probably did not begin to dress with restraint until after the council at Clarendon in January 1164, and that he continued to keep a household with all the trappings of grandeur until after he fled England. Furthermore, he remained a pluralist, for, although he gave up the chancellorship, he retained his other offices. Such pomp and positions certainly were not unusual for twelfth-century bishops, but they were just the things about which the Cistercian reformers complained.

86. Robertson, *Materials*, 5: 41 (Letter 25).

87. Ibid., 5: 56–57, 113 (Letters 35, 60).

88. Ibid., 5: 113 (Letter 60).

89. See McGinn, *Golden Chain*, pp. 38–39; Robertson, *Materials*, 5: 110–16 (Letter 60); Preiss, *Die politische Tätigkeit*, pp. 94–96. For Henry, see Lenssen, "A propos de Cîteaux et de S. Thomas de Cantorbéry." When John of Salisbury left England, he went first to Rheims, where he received support from the archbishop Henry; Robertson, *Materials*, 5: 98–99 (Letter 45).

90. John of Salisbury commented that Becket's time at Pontigny would give him the opportunity to improve both his Latin and his character; Robertson, *Materials*, 5: 163–64. In 1166, Gilbert Foliot and his allied English bishops commented in a letter to Becket that they were pleased he was atoning for his previous behavior with fasts, prayers, and tears at Pontigny, and hoped that his penitential mood would continue so that a negotiated settlement of the quarrel would be possible; Gilbert Foliot, Letter 167, *Letters and Charters*, p. 223.

91. Robertson, *Materials*, 5: 160 (Letter 148); Preiss, *Die politische Tätigkeit*, p. 82.

92. Robertson, *Materials*, 5: 365 (Letter 188). It is worth noting that we have only Henry's account of the meeting, which he described in a letter of May 1166, when he threatened Gilbert for not upholding his end of the agreement.

93. McGinn, *Golden Chain*, p. 45.

94. The Cistercians' position parallels that of Alexander III, who, in June 1165, wrote to Becket asking that he not do anything to provoke Henry; Robertson, *Materials*, 5: 179–80 (Letter 95). Alexander was about to move south to Italy, and he was worried about Henry's support.

95. Ibid., 5: 266–82 (Letters 152–54). It is not clear which two of these three letters Urban carried.

96. Ibid., 5: 365–66 (Letter 188). Henry's threats against the Cistercians are

mentioned in a number of letters from the summer of 1166, including a request from Alexander III to the abbots of Cîteaux, Pontigny, and all other Cistercian abbeys that they not succumb to Henry's threats. Ibid., 5: 385, 387, 389, 426–27 (Letters 194–96, 212).

97. Unlike Frederick Barbarossa, who could not disturb the Alexandrine abbeys if they were protected by their bishops, Henry II clearly had the power to make good on his threats. Alexander annulled Becket's excommunications by the fall of 1165, which could be evidence that he thought Becket had pushed too hard or a sign that Alexander had to compromise because of his political need for Henry's support.

98. "Quod occasione abbatis eidem monasterio praesidentis, qui non eam gratiam et reverentiam in oculis regum et principum promeruit, quam antecessores ejus promoruisse noscuntur, ipsi monasterio non modicum derogatur, et totus ordo non minimum exinde incommodum sustinet et jacturam." Alexander III, Letter 324, *PL* 200: 349.

99. Alexander III, Letter 325, *PL* 200: 350–51.

100. Alexander III, Letters 325, 340, *PL* 200: 350–51, 368–69.

101. *Chronicon Clarevallense*, *PL* 185: 1248; Robertson, *Materials*, 5: 447–48 (Letter 217); McGinn, *Golden Chain*, pp. 43–44.

102. *Statuta*, 1: 75–76, cites Manrique, whose source is the fifteenth-century *Dialogus de prospero et adverso statu Ordinis Cisterciensis*; the *Chronicon Clarevallense* is equivocal about Geoffrey's departure, commenting that he resigned, "videas contra se, sive juste, sive injuste quorumdam odia concitata": *PL* 185: 1248. See Lenssen, "A propos de Cîteaux et de S. Thomas de Cantorbéry," pp. 99–100. Bouchard, *Sword, Miter, and Cloister*, follows Manrique.

103. Geoffrey became abbot of Fossenova in 1170 and abbot of Hautecombe in 1176.

104. Preiss, *Die politische Tätigkeit*, pp. 89–90.

105. Lenssen, "A propos de Cîteaux et de S. Thomas de Cantorbéry," pp. 106–7. For Geoffrey's trip in 1164, see Preiss, *Die politische Tätigkeit*, p. 79.

106. Robertson, *Materials*, 3: 87–88.

107. After the failure to meet with Becket at Gisors in April, Henry began to negotiate with Frederick and told his legates at the council at Würzburg to swear that he would abandon Alexander for Pascal; Barlow, *Thomas Becket*, p. 136.

108. It is worth noting that Aelred of Rievaulx, in the last years of his life, dedicated his homilies *De oneribus* on the prophet Isaiah to Gilbert Foliot; *PL* 195: 361. Gilbert's principled position may well have been one that many Cistercians found attractive.

109. For this interpretation, see McGinn, *Golden Chain*, p. 44, who is following the interpretation of Preiss, *Die politische Tätigkeit*, p. 98.

110. Robertson, *Materials*, 6: 48–24, 151, 214 (Letters 246–48, 285, 315), among others. Becket became so intemperate about William that John of Salisbury told him to use a humbler style in his correspondence with the cardinal (6: 217 [Letter 317]). William appeared to take Henry's part as early as November 1164, when he represented the king before the papal curia and defended the Constitutions of Clarendon; Barlow, *Thomas Becket*, p. 122.

111. Robertson, *Materials*, 6: 525 (Letter 469).

112. Barlow, *Thomas Becket*, p. 186.

113. Robertson, *Materials* 7: 82, 90, 231 (Letter 564, 568, 641); Barlow, *Thomas Becket*, pp. 186, 189, 200–201; Preiss, *Die politische Tätigkeit*, pp. 106–9.

114. Robertson, *Materials*, 7: 225 (Letter 638).

115. When Henry and Becket met at Montmirail in January 1169, Becket's advisers, after much debate, thought they had convinced the archbishop to omit the *salvo* clause, but after Becket met with the king and submitted his case to royal judgment, he nonetheless added the words "saving the honor of God." As Barlow points out, this was Becket's initial condition, and he continued to stand by it (pp. 180–81). Similarly, the two men planned to meet at Montemarte in November 1169, but Henry refused to give Becket the kiss of peace because he had vowed not to, whereas Becket insisted on the kiss because he saw it as a warranty of Henry's intentions; Barlow, *Thomas Becket*, p. 194–95.

116. Preiss, *Die politische Tätigkeit*, pp. 130–31; Barlow, *Thomas Becket*, pp. 253–55, 260.

117. Henry of Marcy, Letter 6, *PL* 204: 220.

118. Robertson, *Materials*, 6: 152; Caesarius of Heisterbach, *Dialogue on Miracles* 8.69, 2: 70–71. The Cistercians are also given credit for aiding the rapid spread of Becket's cult; Smalley, *Becket Conflict*, p. 192. By 1185, the order observed the feast of the new saint, although initially only the English houses celebrated it as a feast with two masses; *Statuta*, 1: 102 (1185, no. 36). Only in 1191 did it become a major feast throughout the order; *Statuta*, 1: 144 (1191, no. 63).

119. For the phrase "spirit of *Realpolitik*," see McGinn, *Golden Chain*, p. 44, where he follows the interpretation of Preiss, *Die politische Tätigkeit*, pp. 92, 98, 155.

120. Baldwin of Ford, *De corruptis moribus cleri et populi*, *PL* 204: 415–18, CFS, 39: 68–76. Smalley believed the treatise was written after Baldwin became archbishop of Canterbury in 1184; *Becket Conflict*, p. 219.

CHAPTER 9

1. No longer are medieval heretics considered "Manichees." For a careful study of the different strands of eleventh- and twelfth-century dissent, see

Moore, *Origins of European Dissent*. See also Russell, *Dissent and Reform*; Lambert, *Medieval Heresy*.

2. Eberwin of Steinfeld, *PL* 182: 676–80. Translated in Wakefield and Evans, *Heresies*, pp. 127–32 (no. 15).

3. Ibid.

4. Moore, *Origins of European Dissent*, p. 168.

5. "Quae nocere quam vincere malunt, et ne apparere quidem volunt, sed serpere?" Bernard of Clairvaux, *Ser. sup. cant.* 65.2, *SBO* 2: 173, CFS, 31: 180.

6. Bernard of Clairvaux, *Ser. sup. cant.* 65.5, *SBO* 2: 175–76, CFS, 31: 185–86.

7. 1 Tim. 4.1–4. See Bernard of Clairvaux, *Ser. sup. cant.* 66.2, *SBO* 2: 179, CFS, 31: 192.

8. "In victu autem et habitu habentes formam pietatis, sed virtutem eius abnegantes [2 Tim. 3.5], eo decipiunt plures, quo transfigurant se in angelos lucis, cum sint Satanae." Bernard of Clairvaux, Letter 189, *SBO* 8: 14 (James, no. 239). "Sub vestimentis ovium lupus rapax"; "Nec mirum tamen si serpens ille callidus decepit te, quippe speciem pietatis habens, cuius virtutem penitus abnegavit." Letter 214, *SBO* 8: 125–26 (James, no. 317).

9. Moore, *Origins of European Dissent*, p. 251. For the "secret conventicles," see the account of the heretics at Châlons-sur-Marne in Wakefield and Evans, *Heresies*, p. 90. See also the account of the heretics at Orléans in 1022 (pp. 74–81).

10. See Geoffrey's letter back to the monks at Clairvaux, written in 1145, *PL* 185: 410–16, and his later account in the *Vita prima*, *PL* 185: 312–13.

11. Leclercq, "Le témoignage," pp. 194–95. See also Geoffrey's description of the Cathars (p. 196).

12. "Non habent certos aditus, semitas ambulant circulares; et in quodam suarum fraudium labyrintho monstra novissima reconduntur. Tamquam damula de manu diffugiunt, et instar colubri tortuosi quo eos plus astrinxeris facilius elabuntur." Henry of Marcy, Letter 29, *PL* 204: 235.

13. Bernard of Clairvaux, *Ser. sup. cant.* 65.1, *SBO* 2: 172, CFS, 31: 180.

14. "Egressus est de caverna sua coluber tortuosus." Bernard of Clairvaux, Letter 331, *SBO* 8: 269 (James, no. 243). "Cuius virulenta folia utinam adhuc laterent in scriniis, et non in triviis legerentur." Letter 189, *SBO* 8: 13 (James, no. 239).

15. "Iste vero iam providit quomodo virus suum transfundat in posteros, quomodo noceat generationi omni quae ventura est." Bernard of Clairvaux, Letter 332, *SBO* 8: 271–72 (James, no. 244).

16. "Presertim animos iuueniles nouitate gaudentes: sine claue que Christus est in diuinas paginas irruentes: sine spiritu qui solus ea nouit scrutantes ipsa etiam alta dei." *Libellus contra capitula Gisleberti episcopi Pictavensis* 1.2, p. 38; see also 1.14, p. 38.

17. See, e.g., the account of the synod held at Arras by Bishop Gerard of Cam-

brai in 1025, translated in Wakefield and Evans, *Heresies*, pp. 82–85. See also Duby, *Three Orders*, pp. 29–36.

18. "Populo stulto et insipienti." Bernard of Clairvaux, Letter 241, *SBO* 8: 126. "Nec rationibus convincuntur, quia non intelligunt, nec auctoritatibus corriguntur, quia non recipiunt, nec flectuntur suasionibus, qui subversi sunt." *Ser. sup. cant.* 66.12, *SBO* 2: 186, CFS, 31: 203.

19. For studies of the Church's reaction to heresy, see Moore, *Origins of European Dissent*, pp. 243–83; Maisonneuve, *Etudes sur les origines de l'inquisition*; Manselli, "De la *persuasio* à la *coercitio*"; Peters, *Inquisition*, esp. pp. 40–74.

20. Moore, *Origins of European Dissent*, p. 90; Geoffrey of Auxerre, *Epistola*, *PL* 185: 412.

21. Geoffrey of Auxerre, *Epistola*, *PL* 185: 412.

22. For an account of the council at Rheims, see John of Salisbury, *Historia pontificalis* 8–11, pp. 15–25.

23. Moore, *Origins of European Dissent*, p. 253. For accounts of this council, see Sigebert of Gembloux, *Chronica*, p. 390; William of Newburgh, *Historia rerum Anglicarum*, RS 82.1: 60–64. Geoffrey of Auxerre discusses Bernard's actions at the council at Rheims but does not mention Eon.

24. Leclercq, "Le témoignage," pp. 194–95.

25. "Si non vis scandalizare Ecclesiam, eice feminam. Alioquin ex hoc uno cetera, quae non adeo manifesta sunt, procul dubio credibilia fiunt." Bernard of Clairvaux, *Ser. sup. cant.* 65.6, *SBO* 2: 176, CFS, 31: 186.

26. "Homo apostata est, qui relicto religionis habitu. . . . cum meretricibus inventus est praedicator insignis, et interdum etiam cum coniugatis." Bernard of Clairvaux, Letter 241, *SBO* 8: 126–27 (James, no. 317). "Monachum sine regula, sine sollicitudine praelatum, sine disciplina abbatem, Petrum Abaelardum, disputantem cum pueris, conversantem cum mulierculis." Letter 332, *SBO* 8: 271 (James, no. 244). Geoffrey of Auxerre also stressed the danger of unregulated women in his description of the followers of Peter Waldo; Leclercq, "Le témoignage," pp. 195–96.

27. Bernard of Clairvaux, *Ser. sup. cant.* 65.4, *SBO* 2: 175, CFS, 31: 184. For a study of chaste marriages, and a discussion of the challenge they posed to the clergy, see Elliott, *Spiritual Marriage*, esp. pp. 137–42.

28. Geoffrey of Auxerre, *Epistola*, *PL* 185: 414. This is also the argument of Moore, *Origins of European Dissent*, p. 275.

29. Geoffrey of Auxerre, *Epistola*, *PL* 185: 410–16.

30. Moore, *Origins of European Dissent*, pp. 276–77.

31. "In convictu et contubernio feminarum." Bernard of Clairvaux, *Ser. sup. cant.* 66.14, *SBO* 2: 187, CFS, 31: 206. See also *Ser. sup. cant.* 65.7.

32. Geoffrey of Auxerre, *Epistola*, *PL* 185: 412.

33. "Tua quoque potenti dextera cooperante"; Bernard of Clairvaux, Letters 241, 242, *SBO* 8: 127, 128 (James, nos. 317, 318).

34. Mansi, *Sacrorum conciliorum* 21: 718; Maisonneuve, *Etudes sur les origines de l'inquisition*, pp. 125–26.

35. "Etenim de quo constat quod ad amorem Dei non sit deinceps rediturus, sapit sibi necesse est, non prope iam nihil, sed nihili ex toto, utpote quod in aeternum nihili est. Illo igitur excepto, qui non modo iam non diligendus, insuper et odio habendus est, secundum illud: Nonne qui oderunt te, Domine, oderam, et super inimicos tuos tabescebam?" Bernard of Clairvaux, *Ser. sup. cant.* 50.7, *SBO* 2: 82, CFS, 31: 36.

36. "Oportet autem, ait, haereses et schismata esse, ut qui probati sunt manifesti fiant." Bernard of Clairvaux, Letters 189, 336, *SBO* 8: 15–16, 275 (James, nos. 239, 248).

37. Bernard of Clairvaux, Letter 189, *SBO* 8: 15–16 (James, no. 239).

38. "Quamquam melius procul dubio gladio coercentur, illius videlicet qui non sine causa gladium portat, quam in suum errorem multos traicere permittantur. Dei enim minister ille est, vindex in iram ei qui male agit." Bernard of Clairvaux, *Ser. sup. cant.* 66.12, *SBO* 2: 186–87, CFS, 31: 204.

39. "Ui armata per laicos exturbare." Peter the Venerable, *Tractatus contra petrobrusianos*, *CCCM* 10: 3.

40. "Satisfaciet forsitan lecta epistola occultis aliquorum catholicorum cogitatibus, et mentes eorum aut ab ignoto hominibus fidei languore sanare, aut contra eos, quorum lingua a propheta gladius acutus dicitur, premunire poterit." Peter the Venerable, *Tractatus contra petrobrusianos*, *CCCM* 10: 4. For a discussion of Peter the Venerable's own religious doubts, see Langmuir, "Peter the Venerable: Defense against Doubts," *Toward a Definition of Antisemitism*, pp. 197–208.

41. Henry of Marcy, Letter 29, *PL* 204: 235.

42. Gervase of Canterbury, *Chronica*, RS 73.1: 270. See Moore, *Origins of European Dissent*, p. 212.

43. For the importance of this expedition for early inquisitorial procedure, see Maisonneuve, *Etudes sur les origines de l'inquisition*, pp. 132–33. For the Maurand family, see Mundy, *Liberty and Political Power*, pp. 60–62.

44. Peter of Saint Chrysogonus, *PL* 199: 1121–24.

45. Henry of Marcy, Letter 39, *PL* 204: 235–40. In fact, at the point that the legate began to hear the cases of other suspects, Henry asked for permission to return north.

46. "Quomodo enim, adveniente Spiritu sancto, in adversariis ejus spiritus remaneret? Cernere erat hominem quasi morbo paralysi dissolutum, nec loquelam retinuisse, nec sensum, quamvis tantae facundiae fuisse diceretur ab omnibus, quod omnes in dicendo solitus sit superare." Henry of Marcy, Letter 39, *PL* 204: 238.

47. See Brown, "Society and the Supernatural."

48. "Aperiuntur ora fidelium, et catholicae plebis labia in tua, Christe, praeconia resolvuntur, velut tunc primum in eadem urbe fidei splendor erumperet,

et in spem salutis aeternae desperata dudum civitas respiraret. Et tunc igitur et deinceps verbum fidei crescebat, et multiplicabatur in dies; ita ut universa urbis facies laetior videretur, quae in candorem lucidae virtutis de tenebris evadebat erroris." Henry of Marcy, *PL* 204: 238.

49. Moore, *Origins of European Dissent*, p. 218.

50. "Sed reversus ad uomitum colligere et disseminare discipulos non desistit." Leclercq, "Le témoignage," p. 195. See also Dondaine, "Aux origines du Valdéisme."

51. Maisonneuve, *Etudes sur les origines de l'inquisition*, p. 133; Moore, *Origins of European Dissent*, p. 257.

52. See *Decrees of the Ecumenical Councils*, 1: 224–25; Foreville, *Latran I, II, III*, pp. 145–51.

53. Moore, *Origins of European Dissent*, p. 257; Maisonneuve, *Etudes sur les origines de l'inquisition*, p. 135.

54. See Congar, "Henri de Marcy," pp. 80–81.

55. Bernard of Clairvaux, Letter 363, *SBO* 8: 312 (James, no. 391).

56. "Ut Christi ulciseantur injurias, ponantque desertum illud quasi hortum Domini, et solitudinem ejus in delicias paradisi." Henry of Marcy, Letter 29, *PL* 204: 240.

57. Bernard of Clairvaux, Letter 189, *SBO* 8: 14 (James, no. 329).

58. "Quod dubitas, O David? quid trepidas, vir fidelis? Sume tibi fundam et lapidem, percutiatur protinus in fronte blasphemus, et caput nequam, quod impudenter erigitur, suo tuis manibus mucrone tollatur. Si enim in hoc certamine pars Christi vincitur, si vel ad modicum et in puncto mater Ecclesia conculcatur, scimus profecto causae nostrae desse meritum, sed patronum. Scimus quod non negabitur agonistae nostro triumphus, si in amore Christi militet pugnaturus." Henry of Marcy, Letter 29, *PL* 204: 235.

CONCLUSION

1. John of Salisbury, *Historia pontificalis* 12, pp. 26.

2. Similarly, Smalley reminds us not to let the polemic obscure the fact that twelfth-century masters such as Anselm and Ralph of Laon prepared scholars for ecclesiastical positions in "schools of piety"; *Becket Conflict*, pp. 21–23.

3. See McLaughlin, "Consorting with Saints," pp. 282–465.

4. Farmer, *Communities of St. Martin*, pp. 117–50; Van Engen, *Rupert of Deutz*, pp. 299–323.

5. Guido I, prior of La Chartreuse, *Consuetudines cartusiae* 7, 14, 41, *SC* 313: 176–77, 296–97, 244–46.

6. Little, *Religious Poverty*, pp. 75–83; for the hermit who lived on what he could find in the woods, see *Vita beati Bernardi fundatoris, PL* 172: 1380.

7. Smalley, *Becket Conflict*, esp. pp. 92–102, 174–86; Baldwin, *Masters, Princes and Merchants*; Ferruolo, *Origins of the University*.

8. Smalley, *Becket Conflict*, p. 25.

9. For later uses of the Cistercians' moral conception of the Church, see Grosseteste's critique of the thirteenth-century papal government; Southern, *Robert Grosseteste*.

10. Walter Map, *De nugis curialium* 1.25, pp. 89.

11. "Sed vocatus, sed tractus." Bernard of Clairvaux, Letter 48, *SBO* 7: 138 (James, no. 51). Bernard and Hugh of Pontigny made a similar point when writing the pope on behalf of Bishop Stephen of Paris, claiming that "a great necessity has drawn us from our cloister into the public, where we speak of what we have seen (Magna siquidem nos necessitas de claustris ad publicum traxit, ubi et quod loquimur vidimus)." Bernard of Clairvaux, Letter 46, *SBO* 7: 135 (James, no. 49).

12. "Gaudeo nempe, quod et vestrae prudentiae nostram in talibus occupationem displicere cognovi. Et quidem iustissime et amicissime. Age ergo si ita vultis, immo quia sic cernitis ac decernitis, et amico expedire, et monacho convenire; date, quaeso, operam, quatenus una utriusque voluntas citius impleatur, quo et vobis videlicet satisfiat ad iustitiam, et mihi ad salutem animae consulatur. Indicatur, si placet, clamosis et importunis ranis de cavernis non egredi, sed suis contentas esse paludibus. Non audiantur in conciliis, in palatiis non inveniantur; ad causas, ad negotia nulla necessitas, nulla trahere possit auctoritas." Bernard of Clairvaux, Letter 48, *SBO* 7: 139 (James, no. 51).

13. "Ego enim quaedam Chimaera mei saeculi, nec clericum gero nec laicum. Nam monachi iamdudum exui conversationem, non habitum. Nolo scribere de me quod vos per alios audisse existimo, quid actitem, quid studeam, per quae discrimina verser in mundo, immo per quae iacter praecipitia. Si quominus audistis, precor ut inquiratis et, secundum quod audieritis, et consilium impendatis, et orationum suffragia." Bernard of Clairvaux, Letter 250, *SBO* 8: 147 (James, no. 326).

14. Goodrich makes the point that Bernard was most likely to lament his political activities when writing to more contemplative monks such as the Carthusians; "Reliability of the *Vita prima*," pp. 172–73.

15. Dimier, "Mourir à Clairvaux!"

16. First Henry considered Luke 11.24, "I will return to my house from which I came"; then Song 5.3–4: "I had put off my garment, how could I put it on? I had bathed my feet, how could I soil them?" But then he remembered John 21.18, "When you were young, you girded yourself and walked where you would, but when you are old, another girds you and leads you where you do not wish to go." *Tractatus de peregrinante civitate dei*, *PL* 204: 251.

17. "In hac fratres meos et filios Claraevallenses, quorum absentiam de-

plorabam, praesentes reperi; in hac omnes bonos in hoc mundo peregrinantes ascriptos cives inveni. Quid igitur restare aliud jam videtur, nisi ut post multos et varios fluctus superius descriptos, civitate tandem habitationis inventa, seminare agros, plantare vineas, et fructum nativitatis facere studeamus?" Henry of Marcy, *Tractatus de peregrinante civitate dei, PL* 204: 253.

18. "Ut omnes simul ecclesias unius Catholicae inveniatur ambitus continere"; Geoffrey of Auxerre, *Sermo ad praelatos in concilio convocatos, PL* 184: 1101.

19. "Non humana praesumptio, sed timor Dei, ne exigua haec Cisterciensis Ordinis rota ad nihilum nobis posset ultra prodesse, si non esset rota in media rotae"; "Nihil enim ad aeternam animarum salutem, pro qua Deo vivimus, et custodire decrevimus vias duras, prodesset monastica conversatio, si ecclesiastica nobis communio non adesset. Sed neque illud dubium, quod nequeat membrum illud esse de corpore, quod noluerit esse sub capite." Ibid., *PL* 184: 1101.

20. "In concilio de scismate," B.N. n.a. lat. 1476, ff. 89r–90v. See also Leclercq, "Le témoignage," pp. 197–98.

Bibliography

MANUSCRIPT SOURCES

Aube, Archives Départementales

3 H 9: Cartulary, Clairvaux
3 H 10: Cartulary, Clairvaux
4 H 1: Cartulary, L'Arrivour

Côte d'Or, Archives Départementales

11 H 9: Cartulary 210, Fontenay
11 H 63: Cartulary 169, Cîteaux
11 H 64: Cartulary 166, Cîteaux
11 H 881: Notice, Cîteaux
12 H 36: Charters, Bussière

Haute Marne, Archives Départementales

1 H 4: Cartulary, Auberive
3 H 2: Charters, Boulancourt
6 H 2: Cartulary, Longuay
8 H 1: Pancarte, Morimond
8 H 22: Charters, Morimond
8 H 27: Pancarte, Morimond

Paris, Bibliothèque Nationale

MS lat. 3301c: Sermons, Hugh, abbot of Pontigny
MS lat. 3338: Exempla and miracles from Clairvaux
MS lat. 5468: Cartulary, Vauluisant
MS lat. 9874: Cartulary, Saint-Seine
MS lat. 9887: Cartulary, Pontigny
MS lat. 9901: Cartulary, Vauluisant

MS lat. 11867: Letter collection attributed to Master Transmundus
MS lat. 12824: Cartulary of Saint-Seine
MS lat 14859. Sermon by anonymous Cistercian abbot, translated into Latin by Alan of Lille
MS lat. 15912: Collection of moral examples
MS lat. 17100: Cartulary, Saint Mammes of Langres
MS lat. 18178: Geoffrey of Auxerre, *Sermones de tempore*
MS n.a. lat. 1476: Sermons, Geoffrey of Auxerre
MS n.a. lat. 18373: Cartulary, Foigny

Troyes, Bibliothèque Municipale

MS lat. 503: Sermons, Geoffrey of Auxerre
MS lat. 893: Letter collection attributed to Master Transmundus
MS lat. 946: *Liber visionum et miraculorum*

PRINTED SOURCES

Achery, Luc d'. *Spicilegium; sive Collectio veterum aliquot scriptorum qui in Galliae bibliothecis delituerant.* Paris, 1723. Reprint, Farnborough, Eng., 1967–68.
Aelred of Rievaulx. *Dialogue on the Soul.* Trans. C. H. Talbot. CFS, 22. Kalamazoo, Mich., 1981.
————. *Genealogia regum Anglorum. PL* 195: 711–38.
————. *The Mirror of Charity.* Trans. Elizabeth Connor. CFS, 17. Kalamazoo, Mich., 1990.
————. *Opera omnia: Opera ascetica.* Ed. A. Hoste and C. H. Talbot. *CCCM* 1. Turnhout, 1971.
————. *Opera omnia: Sermones I–XLVI.* Ed. Gaetano Raciti. *CCCM* 2a. Turnhout, 1979.
————. *Sermones de oneribus. PL* 195: 361–501.
————. *Sermones inediti B. Aelredi abbatis Rievallensis.* Ed. C. H. Talbot. Series Scriptorum S. Ordinis Cisterciensis 1. Rome, 1952.
————. *Spiritual Friendship.* Trans. Mary Eugenia Laker. CFS, 5. Washington, D.C., 1974.
————. *Vita s. Edwardi regis. PL* 195: 737–90.
Alan of Auxerre. *Epistolae et chartae. PL* 201: 1385–88.
————. *S. Bernardi vita secunda. PL* 185: 469–524.
Alcuin. *De virtutibus et vitiis. PL* 101: 613–58.
Alexander III. *Epistolae et privilegia. PL* 200: 69–1466.
Amadeus of Lausanne. *De laudibus beatae Mariae/Huit homélies Mariales.* Ed. Jean Deshusses, trans. into French by Antoine Dumas. *SC* 72. Paris, 1960.
Arbaumont, J. d', ed. *Cartulaire du prieuré de Saint-Etienne de Vignory.* Langres, 1882.

Arnold of Bonneval. *S. Bernardi vita prima.* Book 2. *PL* 185: 267–302.

Augustine of Hippo. *The City of God.* Trans. Henry Bettenson. Harmondsworth, Eng., 1972.

———. *Confessions.* Trans. R. S. Pine-Coffin. Harmondsworth, Eng., 1961.

———. *De doctrina christiana.* In *Oeuvres de Saint Augustin*, 11: 168–541. Ed. and trans. into French by G. Combès and J. Farges. Paris, 1949.

———. *The Literal Meaning of Genesis.* 2 vols. Trans. John Hammond Taylor. New York, 1982.

Baldwin of Ford. *Spiritual Tractates.* 2 vols. Trans. David N. Bell. CFS, 38, 41. Kalamazoo, Mich., 1986.

———. *Tractatus varii. PL* 204: 403–572.

Benedict of Nursia. *Regula Benedicti.* In Timothy Fry, ed., *RB 80: The Rule of Saint Benedict in Latin and English.* Collegeville, Minn., 1981.

Bernard, Auguste, ed. *Cartulaire de l'abbaye de Savigny.* Paris, 1853.

Bernard of Clairvaux. "Cistercians and Cluniacs: St. Bernard's *Apologia* to Abbot William." Trans. M. Casey. In *Treatises I*, pp. 33–69. CFS, 1. Spencer, Mass., 1970.

———. *Five Books on Consideration: Advice to a Pope.* Trans. John D. Anderson and Elizabeth T. Kennan. CFS, 37. Kalamazoo, Mich., 1976.

———. *The Letters of St. Bernard of Clairvaux.* Trans. B. S. James. Chicago, 1953.

———. "In Praise of the New Knighthood." Trans. Conrad Greenia. In *Treatises III*, pp. 127–67. CFS, 19. Kalamazoo, Mich., 1977.

———. *The Life and Death of St. Malachy the Irishman.* Trans. Robert T. Meyer. CFS, 10. Kalamazoo, Mich., 1978.

———. "Monastic Obligations and Authority: St. Bernard's Book on Precept and Dispensation." Trans. Conrad Greenia. In *Treatises I*, pp. 103–50. CFS, 1. Spencer, Mass., 1970.

———. "On Grace and Free Choice." Trans. Daniel O'Donovan. In *Treatises III*, pp. 53–111. CFS, 19. Kalamazoo, Mich., 1977.

———. "On Loving God." Trans. Robert Walton. In *Treatises II*, pp. 93–132. CFS, 13. Kalamazoo, Mich., 1973.

———. *S. Bernardi opera.* Ed. Jean Leclercq, C. H. Talbot, N. M. Rochais. 8 vols. Editiones Cistercienses. Rome, 1957–77.

———. *Sermons on Conversion.* Trans. M.-B. Saïd. CFS, 25. Kalamazoo, Mich., 1981.

———. "The Steps of Humility and Pride." Trans. M. Ambrose Conway. In *Treatises II*, pp. 25–82. CFS, 13. Kalamazoo, Mich., 1973.

Besson, Joseph. *Mémoires pour l'histoire ecclésiastique des diocèses de Genève, Tarentaise, Aoste, Maurienne et du décanat de Savoye.* New ed. Moutiers, 1871.

Bethell, D. L. "An Unpublished Letter of St. Stephen Harding." *Downside Review* 79 (1961): 349–50.

Bligny, Bernard, ed. *Recueil des plus anciens actes de la Grande-Chartreuse, 1086–1196.* Grenoble, 1958.

Bourrier, M., ed. *Chartes de l'abbaye de Saint-Etienne de Dijon de 1140 à 1155.* Dijon, 1912.

Bouton, Jean de la Croix, and Jean Baptiste Van Damme, eds. *Les plus anciens textes de Cîteaux.* Achel, 1974.

Caesarius of Heisterbach. *The Dialogue on Miracles.* 2 vols. Trans. H. von E. Scott and C. C. Swinton Bland. London, 1929.

Canat de Chizy, Paul, ed. *Cartulaire du prieuré de Saint-Marcel-lès-Châlon.* Châlon-sur-Saône, 1894.

Canivez, Joseph Marie, ed. *Statuta capitulorum generalium ordinis cisterciensis ab anno 1116 ad annum 1786,* 1, *1116–1220.* Louvain, 1933.

Carta caritatis prior. In Jean de la Croix Bouton and Jean Baptiste Van Damme, eds., *Les plus anciens textes de Cîteaux,* 89–102. Achel, 1974.

Charmasse, Anatole de, ed. *Cartulaire de l'église d'Autun.* Paris, 1865.

———. *Cartulaire de l'évêché d'Autun.* Paris, 1880.

Chartraire, Eugène, ed. *Cartulaire du Chapitre de Sens.* Société Archéologique de Sens. Documents 3. Sens, 1904.

Chevalier, Cyr Ulysse-Joseph, ed. *Cartulaire du prieuré de Paray-le-Monial.* Paris, 1890.

Chevrier, Georges, and Maurice Chaume, eds. *Chartes et documents de Saint Bénigne de Dijon.* Dijon, 1943.

Chrétien de Troyes. *Erec and Enide.* Ed. and trans. Carleton W. Carroll. Garland Library of Medieval Literature 25. New York, 1987.

———. *The Knight with the Lion, or Yvain.* Ed. and trans. William W. Kibler. New York, 1985.

Chronicon Clarevallense. PL 185: 1247–52.

Chronicon Mauriniacensi. RHGF 12: 68–88. Paris, 1882.

Conrad of Eberbach. *Exordium magnum cisterciense.* Ed. Bruno Griesser. Series Scriptorum S. Ordinis Cisterciensis 2. Rome, 1961.

Decrees of the Ecumenical Councils, 1. Ed. Norman P. Tanner. London, 1990.

Dimier, Anselme. *Bibliographie générale de l'ordre cistercien: Recueil de textes pour servir à l'histoire de S. Pierre II de Tarentaise.* Documentation Cistercienne 21. Rochefort, 1978.

———. "Un témoin tardif peu connu du conflit entre Cisterciens et Clunisiens." In G. Constable and J. Kritzeck, eds., *Petrus Venerabilis, 1156–1956,* pp. 81–94. Studia Anselmiana 40. Rome, 1956.

Diversorum ad S. Bernardum et alios. PL 182: 675–716.

Duby, Georges. *Recueil des pancartes de l'abbaye de la Ferté-sur-Grosne (1113–1178).* Annales de la Faculté des Lettres, n.s. 3. Aix-en-Provence, 1953.

Eugenius III. *Epistolae et privilegia. PL* 180: 1013–1606.

Exordium cistercii et summa cartae caritatis. In Jean de la Croix Bouton and Jean Baptiste Van Damme, eds., *Les plus anciens textes de Cîteaux,* pp. 110–25. Achel, 1974.

Exordium parvum. In Jean de la Croix Bouton and Jean Baptiste Van Damme, eds., *Les plus anciens textes de Cîteaux,* pp. 54–86. Achel, 1974.

Fyot de la Marche, Claude. *Histoire de l'église abbatiale et collégiale de Saint Estienne de Dijon.* Dijon, 1696.

Gallia Christiana in provincias ecclesiasticas distributa. Ed. Dionysii Sammarthani. Paris, 1715–1865. Reprint, Gregg Press, 1970.

Garrigues, Martine. *Le premier cartulaire de l'abbaye cistercienne de Pontigny (XIIe–XIIIe s.).* Collection de documents inédits sur l'histoire de France 14. Paris, 1981.

Geoffrey of Auxerre. *Expositio in cantica canticorum.* 2 vols. Ed. Ferruccio Gastaldelli. Temi e Testi 19–20. Rome, 1974.

———. "Les *Fragmenta de vita et miraculis s. Bernardi.*" *Analecta Bollandiana* 50 (1932): 83–122.

———. *Libellus de condemnatione errorum Gilberti Porretani. PL* 185: 587–618.

———. *Libellus contra capitula Gisleberti episcopi Pictavensis.* In N. M. Häring, "The Writings Against Gilbert of Poitiers by Geoffrey of Auxerre." *Analecta Cisterciensia* 22 (1966): 3–83.

———. "Quattro sermoni 'ad abbates' di Goffredo di Auxerre." Ed. F. Gastaldelli. *Cîteaux* 34 (1983): 161–200.

———. *S. Bernardi vita prima.* Books 3–6. *PL* 185: 301–68, 395–416.

———. *Sermo ad praelatos in concilio convocatos. PL* 184: 1095–1102.

———. "Tre sermoni di Goffredo di Auxerre su San Benedetto." In F. Gastaldelli, "Regola, spiritualità e crisi dell'ordine cisterciense in tre sermoni di Goffredo di Auxerre su San Benedetto." *Cîteaux* 31 (1980): 193–225.

———. *Vita sancti Petri archiepiscopi Tarentasiensi. AASS,* Mai 2: 320–35.

Gerald of Wales. *De principis instructione.* Ed. George F. Warner. Rolls Series 21.8. London, 1891.

———. *Speculum ecclesiae.* Ed. J. S. Brewer, J. F. Dimock, and G. F. Warner. Rolls Series 21. London, 1861–91.

Gervase of Canterbury. *Chronica.* 2 vols. Rolls Series 73. London, 1879.

Gesta concilio Trencensi. RHGF 14: 231–33. Paris, 1882.

Gesta pontificum Autissiodorensium. In L. M. Duru, ed., *Bibliothèque historique de l'Yonne,* 1. Auxerre, 1850.

Gestis pontificum Cenomannensium. RHGF 12: 539–57. Paris, 1882.

Gilbert Foliot. *The Letters and Charters of Gilbert Foliot.* Ed. Z. N. Brooke, Adrian Morey, C. N. L. Brooke. Cambridge, Eng., 1967.

Gilbert of Hoyland. *Epistolae. PL* 184: 289–98.

———. *Sermones in canticum Salomonis. PL* 184: 11–252.

———. *Sermons on the Song of Songs.* 3 vols. Trans. Lawrence C. Braceland. CFS, 14, 20, 26. Kalamazoo, Mich., 1978–79.

———. *Tractatus ascetici. PL* 184: 251–98.

———. *Treatises, Epistles, and Sermons.* Trans. Lawrence C. Braceland. CFS, 34. Kalamazoo, Mich., 1981.

Gregory the Great. *Dialogues.* 3 vols. Ed. Adalbert de Vogüé. Trans. into French by Paul Antin. *SC* 251. Paris, 1978–80.

———. *Homélies sur Ezéchiel.* Ed. and trans. into French by Charles Morel. *SC* 327. Paris, 1986.

———. *Regulae pastoralis/Règle pastorale.* 2 vols. Ed. and trans. into French by Floribert Rommel and Charles Morel. *SC* 382. Paris, 1992.

Griesser, Bruno. "Die *'Ecclesiastica officia Cisterciensis ordinis'* des Cod. 1711 von Trient." *ASOC* 12 (1956): 10–288.

Guerric of Igny. *Liturgical Sermons.* 2 vols. Trans. Monks of Mount Saint Bernard Abbey. CFS, 8, 32. Spencer, Mass., 1970–71.

———. *Sermons.* 2 vols. Ed. John Morson and Hilary Costello. Trans. into French by Placide Deseille. *SC* 166, 202. Paris, 1970–73.

Guesnon, A., ed. "Le cartulaire de l'évêché d'Arras, analysé chronologiquement." *Mémoires de l'Académie des sciences, lettres et arts d'Arras.* 2d ser., 33 (1902): 165–323.

Guido I, prior of La Chartreuse. *Consuetudines cartusiae / Coutumes de Chartreuse.* Ed. and trans. into French by a Chartreux. *SC* 313. Paris, 1984.

Guignard, Philippe, ed. *Les monuments primitifs de la règle cistercienne.* Dijon, 1878.

Henry of Marcy. *Epistolae. PL* 204: 215–52.

———. *Tractatus de peregrinante civitate dei. PL* 204: 251–402.

Herbert of Clairvaux. *De miraculis. PL* 185: 1271–1384.

Hugh of Saint Victor. *De sacramentis christianae fidei. PL* 176: 173–618.

Humbert of Moyenmoutier. *Adversus simoniacos libri tres. PL* 143: 1007–12.

Idung of Prüfening. *Cistercians and Cluniacs: The Case for Cîteaux.* Trans. Jeremiah F. O'Sullivan. CFS, 33. Kalamazoo, Mich., 1977.

———. *Dialogus duorum monachum.* Ed. R. B. Huygens. Spoleto, 1980.

Innocent II. *Epistolae et privilegia. PL* 179: 53–674.

Isaac of Stella. *Letter on the Soul.* Trans. Bernard McGinn. In Bernard McGinn, ed., *Three Treatises on Man: A Cistercian Anthropology,* pp. 155–77. CFS, 24. Kalamazoo, Mich., 1977.

———. *Sermons.* 3 vols. Ed. Anselm Hoste and Gaetano Raciti. Trans. into French by Gaston Salet and Gaetano Raciti. *SC* 130, 207, 339. Paris, 1967–87.

————. *Sermons on the Christian Year*, 1. Trans. Hugh McCaffery. CFS, 11. Kalamazoo, Mich., 1979.

Jaffé, Philip. *Regesta pontificum Romanorum*. Ed. S. Löwenfeld, R. Kaltenbrunner, and P. Ewald. Leipzig, 1885–88.

John (bishop of Orléans). *De institutione laicali*. PL 106: 121–278.

John of Lodi. *Vita Petri Damiani*. PL 144: 113–46.

John of Salisbury. *Historia pontificalis*. Ed. and trans. Marjorie Chibnall. Edinburgh, 1956.

————. *Policraticus, sive De nugis curialum et vestigiis philosophorum*. 2 vols. Ed. C. C. J. Webb. Oxford, 1909.

Lalore, Charles, ed. *Chartes de l'abbaye de Mores*. Troyes, 1873.

————. *Collection des principaux cartulaires du diocèse de Troyes*. 7 vols. Paris, 1875–90.

Lanfranc. *The Monastic Constitutions*. Ed. and trans. David Knowles. London, 1951.

Laurent, Jacques. *Cartulaires de l'abbaye de Molesme: 916–1250*. Paris, 1907.

Leclercq, Jean, ed. "Lettres d'Odon d'Ourscamp: Cardinal Cistercien." *Studia Anselmiana* 36 (1955): 145–57.

Lettres des premiers Chartreux. 2 vols. Ed. and trans. into French by a Chartreux. SC 10, 274. Paris, 1962, 1980.

Libellus de diuersis ordinibus et professionibus qui sunt in aecclesia. Ed. and trans. Giles Constable and Bernard Smith. Oxford, 1972.

Loisne, Auguste Menche de, ed. *Le cartulaire du chapitre d'Arras*. Arras, 1896.

Longère, J., ed. "Un sermon inédit d'Odon de Soissons." *Cîteaux* 31 (1980): 163–80.

Lucius III. *Epistolae et privilegia*. PL 201: 1071–1376.

McGinn, Bernard, ed. *Three Treatises on Man: A Cistercian Anthropology*. CFS, 24. Kalamazoo, Mich., 1977.

Mansi, Joannes Dominic. *Sacrorum conciliorum nova et amplissima collectio*. Paris, 1903. Reprint, Graz, Austria, 1960–61.

Marie de France. *The Lays of Marie de France*. Trans. Robert Hanning and Joan Ferrante. Durham, N.C., 1978.

Marlier, J., ed. *Chartes et documents concernant l'abbaye de Cîteaux, 1098–1198*. Rome, 1969.

Martin, Jean Baptiste, ed. *Conciles et bullaire du diocèse de Lyon*. Lyon, 1905.

Meyer, Paul, ed. *L'histoire de Guillaume le Maréchal*. 3 vols. Société de l'histoire de la France. Paris, 1891–1901.

Nicholas of Clairvaux. *Epistolae*. PL 196: 1593–1654.

Orderic Vitalis. *Historia aecclesiastica / The Ecclesiastical History of Orderic Vitalis*. Ed. and trans. Marjorie Chibnall. Oxford, 1973.

Otloh of Saint Emmeram. *De doctrina spirituali*. PL 146: 263–300.

Otto of Freising. *Chronica sive historia de duabus civitatibus*. Ed. Adolf Hofmeister. Hannover, 1912.

———. *The Deeds of Frederick Barbarossa*. Trans. Charles Christopher Mierow. New York, 1953.

———. *The Two Cities: A Chronicle of Universal History to the Year 1146 A.D.* Trans. Charles Christopher Mierow, ed. Austin P. Evans and Charles Knapp. New York, 1928.

Peter Abelard. *Historia calamitatum*. Ed. J. Monfrin. Paris, 1967.

Peter Damian. *De fuga dignitatum ecclesiasticarum*. *PL* 145: 455–64.

———. *Liber Gomorrhianus/Book of Gomorrah*. Trans. Pierre Payer. Waterloo, Ont., 1982.

———. *Vita beati Romualdi*. Ed. Giovanni Tabacco. Istituto Storico Italiano per il Medio Evo 94. Rome, 1957.

Peter Monoculus, *Epistolae*. *PL* 201: 1393–1404.

Peter of Celles. *Epistolae*. *PL* 202: 405–636.

Peter of Saint Chrysogonus. *Epistolae*. *PL* 199: 1119–24.

Peter the Venerable. *The Letters of Peter the Venerable*. 2 vols. Ed. Giles Constable. Cambridge, Mass., 1967.

———. *De miraculis libri duo*. Ed. Dyonisia Bouthiellier. *CCCM* 83. Turnhout, 1988.

———. *Statuta Petri Venerabilis*. Ed. Giles Constable with J. D. Brady and D. C. Waddell. In *Consuetudines Benedictinae variae*. Corpus Consuetudinum Monasticarum 6. Sieburg, 1975.

———. *Tractatus contra petrobrusianos*. Ed. James Fearns. *CCCM* 10. Turnhout, 1968.

Poulalier, Adrien Bièvre, ed. *Chartes de l'abbaye de Saint-Etienne de Dijon de 1098 à 1140*. Dijon, 1912.

Quantin, Maximilien, ed. *Cartulaire général de l'Yonne*. 3 vols. Auxerre, 1854–73.

———. *Recueil de pièces par faire suite au Cartulaire général de l'Yonne*. Auxerre, 1873.

Radice, B., trans. *The Letters of Abelard and Heloise*. Harmondsworth, Eng., 1974.

Robertson, James Craigie, ed. *Materials for the History of Thomas of Becket, Archbishop of Canterbury*. 7 vols. Rolls Series 67. London, 1875–85.

Rupert of Deutz. *Super quaedam capitula regulae divi Benedicti abbatis*. *PL* 170: 477–538.

S. Joannis Gualberti vita. *PL* 146: 667–706.

Sigebert of Gembloux. *Chronica et continuato*. *Monumenta Germaniae Historia Scriptores* 6: 300–90. Hannover, 1844.

Spahr, Kolumban. *Das Leben des hl. Robert von Molesme: Eine Quelle zur Vorgeschichte von Cîteaux*. Fribourg, Switzerland, 1944.

Stephen (bishop of Paris). *Epistolae*. *PL* 173: 1411–20.

Suger of Saint-Denis. *Vie de Louis VI le Gros.* Ed. and trans. into French by Henri Waquet. Paris, 1964.

——. *Epistolae. PL* 186: 1347–1440.

Ulrich. *Antiquiores consuetudines Cluniacensis monasterii. PL* 149: 643–778.

Vita beati Bernardi fundatoris congregationis de Tironio in Gallia. PL 172: 1367–1446.

Vita s. Johannis Valentinensis episcopi. In Edmund Martene and Ursinus Durand, eds., *Thesaurus novus anecdotorum* 3. 1693–1702. Paris, 1714. Reprint, New York, 1968.

Vita s. Petri prioris Juliacensis puellarum monasterii, et monachi Molesmensis. PL 185: 1257–70.

Walter Daniel. *The Life of Ailred of Rievaulx.* Trans. F. M. Powicke. New York, 1951.

Walter Map. *De nugis curialium.* Ed. and trans. M. R. James, rev. C. N. L. Brooke and R. A. B. Mynors. Oxford, 1983.

Waquet, Jean. *Recueil de chartes de l'abbaye de Clairvaux.* Troyes, 1950.

William of Malmesbury. *De gestis regum Anglorum libri quinque.* 2 vols. Ed. William Stubbs. Rolls Series 90. London, 1887–89.

——. *Historia novella.* Ed. William Stubbs. Rolls Series 90.2. London, 1889.

William of Newburgh. *Historia rerum Anglicarum.* Ed. Richard Howlett. Rolls Series 82.1. London, 1884.

William of Saint-Thierry. *Exposition on the Song of Songs.* Trans. Columba Hart. CFS, 6. Spencer, Mass., 1970.

——. *The Golden Epistle: A Letter to the Brethren at Mont Dieu.* Trans. Theodore Berkeley. CFS, 12. Spencer, Mass., 1971.

——. *De natura corporis et animae. PL* 180: 695–726.

——. *Expositio in canticum canticorum.* Ed. J.-M. Déchanet. *SC* 82. Paris, 1962.

——. "The Nature of the Body and Soul." Trans. Benjamin Clark. In Bernard McGinn, ed., *Three Treatises on Man*, pp. 103–52. CFS, 24. Kalamazoo, Mich., 1977.

——. *On Contemplating God.* In *The Works of William of St. Thierry* 1. Trans. Sister Penelope. CFS, 3. Spencer, Mass., 1971.

——. *S. Bernardi vita prima.* Book 1. *PL* 185: 225–68.

Wilmart, André. "Une riposte de l'ancien monachisme au manifeste de Saint Bernard." *Revue Bénédictine* 46 (1934): 296–344.

SECONDARY SOURCES

Alfonso, Isabel. "Cistercians and Feudalism." *Past and Present* 133 (1991): 3–30.

Alverny, Marie-Thérèse d'. *Alain de Lille: Textes inédits.* Paris, 1965.

Amélineau, E. "Saint Bernard et le schisme d'Anaclet II (1130–1138)." *Revue des questions historiques* 30 (1881): 47–112.

Anciaux, Paul. *La théologie du sacrement de pénitence au XIIe siècle.* Louvain, 1949.

Arbois de Jubainville, M. H. d'. *Etudes sur l'état intérieur des abbayes cisterciennes, et principalement de Clairvaux au XIIe et XIIIe siècle.* Paris, 1858.

Auberger, Jean-Baptiste. *L'unanimité cistercienne primitive: Mythe ou réalité?* Cîteaux: Studia et Documenta 3. Achel, 1986.

Aubert, Marcel. *L'architecture cistercienne en France.* Paris, 1943.

Auerbach, Erich. *Mimesis: The Representation of Reality in Western Literature.* Trans. Willard R. Trask. Princeton, 1953.

Baker, Derek. "'*Viri religiosi*' and the York Election Dispute." In G. J. Cuming and Derek Baker, eds., *Councils and Assemblies*, pp. 87–100. Studies in Church History 7. Cambridge, Eng., 1971.

Baldwin, John W. *The Government of Philip Augustus.* Berkeley, 1986.

———. "Masters at Paris from 1179 to 1215: A Social Perspective." In Robert L. Benson and Giles Constable, eds., *Renaissance and Renewal in the Twelfth-Century*, pp. 138–72. Cambridge, Mass., 1982.

———. *Masters, Princes and Merchants: The Social Views of Peter the Chanter and His Circle.* Princeton, 1970.

Barber, Malcolm. "The Origins of the Order of the Temple." *Studia Monastica* 12 (1970): 219–40.

Barlow, Frank. *Thomas Becket.* London, 1986.

Barraclough, Geoffrey. *The Medieval Papacy.* New York, 1968.

Bartlett, Robert. *Trial by Fire and Water: The Medieval Judicial Ordeal.* New York, 1986.

Batany, Jean. "Les moines blancs dans les états du monde." *Cîteaux* 15 (1964): 5–25.

Beck, Hans-Georg, et al. *From the High Middle Ages to the Eve of the Reformation.* Vol. 4 of *Handbook of Church History.* Trans. A. Biggs. New York, 1970.

Bedos-Rezak, Brigitte. "Diplomatic Sources and Medieval Documentary Practices: An Essay in Interpretive Methodology." In John Van Engen, ed., *The Past and Future of Medieval Studies.* South Bend, Ind., 1994.

Bell, Daniel N. "Heaven on Earth: Celestial and Cenobitic Unity in the Thought of Baldwin of Ford." In E. Rozanne Elder, ed., *Heaven on Earth*, pp. 1–21. CSS, 68. Kalamazoo, Mich., 1983.

Belotte, Michel. "Les possessions des évêques de Langres dans la région de Mussy-sur-Seine et de Châtillon-sur-Seine du milieu du XIIe au milieu du XIVe siècle." *Annales de Bourgogne* 37 (1965): 170–71.

Benson, Robert L. *The Bishop-Elect: A Study in Medieval Ecclesiastical Office.* Princeton, 1968.

Benton, John F. "Consciousness of Self and Perceptions of Individuality." In

Robert L. Benson and Giles Constable, eds., *Renaissance and Renewal in the Twelfth Century*, pp. 263–95. Cambridge, Mass., 1982.

————. *Self and Society in Medieval France: The Memoirs of Abbot Guibert of Nogent.* New York, 1970.

Berlière, Ursmer. "L'exercice du ministère paroissial par les moines dans le haut moyen-âge." *Révue Bénédictine* 39 (1927): 227–50.

————. "Les fraternités monastiques et leur rôle juridique." *Mémoires de l'Academie Royale de Belgique.* 2d ser. 11, no. 3 (1920): 1–20.

————. *L'ordre monastique des origines au XIIe siècle.* Lille, 1924.

Berman, Constance H. "The Foundation and Early History of the Monastery of Silvanès: The Economic Reality." In John R. Sommerfeldt, ed., *Cistercian Ideals and Reality*, pp. 280–318. CSS, 60. Kalamazoo, Mich., 1978.

————. "The Development of Cistercian Economic Practice During the Lifetime of Bernard of Clairvaux: The Historical Perspective on Innocent II's 1132 Privilege." In John R. Sommerfeldt, ed., *Bernardus Magister*, pp. 303–13. CSS, 135. Spencer, Mass., 1992.

————. *Medieval Agriculture, the Southern French Countryside and the Early Cistercians.* Transactions of the American Philosophical Society 76. Philadelphia, 1986.

————. "Origins of the Filiation of Morimond in Southern France: Redating Foundation Charters of Gimont, Villelongue, Berdoues, L'Escaledieu, and Bonnefort." *Cîteaux: Commentarii cistercienses* 41 (1990): 256–77.

Bernard de Clairvaux. Commission d'Histoire de l'Ordre de Cîteaux. Paris, 1953.

Bernard de Clairvaux: Histoire, mentalités, spiritualité. SC 380. Paris, 1992.

Bernard of Clairvaux: Studies Presented to Dom Jean Leclercq. CSS, 23. Washington, D.C., 1973.

Bernhardi, Wilhelm. *Lothar von Supplinburg.* Berlin, 1879. Reprint, 1975.

Bienvenu, Jean-Marc. *L'étonnant fondateur de Fontevraud: Robert d'Arbrissel.* Paris, 1981.

Biersack, Aletta. "Local Knowledge, Local History: Geertz and Beyond." In Lynn Hunt, ed., *The New Cultural History*, pp. 87–91. Berkeley, 1989.

Blake, E. O. "The Formation of the 'Crusade Idea.'" *Journal of Ecclesiastical History* 21 (1970): 11–31.

Bligny, Bernard. *Saint Bruno: Le premier chartreux.* Rennes, 1984.

Bloch, Herbert. "The Schism of Anacletus II and the Glanfeuil Forgeries of Peter the Deacon of Monte Cassino." *Traditio* 8 (1952): 159–264.

Bloch, Marc. *Feudal Society.* Trans. L. A. Manyon. 2 vols. Chicago, 1961.

Bolton, Brenda. *The Medieval Reformation.* London, 1983.

Bouchard, Constance Brittain. "Cistercian Ideals versus Reality: 1134 Reconsidered." *Cîteaux: Commentarii cistercienses* 39 (1988): 217–31.

————. *Holy Entrepreneurs: Cistercians, Knights, and Economic Exchange in Twelfth-Century Burgundy.* Ithaca, 1991.

————. "Merovingian, Carolingian and Cluniac Monasticism: Reform and Renewal in Burgundy." *Journal of Ecclesiastical History* 41 (1990): 365–88.

————. "The Origins of the French Nobility: A Reassessment." *American Historical Review* 86 (1981): 501–32.

————. *Spirituality and Administration: The Role of the Bishop in Twelfth-Century Auxerre.* Speculum Anniversary Monographs 5. Cambridge, Mass., 1979.

————. *Sword, Miter, and Cloister: Nobility and the Church in Burgundy, 980–1198.* Ithaca, 1987.

————. "Twelfth-Century Burgundy: The Great Unknown?" In Francis R. Swietek and John R. Sommerfeldt, eds., *Studiosorum Speculum: Studies in Honor of Louis J. Lekai, O.Cist.,* pp. 33–51. CSS, 141. Kalamazoo, Mich., 1993.

Bourgain, Louis. *La chaire française au XIIe siècle d'après les manuscrits.* Paris, 1879.

Bouton, Jean de la Croix. *Bibliographie Bernardine 1891–1957.* Paris, 1958.

Bredero, Adriaan Hendrick. "The Canonization of Bernard of Clairvaux." In John R. Sommerfeldt, ed., *Cistercian Ideals and Reality,* pp. 80–105. CSS, 60. Kalamazoo, Mich., 1978.

————. *Cluny et Cîteaux au douzième siècle: L'histoire d'une controverse monastique.* Amsterdam, 1985.

————. "Etudes sur la *Vita prima* de Saint Bernard." *ASOC* 17 (1961): 3–72, 215–60; 18 (1962): 3–59.

————. "Saint Bernard and the Historians." In M. Basil Pennington, ed., *St. Bernard of Clairvaux,* pp. 27–62. CSS, 28. Kalamazoo, Mich., 1977.

————. "Saint Bernard in His Relations with Peter the Venerable." In John R. Sommerfeldt, ed., *Bernardus Magister,* pp. 315–47. CSS, 135. Spencer, Mass., 1992.

Brooke, Christopher. *The Monastic World 1000–1300.* London, 1974.

Brown, Peter. *Augustine of Hippo.* London, 1967.

————. *The Body and Society: Men, Women and Sexual Renunciation in Early Christianity.* New York, 1988.

————. "The Rise and Function of the Holy Man in Late Antiquity." *Journal of Roman Studies* 41 (1971): 80–101.

————. "Society and the Supernatural: A Medieval Change." *Daedalus* 104 (1975): 133–51.

Bulliot, Jacques Gabriel. *Essai historique sur l'abbaye de Saint-Martin d'Autun de l'ordre de Saint-Benoît.* Autun, 1849.

Bur, Michel. *La formation du comté de Champagne v. 950–v. 1150.* Nancy, 1977.

Burnaby, John. *Amor Dei: Study of the Religion of St. Augustine.* London, 1938.

Burns, J. H., ed. *The Cambridge History of Medieval Political Thought, c.350–c.1450.* Cambridge, Eng., 1988.

Butler, Edward Cuthbert. *Benedictine Monachism*. London, 1919.

Bynum, Caroline Walker. *Docere verbo et exemplo: An Aspect of Twelfth-Century Spirituality*. Harvard Theological Studies 31. Missoula, Mont., 1979.

———. *Fragmentation and Redemption: Essays on Gender and the Human Body in Medieval Religion*. New York, 1991.

———. *Holy Feast and Holy Fast: The Religious Significance of Food to Medieval Women*. Berkeley, 1987.

———. *Jesus as Mother: Studies in the Spirituality of the High Middle Ages*. Berkeley, 1982.

Cantor, N. F. "The Crisis of Western Monasticism." *American Historical Review* 66 (1960): 47–67.

Casey, Michael. *Athirst for God: Spiritual Desire in Bernard of Clairvaux's Sermons on the Song of Songs*. CSS, 77. Kalamazoo, Mich., 1988.

Chaume, Maurice. "Les origines familiales de Saint Bernard." In *Saint Bernard et son temps*, pp. 75–112. Association bourguignonne des sociétés savantes, Congrès de 1927. Dijon, 1928.

Chauvin, R. "Réalités et évolution de l'économie cistercienne dans le duché et comté de Bourgogne au moyen âge: essai de synthèse." In *L'économie cistercienne: Géographie—mutations du moyen âge aux temps moderns*, pp. 13–52. Flaran 3. Auch, 1983.

Cheney, Mary G. "The Recognition of Pope Alexander III: Some Neglected Evidence." *English Historical Review* 84 (1969): 474–97.

Chenu, Marie-Dominique. *Nature, Man and Society in the Twelfth Century*. Ed. and trans. Jerome Taylor and Lester Little. Chicago, 1968.

Chodorow, Stanley. *Christian Political Theory and Church Politics in the Mid-Twelfth Century: The Ecclesiology of Gratian's Decretum*. Berkeley, 1972.

Clair, R. "Saint Pierre de Tarentaise et Saint Amédée de Lausanne." *Cîteaux* 25 (1974): 287–98.

Clanchy, M. T. *From Memory to Written Record: England 1066–1307*. London, 1979.

Clerval, A. *Les écoles de Chartres au moyen âge*. Paris, 1895.

Congar, Yves. "L'ecclésiologie de S. Bernard." *ASOC* 9 (1953): 136–90.

———. "Henri de Marcy, abbé de Clairvaux, cardinal évêque d'Albano et légat pontifical." *Studia Anselmiana* 43 (1958): 1–90.

Constable, Giles. "Cluniac Tithes and the Controversy between Gigny and Le Miroir." *Revue Bénédictine* 70 (1960): 591–624.

———. "The Disputed Election at Langres in 1138." *Traditio* 13 (1957): 119–52.

———. "Eremitical Forms of Monastic Life." In *Instituzioni monastiche e instituzioni canonicali*. Miscellanea del Centro di studi medioevali 9. Milan, 1980.

———. "*Famuli* and *Conversi* at Cluny." *Revue Bénédictine* 83 (1973): 326–50.

————. "Monastic Legislation at Cluny in the Eleventh and Twelfth Centuries." In *Cluniac Studies*. Reprint, London, 1980.

————. "The Monastic Policy of Peter the Venerable." In *Pierre Abélard, Pierre le Vénérable*, pp. 119–42. Colloques Internationaux du Centre National de la Recherche Scientifique 546. Paris, 1975.

————. *Monastic Tithes from their Origins to the Twelfth Century*. Cambridge, Eng., 1964.

————. "Renewal and Reform in Religious Life." In Robert L. Benson and Giles Constable, eds., *Renaissance and Renewal in the Twelfth Century*, pp. 37–67. Cambridge, Mass., 1982.

————. "The Study of Monastic History Today." In Vaclav Mudroch and G. S. Couse, eds., *Essays on the Reconstruction of Medieval History*, pp. 21–52. Montreal, 1974.

Cowdrey, H. E. J. *The Age of Abbot Desiderius: Montecassino, the Papacy, and the Normans in the Eleventh and Early Twelfth Centuries*. Oxford, 1983.

————. *The Cluniacs and the Gregorian Reform*. Oxford, 1970.

————. "Legal Problems Raised by Agreements of Confraternity." In Karl Schmid and Joachim Wollasch, eds., *Memoria: Der Geschichtliche Zeugniswert des liturgischen Gedenkens im Mittelalter*, pp. 232–54. Munich, 1984.

————. "The Peace of God and the Truce of God in the Eleventh Century." *Past and Present* 46 (1970): 42–64.

————. " 'Quidem frater Stephanus nomine, angelicus natione': The English Background of Stephen Harding." *Revue Bénédictine* 101 (1991): 322–40.

Crozet, René. "L'épiscopat de France de l'ordre de Cîteaux au XIIe siècle." *Cahiers de civilisation médiévale* 18 (1975): 263–68.

Dalarun, Jacques. *L'impossible sainteté: La vie retrouvée de Robert d'Arbrissel (v. 1045–1116) fondateur de Fontevraud*. Paris, 1985.

Darnton, Robert. "The Symbolic Element in History." *Journal of Modern History* 58 (1986): 218–34.

Delatte, Paul. *Commentaire sur la règle de Saint Benoît*. Paris, 1913.

Delfgaauw, Pacifique. "La nature et les degrés de l'amour selon saint Bernard." In *Saint Bernard théologien: Actes du congrès de Dijon 15–19 septembre 1953*. *ASOC* 11 (1953): 234–52.

Dereine, Charles. "Odon de Tournai et la crise du cénobitisme au XIe siècle." *Revue du moyen âge latin* 4 (1948): 137–54.

Dimier, Anselme. *Amédée de Lausanne: Disciple de Saint Bernard*. Abbaye de Saint Wandrille, 1949.

————. "Architecture et spiritualité cisterciennes." *Revue du moyen âge* 3 (1947): 255–74.

————. *Les moines bâtisseurs: Architecture et vie monastique*. Paris, 1964.

————. "Mourir à Clairvaux!" *COCR* 17 (1955): 272–85.

————. "Saint Bernard et le recrutement de Clairvaux." *Revue Mabillon* 42 (1952): 17–30, 56–68, 69–78.

————. "Saint Pierre Ier de Tarentaise." *Cistercienser Chronik* 47 (1935): 1–7.

————. "Violences, rixes et homicides chez les Cisterciens." *Revue des sciences religieuses* 46 (1972): 38–57.

Dondaine, Antoine. "Aux origines du Valdéisme: Une profession de foi de Valdès." *Archivum fratrum praedicatorum* 16 (1946): 30–31.

Donkin, R. A. "Settlement and Depopulation on Cistercian Estates during the Twelfth and Thirteenth Centuries, especially in Yorkshire." *Bulletin of the Institute of Historical Research* 33 (1960): 141–65.

Donnelly, James. *The Decline of the Medieval Cistercian Laybrotherhood.* New York, 1949.

Dubois, Jacques. "L'institution des convers au XIIème s.: Forme de vie monastique propre aux laïcs." In *I laïci nella "Societas christiana" dei secoli XI e XII.* Miscellanea del Centro di studi medioevali 5. Milan, 1968.

Duby, Georges. *The Chivalrous Society.* Trans. Cynthia Postan. Berkeley, 1977.

————. "The Culture of the Knightly Class: Audience and Patronage." In Robert L. Benson and Giles Constable, eds., *Renaissance and Renewal in the Twelfth Century,* pp. 248–62. Cambridge, Mass., 1982.

————. *The Early Growth of the European Economy.* Trans. Howard Clarke. Ithaca, 1974.

————. "Economie domainale et économie monétaire: Le budget de l'abbaye de Cluny entre 1080 et 1135." *Annales E. S. C.* 7 (1952): 155–71.

————. *Rural Economy and Country Life in the Medieval West.* Trans. Cynthia Postan. Columbia, S.C., 1968.

————. *Saint Bernard: L'art cistercien.* Paris, 1976.

————. *La société aux XIe et XIIe siècles dans la région mâconnaise.* Paris, 1953.

————. *The Three Orders: Feudal Society Imagined.* Trans. Arthur Goldhammer. Chicago, 1980.

————. *William Marshal: The Flower of Chivalry.* Trans. Richard Howard. New York, 1985.

Ducourneau, J. Othon. "De l'institution et des *Us* des convers dans l'ordre de Cîteaux." In *Saint Bernard et son temps,* pp. 139–201. Association bourguignonne des sociétés savantes, Congrès de 1927. Dijon, 1928.

————. "Les origines cisterciennes." *Revue Mabillon* 22 (1932): 133–64, 233–52; 23 (1933): 1–32, 81–111, 153–89.

Dumont, Charles. "Seeking God in Community According to St. Aelred." *Cistercian Studies* 6 (1971): 289–317.

Dunbabin, Jean. *France in the Making.* Oxford, 1985.

Duvernay, Roger. "Cîteaux, Vallombreuse, et Etienne Harding." *ASOC* 8 (1952): 379–494.

Elder, E. Rozanne, and John R. Sommerfeldt, eds. *The Chimaera of His Age: Studies on Bernard of Clairvaux.* CSS, 63. Kalamazoo, Mich., 1980.

Elliott, Dyan. *Spiritual Marriage: Sexual Abstinence in Medieval Wedlock.* Princeton, 1993.

Erdmann, Carl. *The Origin of the Idea of Crusade.* Trans. Marshall W. Baldwin and Walter Goffart. Princeton, 1977.

Evans, Gillian. "The '*De consideratione*' of Bernard of Clairvaux: A Preliminary Report." *Cîteaux* 35 (1984): 129–34.

————. *The Mind of St. Bernard of Clairvaux.* Oxford, 1983.

Farmer, Sharon. *Communities of St. Martin: Legend and Ritual in Medieval Tours.* Ithaca, 1991.

————. "Persuasive Voices: Clerical Images of Medieval Wives." *Speculum* 61 (1986): 517–43.

Feiss, Hugh. "Bernardus Scholasticus: The Correspondence of Bernard of Clairvaux and Hugh of Saint Victor on Baptism." In John R. Sommerfeldt, ed., *Bernardus Magister*, pp. 349–78. CSS, 135. Spencer, Mass., 1992.

Ferruolo, Stephen C. *The Origins of the University: The Schools of Paris and their Critics, 1100–1215.* Stanford, 1985.

Fiske, Adele M. *Friends and Friendship in the Monastic Tradition.* Cuernavaca, Mexico, 1970.

————. "St. Bernard of Clairvaux and Friendship." *Cîteaux* 11 (1960): 85–104.

Fliche, Austin. "L'influence de Grégoire VII et des idées grégoriennes sur la pensée de Saint Bernard." In *Saint Bernard et son temps*, pp. 137–50. Association bourguignonne des sociétés savantes, Congrès de 1927. Dijon, 1927.

Flood, Bernard. "St. Bernard's View of Crusade." *Cistercian Studies* 9 (1974): 22–35.

Folz, Robert. "Pierre le Vénérable et la liturgie." In *Pierre Abélard, Pierre le Vénérable*, pp. 143–64. Colloques Internationaux du Centre National de la Recherche Scientifique 546. Paris, 1975.

Foreville, Raymonde. *Latran I, II, III et Latran IV.* Paris, 1965.

Fossier, Robert. "L'économie cistercienne dans les plaines du nord-ouest de l'Europe." In *L'économie cistercienne: Géographie—mutations du moyen âge aux temps moderns*, pp. 53–74. Flaran 3. Auch, 1983.

————. "La fondation de Clairvaux et la famille de Saint Bernard." In *Mélanges Saint Bernard: 24e Congrès de l'Association bourguignonne des sociétés savantes*, pp. 19–27. Dijon, 1953.

————. "La vie économique de Clairvaux des origines à la fin de la guerre de cent ans: 1115–1471." Thèse, Ecole des Chartes, 1949.

Foucault, Michel. *The History of Sexuality.* Trans. Robert Hurley. New York, 1978.

Fournier, Paul, and Gabriel Le Bras. *Histoire des collections canoniques en Occident depuis les Fausses décrétales jusqu'au Décret de Gratien.* Paris, 1931–32.

Gams, Pius Boniface. *Series episcoporum ecclesiae Catholicae.* Leipzig, 1931.

Geary, Patrick. *Before France and Germany.* Oxford, 1988.

Geertz, Clifford. *The Interpretation of Cultures.* New York, 1973.

Gilchrist, J. "Canon Law Aspects of the Gregorian Reform Progamme." *Journal of Ecclesiastical History* 13 (1962): 21–38.

Gilson, Etienne. *The Mystical Theology of Saint Bernard.* Trans. A. H. C. Downes. New York, 1940.

———. *The Spirit of Mediaeval Philosophy.* Trans. A. H. C. Downes. London, 1950.

Gimpel, Jean. *The Medieval Machine.* New York, 1976.

Godefrey, J. "L'histoire du prieuré de Saint-Ayoul de Provins et le récit des miracles du saint." *Revue Mabillon* 27 (1937): 96–107; 28 (1938): 29–48, 84–98, 112–17.

Gold, Penny Schine. *The Lady and the Virgin: Image, Attitude and Experience in Twelfth-Century France.* Chicago, 1985.

Goodenough, Ward E. "Toward an Anthropologically Useful Definition of Religion." In Allan W. Eister, ed., *Changing Perspectives in the Scientific Study of Religion*, pp. 165–84. New York, 1974.

Goodrich, W. Eugene. "Caritas and Cistercian Uniformity: An Ideological Connection." *Cistercian Studies* 20 (1985): 31–43.

———. "The Cistercian Founders and the Rule: Some Reconsiderations." *Journal of Ecclesiastical History* 35 (1984): 358–75.

———. "The Limits of Friendship: A Disagreement between St. Bernard and Peter the Venerable on the Role of Charity in Dispensation from the Rule." *Cistercian Studies* 16 (1981): 81–97.

———. "The Reliability of the *Vita prima S. Bernardi*, The Image of Bernard in Book I of the *Vita prima* and His Own Letters: A Comparison." *Analecta Cisterciensia* 43 (1987): 153–80.

Gray, J. W. "The Problem of Papal Power in the Ecclesiology of S. Bernard." *Transactions of the Royal Historical Society* 5 (1974): 1–17.

Grotz, Hans. "Kriterien auf dem Prüfstand: Bernhard von Clairvaux angesichts zweier kanonisch strittiger Wahlen." In Hubert Mordek, ed., *Aus Kirche und Reich: Studien zu Theologie, Politik und Recht im Mittelalter*, pp. 237–63. Festschrift für Friedrich Kempf. Sigmaringen, 1983.

Grundmann, Herbert. *Religiöse Bewegungen im Mittelalter.* 2d ed. Hildesheim, Germany, 1961.

Hallam, Elizabeth. *Capetian France, 987–1328.* London, 1980.

Haller, Johannes. *Das Papsttum: Idee und Wirklichkeit* 3. Basel, 1952.

Hallinger, Kassius. *Gorze-Kluny.* Rome, 1950–51.

———. "Woher kommen die Laienbrüder?" *Analecta Cisterciensia* 12 (1956): 1–104.

Hanawalt, Barbara. *The Ties That Bound: Peasant Families in Medieval England.* New York, 1986.

Häring, N. M. "The Writings Against Gilbert of Poitiers by Geoffrey of Auxerre." *ASOC* 22 (1966): 3–83.

Head, Thomas F. *Hagiography and the Cult of Saints: The Diocese of Orléans 800–1200.* Cambridge, Eng., 1990.

Head, Thomas, and Richard Landes, eds. *Essays on the Peace of God: The Church and People in Eleventh-Century France.* Historical Reflections / Réflexions Historiques 14. Waterloo, Ont., 1987.

Heath, Robert G. *Crux Imperatorum Philosophia: Imperial Horizons of the Cluniac Confraternitas, 964–1109.* Pittsburgh, 1976.

Heathcote, Sheila J. "The Letter Collections Attributed to Master Transmundus." *ASOC* 21 (1965): 35–109, 167–238.

Higounet, C. "Essai sur les granges cisterciennes." In *L'économie cistercienne: Géographie—mutations du moyen âge aux temps moderns,* pp. 157–80. Flaran 3. Auch, 1983.

Hill, Bennett D. "Archbishop Thomas Becket and the Cistercian Order." *ASOC* 27 (1971): 64–80.

———. *English Cistercian Monasteries and their Patrons in the Twelfth Century.* Urbana, 1968.

Hobsbawm, Eric, and Terence Ranger, eds. *The Invention of Tradition.* Cambridge, Eng., 1983.

Holdsworth, Christopher. "A Cistercian Monastery and Its Neighbors." *History Today* 30 (1980): 32–37.

Holtzmann, Walther, ed. *Papsturkunden in England.* Berlin, 1935.

Hostie, Raymond. *Vie et mort des ordres religieux: Approches psycho-sociologiques.* Paris, 1972.

Hunt, Lynn, ed. *The New Cultural History.* Berkeley, 1989.

Hunt, Noreen. *Cluny under Saint Hugh, 1049–1109.* London, 1967.

Hutchison, Carole. *The Hermit Monks of Grandmont.* CSS, 118. Kalamazoo, Mich., 1989.

Iogna-Prat, Dominique. *Agni immaculati: Recherches sur les sources hagiographiques relatives à Saint Maieul de Cluny.* Paris, 1988.

Jacqueline, Bernard. *Episcopat et papauté chez Saint Bernard de Clairvaux.* Paris, 1975.

———. "Saint Bernard de Clairvaux et la curie romaine." *Revista di Storia della Chiesa in Italia* 7 (1953): 227–44.

———. "Yves de Chartres et Saint Bernard." In *Etudes d'histoire du droit canonique dédiées à Gabriel Le Bras,* 1: 79–84. Paris, 1965.

James, William. *The Varieties of Religious Experience.* Reprint, New York, 1982.

Janauschek, Leopold. *Originum cisterciensium* I. Vienna, 1877. Reprint, Ridgewood, N.J., 1964.

Javelet, Robert. *Image et ressemblance au douzième siècle, de Saint Anselme à Alain de Lille.* 2 vols. Paris, 1967.

Jestice, Phyllis Gwen. "Holiness and Society in Medieval Europe, 800–1100." Ph.D. diss., Stanford University, 1989.

Jobin, Jean Baptiste. *Saint Bernard et sa famille.* Paris, 1891.

Johnson, Penelope. *Prayer, Patronage, and Power: The Abbey of La Trinité, Vendôme, 1032–1187.* New York, 1981.

Jordan, Karl. "Die Entstehung der römische Kurie." *Zeitschrift der Savigny-Stiftung für Rechtsgeschichte, Kanonistische Abteilung* 59 (1939): 96–152.

Kennan, Elizabeth. "The '*De consideratione*' of St. Bernard of Clairvaux and the Papacy in the Mid-Twelfth Century." *Traditio* 23 (1967): 73–115.

Kinder, Terryl. "Construction at Pontigny: Whence Came the Ribbed Vaults and Other Changes." Paper delivered at the 18th International Congress on Medieval Studies, May 7, 1983, Kalamazoo. Abstracted in "Aspects of Cistercian Art." *Cîteaux: Commentarii cisterciensis* 34 (1983): 326.

King, Archdale A. *Cîteaux and Her Elder Daughters.* London, 1954.

———. *Liturgies of the Religious Orders.* London, 1955.

Klewitz, Hans Walter. "Das Ende des Reformpapsttums." In *Reformpapsttum und Kardinalkolleg,* pp. 207–53. Darmstadt, 1957.

Knowles, David. *Christian Monasticism.* New York, 1969.

———. *Cistercians and Cluniacs: The Controversy between St. Bernard and Peter the Venerable.* New York, 1955.

———. *The Monastic Order in England: A History of its Development from the Times of St. Dunstan to the Fourth Lateran Council 943–1216.* Cambridge, Eng., 1941.

———. "The Primitive Cistercian Documents." In *Great Historical Enterprises,* pp. 199–222. London, 1963.

———. "The Reforming Decrees of Peter the Venerable." In G. Constable and J. Kritzeck, eds., *Petrus Venerabilis, 1156–1956,* pp. 1–20. *Studia Anselmiana* 40. Rome, 1956.

———. *Thomas Becket.* Stanford, 1971.

Koziol, Geoffrey. *Begging Pardon and Favor: Ritual and Political Order in Early Medieval France.* Ithaca, 1992.

Kuttner, Stephan. "A Forgotten Definition of Justice." *Studia Gratiana* 20 (1976): 75–109.

Lackner, Bede. *The Eleventh-Century Background of Cîteaux.* CSS, 8. Washington, D.C., 1972.

———. "The Liturgy of Early Cîteaux." In *Studies in Medieval Cistercian*

History Presented to Jeremiah F. O'Sullivan, pp. 1–34. CSS, 13. Spencer, Mass., 1971.

Lambert, Malcolm. *Medieval Heresy: Popular Movements from Bogomil to Hus.* New York, 1976.

Lang, A. Proulx. "The Friendship between Peter the Venerable and Bernard of Clairvaux." In *Bernard of Clairvaux: Studies Presented to Dom Jean Leclercq,* pp. 35–53. CSS, 23. Washington, D.C., 1973.

Langmuir, Gavin I. *History, Religion and Antisemitism.* Berkeley, 1990.

————. *Toward a Definition of Antisemitism.* Berkeley, 1990.

Laudage, Johannes. *Priesterbild und Reformpapsttum im 11. Jahrhundert.* Cologne, 1984.

Lawrence, Clifford Hugh. *Medieval Monasticism: Forms of Religious Life in Western Europe in the Middle Ages.* London, 1984.

Lebeuf, Jean. *Mémoires concernant l'histoire civile et ecclésiastique d'Auxerre et son ancien diocèse.* 2 vols. 1747. Reprint, M. Challe and M. Quantin, eds., Auxerre-Paris, 1848–55. Reprint, 4 vols., Marseille, 1978.

Leclercq, Jean. "Epîtres d'Alexandre III sur les Cisterciens." *Revue Bénédictine* 64 (1954): 68–70.

————. *Etudes sur Saint Bernard et le texte de ses écrits. ASOC* 9 (1953).

————. *La femme et les femmes dans l'oeuvre de Saint Bernard.* Paris, 1982.

————. "The Intentions of the Founders of the Cistercian Order." *Cistercian Studies* 4 (1969): 21–61.

————. "Lettres de S. Bernard: Histoire ou littérature?" *Studi medievali* 12 (1971): 1–74.

————. *The Love of Learning and the Desire for God: A Study of Monastic Culture.* Trans. Catherine Misrahi. Reprint, New York, 1962.

————. *Le mariage vu par les moines au xiie siècle.* Paris, 1983.

————. "The Monastic Crisis of the Eleventh and Twelfth Centuries." Noreen Hunt, ed., *Cluniac Monasticism in the Central Middle Ages,* pp. 217–37. London, 1971.

————. *Monks and Love in Twelfth-Century France: Psycho-Historical Essays.* Oxford, 1979.

————. *Recueil d'études sur Saint Bernard et ses écrits.* 3 vols. Rome, 1962–69.

————. "St. Bernard and the Rule of St. Benedict." In M. Basil Pennington, ed., *The Rule and Life: An Interdisciplinary Symposium,* pp. 151–68. CSS, 12. Spencer, Mass., 1971.

————. *Saint Bernard of Clairvaux and the Cistercian Spirit.* Trans. Claire Lavoie. CSS, 16. Kalamazoo, Mich., 1976.

————. *A Second Look at Bernard of Clairvaux.* Trans. Marie-Bernard Saïd. CSS, 105. Kalamazoo, Mich., 1990.

————. "Le témoignage de Geoffroy d'Auxerre sur la vie cistercienne." *Studia Anselmiana* 31 (1953): 174–201.

Lecoy de la Marche, A. *Le chaire française au moyen-âge*. 2d ed. Paris, 1886.

Lefèvre, J. A. "L'évolution des *Usus conversorum* de Cîteaux." *COCR* 17 (1955): 65–97.

————. "Que savons-nous du Cîteaux primitif?" *Revue d'histoire ecclésiastique* 51 (1956): 4–51.

————. "La véritable *Carta caritatis* primitive et son évolution." *COCR* 14 (1954): 5–29.

————. "Le vrai récit des origines cisterciennes, est-il l'*Exordium parvum*?" *Le moyen âge* 61 (1955): 79–120, 329–60.

Le Goff, Jacques. *The Birth of Purgatory*. Trans. Arthur Goldhammer. Chicago, 1984.

————. *Intellectuals in the Middle Ages*. Trans. Teresa Lavender Fagan. Cambridge, Mass., 1993.

————. *Time, Work and Culture in the Middle Ages*. Trans. Arthur Goldhammer. Chicago, 1980.

Lekai, Louis. *The Cistercians: Ideals and Reality*. Kent, Ohio, 1977.

————. "Ideals and Reality in Early Cistercian Life and Legislation." In John R. Sommerfeldt, ed., *Cistercian Ideals and Reality*, pp. 4–29. CSS, 60. Kalamazoo, Mich., 1978.

————. "Medieval Cistercians and their Social Environment: The Case of Hungary." *ASOC* 32 (1976): 251–80.

————. "The Rule and the Early Cistercians." *Cistercian Studies* 5 (1970): 243–51.

Lemarignier, Jean-François. *Etude sur les privilèges d'exemption et de jurisdiction ecclésiastique des abbayes normandes depuis les origines jusqu'en 1140*. Paris, 1937.

————. "L'exemption monastique et les origines de la réforme grégorienne." In *A Cluny: Congrès scientifique*, pp. 288–340. Dijon, 1950.

————. *Recherches sur l'hommage en marche et les frontières féodales*. Lille, 1945.

Lenssen, Séraphin. "A propos de Cîteaux et de S. Thomas de Cantorbéry: L'abdication du bienheureux Geoffroy d'Auxerre comme abbé de Clairvaux." *COCR* 17 (1955): 98–110.

————. "Saint Robert, fondateur de Cîteaux." *COCR* 4 (1937): 2–16, 81–96, 161–177.

Lescher, Bruce. "Laybrothers: Questions Then, Questions Now." *Cistercian Studies* 23 (1988): 63–85.

Leyser, Henrietta. *Hermits and the New Monasticism*. London, 1984.

Lipkin, Joel. "The Entrance of the Cistercians into the Church Hierarchy 1098–1227: The Bernardine Influence." In E. Rozanne Elder and John R.

Sommerfeldt, eds., *The Chimaera of His Age: Studies on Bernard of Clairvaux*, pp. 61–75. CSS, 63. Kalamazoo, Mich., 1980.

Little, Lester K. *Religious Poverty and the Profit Economy in Medieval Europe.* Ithaca, 1978.

Locatelli, René. "L'expansion de l'ordre cistercien." In *Bernard de Clairvaux: Histoire, mentalités, spiritualité*, pp. 103–40. SC 380. Paris, 1992.

———. "L'implantation cistercienne dans le comté Bourgogne jusqu'au milieu du XVIe siècle." *Cahiers d'histoire* 20 (1975): 167–220.

Lynch, J. H. "The Cistercians and Underage Novices." *Cîteaux* 24 (1973): 283–97.

Mahn, Jean Berthold. *L'ordre cistercien et son gouvernement des origines au milieu du XIIIe siècle (1098–1265).* Paris, 1945.

Maisonneuve, Henri. *Etudes sur les origines de l'inquisition.* Paris, 1960.

Maleczek, Werner. "Das Kardinal Kollegium unter Innocenz II. und Anaklet II." *Archivum historiae pontificiae* 19 (1981): 27–78.

Mannion, Anne. "*Novalia*: A Study of Cistercian Economic Policy and Practices from 1098–1215." Ph.D. diss., Fordham University, 1980.

Manselli, Raoul. "De la *persuasio* à la *coercitio*." In *Le crédo, la morale, et l'inquisition*, pp. 175–97. Cahiers de Fanjeaux 6. Toulouse, 1971.

Markus, Robert A. *The End of Ancient Christianity.* Cambridge, Eng., 1990.

———. "Gregory the Great's *Rector* and His Genesis." In Jacques Fontaine, Robert Gillet, and Stan Pellistrandi, eds., *Grégoire le Grand*, pp. 137–46. Colloques Internationaux du Centre National de la Recherche Scientifique, Chantilly, 1982. Paris, 1986.

———. "The Latin Fathers." In J. H. Burns, ed., *The Cambridge History of Medieval Political Thought, c.350–c.1450*, pp. 92–122. Cambridge, Eng., 1988.

———. *Saeculum: History and Society in the Theology of St. Augustine.* Cambridge, Eng., 1970.

———. "The Sacred and the Secular: From Augustine to Gregory the Great." *Journal of Theological Studies*, n.s. 36 (1985): 84–96.

Matter, E. Ann. *The Voice of My Beloved: The Song of Songs in Western Medieval Christianity.* Philadelphia, 1990.

Mayr-Harting, H. "Functions of a Twelfth-Century Recluse." *History* 60 (1975): 337–52.

McCrank, Lawrence J. "The Frontier of the Spanish Reconquest and the Land Acquisitions of the Cistercians of Poblet 1150–1276." *ASOC* 29 (1973): 57–78.

McGinn, Bernard. *The Golden Chain: A Study in the Theological Anthropology of Isaac of Stella.* CSS, 15. Washington, D.C., 1972.

McGuire, Brian Patrick. *The Difficult Saint: Bernard of Clairvaux and His Tradition.* CSS, 126. Kalamazoo, Mich., 1991.

———. *Friendship and Community: The Monastic Experience 350–1250.* CSS, 95. Kalamazoo, Mich., 1988.

———. "A Lost Clairvaux Exemplum Collection Found: The *Liber visionum et miraculorum* Compiled under Prior John of Clairvaux, 1171/79." *ASOC* (1983): 27–62.

———. "Monastic Friendship and Toleration in Twelfth-Century Cistercian Life." In W. J. Sheils, ed., *Monks, Hermits and the Ascetic Tradition*, pp. 147–60. Studies in Church History 27. Padstow, Eng., 1985.

———. "Structure and Consciousness in the *Exordium magnum cisterciense*: The Clairvaux Cistercians after Bernard." *Cahiers de l'Institut du Moyen Age Grec et Latin* 30 (1979): 31–90.

McLaughlin, M. M. "Survivors and Surrogates: Children and Parents from the Ninth to the Thirteenth Centuries." In Lloyd deMause, ed., *The History of Childhood*, pp. 101–81. New York, 1974.

McLaughlin, Megan. *Consorting with Saints: Prayer for the Dead in Early Medieval France.* Ithaca, 1994.

———. "Consorting With Saints: Prayer for the Dead in Early Medieval French Society." Ph.D. diss., Stanford University, 1985.

Meagher, Luanne. "The Letters of Nicholas of Clairvaux." In E. Rozanne Elder, ed., *Heaven and Earth*, pp. 128–39. CSS, 68. Kalamazoo, Mich., 1983.

Meer, Frederik van der. *Atlas de l'ordre cistercien.* Paris, 1965.

Mélanges Saint Bernard: 24e Congrès de l'Association bourguignonne des sociétés savantes. Dijon, 1954.

Mikkers, Edmond. "De vita et operibus Gilberti de Hoylandia." *Cîteaux* 14 (1963): 33–34, 265–79.

Moffatt, James. *Love in the New Testament.* London, 1929.

Momigliano, Arnaldo. *On Pagans, Jews, and Christians.* Middletown, Conn., 1987.

Moore, John C. "The Origins of Western Ideas: Irving Singer's *The Nature of Love: Plato to Luther.*" *Journal of the History of Ideas* 29 (1968): 149–50.

Moore, R. I. *The Formation of a Persecuting Society.* Oxford, 1987.

———. *The Origins of European Dissent.* Oxford, 1977. Rev. ed., 1985.

Morey, Adrian, and C. N. L. Brooke. *Gilbert Foliot and His Letters.* Cambridge, Eng., 1965.

Morin, G. "Rainaud l'ermite et Ives de Chartres: Une épisode de la crise du cénobitisme au XI–XIIe siècle." *Revue Bénédictine* 40 (1928): 99–115.

Morris, Colin. *The Discovery of the Individual 1050–1200.* New York, 1972.

———. *The Papal Monarchy: The Western Church from 1050–1250.* Oxford, 1989.

Morrison, Karl. *Tradition and Authority in the Western Church, 300–1140.* Princeton, 1969.

Morson, John, and Hilary Costello, "Introduction." In Guerric of Igny, *Liturgical Sermons*, 1, CFS, 8: vii–xviii.

Mostert, Marco. *The Political Theology of Abbo of Fleury*. Hilversum, The Netherlands, 1987.

Mundy, John H. *Liberty and Political Power in Toulouse, 1050–1230*. New York, 1954.

Murray, A. Victor. *Abelard and St. Bernard: A Study in Twelfth Century "Modernism."* Manchester, 1967.

Murray, Alexander. *Reason and Society in the Middle Ages*. Oxford, 1978.

Nelson, Janet. "Kingship and Empire." In J. H. Burns, ed., *The Cambridge History of Medieval Political Thought, c.350–c.1450*, pp. 211–51. Cambridge, Eng., 1988.

Niermeyer, J. F. *Mediae latinitatis lexicon minus*. Leiden, 1976.

Nygren, Anders. *Agape and Eros*. Trans. Philip S. Watson. Philadelphia, 1953.

O'Dwyer, Barry William. "Bernard as an Historian: The Life of Saint Malachy of Armagh." *Journal of Religious History* 10 (1978): 128–61.

Oliger, Paul Remy. *Les évêques réguliers: Recherche sur leur condition juridique depuis les origines du monachisme jusqu'à la fin du moyen-âge*. Paris-Louvain, 1958.

Othon, le R. P. "De l'institution et des us des convers." In *Saint Bernard et son temps*, pp. 139–201. Association bourguignonne des sociétés savantes, Congrès de 1927. Dijon, 1928.

Oursel, Charles. *La miniature du XIIe siècle à l'abbaye de Cîteaux*. Dijon, 1926.

Pacaut, Marcel. *Alexandre III: Etude sur la conception du pouvoir pontifical dans sa pensée et dans son oeuvre*. Paris, 1956.

———. *Louis VII et les élections épiscopales dans le royaume de France*. Paris, 1957.

———. *La théocratie: l'église et le pouvoir au moyen âge*. Paris, 1957.

Palumbo, Pier Fausto. *Lo scisma del MCXXX*. Rome, 1942.

Pennington, M. Basil, ed. *The Cistercian Spirit: A Symposium*. CSS, 3. Spencer, Mass., 1970.

———. *Saint Bernard of Clairvaux: Studies Commemorating the Eighth Centenary of His Canonization*. CSS, 28. Kalamazoo, Mich., 1977.

Peters, Edward. *Heresy and Authority in Western Europe: Documents in Translation*. Philadelphia, 1980.

———. *Inquisition*. London, 1988.

Petit, Ernest. *Histoire des ducs de Bourgogne de la race capétienne*. 6 vols. Paris, 1885–98.

Poly, Jean-Pierre, and Eric Bournazel. *The Feudal Transformation, 900–1200*. Trans. Caroline Higgitt. New York, 1991.

Poole, Austin L. *From Domesday Book to Magna Carta*. 2d ed. Oxford, 1955.

Powicke, F. M. "Maurice of Rievaulx." *English Historical Review* 36 (1921): 17–29.

Prat, Ferdinand. "Charité; I: La charité dans la Bible." In *Dictionnaire de spiritualité: Ascétique et mystique, doctrine et histoire*, 2: 508–9. Paris, 1953.

Prawer, Joshua. *Histoire de royaume latin de Jérusalem*. 2 vols. Paris, 1969–70.

Preiss, Martin. *Die politische Tätigkeit und Stellung der Cisterzienser im Schisma von 1159–1177*. Historische Studien 248. Berlin, 1934.

Preus, J. Samuel. *Explaining Religion: Criticism and Theory from Bodin to Freud*. New Haven, 1987.

Raciti, Gaetano. "Isaac de l'Etoile." In *Dictionnaire de spiritualité: Ascétique et mystique, doctrine et histoire*, 7: 2011–38. Paris, 1953.

———. "Isaac de l'Etoile et son siècle." *Cîteaux* 12 (1961): 281–306; 13 (1962): 18–34, 133–45, 205–26.

Renna, Thomas. "St. Bernard's Idea of Peace in Historical Perspective, 750–1150." *Res publica litterarum* 6 (1983): 189–95.

———. "St. Bernard's View of the Episcopacy in Historical Perspective, 400–1150." *Cistercian Studies* 15 (1980): 39–49.

Reynolds, Susan. *Kingdoms and Communities in Western Europe, 900–1300*. Oxford, 1984.

Richard, Jean. "Le milieu familial." In *Bernard de Clairvaux*, pp. 3–15. Commission d'Histoire de l'Ordre de Cîteaux. Paris, 1953.

Ricoeur, Paul. "Structure, Word, Event." Trans. Robert Sweeney. In *The Conflict of Interpretations: Essays in Hermeneutics*, pp. 79–96. Evanston, 1974.

Riley-Smith, Jonathan. *The First Crusade and the Idea of Crusading*. London, 1986.

Robinson, I. S. *Authority and Resistance in the Investiture Contest*. Manchester, 1978.

———. "Church and Papacy." In J. H. Burns, ed., *The Cambridge History of Medieval Political Thought c.350–c.1450*, pp. 252–307. Cambridge, Eng., 1988.

Robson, C. A. *Maurice of Sully and the Medieval Vernacular Homily*. Oxford, 1952.

Rochais, Henri. "Enquête sur les sermons divers et les sentences de S. Bernard." *ASOC* 18 (1962): 1–183.

Rochais, Henri, and Eugène Manning. *Bibliographie de Saint Bernard*. Documentation Cistercienne 21. Rochefort, Belgium, 1979.

Roehl, Richard. "Plan and Reality in a Medieval Monastic Economy: The Cistercians." *Studies in Medieval and Renaissance History* 9 (1972): 83–113.

Rosenwein, Barbara H. "Feudal War and Monastic Peace: Cluniac Liturgy as Ritual Aggression." *Viator* 2 (1971): 129–57.

———. *Rhinoceros Bound: Cluny in the Tenth Century*. Philadelphia, 1982.

———. "Rules and the 'Rule' at Tenth-Century Cluny." *Studia Monastica* 19 (1977): 307–20.

———. *To Be the Neighbor of St. Peter: The Social Meaning of Cluny's Property, 909–1049*. Ithaca, 1989.

Rosenwein, Barbara H., and Lester Little. "Social Meaning in the Monastic and Mendicant Spiritualities." *Past and Present* 63 (1974): 4–32.

Roussel (l'abbé). *Nouvelle étude sur le diocèse de Langres et ses évêques.* Langres, 1889.

Rudolph, Conrad. *The "Things of Greater Importance": Bernard of Clairvaux's Apologia and the Medieval Attitude Toward Art.* Philadelphia, 1990.

Russell, Jeffrey Burton. *Dissent and Reform in the Early Middle Ages.* Berkeley, 1965.

Sahlins, Marshall. *Historical Metaphors and Mythical Realities: Structure in the Early History of the Sandwich Islands Kingdom.* ASAO Special Publications 1. Ann Arbor, 1981.

———. *Islands of History.* Chicago, 1985.

Saltman, Avrom. *Theobald, Archbishop of Canterbury.* London, 1956.

Schneider, Bruno. "Cîteaux und die benediktinische Tradition: Die Quellenfrage des *Liber usum* im Lichte der *Consuetudines monasticae.*" *ASOC* 16 (1960): 171–54; 17 (1961): 98–114.

Singer, Irving. *The Nature of Love: Plato to Luther.* New York, 1966.

Smalley, Beryl. *The Becket Conflict and the Schools: A Study of Intellectuals in Politics.* Oxford, 1973.

———. *The Study of the Bible in the Middle Ages.* Oxford, 1952. Reprint, Notre Dame, 1964.

Snaith, Norman H. *The Distinctive Ideas of the Old Testament.* London, 1944.

Somerville, Robert. *Pope Alexander III and the Council of Tours.* Center for Medieval and Renaissance Studies 12. Berkeley, 1977.

Sommerfeldt, John R. "The Social Theory of Bernard of Clairvaux." In *Studies in Medieval Cistercian History Presented to Jeremiah F. O'Sullivan*, pp. 35–48. CSS, 13. Spencer, Mass., 1991.

———. *The Spiritual Teachings of Bernard of Clairvaux.* CSS, 125. Kalamazoo, Mich., 1991.

———, ed. *Bernardus Magister.* CSS, 135. Spencer, Mass., 1992.

———. *Cistercian Ideals and Reality.* CSS, 60. Kalamazoo, Mich., 1978.

Southern, R. W. *The Making of the Middle Ages.* New Haven, 1953.

———. *Robert Grosseteste: The Growth of an English Mind in Medieval Europe.* 2d ed. Oxford, 1992.

———. *Saint Anselm and His Biographer: A Study of Monastic Life and Thought.* Cambridge, Eng., 1963.

———. *Western Society and the Church in the Middle Ages.* Harmondsworth, Eng., 1970.

Spence, Jonathan D. *The Memory Palace of Matteo Ricci.* New York, 1984.

Squire, Aelred. *Aelred of Rievaulx: A Study.* London, 1969.

————. "The Literary Evidence for the Preaching of Aelred of Rievaulx." *Cîteaux* 11 (1960): 165–79, 245–51.

Stainmesse, B. "La formation du temporel de l'abbaye de Clairvaux (des origines au début du XIIIe s.)." Résumé sommaire. *Annales de Bourgogne* 22 (1950): 135.

Stickler, Alfons M. "Concerning the Political Theories of the Medieval Canonists." *Traditio* 7 (1949–51): 450–63.

Stiegmann, Emero. "A Tradition of Aesthetics in Saint Bernard." In John R. Sommerfeldt, ed., *Bernardus Magister*, pp. 129–47. CSS, 135. Spencer, Mass., 1992.

Stock, Brian. *The Implications of Literacy: Written Language and Models of Interpretation in the Eleventh and Twelfth Centuries*. Princeton, 1982.

Straw, Carole. *Gregory the Great: Perfection in Imperfection*. Berkeley, 1988.

Strayer, Joseph R. *On the Medieval Origins of the Modern State*. Princeton, 1970.

Stroll, Mary. *The Jewish Pope: Ideology and Politics in the Papal Schism of 1130*. Leiden, 1987.

Tabuteau, Emily. *Transfers of Property in Eleventh-Century Norman Law*. Chapel Hill, 1988.

Talbot, C. H. "Associations of Clairvaux, Clairmarais and Ter Doest." *Cîteaux in de Nederlanden* 5 (1954): 233–45.

————. "The Sermons of Hugh of Pontigny." *Cîteaux in de Nederlanden* 7 (1956): 5–31.

Tellenbach, Gerd. *Church, State and Christian Society at the Time of the Investiture Contest*. Trans. R. F. Bennett. Oxford, 1940.

Tierney, Brian. *The Crisis of Church and State, 1050–1300*. Englewood Cliffs, N.J., 1964.

————. "Some Recent Works on the Political Theories of the Medieval Canonists." *Traditio* 10 (1954): 594–625.

Troeltsch, Ernst. *The Social Teaching of the Christian Churches*, 1. Trans. Olive Wyon. New York, 1931. Reprint, Chicago, 1981.

Turner, Victor. *Dramas, Fields, and Metaphors: Symbolic Action in Human Society.* Ithaca, 1974.

————. *The Ritual Process: Structure and Anti-structure*. Chicago, 1969.

Turner, Victor, and Edith Turner. *Image and Pilgrimage in Christian Culture*. New York, 1978.

Ullmann, Walter. *The Growth of Papal Government in the Middle Ages*. 3d ed. London, 1970.

————. *A History of Political Thought: The Middle Ages*. Harmondsworth, Eng., 1965.

Vacandard, Elphège. *Vie de Saint Bernard, abbé de Clairvaux*. Paris, 1920.

Valvekens, J. B. "Les actes de confraternité de 1142 et 1153 entre Cîteaux et Prémontré." *Analecta Praemonstratensia* 42 (1966): 326–30.

Van Damme, Jean Baptiste. "Autour des origines cisterciennes." *COCR* 20 (1958): 37–60, 153–68, 374–90; 21 (1959): 228–50, 302–29.

———. "Saint Etienne Harding mieux connu." *Cîteaux* 14 (1963): 307–13.

———. "Vir Dei Albericus." *ASOC* 20 (1964): 153–64.

Van Engen, John H. "The 'Crisis of Cenobitism' Reconsidered: Benedictine Monasticism in the Years 1050–1150." *Speculum* 61 (1986): 269–304.

———. *Rupert of Deutz*. Berkeley, 1983.

Vergier, J. "Le cloître et les écoles." In *Bernard de Clairvaux: Histoire, mentalités, spiritualité*, pp. 459–73. SC 380. Paris, 1992.

Vicaire, M.-H. *L'imitation des apôtres: moines, chanoines, mendiants (IVe– XIIIe siècles)*. Paris, 1963.

Vogüé, Adalbert de. *Community and Abbot in the Rule of Saint Benedict*. 2 vols. Trans. Charles Philippi. CSS, 5.1–2. Kalamazoo, Mich., 1979–88.

———. *The Rule of Saint Benedict: A Doctrinal and Spiritual Commentary*. Trans. John Baptist Hasbrouck. CSS, 54. Kalamazoo, Mich., 1983.

Walter, Johannes Wilhelm von. *Die ersten Wanderprediger Frankreichs*. 2 vols. Studien zur Geschichte der Theologie und der Kirche 9. Leipzig, 1903–6.

Waddell, Chrysogonus. "Early Cistercian Experience of Liturgy." In M. Basil Pennington, ed., *The Rule and Life: An Interdisciplinary Symposium*, pp. 77–116. CSS, 12. Spencer, Mass., 1971.

———. "The *Exordium cistercii* and the *Summa carta caritatis*: A Discussion Continued." In John R. Sommerfeldt, ed., *Cistercian Ideals and Reality*, pp. 34–61. CSS, 60. Kalamazoo, Mich., 1978.

———. "Notes Towards the Exegesis of a Letter by Saint Stephen Harding." In E. Rozanne Elder, ed., *Noble Piety and Reformed Monasticism*, pp. 10–39. CSS, 65. Kalamazoo, Mich., 1981.

———. "The Pre-Cistercian Background of Cîteaux and the Cistercian Liturgy." In E. Rozanne Elder, ed., *Goad and Nail*, pp. 109–32. CSS, 10. Kalamazoo, Mich., 1985.

———. "Simplicity and Ordinariness: The Climate of Early Cistercian Hagiography." In John R. Sommerfeldt, ed., *Simplicity and Ordinariness*, pp. 1–47. CSS, 61. Kalamazoo, Mich., 1980.

———. "Toward a New Provisional Edition of the Statutes of the Cistercian General Chapter, c. 1119–1189." In Francis R. Swietek and John R. Sommerfeldt, eds. *Studiosorum Speculum: Studies in Honor of Louis J. Lekai, O.Cist.*, pp. 384–419. CSS, 141. Kalamazoo, Mich., 1993.

Waddell, Helen. *The Wandering Scholars*. London, 1927.

Wakefield, Walter L., and Austin P. Evans. *Heresies of the High Middle Ages.* 2d ed. New York, 1991.

Wallace-Hadrill, J. M. *Early Germanic Kingship in England and on the Continent.* Oxford, 1971.

Ward, Benedicta. "The Desert Myth: Reflections on the Desert Ideal in Early Cistercian Monasticism." In M. Basil Pennington, ed., *One Yet Two: Monastic Tradition East and West,* pp. 183–99. CSS, 29. Kalamazoo, Mich., 1976.

Watt, J. A. "Spiritual and Temporal Powers." In J. H. Burns, ed., *The Cambridge History of Medieval Political Thought, c.350–c.1450,* pp. 367–423. Cambridge, Eng., 1988.

Werner, Ernst. "Bemerken zu einer neuen These über die Herkunft der Laienbrüder." *Zeitschrift für Geschichtswissenschaft* 6 (1958): 355–59.

White, Hayden. "The Gregorian Ideal and St. Bernard of Clairvaux." *Journal of the History of Ideas* 21 (1960): 321–48.

White, Lynn. *Medieval Technology and Social Change.* Oxford, 1962.

White, Stephen D. *Custom, Kinship, and Gifts to Saints: The Laudatio Parentum in Western France, 1050–1150.* Chapel Hill, 1988.

Willi, Dominicus. "Päpste, Kardinäle und Bischöfe aus dem Cistercienser-Orden." *Cistercienser chronik* 23 (1911): 225–37, 263–73, 294–312, 323–39, 355–70; 24 (1912): 9–15, 36–52, 73–75.

Williams, Daniel Day. *The Spirit and the Forms of Love.* New York, 1968.

Williams, George H. *Wilderness and Paradise in Christian Thought.* New York, 1962.

Williams, Watkin. "Arnold of Morimond." *Journal of Theological Studies* 40 (1939): 370–71.

———. "The Political Philosophy of St. Bernard of Clairvaux." *Blackfriars* 24: 466–69.

———. *Saint Bernard of Clairvaux.* Manchester, 1935.

Wilmart, A. "Une riposte de l'ancien monachisme au manifeste de Saint Bernard." *Revue Bénédictine* 46 (1934): 296–344.

Wollasch, Joachim. "Ein cluniacensisches Totenbuch aus der Zeit Abt Hugos von Cluny." *Frühmittelalterliche Studien* 1 (1967): 406–43.

Workman, Herbert B. *The Evolution of the Monastic Ideal: From the Earliest Times down to the Coming of the Friars.* London, 1913. Reprint, Boston, 1962.

Zaluska, Yolanda. *L'enluminure et le scriptorium de Cîteaux au XIIe siècle.* Cîteaux: Studia et Documenta 4. Cîteaux, 1989.

Index

In this index an "f" after a number indicates a separate reference on the next page, and an "ff" indicates separate references on the next two pages. A continuous discussion over two or more pages is indicated by a span of page numbers, e.g., "57–59." *Passim* is used for a cluster of references in close but not consecutive sequence.

Library of Congress Cataloging-in-Publication Data

Newman, Martha G.
The boundaries of charity : Cistercian culture and ecclesiastical
reform, 1098–1180 / Martha G. Newman.
  p.   cm.
Includes bibliographical references and index.
ISBN 0-8047-2512-8
1. Cistercians—Europe—History.   2. Europe—Church
history—600–1500.   1. Title.
BX3415.N48   1996
271′.1204′09021—dc20
                                        95-14016
                                             CIP

∞ This book is printed on acid-free, recycled paper.